Separation Agreement

David R. Greig, LAWYER

Self-Counsel Press
(a division of)
International Self-Counsel Press Ltd.
Canada   USA

Self-Counsel Press acknowledges the financial support of the Government of Canada through the Canada Book Fund (CBF) for our publishing activities.

Printed in Canada.

First edition: 2000; Reprinted: 2001 (2), 2002, 2004 (2)
Second edition: 2006
Third edition: 2007; Reprinted: 2008, 2009, 2010, 2011, 2012, 2013
Fourth edition: 2014; Reprinted: 2015; 2016

Library and Archives Canada Cataloguing in Publication

Greig, David R.
   Separation agreement / David R. Greig. — 4th ed.

(Self-counsel legal series)
CD-ROM in pocket of cover.
ISBN 978-1-77040-228-7

1. Separation (Law) — Canada — Popular works. 2. Separation (Law) — Canada — Forms. I. Title.
II. Series.

KE585.G73 2007   346.7101'668   C2006-906686-8
KF535.Z9G73 2007

Self-Counsel Press
(a division of)
International Self-Counsel Press Ltd.

North Vancouver, BC
Canada

Bellingham, WA
USA

CONTENTS

DISCLAIMER

The author, the publisher, and the vendor of these forms make no representations or warranties regarding the outcome or the use to which these forms are put and are not assuming any liability for any claims, losses, or damages arising out of the use of these forms. The user of these forms should not rely on the author or publisher of these forms for any professional advice.

INTRODUCTION

Separation can be a time of great upset. Memories, broken promises, and hurt feelings lead to disappointment and create confusion. Separating couples, who have managed to work together for decades, often cannot agree on anything. Arguments about children, money, and property can quickly escalate into costly court battles which further aggravate the acrimony and upset.

Ironically, the decisions that need to be made at the time of separation require calm consideration and objective assessment. These decisions will create significant and lasting financial consequences for the parties and their children.

Getting past the emotional turmoil of separation is not what this book is about. There are other books, counselors, and psychologists for that. The focus here, instead, is on assisting couples who choose to move on with their lives in a productive way after separation. It's about how to reduce your reasoned resolve to a written contract that will be reliable.

When you and your spouse separate, you have an opportunity to settle all the outstanding issues by agreement and to document that agreement in writing. A separation agreement is simply a contract that records the specific written details of that agreement so that the terms are known to you and others now, and in the future.

An agreement that sensibly resolves all relevant issues can restore calm. It may also —

(a) offer significant tax advantages;

(b) simplify divorce proceedings;

(c) add certainty to financial planning; and

(d) assist in estate planning.

The law is constantly changing. Readers should keep this in mind as they work through their separation agreement.

In British Columbia, for instance, a major change occurred in March of 2013, when the long-standing *Family Relations Act* was completely replaced by the *Family Law Act*. The FLA achieves many objectives, including an emphasis on encouraging settlement and out-of-court resolution. In addition, the FLA focuses on a "child centered" approach to parenting issues, and adds many new definitions and terms. Now, instead of describing the residency of a child in terms of "custody and access," the law explains that persons responsible for making decisions about children are called "guardians" with "parental responsibilities." These guardians have defined "parenting responsibilities" and share "parenting time." They bear a duty to act in the best interests of the children, which is now the only consideration in determining what's "right" for a child.

Details about this new legislation can be gathered from a variety of sources, including online resources offered by family law firms, the Legal Services society, and the BC Superior Court website. Simply search "BC *Family Law Act*" and you will have several excellent sources to review. Not every source on the Internet is accurate. One good site is www.lss.bc.ca. If in doubt, see a lawyer.

The BC FLA is designed to facilitate resolution, by parties, in the absence of acrimonious litigation. Section 4 specifically provides that one of the purposes is to "encourage parties to a family law dispute to resolve the dispute through agreements and appropriate family dispute resolution before making an application to court (and) to encourage parents and guardians to resolve conflict other than through court intervention."

This act, of course, does not affect the law in any other province. Similarly, it cannot and does not replace or change the federal *Divorce Act*. Our national *Divorce Act* continues to utilize the older language known to all: phrases such as "custody," "access," and "guardianship" prevail across the nation. For that reason, in this publication, we have continued to use the language of the *Divorce Act* in the draft agreement that accompanies this book. Readers in British Columbia who wish to avail themselves of the new legislation (the *Family Law Act*) will need to use some caution when drafting their agreement. It is important to note, however, that agreements made under the "old" law will not suddenly become invalid with the implementation of new law. Similarly, separating married parents who choose to use language that is consistent with the federal *Divorce Act* can anticipate enforceability in accordance with that law.

In the event of any conflict between any provincial law and the federal *Divorce Act*, the latter will prevail. For that and other reasons, it is likely that the effect of the new BC law will be of somewhat limited effect (at least initially) for married folks who reside in British Columbia. In the coming years, parties who separate and litigate will ask judges to interpret, apply, and define these new provisions. It may be some time before the full impact and ambit of the new legislation is known.

Elsewhere in Canada, provincial family laws and the federal *Divorce Act* will continue to operate together in a sometimes awkward (but often harmonious) relationship. Together, these various principles provide a combination of rules and concepts that can, at times, be confusing.

If you and your spouse are married and residing in BC, your parenting arrangements can still be determined under and in accordance with the federal *Divorce Act*. You may make an election to have the new *Family Law Act* prevail, but it's not necessary. When it comes to dividing family assets, however, the applicable rules and regulations governing that division will be found in provincial legislation. For British Columbians, that's the new *Family Law Act*. The genesis of this confusing mix of overlapping laws is our Constitution.

Under our Canadian Constitution, the federal and provincial lawmakers each have certain and defined topics over which they have "control." So, for instance, Criminal law is a federal topic, and is governed by our national Criminal Code. No province can make rules about Criminal law. That would be unconstitutional. Motor vehicle law, however, is a provincial topic, and each province makes vehicular legislation. Conflict can and does arise when a province purports to enact law about the criminal misuse of a vehicle (i.e. impaired driving). The same is true in family law when there is overlap and uncertainty between competing principles.

When it comes to family law, the overlap is more confusing. Our Constitution provides that "property and civil rights" are a provincial topic — and so every province has the exclusive right to decide matters pertaining to the division of property on marriage breakdown. Divorce, however, is a federally governed matter, and so the federal *Divorce Act* governs that topic. Unfortunately, the law is less certain when it comes to corollary relief (the issues which are ancillary to the divorce). There, the picture becomes hazy. The federal *Divorce Act* contains provisions respecting custody, access, guardianship, and spousal and child support. It does not purport to govern property division, (because that's one of the provincial topics under "property and civil rights").

All provinces and territories are powerless on the divorce topic, but they do have the capacity to make legislation governing other aspects of family law. Oddly, this means that the provinces can also make law regarding custody, access, guardianship, and spousal and child support, as long as they do not deal with "divorce" itself. And, of course, every province has exclusive jurisdiction to make all the laws about property division on marriage breakdown.

To make matters more confusing, however, the Supreme Courts in each province work in concert with the provincial courts, but the scope of the provincial court authority is limited by Constitutional law principles. Provincial courts cannot grant divorces, but they can make orders about the care of children and support. Provincial courts have very limited power, however, when it comes to dividing property (even though that would seem inconsistent with the other Constitutional law concepts about "property and civil rights" described above). The Supreme Court in each province has the capacity to determine all matters relating to marriage breakdown (and the breakdown of a "common law" relationship), and will decide the matters based on provincial laws, federal laws, and the common law.

This means that both the federal and provincial governments can enact laws on the common topics (children and support), but only the provinces can make law on property division, and only the federal government can make divorce law.

For British Columbians who separate after March 2013, the BC *Family Law Act* will determine the division of property. The old *Family Relations Act* is "gone," and so the division of property for married folks and "common law" couples in BC will be determined exclusively under the FLA.

Questions about "which government prevails and what law applies" engage a legal topic called jurisdiction. It's a confusing area of law, and well beyond the scope of this publication. A general summary of the big jurisdictional principles that separation topics in this book might include the following:

(a) Divorce is exclusively a federal topic. A divorce can only be granted under the federal *Divorce Act*, and can only be granted by a Supreme Court.

(b) Children's issues, including custody, access, guardianship, and support, are topics common to both the federal *Divorce Act*, and the laws of each province and territory. As a result, children's issues can be settled or determined under provincial family law rules, or under the federal *Divorce Act* if the parties are married.

(c) If the parties are unmarried, the children's issues cannot be determined under the federal *Divorce Act* (because the spouses were never married), and so provincial laws govern.

(d) Married and unmarried spouses can elect to have their children's issues spousal support addressed in either Supreme Court or provincial court.

(e) Property matters will be governed by provincial law (and in some cases, by the "common law"). The federal *Divorce Act* has no role in the division of property.

(f) Virtually all property matters must be determined by a Supreme Court.

If you are confused about these concepts, you're not alone. Questions about jurisdiction are not uncommon, and can be worrisome. Unfortunately, these issues should be addressed early in the separation process because determining which laws apply will affect the range of options available, and establish which language is most suitable. An experienced family law lawyer can address any jurisdictional concerns.

Do the courts recognize separation agreements?

Canadian courts and legislatures have tried to encourage parties to settle their disputes through negotiated contracts. Separation agreements are one such type of contract. Judges have shown a willingness to promote the validity of such contracts by judicial reluctance to interfere. If your agreement is fair, properly executed, and sensible, it will probably stand the test of time and withstand judicial review. There are, however, several exceptions to this general rule:

(a) If you and your spouse agree on issues relating to children (i.e., support and parenting) that are not in the best interests of the child, the court can make changes.

(b) If there is a lack of disclosure or deliberate deception respecting assets, liabilities, income, or expenses, the property division and support agreement may be reviewed.

(c) If the agreement is plainly unfair (i.e., one spouse releases all claims to support without compensation), the court can upset it.

Who is a spouse under current law?

This book is intended to apply to married couples who are separated or are considering separation. While many of the principles described herein apply equally to "common law" (unmarried) couples, that is not true everywhere in Canada. Across the nation, the rules that apply to common-law couples are changing, so for those persons, up-to-date legal advice is essential.

Recent amendments to Canadian law now permit the formalization of marriage between same-sex partners. In the event of a breakdown of such relations (where the parties are married under the new law and have recently separated), the use of the terms "husband" and "wife" may be inappropriate. Those terms can be supplanted by the given names of each spouse, or by simple reference to "Spouse 1" and "Spouse 2." A more difficult issue arises as to the retroactive application of the law respecting support and property division. If your same-sex marriage has come to an end, consultation with counsel may be advisable.

A separation agreement form specific to same-sex partners is included in the download kit that accompanies this book.

PREPARING YOUR SEPARATION AGREEMENT

What is in a separation agreement?

Most separation agreements consist of the same essential points: They start with the date and the full names of the parties to the agreement. *Recitals*, which describe the background or particulars of the agreement, follow. Next, the terms of the arrangement (the *covenants*) form the main body of the agreement. Finally, the document ends with the execution area, the parties sign with a witness.

Examine the sample at the end of this guide and identify each of these components. Schedule A describes the assets and liabilities of the parties and should be added to the back of the agreement.

Completing the agreement

This book contains a blank copy of the basic separation agreement. There is also a web accessible download kit that contains the blank forms in electronic format for you to use. Once you have familiarized yourself with the agreement, use one copy of the form to prepare a draft or rough copy by filling in all the variables that apply to your particular circumstance.

When you are satisfied with the agreement and your spouse has agreed to the terms, use a second copy of the agreement to prepare your final draft, keeping the following in mind:

(a) add any terms that you want included in the agreement, but ensure that such additions make good sense and clearly describe what is intended.

(b) names, addresses, and dates must be provided in full and must be accurate.

(c) delete any clauses that do not apply by drawing a line through the words or sentences that you intend to omit. After copies of the document are made, both you and your spouse should initial each one of these deletions.

(d) when two alternative words are presented (such as he/she) be sure to cross out the one that does not apply.

(e) all disclosure particulars should be fully and fairly described. Failure to disclose an asset may invalidate the agreement.

(f) the agreement must "make sense" and be understandable to an outsider. Even if the parties think that they understand the agreement perfectly, what is intended may not be obvious years later if a dispute arises. Because a judge may be called upon to interpret the agreement, the terms and conditions must be clear and capable of only one meaning. Sometimes, having a friend review the agreement *before* it's executed can be helpful. If you still have concerns, have the document reviewed by a lawyer.

If you do not understand a particular clause of the agreement or are confused about an issue, investigate further. Do not agree to anything you do not understand. If you remain uncertain or confused, talk to a lawyer.

While you can add terms to your separation agreement at any point in the agreement, the wording should be clear, legible, and sensible. In order for the amendments to be valid, they must be initialed by both parties. For example, should you wish to add an item to the property clauses, you should type or handwrite the additional wording and then initial the amendment in the margin as shown below:

 Both parties will continue to jointly own and use (to their mutual benefit) the Puerto Vallarta time share.

Obviously, it's better if there are no "last minute" deletions – handwritten changes should be avoided.

Signing and witnessing the agreement

Once you have completed the main body of the agreement, check it for accuracy but do not sign or date the agreement. Before you sign, make as many copies of the agreement as you will need. Good quality photocopies are sufficient for this purpose, or you can print the copies you have completed on your computer. You will need at least two copies of the agreement, one for your spouse and one for you. If you sign the agreement before you make the copies, the signatures will not be original signatures and may not be valid.

For the signing of the agreement, you will *each* need a witness who is an adult (i.e., 19 or older) and is competent (i.e., understands what is being done). <u>In front of your witness</u>, date the agreement, initial all deletions, and sign it. Have your witness sign where indicated. Your spouse then repeats the procedure with his or her witness. Do not use one common witness!

If you and your spouse are using lawyers, you should each take the separation agreement to your respective lawyers and have them look at the agreement before signing. Then, each lawyer can act as a witness and keep a copy of the agreement in your file.

After your separation agreement is signed and witnessed, both parties should keep an original.

FIVE KEY ISSUES TO ADDRESS
IN YOUR SEPARATION AGREEMENT

When parties separate, they generally need to address five key issues. These are: parenting of children (often called "custody"), access (sometimes called "visitation" or "parenting time"), guardianship (see below), support, and property division.

Custody

"Custody" is a word found in the federal *Divorce Act*, and in some provincial legislation. This term explains and describes where a child will normally reside after the parents have separated.

The federal *Divorce Act* uses the word "custody" to explain the residency of children. The language that is used to describe where a child will reside varies from one province to the next, but the basic substance of the law is pretty well uniform across the country. Generally speaking, the law tends to support the proposition that unless it is contrary to the best interests of the child, the child is entitled to the benefit of maximal contact with both parents. Quite often, that means shared parenting and something "similar" to joint custody. While many well intentioned parents will disagree on what specifics should prevail in their case, our legal system focuses the inquiry on what's best for the child. Joint custody and a "50/50" sharing are not presumed, but that is a common solution which many judges and parents implement because it often is in the best interests of the child.

Unfortunately, many divorcing parents have difficulty separating their own needs and wants from the "best interests" of the child. Often, there is a power struggle or control issue in play. As well, parents sometimes believe that they "need" custody in order to receive child support.

Our Canadian laws require a parenting arrangement that is in the best interest of the child — it's not "about" what's best for the parents, or most convenient for one or the other. It's also not "about" money – or who has the better house, job, or education. Custody is decided first, then support.

Separating parents need to focus on the best interests of the child and must try to work cooperatively. That's easier said than done, however, but many parents find that a counsellor or mediator can help. When discussing and negotiating this issue, keep in mind the following principles:

(a) regardless of what terms you and your spouse may settle upon, the court maintains the power to review the agreement at any time, and can adjust parenting arrangements as circumstances changes. Parenting topics (unlike property settlements) are always reviewable.

(b) as a consequence, it's unlikely that the parenting "deal" you settle on now will last forever. Your children will grow up, and as they do, their desires, interests, and your own circumstances will change. Keep that in mind as you discuss the arrangements with your former spouse.

7

(c) the wishes of your child are a relevant consideration, but rarely determinative. The views of a young child are significantly less important than the desires of a mature 14 year old.

(d) there are no "presumptions" which universally apply to all children, but often, courts will try to keep siblings together, and may seek to avoid schemes which require a great deal of "back and forth." While short visits and regular exchanges may be proper and preferred for infants, teens are unlikely to be well served by a daily change of residence.

(e) courts are typically unimpressed by mud-slinging allegations of bad character or new lovers, but will be cautious about any case where there is family violence, or demonstrable evidence of drug or alcohol abuse.

(f) a parent who has custody of a child more than 40 percent of the time may not be required to pay base child support (as described later), but will nonetheless be required to contribute to special and extraordinary expenses. So, while it is true that custody arrangements and "parenting time" can make a big difference in determining base child support, the proper decision about what's in the best interest of the child should not be determined by that fact. Remember custody comes first. Once that's known, the focus will be on support. The support issue can be assessed thereafter. Having said all that, the law on this point can be confusing, and so if you and your spouse need assistance addressing the concerns, get help. An experienced family law lawyer can explain the law and the options, often in a brief consultation.

(g) If the residency of the parents (and children) is likely to change, and if the move is contentious, you should consult counsel. Mobility (or "relocation." as it is sometimes called) is a tricky legal topic which is often determined according to the interplay between the case law and the common law. The Supreme Court of Canada case of *Gordon v. Goertz* remains important, so care must be taken when mobility or relocation is an issue. Notice is the key.

(h) While the arrangements that you have settled on regarding property division cannot later be changed, the terms regarding custody and access can be reviewed from time to time. For instance, during the "turbulent" adolescent and teen years, it's not uncommon for children to "decide" that they want to change residences. In such circumstances, if it's determined that such a change is in the best interests of the child, an amendment to the agreement can be made, and the child can move. Typically, such modifications also involve an adjustment to the child support arrangements.

(i) Some separated parents choose to utilize improvisational and neutral language in the description of their custodial arrangements. Phrases such as "shared parenting" are sometimes incorporated to set out the agreed-upon terms. This kind of creativity may make good practical sense to parties, but deviating from the conventional language (such as "custody and access") may be troublesome if issues arise concerning child support and mobility. If you and your spouse want to use special language to describe your parenting arrangement, it's best to obtain legal advice.

(j) "Split custody" is a term used to describe the arrangement where each parent has custody of (at least) one child. That situation triggers specific support obligations which are defined in paragraph 8 of the Federal Child Support Guidelines. Parents who are sharing custody of several children should take advice on the operation of these provisions, to insure compliance with the law.

Access

Access terms set out the arrangement you and your spouse have settled on for visitation. Some couples agree on a general description; for example, "the Husband shall have reasonable and generous access." If you and your spouse have an amicable relationship and are able to communicate and cooperate, you may not need specificity. If, however, bickering and misunderstanding punctuate your post-separation spousal relationship, you should write out the specifics in your agreement. Describe the arrangement for weekends, holidays, birthdays, and religious holidays. Set out the specifics of the summer holidays, and who will perform the pick-up and drop-off. Be fair, be sensible, and, most important, be clear. Many couples spend thousands of dollars on legal fees arguing over these topics.

Readers in British Columbia who have children out of wedlock, or those who wish to avail themselves of the provisions of the new *Family Law Act*, will need to be careful here. The terms "custody," "access," and "guardianship" (found in the *Divorce Act*) have been replaced with terminology that is quite different from the federal law. If you employ the "old" language of the *Divorce Act* in a new BC agreement, you will not likely have created an invalid bargain, but you could have problems. Care should be taken to get it right. If you are planning to have your situation governed by the FLA, you should use the proper terminology. Review the applicable provisions, and check out one of several informative websites for additional aid, and the complete text of the Act. If you still have questions, see a lawyer.

When you take those steps, you'll see that section 37 of the FLA provides that the only thing to be considered in making an order or agreement for the care of a child is the best interests of the child. All of the child's needs and circumstances are to be taken into consideration. Parents (who are guardians of children) may exercise all parental responsibilities with respect to a child and must do so with these considerations in mind. Sections 40 and 41 describe this. Access is now called "parenting time," and parenting arrangements describe how the time is to be shared.

Despite the change in nomenclature, the same principles will continue to apply, and parents will be encouraged to find sensible parenting arrangements that are sensitive to the specific needs and interests of children.

Under the BC Law, all parents are automatically guardians, unless the parent has never resided with the child. All guardians— and so, by definition, almost all parents—will enjoy parenting responsibilities and parenting time. Whether any of this new language will reduce conflict or encourage cooperation and hasten the resumption of peace in families in crisis remains a lofty objective and a perplexing question. For the purposes of this book, we have elected to continue with the language of the federal *Divorce Act*, in the sample agreement in part because those provisions are tested, known, and predictably reliable. British Columbian who wish to import the new language of the *Family Law Act* in their agreement should do so with caution.

Guardianship

In most jurisdictions, the arrangement on guardianship resolves two legal questions:

(a) Who will have custody of the child if one parent dies?

(b) Who will be involved in the decision-making process on topics affecting the health, welfare, and education of the child?

For most couples, an agreement that provides for joint guardianship is sensible.

Again, British Columbians wishing to utilize the new *Family Law Act* will need to be circumspect here, since the legal meaning of guardianship has now changed. If you wish to utilize the FLA terms in your separation agreement, you will likely require independent legal advice with respect to the applicable nomenclature.

Support

Your separation agreement should address both spousal and child support.

Spousal support

Commonly called alimony in the United States, spousal support is compensation paid by one spouse to the other to relieve economic inequality that may exist at the end of a relationship. Support can be paid in a lump sum or periodic basis and may be tax deductible if properly structured. Periodic spousal support is tax deductible by the payor, and counts as taxable income in the hands of the recipient. In some cases, spousal support continues indefinitely, while other spouses agree to support for a limited time or agree to review the arrangement some time in the future. Depending on your circumstances, the obligation to pay and the right to receive support can be

significant, and so some advice on the topic may be necessary.

If a husband pays $200 per month to his spouse for her support, $2,400 per annum is deducted from the husband's taxable income, and an equal amount is added to the wife's income. Some qualifications to this general rule exist:

(a) The parties must be separated;

(b) The payments must be periodic (not a lump sum);

(c) The payments must be pursuant to a court order or written agreement. A separation agreement qualifies;

(d) If the payments are made to a third party and not the spouse directly (e.g., a mortgage company), certain restrictions apply.

Under the current federal *Divorce Act*, an identified object of spousal support is the promotion of economic self-sufficiency. Until recently, that factor was given considerable weight by the courts, and often resulted in the making of time-limited spousal support orders that terminated at some future time.

The law respecting spousal support continues to evolve. Several years ago, the Federal Department of Justice commissioned and then published a report concerning spousal support. This report, entitled "Spousal Support Advisory Guidelines" attempts to add certainty to the *quantum* of spousal support properly payable on separation, and to offer a formula for that determination.

The report is now aged and is 182 pages long, and complex. It is, however, extremely helpful, and contains useful information about the suggested formula, and also the case law and principles on which it is based. Courts across the country have used and applied the formula contained within the report. Persons who have the opportunity to read the material should do so. The report can be found online at www.justice.gc.ca.

Some provinces have treated the Spousal Support Advisory Guidelines as very persuasive, while other provinces have been less enthusiastic. Either way, they are an important guidepost.

When considering the report, it's important to remember the following:

(a) Unlike the Child Support Guidelines (which *are* law), these spousal guidelines are not binding.

(b) The spousal guidelines do not necessarily apply to "common law" (unmarried) spouses, and offer no formula for determining entitlement.

(c) There are two formulas described: one for separating spouses without children, and one for families with children. The former is relatively easy to apply, the latter more complex.

(d) These guidelines offer a "range" for support within which various factors and considerations can be taken into account.

Remember that the spousal support guidelines are not binding and not "firm law". Debate continues to range about whether the spousal support guidelines or the principles behind them will ever become law. While that debate carries on, we know that the old rule that spousal support was never to become a "pension for life" is now gone. At the end of a long-term traditional marriage, spousal support may continue indefinitely. This is particularly so when it can be demonstrated that one spouse has suffered a continuing economic disadvantage because of a career compromise made in order to take on family obligations, such as raising children.

Time limited support (that is, support that continues for a finite number of years) may be appropriate in marriages of shorter duration, and if the parties each have some means. When the marriage endures for seven or eight years or longer, however, the fairness of term support is suspect. In mid-term and long-term marriages, support that is automatically extinguished at some pre-determined time is a rarity, and few judges support such arrangements. That does not mean that parties cannot agree to term support at the end of a long marriage, but it does mean that a court might not approve of such a provision. A more common clause is one which provides for a review (of quantum, or entitlement) in a certain number of years. This sensible alternative has the unfortunate consequence of requiring the parties to re-engage in the process again, in a few years time, but at least it's flexible.

There may be great value in the certainty of a final "deal" which is imperfect, but ends the war. Your particular circumstances, aspirations, and worries will be relevant. As always, use Internet resources with caution. The Federal Department of Justice website and www. mysupportcalculator.ca are both quite good.

Child support

Support paid by a spouse for the benefit of children is not deductible by the person making the payments, nor is the payment taxable income in the hands of the recipient. Legislative changes now provide tables (Child Support Guidelines) that set out the mandatory quantum of support. For your convenience, these tables are reproduced at the back of this book. The Department of Justice has released a step-by-step booklet explaining the Federal Child Support Guidelines. The web accessible download kit for this book provides a link at www.self-counsel.com/updates/separate/15kit. htm whereby you can download this booklet, or you can visit the Justice Canada website at www.justice.gc.ca.

The child support legislation was designed to simplify and make uniform all child support payments. In many cases, it has achieved that objective. If, however, you and your spouse have a shared or split custody regime, the tables are not easy to understand and the law can be confusing.

In most circumstances, child support consists of two amounts: the *base* and the allowance for *specials*. To calculate the *base*, turn to the Child Support Guidelines at the end of this book, and refer to the table for the province in which the payor resides. Ascertain the payor's income by looking at line 150 of his or her last tax return, determine the number of children who qualify for support, and then find the corresponding amount of child support. That is the base amount that must be paid. Remember: the guideline amount is a floor, not a ceiling. A spouse can always pay more, but except in extremely unusual circumstances (such as in cases of undue hardship), rarely less.

To calculate the *special,* ascertain the costs of daycare, ongoing medical and dental expenses for the child, and extracurricular expenses. These costs are then shared between the parents in proportion to their incomes. For instance, if the custodial mother earns $20,000 per annum, and the father earns $30,000, the father must add to his base support amount three-fifths (or 60 percent) of the cost of these special expenses.

In the above example, assume that there are two children, and the parties live in British Columbia. According to the guidelines, the base payable by the father (based on his income of $30,000) is $463 per month. If the specials are $50 per month, the amount the father pays to the mother is $463 plus three-fifths (or 60 percent) of $50, for a total of $493.

The courts have little discretion to avoid the application of the guidelines. In this regard, we must explain: the child support "guidelines" are not guidelines at all, they are law. The spousal support guidelines are, by contract, exactly that — guidelines. Try not to confuse the concepts, even though the language is nonsensical.

A child support agreement that is inconsistent with the guidelines will attract the critical attention of the court, and can constitute an absolute bar to the granting of a divorce. In some provinces, however, parents have the right to agree on a scheme that is not necessarily in compliance with the Guidelines, provided that reasonable arrangements for the support and maintenance of the child have been made. Those alternate "reasonable arrangements" may involve some special clause to divide property in a beneficial way, or provide "lump sum" support, or some other scheme. What will constitute reasonable arrangements will depend on circumstances.

Property division

When you and your spouse separate, your family assets (and any debts you may have accumulated) need to be divided. Of this there can be no doubt — owning real property with a friend is a very bad idea — continuing to own property with a former lover is worse.

The laws respecting the division of family assets (at the end of a marriage) vary from province to province. Generally speaking, however, there is a presumption in favour of an equal division of assets if those assets were acquired or used by the family during the currency of the relationship. In addition, most jurisdictions employ a legislative scheme that requires the parties to fairly allocate their obligations (debts). These principles are best described as a presumption in favour of equivalency. In some circumstances, however, a simple "equal division" may be unfair. For instance, where one party came into the relationship with significant assets and the other party was penniless, an equal division of assets at the end of a short marriage may be unfair.

In British Columbia, the FLA provides that the assets which one party brought to a relationship before it began will survive the relationship and at the end that party can claim an exclusion to the extent of that value. Family property, under this new legislation, is all property except for "excluded property" which a party owned prior to cohabitation and would also include gifts, inheritance, personal injury awards and property held in trust. A close examination of Parts 5 and 6 of the *Family Law Act* will be important for British Columbians who are attempting to divide their family property.

Keep in mind that regardless of the specifics of the prevailing legislation, consenting and informed adults can always make a compromise or "contract" as long as it's generally fair and properly done. One of the best ways to ensure that this is accomplished in a supportable way, is to attach a description of the assets and liabilities owned and owed by the parties (at the end of the relationship) as an Appendix to the back of a Separation Agreement. In the sample that is provided, we describe this as "Schedule A." This Schedule can be fairly simple, but should be accurate.

Make sure that each and every asset and liability described in the Schedule is dealt with in the agreement. If there are five assets and four liabilities in the Schedule, for instance, each of these nine items should be addressed and dealt with in the body of the agreement. Leave nothing to the imagination.

In common-law relationships, where the parties are not married, but have lived together in a lasting marriage-like arrangement, the legislative arrangements will likely be wholly inapplicable. The parties will, however, be expected to share property acquired together, based on principles of "trust." The trust laws for Canadian families come from a long line of important cases, including the Supreme Court of Canada decision in Kerr v. Baranow. The Supreme Court of Canada website will lead you to this case, if you are so inclined.

The essence of this principle is that common-law parties who are separating can anticipate a sharing of assets where there is contribution (enrichment) and a corresponding deprivation. Perhaps an example is best:

> *Assume an unmarried couple are together for 14 years. They raise two children during that time. Midpoint in their relationship, they buy a house together. The home is registered in the name of the male spouse (because he works for wages, and has good credit) and not in the name of the female spouse (who has assumed the role of stay-at-home caregiver to the children). On separation, the female spouse may have no legal remedy or status in respect to the house because she's not on the title and is not a wife. She does, however, have a clear entitlement on trust principles. She can allege that she contributed directly and indirectly to the establishment of family equity by staying home and raising the children. She would say that her decision was good for the family, for her spouse, and for the children. This direct and indirect contribution profited the family generally, and that's a form of enrichment. In facilitating this enrichment, she has been correspondingly deprived because she has been out of the labor market, has lost opportunities, and is not on the title of the home. She is entitled to consideration for that. Kerr v. Baranow provides the basis.*

Trust principles are applicable throughout Canada — they are very different in Quebec — but family law legislation about the division of property varies from one province to another. Accordingly, it's important to do some research about the property division rules in the province where you and your spouse reside.

Under Ontario law, when a marriage ends, the contribution of each spouse is recognized. The value or equity in property that was acquired must be divided, and the presumption is in favour of equal division. Also, any increase in the value of property owned by a spouse since the date of marriage is to be shared. The payment from one spouse to the other (to effect the equalization) is called an equalization payment, or an equalization of net family property.

In Ontario, some property is exempt from these rules. Exempt property would consist of property that was inherited, or acquired by gift. Note, however, that if the spouse who receives the gift or inheritance subsequently uses the monies or property in the relationship for a family purpose, the nature of that gift or inheritance becomes "contaminated," and the entirety of the gift will end up in the family law blender.

The British Columbia *Family Law Act* contains similar provisions in sections 81 through 97, and power is given to the court to divide or apportion liabilities for debt.

Depending on where you and your spouse reside, you will need to consider the property division rules in your geographic jurisdiction (province or territory) before specifics are agreed upon. Remember that it is often entirely possible to obtain preliminary legal advice from a competent family law lawyer (on an initial interview) — some lawyers do this for free. Whether you must pay for the advice or not, it's important to get information about property division before negotiating (and certainly before signing the separation agreement). Always be mindful of the risks inherent in taking advice from the Internet.

Some other general principles to remember when discussing how to divide assets:

(1) Good literature is available to help parties discuss their issues and negotiate calmly and frankly (with proper disclosure);

(2) Try to negotiate fairly and only after full disclosure. Keeping secrets about assets and liabilities invariably causes trouble later, and can result in your agreement being declared invalid. Aside from that, it's just plain dishonest. Treat your spouse during separation negotiations as you did on your first date, and expect the same in return;

(3) You should attach a complete description of your assets and liabilities to the Separation Agreement. Use the Schedule A sample as a guide. You do not need to list every pot and pan, or include clothing and photos, but you do need to list all the "big ticket" items;

(4) Do not forget about RRSPs, TFSAs, GICs, bonds, and other investments;

(5) Remember too that RRSPS can be transferred between separating spouses without triggering tax (by use of a T2220 rollover form). This is a significant tax advantage, and should not be squandered. If you have these savings instruments, get legal advice or talk to your banker or accountant.

The family home

If one of your major assets is a home (as is often the case), give careful consideration to this topic. Several solutions are included in the sample separation agreement. Consider all your options carefully.

Remember that if your family home is to be transferred (from joint ownership) to one spouse, the non-owning spouse may still be liable under the mortgage. Accordingly, if your agreement anticipates the transfer of the home in circumstances where the purchaser is not a third party (and so the mortgage will remain on title) you must consider obtaining a release of that obligation. In this, you will need the consent of the lender. Do so before the transfer is complete. Since you will likely need a lawyer or notary to facilitate the transfer, this issue should be discussed with him or her and/ or the lender.

If your agreement provides for the transfer of property from one spouse to the other, keep in mind that there may be significant tax consequences. For example, while transfer of the family home can usually be done on a tax-free basis, that may not be the case with a summer cottage or business asset. Any investment property that has increased in value since the date of purchase may attract tax on the gain (except in particular circumstances). Conversely, savings (e.g., RRSPs, mutual funds) can be split tax free if proper steps are taken. If your agreement anticipates disposition of assets of this type, or any assets having significant value, you should get professional counsel from an accountant or a lawyer.

Pension plans

Canada Pension Plan credits and benefits accumulated during the marriage are usually split equally between the spouses, regardless of the relative contributions each made. Even spouses who have never worked outside the home, and who never contributed directly to the plan, are entitled to half of the pension credits earned during the marriage by the working spouse. The equal division rule also applies when both spouses worked but one paid more into the plan than the other. To qualify, spouses must have lived together for at least 12 consecutive months and separation must have lasted for at least 12 months. A clause in an agreement that says the parties will not share CPP benefits and credits may be unenforceable. If you and your spouse are definitely committed to "opting out" of the usual sharing provisions of the CPP, you should obtain legal advice on the topic.

Note: There may be time limitations on applications to divide CPP credits and benefits. It is best to make the application promptly after separation. Contact your local Service Canada office for further information. You will find their information helpful.

Each spouse is also typically entitled to a one- half interest in the other spouse's employer-sponsored pension plan. When dealing with the division of such a plan, make certain you are complying with the current legislation. The plan administrator can often be very helpful, but if you remain uncertain, seek counsel.

Be careful. Employment pensions can be an extremely valuable asset, and caution and expertise is required when dividing them. If you or your spouse has a valuable employer sponsored pension plan, a good starting point is to discuss the plan and the options with the administrator of the pension plan. These individuals often have sample forms, documents, and helpful advice that is available at no cost.

Because the valuation of pension plans is not simply a matter of adding up contributions and then dividing by two, it may be necessary to engage the services of an actuary to calculate the value of the pension if a trade-off or buyout is anticipated. As well, since there are several different types of pension plans, the way a plan is shared and divided will depend on what kind of plan is being apportioned.

ENFORCING YOUR SEPARATION AGREEMENT

Separation agreements are enforceable under contract law principles. In addition, some jurisdictions allow these agreements to be filed (or registered) in the court as an aid to enforcement. Accordingly, if you encounter a problem with the enforcement of your agreement (i.e., if your spouse is not honouring support commitments made in the agreement), you should speak to the staff at the court registry nearest to where you reside, and ascertain if your agreement can be filed at the registry.

In addition, most provinces maintain publicly funded programs that offer free advice and enforcement action where one party to an agreement or order is refusing or failing to pay spousal or child support. You should inquire about the availability of these programs as well.

If enforcement of the terms of your separation agreement has become problematic, do not delay. Take action immediately, and seek counsel if you have any questions or uncertainties about which way to proceed. Your failure to take action on a breached promise in the agreement could compromise your ability to effect the necessary remedy later.

MISCELLANEOUS

After separation, your will may not fairly reflect your intentions. Be sure to review and revise your will. The Self-Counsel Press title *Write Your Legal Will in 3 Easy Steps is an excellent guide to consider.*

In most jurisdictions, a separation agreement made in the absence of independent legal advice is nonetheless valid and binding. However, it is always wise to review the draft agreement with counsel before executing the agreement. The fees for such review vary widely, but a reasonable range is between $250 to $750. Usually, that's money well spent.

Finally, be frank and fair in the making of your separation agreement. Contracts that are decidedly one-sided or settled when one party is mistaken about material facts are likely to attract critical attention in court. If either of you is unsure about what is fair, do not execute the agreement until you have investigated further.

SAMPLE SEPARATION AGREEMENT

THIS AGREEMENT made the ___4th___ day of ___February___, 20 _--_

BETWEEN:

___JOHN SMITH___,

of the City of ___Anywhere___, in the

Province/Territory of ___British Columbia___

(referred to in this Agreement as "the Husband")

AND:

___SUE SMITH___,

of the City of ___Anywhere___, in the

Province/Territory of ___British Columbia___

(referred to in this Agreement as "the Wife")

RECITALS

WHEREAS:

A.   The parties were married to each other at ___Edmonton___, in the Province/Territory of

___Alberta___, on the ___10th___ day of ___November___, 20 _--_ .

B.   The parties have __2__ children as follows:

Name of Child	Age	Date of Birth
Sally Smith	4	April 1, 20--
Bobby Smith	6	April 2, 20--

C.   The Husband and the Wife agree to live separate and apart and have lived apart since the __20th__ day of ___December___, ___20--___, and intend to continue to live separate and apart according to the terms and conditions described in this agreement.

D.   The assets and liabilities of the Husband and the Wife are completely and accurately described in Schedule A attached to the back of this agreement.

19

E.   The Husband and the Wife intend this agreement to be —

   (i)   a final settlement of their respective rights to and in property owned jointly and/or separately by them; and

   (ii)   a final settlement of the issues of custody, access, guardianship, and support.

NOW THEREFORE THE HUSBAND AND THE WIFE AGREE AS FOLLOWS:

GENERAL

1.   The Husband and the Wife will continue to live separate and apart, and neither will annoy, disturb, or interfere with the other person.

2.   This agreement and everything contained in it shall continue to govern the relationship between the Husband and the Wife, notwithstanding subsequent divorce, dissolution, or annulment of the marriage, by any order or instrument.

3.   This agreement and everything contained in it shall be governed by the Federal *Divorce Act*, and the laws of the Province/Territory of __British Columbia__ .

4.   Any part or provision of this agreement that is found to be void, voidable, or otherwise unenforceable shall be severable from the agreement, and the remainder of the agreement following that finding shall continue in full force and effect.

5.   This agreement may only be amended or varied by a court order, or by written agreement between the Husband and the Wife, which amendment or agreement shall be duly executed by the Husband and the Wife by unrelated or independent persons.

CUSTODY, ACCESS, AND GUARDIANSHIP

6.   (a)   The Husband and/~~or~~ Wife shall have ~~sole~~/joint custody and the ~~Husband~~/Wife shall have primary residency of the following child/ren:

Name of Child	Age	Date of Birth
Sally Smith	4	April 1, 20--
Bobby Smith	6	April 2, 20--

(b)   The Husband ~~and/or Wife~~ shall have reasonable and liberal access to the child/ren on the following terms:

  (i)   five days at Christmas, five days at spring break, half of all statutory holidays, one month in the summer;

  (ii)   Father's Day;

  (iii)   New Year's Eve in even numbered years; and

  (iv)   otherwise, as agreed.

7.   The Husband and the Wife have joint guardianship of the children above described.

SUPPORT

8.   The Husband/~~Wife~~ shall pay to the Wife/~~Husband,~~ for ~~his~~/her own support, the sum of $ 200.00 per month, commencing on the __1st__ day of __April__ , 20 __--__ , and continuing on each and every month thereafter until the __1st__ day of __May__ , 20 __--__ , (or) until such time as the Wife/~~Husband~~ dies, remarries, or commences cohabitation with another person, in what is generally referred to as a common-law relationship, whichever shall occur first.

9.   The Husband/~~Wife~~ shall pay to the Wife/~~Husband~~ for the maintenance of the infant children of the marriage, namely:

Name of Child	Age	Date of Birth
Sally Smith	4	April 1, 20--
Bobby Smith	6	April 2, 20--

the sum of $__472.00__ per month (net of tax), based on the payor's Guideline income of $__30,000.00__ , such payments to be made on the __1st__ day of __March__ , 20 __--__ , and continuing on the __1st__ day of each and every month thereafter, for so long as each child of the marriage remains a child of the marriage.

10.   In addition to the amount above described, the Husband/~~Wife~~ shall pay to the Wife/~~Husband,~~ for special expenses, the sum of $__30.00__ , to be paid at the same time as the payment described in paragraph 9.

ASSETS AND LIABILITIES

11.   (a)   The Husband shall hereafter own and possess the following assets:

Description	Approximate Value
Household items: Living room furniture, all tools, downstairs desk and computer, personal items	$6,000.00
Vehicles: 2010 Ford Taurus	$10,000.00
Savings/RRSPs: All RRSPs	$3,000.00
Other: NIL	NIL

(b)   The Wife shall hereafter own and possess the following assets:

Description	Approximate Value
Household items: All household items not taken by the Husband	$14,000.00
Vehicles: 2008 Plymouth Van	$5,000.00
Savings/RRSPs: NIL	NIL
Other: NIL	NIL

12.   (a)   The Husband shall and does hereafter accept sole and exclusive liability for the following debts:

Institution	Balance	Payments
(i) Visa Card	$2,000.00	$100/month
(ii) CIBC loan	$3,000.00	$135/month

and does now indemnify and save harmless the Wife of and from any and all liability thereunder.

(b)   The Wife shall and does hereafter accept sole and exclusive liability for the following debts:

Institution	Balance	Payments
(i) NIL	NIL	NIL

and does now indemnify and save harmless the Husband of and from any and all liability thereunder.

13.   Neither the Husband nor the Wife shall hereafter pledge the credit of the other or bind the other for debt.

22

MATRIMONIAL HOME AT: ___123 Main Street, Anywhere, BC___

14.   (a)   The Husband/Wife shall have a licence to exclusive occupation and possession of the matrimonial home situate and being at _____ without the obligation to pay rent, until such time as the Husband and the Wife mutually agree to sell the home. If the parties cannot later agree when the home is to be sold, either of them may apply to Court for further determination of same. When the home is sold, the equity or loss resulting therefrom, following the payment of all accounts of real estate commission, mortgage, taxes, and other just discounts, shall be divided equally between the Husband and the Wife.

OR

(b)   Forthwith upon execution of this agreement, the Husband/Wife shall purchase from the Wife/Husband, all interest, right, and title to and in the matrimonial home upon the following terms and conditions:

    (i)   the payment to the Wife/Husband of the sum of $_____

    (ii)   (other terms and conditions): _____

OR

(c)   On the ___1st___ day of ___March___, 20___, the matrimonial home shall be listed for sale and sold as soon thereafter as is reasonable. Until sale, the ~~Husband~~/Wife shall have a licence to exclusive occupation and possession of the matrimonial home, absent rent. For so long as the ~~Husband~~/Wife is in occupation and possession of the matrimonial home, the ~~Wife~~/Husband shall maintain all accounts of mortgage, maintain all taxes, insurance, heat, water, and other charges, and keep the matrimonial home fully insured. Upon sale, the proceeds of sale obtained in accordance with this paragraph shall be distributed as follows:

    (i)   first, to real estate commission

    (ii)   second, to all accounts of mortgage

    (iii)   third, to all taxes, utilities, and other adjustments and discounts

    (iv)   fourth, the balance, if any, to be divided equally between the Husband and the Wife

OR

(d)   On or about the _____ day of _____, 20__, the matrimonial home was sold and proceeds were divided to the satisfaction of the Husband and the Wife, and as a consequence, the Husband and the Wife agree that their respective rights to share in such proceeds have been satisfied, and each agrees not to claim or bring any claim in respect thereto, with respect to property laws in their Province/Territory.

15.   This agreement adequately and completely provides for the present and future needs of the Husband and the Wife, and each covenants and agrees that the arrangement herein described constitutes a full, complete, and final settlement of all rights, causes, claims, and demands with respect to support and property.

ACCEPTANCE

16.   The Husband and the Wife further acknowledge and agree that —

(a)   each and every recital of fact contained herein is true and accurate;

(b)   they each have general knowledge of the other's affairs, assets, and liabilities;

(c)   they have each read and understood this agreement;

(d)   they each sign this agreement as free agents;

(e)   this agreement has been executed without any pressure, influence, or intimidation by anyone; and

(f)   they have each received full and independent legal advice with respect to this agreement and the alternatives available to the execution of it.

OR

being aware of their entitlement to full and independent legal advice, they have, nonetheless, chosen to waive same and elect to proceed with the execution of this agreement absent such advice.

IN WITNESS WHEREOF the Husband and the Wife set their hands this __5th__ day of __February__,

20 _--_ , at the City of __Anywhere__ , in the Province/Territory of __British Columbia__ .

SIGNED BY THE HUSBAND   )

in the presence of:)

__Lisa Johnson__   )   __John Smith__
(Signature of Witness)   )   Signature of Husband

__Lisa Johnson__   )
(Print Name)   )

__456 Blackwood St., Kamloops, BC__   )
(Address)   )

__Golf instructor__   )
(Occupation)   )

SIGNED BY THE WIFE   )

in the presence of:)

__Tom West__   )   __Sue Smith__
(Signature of Witness)   )   Signature of Wife

__Tom West__   )
(Print Name)   )

__789 Upton Ave, Victoria, BC__   )
(Address)   )

__Realtor__   )
(Occupation)   )

SCHEDULE A

ASSETS AND LIABILITIES OF THE SPOUSES

LIST OF ASSETS		LIST OF LIABILITIES	
Description	Approximate Value	Description	Approximate Value
1. House at 123 Main St.	$400,000	1. Mortgage	$100,000
2. 2010 Ford Taurus	$10,000	2. Visa Card	$2,000
3. 2008 Plymouth Van	$5,000	3. CIBC loan	$3,000
4. Household contents	$20,000		
5. RRSPs	$3,000		

APPENDIX
FEDERAL CHILD SUPPORT TABLES

ONTARIO

Federal Child Support Amounts: Simplified Tables
Montants fédéraux de pensions alimentaires pour enfants: Tables simplifiées

Income/ Revenu ($)	Monthly Award/ Paiement mensuel ($) No. of Children/ Nᵇʳᵉ d'enfants				Income/ Revenu ($)	Monthly Award/ Paiement mensuel ($) No. of Children/ Nᵇʳᵉ d'enfants				Income/ Revenu ($)	Monthly Award/ Paiement mensuel ($) No. of Children/ Nᵇʳᵉ d'enfants				Income/ Revenu ($)	Monthly Award/ Paiement mensuel ($) No. of Children/ Nᵇʳᵉ d'enfants			
	1	2	3	4		1	2	3	4		1	2	3	4		1	2	3	4
10820	0	0	0	0	16200	120	231	249	266	21600	173	328	452	499	27000	219	397	545	666
10900	2	4	4	4	16300	122	234	252	270	21700	174	329	454	503	27100	220	398	547	668
11000	21	50	54	58	16400	123	237	256	274	21800	174	331	455	508	27200	221	399	548	670
11100	23	54	59	63	16500	125	241	259	277	21900	175	332	457	512	27300	222	400	550	672
11200	25	59	63	68	16600	127	244	262	281	22000	176	333	459	516	27400	223	402	551	674
11300	27	63	68	73	16700	129	247	266	285	22100	177	334	461	520	27500	223	403	553	676
11400	29	68	73	78	16800	131	250	269	288	22200	178	336	462	524	27600	224	404	554	678
11500	31	72	78	83	16900	133	253	273	292	22300	178	337	464	528	27700	225	405	556	680
11600	32	76	82	88	17000	135	256	276	296	22400	179	338	466	533	27800	226	406	557	682
11700	34	81	87	93	17100	136	258	280	300	22500	180	340	468	537	27900	227	407	559	684
11800	36	85	92	98	17200	136	260	284	305	22600	181	341	469	541	28000	228	408	560	686
11900	38	90	96	103	17300	137	262	288	309	22700	182	342	471	545	28100	229	409	562	688
12000	40	94	101	108	17400	138	264	292	314	22800	183	343	473	549	28200	230	411	563	690
12100	42	98	105	112	17500	138	266	296	318	22900	183	345	475	553	28300	231	412	565	692
12200	44	101	109	116	17600	139	268	301	322	23000	184	346	476	557	28400	232	414	566	694
12300	46	105	113	121	17700	140	270	305	327	23100	185	347	478	561	28500	233	415	568	696
12400	48	109	117	125	17800	140	272	309	331	23200	186	349	479	565	28600	234	417	569	698
12500	49	112	121	129	17900	141	275	313	336	23300	186	350	481	570	28700	234	418	571	700
12600	51	116	125	133	18000	142	277	317	340	23400	187	351	483	574	28800	235	420	573	702
12700	53	120	128	137	18100	143	278	321	345	23500	188	352	485	578	28900	236	421	574	703
12800	55	123	132	142	18200	144	280	326	349	23600	189	354	486	582	29000	237	423	576	705
12900	57	127	136	146	18300	145	281	330	354	23700	190	355	488	586	29100	238	425	578	707
13000	59	130	140	150	18400	146	283	334	359	23800	191	356	490	590	29200	239	426	579	709
13100	61	134	144	154	18500	146	284	339	363	23900	191	358	491	595	29300	240	428	581	711
13200	63	137	147	158	18600	147	286	343	368	24000	192	359	493	599	29400	240	429	582	713
13300	65	141	151	162	18700	148	287	347	373	24100	193	360	495	602	29500	241	431	584	715
13400	67	144	155	166	18800	149	288	351	377	24200	194	362	497	604	29600	242	432	585	717
13500	68	148	159	170	18900	150	290	356	382	24300	194	363	498	607	29700	243	434	587	719
13600	70	151	162	174	19000	151	291	360	386	24400	195	364	500	609	29800	244	435	588	721
13700	72	155	166	178	19100	152	292	364	391	24500	196	366	502	612	29900	245	437	590	723
13800	74	158	170	182	19200	153	294	369	395	24600	197	367	504	614	30000	245	438	591	725
13900	76	162	173	186	19300	154	295	373	400	24700	198	369	505	617	30100	246	439	593	727
14000	78	165	177	190	19400	155	297	378	404	24800	199	370	507	619	30200	247	441	595	729
14100	80	168	180	193	19500	156	298	382	409	24900	199	371	509	622	30300	249	442	597	731
14200	82	171	184	197	19600	156	300	386	414	25000	200	373	511	624	30400	250	444	599	733
14300	84	174	187	200	19700	157	301	391	418	25100	201	374	513	626	30500	251	445	601	735
14400	86	177	190	204	19800	158	303	395	423	25200	202	376	515	628	30600	252	447	603	737
14500	87	180	193	207	19900	159	304	400	428	25300	203	377	516	631	30700	253	448	605	739
14600	89	183	197	211	20000	160	306	404	432	25400	204	378	518	633	30800	254	450	607	741
14700	91	186	200	214	20100	161	307	408	436	25500	205	380	520	635	30900	256	451	609	743
14800	93	189	203	218	20200	162	309	411	440	25600	206	381	522	637	31000	257	452	611	745
14900	95	192	206	221	20300	162	310	415	444	25700	207	382	524	639	31100	258	453	613	747
15000	97	195	210	225	20400	163	311	419	449	25800	208	384	525	642	31200	259	455	615	749
15100	99	198	213	228	20500	164	313	423	453	25900	209	385	527	644	31300	261	456	617	751
15200	101	201	216	232	20600	165	314	426	457	26000	210	386	529	646	31400	262	458	619	753
15300	103	204	220	235	20700	166	316	430	461	26100	211	387	531	648	31500	263	459	621	755
15400	105	207	223	239	20800	166	317	434	465	26200	212	388	532	650	31600	264	461	622	757
15500	106	210	226	242	20900	167	318	438	469	26300	213	389	534	652	31700	265	462	624	759
15600	108	213	229	245	21000	168	320	441	474	26400	213	390	535	654	31800	266	464	626	761
15700	110	216	232	249	21100	169	321	443	478	26500	214	391	537	656	31900	268	465	628	763
15800	112	219	236	252	21200	170	323	445	482	26600	215	392	538	658	32000	269	467	630	765
15900	114	222	239	256	21300	170	324	446	487	26700	216	393	540	660	32100	270	468	632	767
16000	116	225	242	259	21400	171	325	448	491	26800	217	394	541	662	32200	271	470	634	769
16100	118	228	245	263	21500	172	327	450	495	26900	218	395	543	664	32300	273	471	636	771

27

Federal Child Support Amounts: Simplified Tables
Montants fédéraux de pensions alimentaires pour enfants: Tables simplifiées

Income/ Revenu ($)	Monthly Award/ Paiement mensuel ($) No. of Children/ Nᵇʳᵉ d'enfants				Income/ Revenu ($)	Monthly Award/ Paiement mensuel ($) No. of Children/ Nᵇʳᵉ d'enfants				Income/ Revenu ($)	Monthly Award/ Paiement mensuel ($) No. of Children/ Nᵇʳᵉ d'enfants				Income/ Revenu ($)	Monthly Award/ Paiement mensuel ($) No. of Children/ Nᵇʳᵉ d'enfants				Income/ Revenu ($)	Monthly Award/ Paiement mensuel ($) No. of Children/ Nᵇʳᵉ d'enfants			
	1	2	3	4		1	2	3	4		1	2	3	4		1	2	3	4		1	2	3	4
32400	274	473	637	774	37800	334	544	731	885	43200	390	633	821	988	48600	438	723	931	1100					
32500	275	474	639	776	37900	335	545	732	887	43300	391	635	823	990	48700	438	724	933	1102					
32600	276	475	641	778	38000	336	546	734	889	43400	392	637	825	992	48800	439	726	934	1104					
32700	277	477	643	780	38100	337	548	736	891	43500	393	638	827	993	48900	440	727	936	1106					
32800	278	478	645	782	38200	338	549	737	893	43600	394	640	829	995	49000	441	728	938	1108					
32900	280	480	647	784	38300	339	551	739	895	43700	395	642	831	997	49100	442	730	940	1110					
33000	281	481	649	786	38400	341	553	740	896	43800	395	643	833	999	49200	443	731	942	1113					
33100	282	482	651	788	38500	342	554	742	898	43900	396	645	835	1001	49300	444	733	944	1115					
33200	283	484	653	790	38600	343	556	743	900	44000	397	647	837	1003	49400	445	734	947	1118					
33300	284	485	654	793	38700	344	558	745	902	44100	398	649	839	1005	49500	446	736	949	1120					
33400	285	487	656	795	38800	345	559	746	904	44200	399	650	841	1007	49600	447	737	951	1123					
33500	287	488	658	797	38900	346	561	748	906	44300	400	652	843	1009	49700	448	739	953	1125					
33600	288	489	660	799	39000	348	563	749	907	44400	401	654	845	1011	49800	449	740	955	1128					
33700	289	491	662	801	39100	349	565	751	909	44500	402	656	847	1012	49900	449	742	957	1130					
33800	290	492	663	803	39200	350	566	752	911	44600	403	657	849	1014	50000	450	743	959	1133					
33900	291	494	665	806	39300	352	568	754	913	44700	404	659	852	1016	50100	451	745	961	1135					
34000	292	495	667	808	39400	353	570	755	915	44800	404	661	854	1018	50200	452	746	963	1138					
34100	293	496	669	810	39500	354	571	757	917	44900	405	662	856	1020	50300	453	748	966	1140					
34200	294	498	671	812	39600	355	573	758	918	45000	406	664	858	1022	50400	454	749	968	1143					
34300	295	499	672	815	39700	356	575	760	920	45100	407	666	860	1024	50500	455	751	970	1145					
34400	296	500	674	817	39800	357	576	761	922	45200	408	667	862	1026	50600	456	752	972	1148					
34500	297	502	676	819	39900	359	578	763	924	45300	409	669	864	1028	50700	457	754	974	1150					
34600	299	503	678	821	40000	360	579	764	926	45400	410	671	866	1030	50800	458	755	976	1153					
34700	300	504	680	823	40100	361	581	766	928	45500	411	672	868	1031	50900	459	757	979	1155					
34800	301	506	681	826	40200	362	583	767	930	45600	412	674	870	1033	51000	460	758	981	1158					
34900	302	507	683	828	40300	363	584	769	932	45700	413	675	872	1035	51100	461	760	983	1160					
35000	303	508	685	830	40400	364	586	771	934	45800	413	677	874	1037	51200	462	761	985	1163					
35100	304	509	687	832	40500	365	588	772	936	45900	414	679	876	1039	51300	463	763	988	1165					
35200	305	511	689	834	40600	366	590	774	938	46000	415	680	878	1041	51400	464	764	990	1168					
35300	306	512	690	836	40700	367	591	776	941	46100	416	682	880	1043	51500	465	766	992	1170					
35400	308	514	692	839	40800	368	593	777	943	46200	417	683	882	1046	51600	466	767	994	1173					
35500	309	515	694	841	40900	369	595	779	945	46300	418	685	884	1048	51700	466	769	996	1175					
35600	310	516	696	843	41000	370	597	781	947	46400	419	687	886	1050	51800	467	770	999	1178					
35700	311	518	698	845	41100	371	599	783	949	46500	420	688	888	1052	51900	468	772	1001	1180					
35800	312	519	699	847	41200	372	600	784	951	46600	421	690	890	1055	52000	469	773	1003	1183					
35900	313	520	701	849	41300	373	602	786	953	46700	422	692	893	1057	52100	470	774	1005	1186					
36000	315	522	703	851	41400	374	604	787	955	46800	422	693	895	1059	52200	471	776	1007	1188					
36100	316	523	705	853	41500	374	605	789	957	46900	423	695	897	1061	52300	472	777	1009	1191					
36200	317	524	706	855	41600	375	607	790	958	47000	424	697	899	1064	52400	473	779	1012	1193					
36300	318	526	708	857	41700	376	609	792	960	47100	425	699	901	1066	52500	474	780	1014	1196					
36400	319	527	709	859	41800	377	610	793	962	47200	426	701	903	1069	52600	475	782	1016	1198					
36500	320	528	711	861	41900	378	612	795	964	47300	427	702	905	1071	52700	476	783	1018	1201					
36600	321	529	713	863	42000	379	614	797	966	47400	428	704	908	1074	52800	477	785	1020	1203					
36700	322	531	714	865	42100	380	616	799	968	47500	429	706	910	1076	52900	478	786	1022	1206					
36800	323	532	716	867	42200	381	617	801	970	47600	430	708	912	1079	53000	479	787	1024	1208					
36900	324	533	717	869	42300	382	619	803	972	47700	431	709	914	1081	53100	480	788	1026	1211					
37000	325	534	719	871	42400	383	621	805	973	47800	431	711	916	1084	53200	481	790	1028	1213					
37100	326	535	720	873	42500	384	622	807	975	47900	432	713	918	1086	53300	482	791	1031	1216					
37200	327	536	722	875	42600	384	624	809	977	48000	433	715	920	1088	53400	483	793	1033	1218					
37300	328	538	723	876	42700	385	625	811	979	48100	434	716	922	1090	53500	484	794	1035	1221					
37400	329	539	725	878	42800	386	627	813	981	48200	435	718	924	1092	53600	484	796	1037	1223					
37500	330	540	726	880	42900	387	629	815	983	48300	435	719	925	1094	53700	485	797	1039	1226					
37600	331	541	728	882	43000	388	630	817	984	48400	436	720	927	1096	53800	486	799	1041	1228					
37700	333	542	729	884	43100	389	632	819	986	48500	437	722	929	1098	53900	487	800	1044	1231					

ONTARIO — CONTINUED

Federal Child Support Amounts: Simplified Tables
Montants fédéraux de pensions alimentaires pour enfants: Tables simplifiées

Income/ Revenu ($)	Monthly Award/ Paiement mensuel ($) No. of Children/ Nᵇʳᵉ d'enfants				Income/ Revenu ($)	Monthly Award/ Paiement mensuel ($) No. of Children/ Nᵇʳᵉ d'enfants				Income/ Revenu ($)	Monthly Award/ Paiement mensuel ($) No. of Children/ Nᵇʳᵉ d'enfants				Income/ Revenu ($)	Monthly Award/ Paiement mensuel ($) No. of Children/ Nᵇʳᵉ d'enfants			
	1	2	3	4		1	2	3	4		1	2	3	4		1	2	3	4
54000	488	802	1046	1233	59400	540	883	1157	1367	64800	592	963	1261	1502	70200	641	1040	1360	1621
54100	489	803	1048	1236	59500	541	885	1159	1369	64900	593	964	1262	1505	70300	641	1041	1361	1624
54200	490	805	1050	1238	59600	542	886	1160	1372	65000	594	966	1264	1507	70400	642	1042	1363	1626
54300	491	806	1053	1241	59700	543	888	1162	1374	65100	595	968	1266	1509	70500	643	1044	1365	1628
54400	492	808	1055	1243	59800	544	889	1164	1377	65200	596	969	1268	1512	70600	644	1045	1367	1630
54500	493	809	1057	1246	59900	545	891	1166	1379	65300	597	971	1270	1514	70700	645	1047	1368	1632
54600	494	811	1059	1248	60000	546	892	1168	1382	65400	598	972	1272	1516	70800	646	1048	1370	1634
54700	495	812	1061	1251	60100	547	893	1170	1384	65500	599	974	1274	1519	70900	646	1049	1372	1637
54800	496	814	1064	1253	60200	548	895	1172	1387	65600	600	975	1276	1521	71000	647	1051	1374	1639
54900	497	815	1066	1256	60300	549	896	1174	1389	65700	601	977	1277	1523	71100	648	1052	1376	1641
55000	498	817	1068	1258	60400	550	898	1176	1392	65800	602	978	1279	1526	71200	649	1054	1378	1643
55100	499	818	1070	1261	60500	551	899	1177	1394	65900	602	980	1281	1528	71300	650	1055	1380	1646
55200	500	820	1072	1263	60600	552	901	1179	1397	66000	603	981	1283	1530	71400	651	1057	1381	1648
55300	501	821	1074	1266	60700	552	902	1181	1399	66100	604	983	1285	1532	71500	652	1058	1383	1650
55400	502	823	1077	1268	60800	553	904	1183	1402	66200	605	984	1287	1535	71600	653	1060	1385	1652
55500	503	824	1079	1271	60900	554	905	1185	1404	66300	606	986	1289	1537	71700	654	1061	1387	1655
55600	504	826	1081	1273	61000	555	906	1187	1407	66400	607	987	1291	1539	71800	655	1063	1389	1657
55700	505	827	1083	1276	61100	556	907	1189	1409	66500	608	989	1293	1541	71900	656	1064	1391	1659
55800	506	829	1085	1278	61200	557	909	1191	1412	66600	609	990	1294	1544	72000	657	1066	1393	1661
55900	507	830	1087	1281	61300	558	910	1193	1414	66700	610	992	1296	1546	72100	658	1067	1394	1663
56000	508	832	1089	1283	61400	559	912	1195	1417	66800	611	993	1298	1548	72200	658	1068	1396	1664
56100	509	833	1091	1286	61500	560	913	1196	1419	66900	612	995	1300	1551	72300	659	1069	1397	1666
56200	510	835	1093	1288	61600	561	915	1198	1422	67000	613	996	1302	1553	72400	660	1071	1399	1668
56300	511	836	1096	1291	61700	562	916	1200	1424	67100	614	997	1304	1555	72500	661	1072	1400	1670
56400	512	838	1098	1293	61800	563	918	1202	1427	67200	615	999	1306	1557	72600	661	1073	1401	1671
56500	513	839	1100	1296	61900	564	919	1204	1429	67300	615	1000	1307	1559	72700	662	1074	1403	1673
56600	514	841	1102	1298	62000	565	921	1206	1432	67400	616	1002	1309	1562	72800	663	1075	1404	1675
56700	515	842	1104	1301	62100	566	922	1208	1434	67500	617	1003	1311	1564	72900	664	1076	1406	1677
56800	516	844	1106	1303	62200	567	924	1210	1437	67600	618	1005	1313	1566	73000	664	1077	1407	1678
56900	516	845	1109	1306	62300	568	925	1212	1439	67700	619	1006	1315	1568	73100	665	1078	1409	1680
57000	517	847	1111	1308	62400	569	927	1213	1442	67800	620	1008	1316	1570	73200	666	1080	1411	1682
57100	518	849	1113	1310	62500	570	928	1215	1444	67900	620	1009	1318	1572	73300	667	1081	1413	1685
57200	519	850	1115	1313	62600	570	930	1217	1447	68000	621	1010	1320	1574	73400	668	1083	1414	1687
57300	520	852	1117	1315	62700	571	931	1219	1449	68100	622	1011	1322	1576	73500	669	1084	1416	1689
57400	521	853	1119	1318	62800	572	933	1221	1452	68200	623	1013	1324	1578	73600	669	1085	1418	1691
57500	522	855	1121	1320	62900	573	934	1223	1454	68300	624	1014	1325	1581	73700	670	1087	1420	1694
57600	523	856	1123	1323	63000	574	936	1225	1457	68400	624	1015	1327	1583	73800	671	1088	1422	1696
57700	524	858	1124	1325	63100	575	937	1227	1460	68500	625	1017	1329	1585	73900	672	1090	1424	1698
57800	525	859	1126	1328	63200	576	939	1229	1462	68600	626	1018	1331	1587	74000	673	1091	1426	1700
57900	526	861	1128	1330	63300	577	940	1231	1465	68700	627	1019	1333	1589	74100	674	1092	1428	1702
58000	527	862	1130	1332	63400	578	942	1233	1467	68800	628	1021	1334	1592	74200	675	1094	1430	1704
58100	528	864	1132	1334	63500	579	943	1235	1470	68900	629	1022	1336	1594	74300	676	1095	1431	1706
58200	529	865	1134	1337	63600	580	945	1237	1472	69000	630	1023	1338	1596	74400	677	1096	1433	1709
58300	530	867	1136	1339	63700	581	946	1239	1475	69100	631	1024	1340	1598	74500	677	1098	1435	1711
58400	531	868	1138	1342	63800	582	948	1241	1477	69200	632	1026	1342	1600	74600	678	1099	1437	1713
58500	532	870	1140	1344	63900	583	949	1243	1480	69300	633	1027	1343	1602	74700	679	1101	1439	1715
58600	533	871	1141	1347	64000	584	951	1245	1482	69400	634	1028	1345	1605	74800	680	1102	1440	1717
58700	534	873	1143	1349	64100	585	952	1247	1485	69500	634	1030	1347	1607	74900	681	1103	1442	1719
58800	534	874	1145	1352	64200	586	954	1249	1487	69600	635	1031	1349	1609	75000	682	1105	1444	1721
58900	535	876	1147	1354	64300	587	955	1251	1490	69700	636	1032	1350	1611	75100	683	1106	1446	1723
59000	536	877	1149	1357	64400	588	957	1253	1492	69800	637	1034	1352	1613	75200	684	1108	1448	1725
59100	537	879	1151	1359	64500	589	958	1255	1495	69900	638	1035	1354	1615	75300	685	1109	1449	1727
59200	538	880	1153	1362	64600	590	960	1257	1497	70000	639	1037	1356	1617	75400	686	1110	1451	1729
59300	539	882	1155	1364	64700	591	961	1259	1500	70100	640	1038	1358	1619	75500	686	1112	1453	1731

Ontario

Federal Child Support Amounts: Simplified Tables
Montants fédéraux de pensions alimentaires pour enfants: Tables simplifiées

Income/ Revenu ($)	Monthly Award/ Paiement mensuel ($) No. of Children/ N^bre d'enfants				Income/ Revenu ($)	Monthly Award/ Paiement mensuel ($) No. of Children/ N^bre d'enfants				Income/ Revenu ($)	Monthly Award/ Paiement mensuel ($) No. of Children/ N^bre d'enfants				Income/ Revenu ($)	Monthly Award/ Paiement mensuel ($) No. of Children/ N^bre d'enfants			
	1	2	3	4		1	2	3	4		1	2	3	4		1	2	3	4
75600	687	1113	1455	1734	81000	731	1184	1546	1842	86400	773	1250	1631	1942	91800	816	1316	1716	2043
75700	688	1114	1457	1736	81100	732	1185	1548	1844	86500	774	1251	1633	1944	91900	816	1317	1717	2045
75800	689	1116	1458	1738	81200	732	1186	1549	1846	86600	774	1252	1634	1946	92000	817	1318	1719	2047
75900	690	1117	1460	1740	81300	733	1188	1551	1848	86700	775	1254	1636	1948	92100	818	1319	1721	2049
76000	691	1119	1462	1742	81400	734	1189	1553	1850	86800	776	1255	1637	1950	92200	819	1320	1722	2051
76100	692	1120	1464	1744	81500	735	1190	1554	1851	86900	777	1256	1639	1952	92300	819	1322	1724	2053
76200	693	1122	1466	1746	81600	735	1191	1556	1853	87000	777	1257	1640	1954	92400	820	1323	1725	2055
76300	694	1123	1467	1748	81700	736	1193	1557	1855	87100	778	1258	1642	1956	92500	821	1324	1727	2057
76400	695	1124	1469	1751	81800	737	1194	1559	1857	87200	779	1259	1643	1958	92600	822	1325	1729	2058
76500	695	1126	1471	1753	81900	738	1195	1561	1859	87300	779	1261	1645	1960	92700	823	1326	1730	2060
76600	696	1127	1473	1755	82000	738	1196	1562	1861	87400	780	1262	1646	1962	92800	824	1328	1732	2062
76700	697	1129	1475	1757	82100	739	1197	1564	1863	87500	781	1263	1648	1963	92900	824	1329	1733	2064
76800	698	1130	1476	1759	82200	740	1198	1565	1865	87600	782	1264	1649	1965	93000	825	1330	1735	2066
76900	699	1131	1478	1761	82300	740	1200	1567	1867	87700	782	1266	1651	1967	93100	826	1331	1737	2068
77000	700	1133	1480	1764	82400	741	1201	1568	1869	87800	783	1267	1653	1969	93200	826	1332	1738	2070
77100	701	1134	1482	1766	82500	742	1202	1570	1870	87900	784	1268	1654	1971	93300	827	1334	1740	2072
77200	702	1136	1484	1768	82600	743	1203	1571	1872	88000	785	1269	1656	1973	93400	828	1335	1741	2073
77300	703	1137	1485	1770	82700	744	1205	1573	1874	88100	786	1270	1658	1975	93500	829	1336	1743	2075
77400	704	1138	1487	1773	82800	744	1206	1574	1876	88200	787	1271	1659	1977	93600	829	1337	1744	2077
77500	704	1140	1489	1775	82900	745	1207	1576	1878	88300	787	1273	1661	1979	93700	830	1338	1746	2079
77600	705	1141	1491	1777	83000	746	1208	1577	1880	88400	788	1274	1662	1980	93800	831	1339	1747	2081
77700	706	1143	1493	1779	83100	747	1209	1579	1882	88500	789	1275	1664	1982	93900	832	1341	1749	2083
77800	707	1144	1494	1781	83200	748	1210	1580	1884	88600	790	1276	1666	1984	94000	832	1342	1750	2084
77900	708	1145	1496	1783	83300	748	1212	1582	1885	88700	790	1277	1667	1986	94100	833	1343	1752	2086
78000	709	1147	1498	1785	83400	749	1213	1583	1887	88800	791	1279	1669	1988	94200	834	1345	1753	2088
78100	710	1148	1500	1787	83500	750	1214	1585	1889	88900	792	1280	1670	1990	94300	834	1346	1755	2090
78200	711	1150	1501	1789	83600	751	1215	1586	1891	89000	793	1281	1672	1991	94400	835	1347	1756	2092
78300	711	1151	1503	1791	83700	752	1216	1588	1893	89100	794	1282	1674	1993	94500	836	1348	1758	2093
78400	712	1152	1504	1793	83800	752	1218	1589	1895	89200	795	1283	1675	1995	94600	837	1350	1759	2095
78500	713	1153	1506	1795	83900	753	1219	1591	1896	89300	795	1285	1677	1997	94700	837	1351	1761	2097
78600	714	1155	1508	1797	84000	754	1220	1593	1898	89400	796	1286	1678	1999	94800	838	1352	1763	2099
78700	715	1156	1509	1798	84100	755	1221	1595	1900	89500	797	1287	1680	2000	94900	839	1353	1764	2101
78800	715	1157	1511	1800	84200	756	1222	1596	1902	89600	798	1288	1681	2002	95000	840	1355	1766	2103
78900	716	1158	1512	1802	84300	756	1224	1598	1904	89700	798	1289	1683	2004	95100	841	1356	1768	2105
79000	717	1160	1514	1804	84400	757	1225	1599	1905	89800	799	1290	1684	2006	95200	842	1357	1769	2107
79100	718	1161	1516	1806	84500	758	1226	1601	1907	89900	800	1292	1686	2008	95300	842	1359	1771	2108
79200	718	1162	1517	1808	84600	759	1227	1603	1909	90000	801	1293	1687	2010	95400	843	1360	1772	2110
79300	719	1164	1519	1810	84700	760	1228	1604	1911	90100	802	1294	1689	2012	95500	844	1361	1774	2112
79400	720	1165	1520	1811	84800	761	1230	1606	1913	90200	803	1296	1690	2014	95600	845	1362	1776	2114
79500	721	1166	1522	1813	84900	761	1231	1607	1915	90300	803	1297	1692	2015	95700	845	1364	1777	2116
79600	721	1167	1523	1815	85000	762	1232	1609	1917	90400	804	1298	1693	2017	95800	846	1365	1779	2118
79700	722	1169	1525	1817	85100	763	1233	1611	1919	90500	805	1299	1695	2019	95900	847	1366	1780	2119
79800	723	1170	1527	1819	85200	764	1235	1612	1921	90600	806	1301	1696	2021	96000	848	1367	1782	2121
79900	724	1171	1528	1821	85300	764	1236	1614	1922	90700	807	1302	1698	2023	96100	849	1368	1784	2123
80000	724	1172	1530	1823	85400	765	1237	1615	1924	90800	807	1303	1699	2025	96200	850	1369	1785	2125
80100	725	1173	1532	1825	85500	766	1238	1617	1926	90900	808	1304	1701	2026	96300	850	1371	1787	2127
80200	725	1174	1533	1827	85600	767	1240	1619	1928	91000	809	1306	1703	2028	96400	851	1372	1788	2128
80300	726	1176	1535	1829	85700	768	1241	1620	1930	91100	810	1307	1705	2030	96500	852	1373	1790	2130
80400	727	1177	1536	1831	85800	769	1242	1622	1931	91200	811	1308	1706	2032	96600	853	1374	1791	2132
80500	728	1178	1538	1832	85900	769	1243	1624	1933	91300	811	1310	1708	2034	96700	853	1376	1793	2134
80600	728	1179	1540	1834	86000	770	1245	1625	1935	91400	812	1311	1709	2035	96800	854	1377	1794	2136
80700	729	1181	1541	1836	86100	771	1246	1627	1937	91500	813	1312	1711	2037	96900	855	1378	1796	2138
80800	730	1182	1543	1838	86200	771	1247	1628	1939	91600	814	1313	1712	2039	97000	856	1379	1797	2140
80900	731	1183	1544	1840	86300	772	1249	1630	1941	91700	815	1315	1714	2041	97100	857	1380	1799	2142

ONTARIO — CONTINUED

Federal Child Support Amounts: Simplified Tables
Montants fédéraux de pensions alimentaires pour enfants: Tables simplifiées

Income/ Revenu ($)	Monthly Award/ Paiement mensuel ($) No. of Children/ N^{bre} d'enfants				Income/ Revenu ($)	Monthly Award/ Paiement mensuel ($) No. of Children/ N^{bre} d'enfants				Income/ Revenu ($)	Monthly Award/ Paiement mensuel ($) No. of Children/ N^{bre} d'enfants				Income/ Revenu ($)	Monthly Award/ Paiement mensuel ($) No. of Children/ N^{bre} d'enfants			
	1	2	3	4		1	2	3	4		1	2	3	4		1	2	3	4
97200	858	1381	1800	2144	102600	900	1447	1886	2244	108000	942	1514	1970	2344	113400	985	1580	2055	2445
97300	858	1383	1802	2145	102700	900	1448	1887	2246	108100	943	1515	1972	2346	113500	986	1581	2057	2446
97400	859	1384	1803	2147	102800	901	1449	1889	2248	108200	944	1516	1973	2348	113600	987	1582	2059	2448
97500	860	1385	1805	2149	102900	902	1451	1890	2249	108300	944	1518	1975	2350	113700	988	1584	2060	2450
97600	861	1386	1806	2151	103000	903	1452	1892	2251	108400	945	1519	1976	2352	113800	989	1585	2062	2452
97700	862	1387	1808	2153	103100	904	1453	1894	2253	108500	946	1520	1978	2353	113900	989	1586	2063	2454
97800	862	1389	1809	2155	103200	905	1455	1895	2255	108600	947	1521	1979	2355	114000	990	1587	2065	2456
97900	863	1390	1811	2156	103300	905	1456	1897	2257	108700	947	1523	1981	2357	114100	991	1588	2067	2458
98000	864	1391	1813	2158	103400	906	1457	1898	2258	108800	948	1524	1982	2359	114200	992	1589	2068	2460
98100	865	1392	1815	2160	103500	907	1458	1900	2260	108900	949	1525	1984	2361	114300	993	1591	2070	2462
98200	866	1394	1816	2162	103600	908	1460	1902	2262	109000	950	1526	1986	2363	114400	993	1592	2071	2463
98300	866	1395	1818	2164	103700	908	1461	1903	2264	109100	951	1527	1988	2365	114500	994	1593	2073	2465
98400	867	1396	1819	2165	103800	909	1462	1905	2266	109200	952	1528	1989	2367	114600	995	1594	2074	2467
98500	868	1397	1821	2167	103900	910	1463	1907	2268	109300	952	1530	1991	2368	114700	996	1595	2076	2469
98600	869	1399	1822	2169	104000	911	1465	1908	2270	109400	953	1531	1992	2370	114800	997	1597	2077	2471
98700	870	1400	1824	2171	104100	912	1466	1910	2272	109500	954	1532	1994	2372	114900	998	1598	2079	2473
98800	870	1401	1826	2173	104200	913	1467	1911	2274	109600	955	1533	1996	2374	115000	998	1599	2080	2474
98900	871	1402	1827	2175	104300	913	1469	1913	2275	109700	955	1535	1997	2376	115100	999	1600	2082	2476
99000	872	1404	1829	2177	104400	914	1470	1914	2277	109800	956	1536	1999	2378	115200	999	1601	2083	2478
99100	873	1405	1831	2179	104500	915	1471	1916	2279	109900	957	1537	2000	2379	115300	1000	1603	2085	2480
99200	874	1406	1832	2181	104600	916	1472	1917	2281	110000	958	1538	2002	2381	115400	1001	1604	2086	2482
99300	874	1408	1834	2183	104700	917	1474	1919	2283	110100	959	1539	2004	2383	115500	1002	1605	2088	2483
99400	875	1409	1835	2185	104800	917	1475	1920	2284	110200	960	1540	2005	2385	115600	1002	1606	2089	2485
99500	876	1410	1837	2186	104900	918	1476	1922	2286	110300	960	1542	2007	2387	115700	1003	1607	2091	2487
99600	877	1411	1839	2188	105000	919	1477	1923	2288	110400	961	1543	2008	2388	115800	1004	1608	2092	2489
99700	878	1413	1840	2190	105100	920	1478	1925	2290	110500	962	1544	2010	2390	115900	1005	1610	2094	2491
99800	879	1414	1842	2192	105200	921	1479	1926	2292	110600	963	1545	2012	2392	116000	1005	1611	2096	2493
99900	879	1415	1843	2194	105300	921	1481	1928	2294	110700	963	1546	2013	2394	116100	1006	1612	2098	2495
100000	880	1416	1845	2196	105400	922	1482	1929	2295	110800	964	1548	2015	2396	116200	1007	1614	2099	2497
100100	881	1417	1847	2198	105500	923	1483	1931	2297	110900	965	1549	2017	2398	116300	1007	1615	2101	2498
100200	881	1418	1848	2200	105600	924	1484	1932	2299	111000	966	1550	2018	2400	116400	1008	1616	2102	2500
100300	882	1420	1850	2202	105700	925	1485	1934	2301	111100	967	1551	2020	2402	116500	1009	1617	2104	2502
100400	883	1421	1851	2203	105800	925	1487	1936	2303	111200	968	1552	2021	2404	116600	1010	1619	2106	2504
100500	884	1422	1853	2205	105900	926	1488	1937	2305	111300	968	1554	2023	2406	116700	1010	1620	2107	2506
100600	884	1423	1854	2207	106000	927	1489	1939	2307	111400	969	1555	2024	2408	116800	1011	1621	2109	2508
100700	885	1425	1856	2209	106100	928	1490	1941	2309	111500	970	1556	2026	2410	116900	1012	1622	2110	2509
100800	886	1426	1857	2211	106200	929	1491	1942	2311	111600	971	1557	2027	2411	117000	1013	1624	2112	2511
100900	887	1427	1859	2213	106300	929	1493	1944	2313	111700	972	1558	2029	2413	117100	1014	1625	2114	2513
101000	887	1428	1860	2214	106400	930	1494	1945	2315	111800	972	1559	2030	2415	117200	1015	1626	2115	2515
101100	888	1429	1862	2216	106500	931	1495	1947	2316	111900	973	1561	2032	2417	117300	1015	1628	2117	2517
101200	889	1430	1863	2218	106600	932	1496	1949	2318	112000	974	1562	2033	2419	117400	1016	1629	2118	2518
101300	889	1432	1865	2220	106700	933	1497	1950	2320	112100	975	1563	2035	2421	117500	1017	1630	2120	2520
101400	890	1433	1866	2222	106800	934	1499	1952	2322	112200	976	1565	2036	2423	117600	1018	1631	2122	2522
101500	891	1434	1868	2223	106900	934	1500	1953	2324	112300	976	1566	2038	2425	117700	1018	1633	2123	2524
101600	892	1435	1869	2225	107000	935	1501	1955	2326	112400	977	1567	2039	2426	117800	1019	1634	2125	2526
101700	892	1436	1871	2227	107100	936	1502	1957	2328	112500	978	1568	2041	2428	117900	1020	1635	2127	2528
101800	893	1438	1873	2229	107200	936	1504	1958	2330	112600	979	1570	2042	2430	118000	1021	1636	2128	2530
101900	894	1439	1874	2231	107300	937	1505	1960	2332	112700	980	1571	2044	2432	118100	1022	1637	2130	2532
102000	895	1440	1876	2233	107400	938	1506	1961	2333	112800	980	1572	2046	2434	118200	1023	1638	2131	2534
102100	896	1441	1878	2235	107500	939	1507	1963	2335	112900	981	1573	2047	2436	118300	1023	1640	2133	2536
102200	897	1442	1879	2237	107600	939	1509	1964	2337	113000	982	1575	2049	2437	118400	1024	1641	2134	2538
102300	897	1444	1881	2238	107700	940	1510	1966	2339	113100	983	1576	2051	2439	118500	1025	1642	2136	2540
102400	898	1445	1882	2240	107800	941	1511	1967	2341	113200	984	1577	2052	2441	118600	1026	1643	2137	2541
102500	899	1446	1884	2242	107900	942	1512	1969	2343	113300	984	1579	2054	2443	118700	1027	1645	2139	2543

Federal Child Support Amounts: Simplified Tables
Montants fédéraux de pensions alimentaires pour enfants: Tables simplifiées

Income/ Revenu ($)	Monthly Award/ Paiement mensuel ($) No. of Children/ N^bre d'enfants				Income/ Revenu ($)	Monthly Award/ Paiement mensuel ($) No. of Children/ N^bre d'enfants				Income/ Revenu ($)	Monthly Award/ Paiement mensuel ($) No. of Children/ N^bre d'enfants				Income/ Revenu ($)	Monthly Award/ Paiement mensuel ($) No. of Children/ N^bre d'enfants			
	1	2	3	4		1	2	3	4		1	2	3	4		1	2	3	4
118800	1027	1646	2140	2545	124200	1070	1711	2225	2645	129600	1111	1776	2308	2743	135000	1151	1838	2388	2838
118900	1028	1647	2142	2547	124300	1070	1713	2227	2647	129700	1112	1777	2310	2744	135100	1152	1839	2389	2840
119000	1029	1648	2143	2549	124400	1071	1714	2228	2648	129800	1113	1779	2311	2746	135200	1153	1840	2391	2842
119100	1030	1649	2145	2551	124500	1072	1715	2230	2650	129900	1114	1780	2313	2748	135300	1153	1841	2392	2843
119200	1031	1650	2146	2553	124600	1073	1716	2232	2652	130000	1114	1781	2314	2750	135400	1154	1843	2394	2845
119300	1031	1652	2148	2555	124700	1073	1717	2233	2654	130100	1115	1782	2316	2752	135500	1155	1844	2395	2847
119400	1032	1653	2149	2556	124800	1074	1718	2235	2656	130200	1116	1783	2317	2754	135600	1156	1845	2397	2849
119500	1033	1654	2151	2558	124900	1075	1720	2236	2658	130300	1116	1784	2319	2755	135700	1156	1846	2398	2851
119600	1034	1655	2152	2560	125000	1076	1721	2238	2660	130400	1117	1786	2320	2757	135800	1157	1847	2400	2852
119700	1035	1656	2154	2562	125100	1077	1722	2240	2662	130500	1118	1787	2322	2759	135900	1158	1848	2401	2854
119800	1035	1658	2156	2564	125200	1078	1724	2241	2664	130600	1119	1788	2323	2761	136000	1159	1850	2403	2856
119900	1036	1659	2157	2566	125300	1078	1725	2243	2666	130700	1119	1789	2325	2763	136100	1160	1851	2404	2858
120000	1037	1660	2159	2567	125400	1079	1726	2244	2668	130800	1120	1790	2326	2764	136200	1160	1852	2406	2859
120100	1038	1661	2161	2569	125500	1080	1727	2246	2669	130900	1121	1791	2328	2766	136300	1161	1854	2407	2861
120200	1039	1662	2162	2571	125600	1081	1729	2247	2671	131000	1122	1792	2329	2768	136400	1162	1855	2409	2863
120300	1039	1664	2164	2573	125700	1082	1730	2249	2673	131100	1123	1793	2331	2770	136500	1163	1856	2410	2865
120400	1040	1665	2165	2575	125800	1082	1731	2250	2675	131200	1123	1794	2332	2771	136600	1163	1857	2412	2866
120500	1041	1666	2167	2576	125900	1083	1732	2252	2677	131300	1124	1796	2334	2773	136700	1164	1858	2413	2868
120600	1042	1667	2169	2578	126000	1084	1734	2253	2679	131400	1125	1797	2335	2775	136800	1165	1860	2415	2870
120700	1043	1668	2170	2580	126100	1085	1735	2255	2681	131500	1126	1798	2337	2777	136900	1165	1861	2416	2872
120800	1044	1669	2172	2582	126200	1086	1736	2256	2683	131600	1126	1799	2338	2778	137000	1166	1862	2418	2873
120900	1044	1671	2173	2584	126300	1086	1738	2258	2685	131700	1127	1800	2340	2780	137100	1167	1863	2420	2875
121000	1045	1672	2175	2586	126400	1087	1739	2259	2686	131800	1128	1801	2341	2782	137200	1168	1864	2421	2877
121100	1046	1673	2177	2588	126500	1088	1740	2261	2688	131900	1129	1803	2343	2784	137300	1168	1865	2423	2878
121200	1047	1675	2178	2590	126600	1089	1741	2262	2690	132000	1129	1804	2344	2785	137400	1169	1867	2424	2880
121300	1048	1676	2180	2591	126700	1090	1743	2264	2692	132100	1130	1805	2345	2787	137500	1170	1868	2426	2882
121400	1048	1677	2181	2593	126800	1090	1744	2266	2694	132200	1130	1806	2347	2789	137600	1171	1869	2427	2884
121500	1049	1678	2183	2595	126900	1091	1745	2267	2696	132300	1131	1807	2348	2790	137700	1171	1870	2429	2886
121600	1050	1680	2184	2597	127000	1092	1746	2269	2697	132400	1132	1808	2350	2792	137800	1172	1871	2430	2887
121700	1051	1681	2186	2599	127100	1093	1747	2270	2699	132500	1132	1810	2351	2794	137900	1173	1872	2432	2889
121800	1052	1682	2187	2601	127200	1093	1748	2272	2701	132600	1133	1811	2353	2796	138000	1174	1873	2433	2891
121900	1053	1683	2189	2602	127300	1094	1749	2273	2702	132700	1134	1812	2354	2797	138100	1175	1874	2435	2893
122000	1053	1685	2190	2604	127400	1095	1750	2275	2704	132800	1135	1813	2356	2799	138200	1175	1875	2436	2894
122100	1054	1686	2192	2606	127500	1096	1752	2276	2706	132900	1135	1814	2357	2801	138300	1176	1877	2438	2896
122200	1054	1687	2193	2608	127600	1096	1753	2278	2708	133000	1136	1815	2358	2803	138400	1177	1878	2439	2898
122300	1055	1689	2195	2610	127700	1097	1754	2279	2709	133100	1137	1816	2359	2805	138500	1178	1879	2441	2900
122400	1056	1690	2196	2611	127800	1098	1755	2281	2711	133200	1138	1817	2361	2806	138600	1178	1880	2442	2901
122500	1057	1691	2198	2613	127900	1098	1756	2282	2713	133300	1138	1818	2362	2808	138700	1179	1881	2444	2903
122600	1057	1692	2199	2615	128000	1099	1757	2284	2715	133400	1139	1820	2364	2810	138800	1180	1882	2445	2905
122700	1058	1694	2201	2617	128100	1101	1758	2286	2717	133500	1140	1821	2365	2812	138900	1181	1884	2447	2907
122800	1059	1695	2202	2619	128200	1101	1759	2287	2718	133600	1141	1822	2367	2813	139000	1181	1885	2448	2908
122900	1060	1696	2204	2621	128300	1101	1760	2289	2720	133700	1141	1823	2368	2815	139100	1182	1886	2450	2910
123000	1060	1697	2206	2623	128400	1102	1762	2290	2722	133800	1142	1824	2370	2817	139200	1183	1887	2451	2912
123100	1061	1698	2208	2625	128500	1103	1763	2292	2724	133900	1143	1825	2371	2819	139300	1183	1888	2453	2913
123200	1062	1699	2209	2627	128600	1104	1764	2293	2725	134000	1144	1827	2373	2820	139400	1184	1889	2454	2915
123300	1062	1701	2211	2628	128700	1104	1765	2295	2727	134100	1145	1828	2374	2822	139500	1185	1891	2456	2917
123400	1063	1702	2212	2630	128800	1105	1766	2296	2729	134200	1145	1829	2376	2824	139600	1186	1892	2457	2919
123500	1064	1703	2214	2632	128900	1106	1767	2298	2730	134300	1146	1830	2377	2825	139700	1186	1893	2459	2920
123600	1065	1704	2215	2634	129000	1107	1769	2299	2732	134400	1147	1831	2379	2827	139800	1187	1894	2460	2922
123700	1065	1705	2217	2636	129100	1108	1770	2301	2734	134500	1148	1833	2380	2829	139900	1188	1895	2462	2924
123800	1066	1707	2219	2638	129200	1108	1771	2302	2736	134600	1148	1834	2382	2831	140000	1189	1896	2463	2926
123900	1067	1708	2220	2639	129300	1109	1773	2304	2737	134700	1149	1835	2383	2832	140100	1190	1897	2465	2928
124000	1068	1709	2222	2641	129400	1110	1774	2305	2739	134800	1150	1836	2385	2834	140200	1190	1898	2466	2929
124100	1069	1710	2224	2643	129500	1111	1775	2307	2741	134900	1150	1837	2386	2836	140300	1191	1899	2468	2931

Federal Child Support Amounts: Simplified Tables
Montants fédéraux de pensions alimentaires pour enfants: Tables simplifiées

Income/ Revenu ($)	Monthly Award/ Paiement mensuel ($) No. of Children/ Nbre d'enfants				Income/ Revenu ($)	Monthly Award/ Paiement mensuel ($) No. of Children/ Nbre d'enfants				Income/ Revenu ($)	Monthly Award/ Paiement mensuel ($) No. of Children/ Nbre d'enfants			
	1	2	3	4		1	2	3	4		1	2	3	4
140400	1192	1901	2469	2933	143700	1216	1939	2517	2991	147000	1241	1977	2567	3049
140500	1193	1902	2471	2935	143800	1217	1941	2519	2993	147100	1242	1978	2569	3051
140600	1193	1903	2472	2936	143900	1217	1942	2520	2995	147200	1242	1979	2570	3053
140700	1194	1904	2474	2938	144000	1218	1943	2522	2996	147300	1243	1980	2572	3054
140800	1195	1905	2475	2940	144100	1219	1944	2523	2998	147400	1244	1982	2573	3056
140900	1196	1906	2477	2941	144200	1220	1945	2525	3000	147500	1245	1983	2575	3058
141000	1196	1908	2478	2943	144300	1220	1946	2526	3001	147600	1245	1984	2576	3060
141100	1197	1909	2479	2945	144400	1221	1948	2528	3003	147700	1246	1985	2578	3062
141200	1197	1910	2481	2947	144500	1222	1949	2529	3005	147800	1247	1986	2579	3063
141300	1198	1912	2482	2948	144600	1223	1950	2531	3007	147900	1248	1987	2581	3065
141400	1199	1913	2484	2950	144700	1223	1951	2532	3008	148000	1248	1989	2582	3067
141500	1199	1914	2485	2952	144800	1224	1952	2534	3010	148100	1249	1990	2584	3069
141600	1200	1915	2487	2954	144900	1225	1953	2535	3012	148200	1250	1991	2585	3070
141700	1201	1916	2488	2955	145000	1226	1954	2537	3014	148300	1250	1993	2587	3072
141800	1202	1918	2490	2957	145100	1227	1955	2538	3016	148400	1251	1994	2588	3074
141900	1202	1919	2491	2959	145200	1227	1956	2540	3017	148500	1252	1995	2590	3076
142000	1203	1920	2492	2961	145300	1228	1958	2541	3019	148600	1253	1996	2591	3077
142100	1204	1921	2493	2963	145400	1229	1959	2543	3021	148700	1254	1997	2593	3079
142200	1205	1922	2495	2965	145500	1230	1960	2544	3023	148800	1254	1999	2594	3081
142300	1205	1923	2496	2966	145600	1230	1961	2547	3024	148900	1255	2000	2596	3083
142400	1206	1925	2498	2968	145700	1231	1962	2547	3026	149000	1256	2001	2597	3084
142500	1207	1926	2499	2970	145800	1232	1963	2549	3028	149100	1257	2002	2598	3086
142600	1208	1927	2501	2972	145900	1232	1965	2550	3029	149200	1257	2003	2600	3088
142700	1208	1928	2502	2974	146000	1233	1966	2552	3031	149300	1258	2004	2601	3089
142800	1209	1929	2504	2975	146100	1234	1967	2554	3033	149400	1259	2006	2603	3091
142900	1210	1930	2505	2977	146200	1235	1968	2555	3035	149500	1260	2007	2604	3093
143000	1211	1931	2507	2979	146300	1235	1969	2557	3036	149600	1260	2008	2606	3095
143100	1212	1932	2508	2981	146400	1236	1970	2558	3038	149700	1261	2009	2607	3096
143200	1212	1933	2510	2982	146500	1237	1972	2560	3040	149800	1262	2010	2609	3098
143300	1213	1935	2511	2984	146600	1238	1973	2561	3042	149900	1263	2011	2610	3100
143400	1214	1936	2513	2986	146700	1238	1974	2563	3043	150000	1263	2012	2611	3102
143500	1215	1937	2514	2988	146800	1239	1975	2564	3045					
143600	1215	1938	2516	2989	146900	1240	1976	2566	3047					

Monthly Award/Paiement mensuel ($)			
One Child/ Un enfant	Two Children/ Deux enfants	Three Children/ Trois enfants	Four Children/ Quatre enfants
1263 plus 0.74% of income over $150,000	2012 plus 1.14% of income over $150,000	2611 plus 1.44% of income over $150,000	3120 plus 1.78% of income over $150,000
1263 plus 0,74% du revenu dépassant 150 000$	2012 plus 1,14% du revenu dépassant 150 000$	2611 plus 1,44% du revenu dépassant 150 000$	3120 plus 1,78% du revenu dépassant 150 000$

NOVA SCOTIA

Federal Child Support Amounts: Simplified Tables
Montants fédéraux de pensions alimentaires pour enfants: Tables simplifiées

Income/ Revenu ($)	Monthly Award/ Paiement mensuel ($) No. of Children/ Nbre d'enfants				Income/ Revenu ($)	Monthly Award/ Paiement mensuel ($) No. of Children/ Nbre d'enfants				Income/ Revenu ($)	Monthly Award/ Paiement mensuel ($) No. of Children/ Nbre d'enfants				Income/ Revenu ($)	Monthly Award/ Paiement mensuel ($) No. of Children/ Nbre d'enfants			
	1	2	3	4		1	2	3	4		1	2	3	4		1	2	3	4
10820	1	1	2	2	16200	87	222	239	257	21600	157	306	428	476	27000	223	393	534	650
10900	2	5	6	6	16300	88	225	243	260	21700	159	308	430	480	27100	224	394	536	652
11000	15	49	53	57	16400	90	228	246	264	21800	160	309	431	485	27200	225	396	538	654
11100	16	53	58	62	16500	91	231	249	267	21900	161	311	433	489	27300	226	397	539	656
11200	18	58	62	67	16600	92	234	252	271	22000	162	312	435	494	27400	227	399	541	658
11300	19	62	67	72	16700	94	237	255	274	22100	163	314	437	498	27500	228	400	543	660
11400	21	66	72	77	16800	95	240	258	277	22200	164	315	439	503	27600	229	402	545	662
11500	22	71	76	82	16900	97	243	262	281	22300	166	317	440	507	27700	230	403	546	664
11600	23	75	81	87	17000	98	246	265	284	22400	167	319	442	512	27800	231	405	548	667
11700	25	79	86	92	17100	99	248	269	288	22500	168	321	444	516	27900	232	406	550	669
11800	26	84	90	97	17200	101	250	273	292	22600	169	322	446	521	28000	233	407	552	671
11900	27	88	95	102	17300	102	252	277	296	22700	171	324	448	525	28100	234	409	554	673
12000	29	93	100	107	17400	103	254	281	300	22800	172	326	450	529	28200	235	410	555	675
12100	30	96	104	111	17500	105	255	285	305	22900	173	327	451	534	28300	236	412	557	677
12200	32	100	107	115	17600	106	257	288	309	23000	174	329	453	538	28400	237	414	559	680
12300	33	103	111	119	17700	107	259	292	313	23100	175	331	455	542	28500	238	415	561	682
12400	35	106	114	122	17800	109	261	296	317	23200	176	332	457	546	28600	239	417	562	684
12500	36	110	118	126	17900	110	263	300	321	23300	178	334	459	551	28700	240	419	564	686
12600	37	113	122	130	18000	111	265	304	325	23400	179	336	462	555	28800	241	420	566	688
12700	39	116	125	134	18100	112	266	308	329	23500	180	337	464	559	28900	242	422	568	690
12800	40	119	129	138	18200	114	267	312	333	23600	181	339	466	563	29000	243	423	569	693
12900	42	123	132	142	18300	115	268	316	338	23700	183	341	468	567	29100	244	425	571	695
13000	43	126	136	146	18400	116	269	319	342	23800	184	343	470	572	29200	245	426	572	697
13100	44	129	139	150	18500	118	270	323	346	23900	185	344	472	576	29300	246	428	574	699
13200	46	132	143	153	18600	119	272	327	350	24000	186	346	475	580	29400	247	430	576	701
13300	47	136	146	157	18700	121	273	331	354	24100	187	348	477	582	29500	248	431	578	703
13400	48	139	150	161	18800	122	274	335	358	24200	188	349	479	585	29600	249	433	579	705
13500	50	142	153	164	18900	123	275	339	363	24300	189	351	481	587	29700	249	435	581	707
13600	51	145	156	168	19000	125	276	342	367	24400	191	353	483	590	29800	250	436	583	709
13700	52	148	160	171	19100	126	277	346	371	24500	192	354	486	592	29900	251	438	584	711
13800	54	151	163	175	19200	128	278	350	375	24600	193	356	488	595	30000	252	440	586	713
13900	55	155	167	179	19300	129	279	354	379	24700	194	358	490	597	30100	253	441	588	715
14000	56	158	170	182	19400	131	280	358	384	24800	195	359	492	600	30200	254	443	590	717
14100	57	161	173	186	19500	132	281	361	388	24900	196	361	494	602	30300	255	444	592	718
14200	59	164	177	189	19600	133	282	365	392	25000	197	363	496	605	30400	255	446	593	720
14300	60	167	180	193	19700	135	283	369	396	25100	198	365	498	607	30500	256	447	595	722
14400	61	171	183	196	19800	136	284	373	400	25200	200	366	500	610	30600	257	449	597	724
14500	63	174	187	200	19900	138	285	377	404	25300	201	368	502	612	30700	258	450	599	726
14600	64	177	190	204	20000	139	286	381	408	25400	202	370	504	615	30800	259	451	601	728
14700	66	180	193	207	20100	140	287	385	412	25500	204	371	506	617	30900	260	453	603	729
14800	67	183	196	211	20200	141	288	388	416	25600	205	373	508	619	31000	261	454	604	731
14900	68	186	200	214	20300	142	289	392	420	25700	206	375	510	622	31100	262	455	606	733
15000	70	189	203	218	20400	143	290	396	424	25800	208	376	513	624	31200	263	457	608	735
15100	71	192	206	221	20500	145	291	399	429	25900	209	378	515	627	31300	264	458	610	736
15200	73	194	209	224	20600	146	293	403	433	26000	211	380	517	629	31400	265	459	611	738
15300	74	197	212	228	20700	147	294	406	437	26100	212	381	519	631	31500	266	461	613	740
15400	76	200	215	231	20800	148	295	410	441	26200	213	383	520	633	31600	266	462	615	742
15500	77	203	218	234	20900	149	296	414	445	26300	214	384	522	635	31700	267	463	617	744
15600	78	205	221	237	21000	150	297	417	449	26400	216	385	524	637	31800	268	465	619	745
15700	80	208	224	241	21100	151	299	419	453	26500	217	386	525	639	31900	269	466	621	747
15800	81	211	227	244	21200	152	300	421	458	26600	218	388	527	641	32000	270	467	623	749
15900	83	213	230	247	21300	154	302	422	462	26700	219	389	529	644	32100	271	468	625	751
16000	84	216	233	250	21400	155	303	424	467	26800	220	390	531	646	32200	272	470	627	753
16100	85	219	236	253	21500	156	305	426	471	26900	221	392	532	648	32300	273	471	628	755

Federal Child Support Amounts: Simplified Tables
Montants fédéraux de pensions alimentaires pour enfants: Tables simplifiées

Income/ Revenu ($)	Monthly Award/ Paiement mensuel ($) No. of Children/ Nbre d'enfants				Income/ Revenu ($)	Monthly Award/ Paiement mensuel ($) No. of Children/ Nbre d'enfants				Income/ Revenu ($)	Monthly Award/ Paiement mensuel ($) No. of Children/ Nbre d'enfants				Income/ Revenu ($)	Monthly Award/ Paiement mensuel ($) No. of Children/ Nbre d'enfants			
	1	2	3	4		1	2	3	4		1	2	3	4		1	2	3	4
32400	273	472	630	757	37800	318	541	720	867	43200	363	612	810	974	48600	407	681	901	1081
32500	274	473	632	759	37900	319	543	722	869	43300	364	613	812	976	48700	408	682	902	1083
32600	275	475	634	761	38000	319	544	724	871	43400	364	614	814	978	48800	409	684	904	1085
32700	276	476	636	763	38100	320	545	726	873	43500	365	616	815	980	48900	410	685	906	1087
32800	277	477	637	765	38200	321	547	727	875	43600	366	617	817	981	49000	411	687	908	1089
32900	278	478	639	767	38300	321	548	729	877	43700	367	618	819	983	49100	412	688	910	1091
33000	278	480	641	769	38400	322	549	731	879	43800	368	620	820	985	49200	413	690	912	1093
33100	279	481	643	771	38500	323	551	733	881	43900	369	621	822	987	49300	414	691	913	1095
33200	280	483	644	773	38600	324	552	734	883	44000	369	622	824	989	49400	415	693	915	1097
33300	280	484	646	775	38700	325	553	736	885	44100	370	623	826	991	49500	416	694	917	1099
33400	281	485	648	777	38800	325	554	738	887	44200	371	624	827	993	49600	416	695	919	1101
33500	282	486	649	779	38900	326	556	739	889	44300	371	626	829	995	49700	417	697	921	1103
33600	283	488	651	781	39000	327	557	741	891	44400	372	627	830	997	49800	418	698	922	1105
33700	284	489	653	783	39100	328	558	743	893	44500	373	628	832	999	49900	419	700	924	1107
33800	284	490	655	785	39200	329	560	744	895	44600	374	629	834	1001	50000	420	701	926	1109
33900	285	492	656	787	39300	330	561	746	897	44700	375	631	835	1003	50100	421	702	928	1111
34000	286	493	658	789	39400	331	562	748	899	44800	376	632	837	1005	50200	422	704	929	1113
34100	287	494	660	791	39500	331	564	749	901	44900	376	633	839	1007	50300	422	705	931	1115
34200	288	495	661	793	39600	332	565	751	903	45000	377	634	840	1009	50400	423	706	933	1117
34300	288	497	663	795	39700	333	566	753	905	45100	378	635	842	1011	50500	424	708	935	1119
34400	289	498	664	797	39800	334	568	754	907	45200	379	637	843	1013	50600	425	709	936	1121
34500	290	499	666	799	39900	335	569	756	909	45300	379	638	845	1015	50700	426	710	938	1123
34600	291	500	668	801	40000	336	570	757	911	45400	380	639	847	1017	50800	427	712	940	1125
34700	292	502	669	803	40100	337	571	759	913	45500	381	640	848	1019	50900	427	713	942	1128
34800	293	503	671	805	40200	338	573	761	915	45600	382	642	850	1021	51000	428	714	943	1130
34900	293	504	673	808	40300	339	574	762	917	45700	383	643	852	1023	51100	429	715	945	1132
35000	294	505	674	810	40400	340	576	764	920	45800	383	644	853	1024	51200	430	717	947	1134
35100	295	506	676	812	40500	341	577	766	922	45900	384	645	855	1026	51300	431	718	948	1136
35200	296	508	677	814	40600	342	578	768	924	46000	385	647	857	1028	51400	431	719	950	1138
35300	296	509	679	816	40700	343	580	769	926	46100	386	648	859	1030	51500	432	721	952	1140
35400	297	510	681	819	40800	344	581	771	928	46200	387	650	860	1032	51600	433	722	954	1143
35500	298	511	683	821	40900	344	583	773	930	46300	388	651	862	1034	51700	434	724	956	1145
35600	299	513	684	823	41000	345	584	775	932	46400	388	652	864	1036	51800	435	725	957	1147
35700	300	514	686	825	41100	346	585	777	934	46500	389	653	865	1038	51900	436	726	959	1149
35800	300	515	688	827	41200	347	586	778	936	46600	390	655	867	1040	52000	437	728	961	1151
35900	301	517	689	829	41300	348	588	780	938	46700	391	656	868	1042	52100	438	729	963	1153
36000	302	518	691	831	41400	348	589	781	940	46800	392	657	870	1044	52200	439	731	964	1155
36100	303	519	693	833	41500	349	590	783	942	46900	393	659	872	1046	52300	440	732	966	1157
36200	304	521	694	835	41600	350	591	784	944	47000	394	660	873	1048	52400	441	734	968	1159
36300	305	522	696	837	41700	351	593	786	945	47100	395	661	875	1050	52500	441	735	970	1162
36400	306	523	698	839	41800	352	594	788	947	47200	396	663	876	1052	52600	442	736	971	1164
36500	306	525	699	841	41900	353	595	789	949	47300	397	664	878	1054	52700	443	738	973	1166
36600	307	526	701	843	42000	353	596	791	951	47400	397	665	880	1056	52800	444	739	975	1168
36700	308	527	702	845	42100	354	597	793	953	47500	398	666	881	1058	52900	445	741	977	1170
36800	309	528	704	847	42200	355	599	794	955	47600	399	668	883	1060	53000	446	742	978	1172
36900	310	530	706	849	42300	356	600	796	957	47700	400	669	885	1062	53100	447	743	980	1174
37000	311	531	707	851	42400	356	601	797	959	47800	401	670	886	1064	53200	448	745	982	1176
37100	312	532	709	853	42500	357	602	799	961	47900	402	672	888	1066	53300	449	746	983	1178
37200	313	534	710	855	42600	358	604	800	963	48000	402	673	890	1068	53400	450	747	985	1180
37300	314	535	712	857	42700	359	605	802	964	48100	403	674	892	1070	53500	451	749	987	1182
37400	314	536	714	859	42800	360	606	804	966	48200	404	676	894	1072	53600	451	750	989	1184
37500	315	538	715	861	42900	361	607	805	968	48300	405	677	895	1074	53700	452	751	991	1186
37600	316	539	717	863	43000	361	609	807	970	48400	406	678	897	1076	53800	453	753	992	1188
37700	317	540	719	865	43100	362	610	809	972	48500	406	680	899	1078	53900	454	754	994	1190

Nova Scotia / Nouvelle-Écosse

Federal Child Support Amounts: Simplified Tables
Montants fédéraux de pensions alimentaires pour enfants: Tables simplifiées

Income/ Revenu ($)	Monthly Award/ Paiement mensuel ($) No. of Children/ N^bre d'enfants				Income/ Revenu ($)	Monthly Award/ Paiement mensuel ($) No. of Children/ N^bre d'enfants				Income/ Revenu ($)	Monthly Award/ Paiement mensuel ($) No. of Children/ N^bre d'enfants				Income/ Revenu ($)	Monthly Award/ Paiement mensuel ($) No. of Children/ N^bre d'enfants			
	1	2	3	4		1	2	3	4		1	2	3	4		1	2	3	4
54000	455	755	996	1192	59400	502	828	1090	1304	64800	548	901	1181	1412	70200	594	972	1274	1521
54100	456	756	998	1194	59500	503	830	1091	1306	64900	549	902	1183	1414	70300	595	973	1276	1523
54200	457	758	999	1196	59600	504	831	1093	1308	65000	550	903	1185	1417	70400	595	974	1278	1525
54300	457	759	1001	1198	59700	505	833	1095	1310	65100	551	904	1187	1419	70500	596	975	1280	1527
54400	458	761	1003	1200	59800	506	834	1096	1312	65200	552	906	1188	1421	70600	597	977	1281	1529
54500	459	762	1005	1202	59900	507	835	1098	1314	65300	553	907	1190	1423	70700	598	978	1283	1531
54600	460	763	1006	1204	60000	507	837	1100	1316	65400	553	908	1192	1425	70800	599	979	1285	1533
54700	461	765	1008	1207	60100	508	838	1102	1318	65500	554	910	1193	1427	70900	600	981	1287	1535
54800	462	766	1010	1209	60200	509	840	1103	1320	65600	555	911	1195	1429	71000	601	982	1288	1537
54900	462	767	1012	1211	60300	510	841	1105	1322	65700	556	912	1197	1431	71100	602	983	1290	1539
55000	463	769	1013	1213	60400	511	842	1107	1324	65800	557	914	1198	1433	71200	603	985	1291	1541
55100	464	770	1015	1215	60500	511	844	1108	1326	65900	558	915	1200	1435	71300	603	986	1293	1543
55200	465	772	1017	1217	60600	512	845	1110	1328	66000	558	916	1202	1437	71400	604	987	1295	1545
55300	466	773	1018	1219	60700	513	846	1112	1330	66100	559	917	1204	1439	71500	605	989	1297	1547
55400	466	774	1020	1221	60800	514	848	1113	1332	66200	560	919	1206	1441	71600	606	990	1298	1549
55500	467	776	1022	1224	60900	515	849	1115	1334	66300	561	920	1207	1443	71700	607	992	1300	1551
55600	468	777	1024	1226	61000	516	850	1117	1336	66400	562	921	1209	1445	71800	608	993	1302	1553
55700	469	778	1026	1228	61100	517	851	1119	1338	66500	562	922	1211	1447	71900	608	994	1304	1556
55800	470	780	1027	1230	61200	518	853	1120	1340	66600	563	924	1213	1449	72000	609	996	1305	1558
55900	471	781	1029	1232	61300	519	854	1122	1342	66700	564	925	1214	1451	72100	610	997	1307	1560
56000	472	782	1031	1234	61400	519	855	1124	1344	66800	565	926	1216	1453	72200	611	999	1308	1562
56100	473	783	1033	1236	61500	520	857	1125	1346	66900	566	928	1218	1455	72300	612	1000	1310	1564
56200	474	785	1034	1238	61600	521	858	1127	1348	67000	567	929	1220	1457	72400	612	1001	1312	1566
56300	475	786	1036	1240	61700	522	859	1129	1350	67100	568	930	1222	1459	72500	613	1003	1314	1568
56400	476	787	1038	1242	61800	523	861	1130	1352	67200	569	932	1223	1461	72600	614	1004	1315	1570
56500	476	789	1040	1244	61900	524	862	1132	1354	67300	569	933	1225	1463	72700	615	1005	1317	1572
56600	477	790	1041	1246	62000	524	863	1134	1356	67400	570	934	1227	1465	72800	616	1007	1319	1574
56700	478	791	1043	1248	62100	525	864	1136	1358	67500	571	936	1229	1467	72900	617	1008	1321	1576
56800	480	793	1045	1250	62200	526	866	1137	1360	67600	572	937	1230	1469	73000	618	1009	1322	1578
56900	480	794	1047	1252	62300	527	867	1139	1362	67700	573	939	1232	1471	73100	619	1010	1324	1580
57000	481	796	1048	1254	62400	528	868	1141	1364	67800	574	940	1234	1473	73200	620	1012	1325	1582
57100	482	797	1050	1256	62500	528	869	1142	1366	67900	574	941	1236	1475	73300	620	1013	1327	1584
57200	483	799	1052	1258	62600	529	871	1144	1368	68000	575	943	1237	1477	73400	621	1014	1329	1586
57300	484	800	1053	1260	62700	530	872	1146	1370	68100	576	944	1239	1479	73500	622	1016	1331	1588
57400	485	802	1055	1262	62800	531	873	1147	1372	68200	577	946	1240	1481	73600	623	1017	1332	1590
57500	486	803	1057	1264	62900	532	875	1149	1374	68300	578	947	1242	1483	73700	624	1018	1334	1592
57600	486	804	1059	1266	63000	533	876	1151	1376	68400	579	948	1244	1485	73800	625	1020	1336	1594
57700	487	806	1061	1268	63100	534	877	1153	1378	68500	579	950	1246	1487	73900	625	1021	1338	1596
57800	488	807	1062	1271	63200	535	879	1154	1380	68600	580	951	1247	1489	74000	626	1022	1339	1598
57900	489	809	1064	1273	63300	536	880	1156	1382	68700	581	952	1249	1491	74100	627	1023	1341	1600
58000	490	810	1066	1275	63400	536	881	1158	1384	68800	582	954	1251	1493	74200	628	1025	1342	1602
58100	491	811	1068	1277	63500	537	883	1159	1386	68900	583	955	1253	1495	74300	629	1026	1344	1604
58200	492	813	1069	1279	63600	538	884	1161	1388	69000	584	956	1254	1497	74400	629	1027	1346	1606
58300	493	814	1071	1281	63700	539	886	1163	1390	69100	585	957	1256	1499	74500	630	1028	1348	1608
58400	494	815	1073	1283	63800	540	887	1164	1392	69200	586	959	1257	1501	74600	631	1030	1349	1610
58500	495	817	1075	1285	63900	541	888	1166	1394	69300	586	960	1259	1503	74700	632	1031	1351	1612
58600	496	818	1076	1288	64000	541	890	1168	1396	69400	587	961	1261	1505	74800	633	1032	1353	1614
58700	496	819	1078	1290	64100	542	891	1170	1398	69500	588	963	1263	1507	74900	634	1034	1355	1616
58800	497	821	1080	1292	64200	543	893	1171	1400	69600	589	964	1264	1509	75000	635	1035	1356	1618
58900	498	822	1082	1294	64300	544	894	1173	1402	69700	590	965	1266	1511	75100	636	1036	1358	1620
59000	499	823	1083	1296	64400	545	895	1175	1404	69800	591	967	1268	1513	75200	637	1038	1359	1622
59100	500	824	1085	1298	64500	545	897	1176	1406	69900	591	968	1270	1515	75300	637	1039	1361	1624
59200	501	826	1086	1300	64600	546	898	1178	1408	70000	592	969	1271	1517	75400	638	1040	1363	1626
59300	502	827	1088	1302	64700	547	899	1180	1410	70100	593	970	1273	1519	75500	639	1042	1365	1628

NOVA SCOTIA — CONTINUED

Federal Child Support Amounts: Simplified Tables
Montants fédéraux de pensions alimentaires pour enfants: Tables simplifiées

Income/ Revenu ($)	Monthly Award/ Paiement mensuel ($) No. of Children/ Nbre d'enfants				Income/ Revenu ($)	Monthly Award/ Paiement mensuel ($) No. of Children/ Nbre d'enfants				Income/ Revenu ($)	Monthly Award/ Paiement mensuel ($) No. of Children/ Nbre d'enfants				Income/ Revenu ($)	Monthly Award/ Paiement mensuel ($) No. of Children/ Nbre d'enfants			
	1	2	3	4		1	2	3	4		1	2	3	4		1	2	3	4
75600	640	1043	1366	1630	81000	686	1115	1458	1739	86400	729	1183	1546	1842	91800	772	1250	1631	1943
75700	641	1045	1368	1632	81100	687	1116	1460	1741	86500	730	1184	1547	1843	91900	773	1251	1632	1945
75800	642	1046	1370	1634	81200	688	1118	1461	1743	86600	731	1185	1549	1845	92000	774	1252	1634	1947
75900	642	1047	1371	1636	81300	688	1119	1463	1745	86700	731	1187	1550	1847	92100	775	1253	1636	1949
76000	643	1049	1373	1638	81400	689	1120	1465	1747	86800	732	1188	1552	1849	92200	776	1254	1637	1951
76100	644	1050	1375	1640	81500	690	1122	1466	1749	86900	733	1189	1554	1851	92300	776	1256	1639	1953
76200	645	1052	1376	1642	81600	691	1123	1468	1751	87000	734	1190	1555	1853	92400	777	1257	1640	1955
76300	646	1053	1378	1644	81700	692	1124	1470	1753	87100	735	1191	1557	1855	92500	778	1258	1642	1956
76400	646	1054	1380	1646	81800	692	1126	1472	1755	87200	736	1192	1558	1857	92600	779	1259	1643	1958
76500	647	1056	1382	1648	81900	693	1127	1473	1757	87300	736	1194	1560	1859	92700	780	1260	1645	1960
76600	648	1057	1383	1650	82000	694	1128	1475	1759	87400	737	1195	1562	1861	92800	780	1262	1647	1962
76700	649	1058	1385	1652	82100	695	1129	1477	1761	87500	738	1196	1563	1863	92900	781	1263	1648	1964
76800	650	1060	1387	1654	82200	696	1130	1478	1763	87600	739	1197	1565	1864	93000	782	1264	1650	1966
76900	651	1061	1388	1656	82300	696	1132	1480	1765	87700	739	1198	1566	1866	93100	783	1265	1652	1968
77000	652	1062	1390	1658	82400	697	1133	1481	1767	87800	740	1200	1568	1868	93200	784	1267	1653	1970
77100	653	1063	1392	1660	82500	698	1134	1483	1769	87900	741	1201	1570	1870	93300	784	1268	1655	1971
77200	654	1065	1393	1662	82600	699	1135	1485	1771	88000	742	1202	1571	1872	93400	785	1269	1656	1973
77300	654	1066	1395	1664	82700	699	1136	1486	1772	88100	743	1203	1573	1874	93500	786	1270	1658	1975
77400	655	1067	1397	1666	82800	700	1138	1488	1774	88200	744	1205	1574	1876	93600	787	1272	1659	1977
77500	656	1069	1399	1668	82900	701	1139	1489	1776	88300	744	1206	1576	1878	93700	788	1273	1661	1979
77600	657	1070	1400	1670	83000	702	1140	1491	1778	88400	745	1207	1577	1880	93800	788	1274	1663	1981
77700	658	1071	1402	1672	83100	703	1141	1493	1780	88500	746	1208	1579	1882	93900	789	1275	1664	1982
77800	658	1073	1404	1674	83200	704	1143	1494	1782	88600	747	1210	1580	1884	94000	790	1277	1666	1984
77900	659	1074	1405	1676	83300	704	1144	1496	1784	88700	747	1211	1582	1885	94100	791	1278	1668	1986
78000	660	1075	1407	1678	83400	705	1145	1497	1785	88800	748	1212	1583	1887	94200	792	1279	1669	1988
78100	661	1076	1409	1680	83500	706	1146	1499	1787	88900	749	1213	1585	1889	94300	792	1281	1671	1990
78200	662	1078	1410	1682	83600	707	1148	1501	1789	89000	750	1215	1586	1891	94400	793	1282	1672	1991
78300	663	1079	1412	1684	83700	707	1149	1502	1791	89100	751	1216	1588	1893	94500	794	1283	1674	1993
78400	663	1080	1414	1686	83800	708	1150	1504	1793	89200	752	1217	1589	1895	94600	795	1284	1676	1995
78500	664	1081	1416	1688	83900	709	1151	1505	1795	89300	752	1219	1591	1897	94700	796	1286	1677	1997
78600	665	1083	1417	1690	84000	710	1153	1507	1796	89400	753	1220	1592	1898	94800	796	1287	1679	1999
78700	666	1084	1419	1692	84100	711	1154	1509	1798	89500	754	1221	1594	1900	94900	797	1288	1681	2001
78800	667	1085	1421	1694	84200	712	1155	1510	1800	89600	755	1222	1595	1902	95000	798	1289	1682	2003
78900	668	1087	1422	1696	84300	712	1157	1512	1802	89700	755	1224	1597	1904	95100	799	1290	1684	2005
79000	669	1088	1424	1698	84400	713	1158	1513	1803	89800	756	1225	1598	1906	95200	800	1291	1685	2007
79100	670	1089	1426	1700	84500	714	1159	1515	1805	89900	757	1226	1600	1908	95300	800	1293	1687	2009
79200	671	1091	1427	1702	84600	715	1160	1517	1807	90000	758	1227	1602	1909	95400	801	1294	1688	2011
79300	671	1092	1429	1704	84700	715	1162	1518	1809	90100	759	1228	1604	1911	95500	802	1295	1690	2013
79400	672	1093	1431	1706	84800	716	1163	1520	1811	90200	760	1230	1605	1913	95600	803	1296	1691	2014
79500	673	1095	1433	1708	84900	717	1164	1522	1813	90300	760	1231	1607	1915	95700	804	1298	1693	2016
79600	674	1096	1434	1710	85000	718	1165	1523	1815	90400	761	1232	1608	1916	95800	805	1299	1694	2018
79700	675	1098	1436	1712	85100	719	1166	1525	1817	90500	762	1233	1610	1918	95900	805	1300	1696	2020
79800	675	1099	1438	1714	85200	720	1168	1526	1819	90600	763	1235	1611	1920	96000	806	1301	1697	2022
79900	676	1100	1439	1716	85300	720	1169	1528	1821	90700	763	1236	1613	1922	96100	807	1302	1699	2024
80000	677	1102	1441	1719	85400	721	1170	1529	1822	90800	764	1237	1614	1924	96200	807	1303	1700	2026
80100	678	1103	1443	1721	85500	722	1171	1531	1824	90900	765	1239	1616	1926	96300	808	1305	1702	2028
80200	679	1105	1444	1723	85600	723	1173	1533	1826	91000	766	1240	1618	1928	96400	809	1306	1703	2029
80300	680	1106	1446	1725	85700	723	1174	1534	1828	91100	767	1241	1620	1930	96500	810	1307	1705	2031
80400	680	1107	1448	1727	85800	724	1175	1536	1830	91200	768	1242	1621	1932	96600	810	1308	1706	2033
80500	681	1109	1450	1729	85900	725	1176	1538	1832	91300	768	1244	1623	1934	96700	811	1309	1708	2035
80600	682	1110	1451	1731	86000	726	1178	1539	1834	91400	769	1245	1624	1936	96800	812	1311	1710	2037
80700	683	1111	1453	1733	86100	727	1179	1541	1836	91500	770	1246	1626	1937	96900	813	1312	1711	2039
80800	684	1113	1455	1735	86200	728	1180	1542	1838	91600	771	1247	1627	1939	97000	813	1313	1713	2040
80900	685	1114	1456	1737	86300	728	1182	1544	1840	91700	772	1249	1629	1941	97100	814	1314	1715	2042

Federal Child Support Amounts: Simplified Tables
Montants fédéraux de pensions alimentaires pour enfants: Tables simplifiées

Income/ Revenu ($)	Monthly Award/ Paiement mensuel ($) No. of Children/ N^bre d'enfants				Income/ Revenu ($)	Monthly Award/ Paiement mensuel ($) No. of Children/ N^bre d'enfants				Income/ Revenu ($)	Monthly Award/ Paiement mensuel ($) No. of Children/ N^bre d'enfants				Income/ Revenu ($)	Monthly Award/ Paiement mensuel ($) No. of Children/ N^bre d'enfants			
	1	2	3	4		1	2	3	4		1	2	3	4		1	2	3	4
97200	815	1315	1716	2044	102600	858	1381	1800	2144	108000	900	1447	1886	2244	113400	942	1513	1970	2344
97300	815	1317	1718	2046	102700	859	1382	1802	2146	108100	901	1448	1888	2246	113500	943	1514	1972	2346
97400	816	1318	1719	2048	102800	860	1383	1803	2148	108200	902	1450	1889	2248	113600	944	1516	1974	2348
97500	817	1319	1721	2049	102900	860	1385	1805	2149	108300	902	1451	1891	2250	113700	945	1517	1975	2350
97600	818	1320	1723	2051	103000	861	1386	1807	2151	108400	903	1452	1892	2252	113800	945	1518	1977	2352
97700	818	1321	1724	2053	103100	862	1387	1809	2153	108500	904	1453	1894	2253	113900	946	1519	1978	2353
97800	819	1322	1726	2055	103200	862	1389	1810	2155	108600	905	1455	1895	2255	114000	947	1521	1980	2355
97900	820	1324	1727	2057	103300	863	1390	1812	2157	108700	906	1456	1897	2257	114100	948	1522	1982	2357
98000	821	1325	1729	2059	103400	864	1391	1813	2158	108800	907	1457	1898	2259	114200	949	1523	1983	2359
98100	822	1326	1731	2061	103500	865	1392	1815	2160	108900	907	1458	1900	2261	114300	949	1525	1985	2361
98200	823	1328	1732	2063	103600	865	1394	1817	2162	109000	908	1460	1901	2263	114400	950	1526	1986	2362
98300	823	1329	1734	2065	103700	866	1395	1818	2164	109100	909	1461	1903	2265	114500	951	1527	1988	2364
98400	824	1330	1735	2066	103800	867	1396	1820	2166	109200	909	1462	1904	2267	114600	952	1528	1989	2366
98500	825	1331	1737	2068	103900	868	1397	1821	2168	109300	910	1464	1906	2269	114700	953	1530	1991	2368
98600	826	1333	1738	2070	104000	868	1399	1823	2170	109400	911	1465	1907	2270	114800	954	1531	1992	2370
98700	826	1334	1740	2072	104100	869	1400	1825	2172	109500	912	1466	1909	2272	114900	954	1532	1994	2372
98800	827	1335	1741	2074	104200	870	1401	1826	2174	109600	912	1467	1910	2274	115000	955	1533	1995	2374
98900	828	1336	1743	2076	104300	870	1403	1828	2175	109700	913	1469	1912	2276	115100	956	1534	1997	2376
99000	829	1338	1744	2077	104400	871	1404	1829	2177	109800	914	1470	1914	2278	115200	957	1535	1998	2378
99100	830	1339	1746	2079	104500	872	1405	1831	2179	109900	915	1471	1915	2280	115300	957	1537	2000	2379
99200	831	1340	1747	2081	104600	873	1406	1833	2181	110000	915	1472	1917	2281	115400	958	1538	2001	2381
99300	831	1342	1749	2083	104700	873	1408	1834	2183	110100	916	1473	1919	2283	115500	959	1539	2003	2383
99400	832	1343	1750	2085	104800	874	1409	1836	2184	110200	917	1474	1920	2285	115600	960	1540	2004	2385
99500	833	1344	1752	2086	104900	875	1410	1838	2186	110300	917	1476	1922	2287	115700	961	1541	2006	2387
99600	834	1345	1753	2088	105000	876	1411	1839	2188	110400	918	1477	1923	2289	115800	962	1543	2007	2388
99700	835	1347	1755	2090	105100	877	1412	1841	2190	110500	919	1478	1925	2290	115900	962	1544	2009	2390
99800	835	1348	1757	2092	105200	878	1413	1842	2192	110600	920	1479	1927	2292	116000	963	1545	2011	2392
99900	836	1349	1758	2094	105300	878	1415	1844	2194	110700	920	1480	1928	2294	116100	964	1546	2013	2394
100000	837	1350	1760	2096	105400	879	1416	1845	2195	110800	921	1482	1930	2296	116200	964	1547	2014	2396
100100	838	1351	1762	2098	105500	880	1417	1847	2197	110900	922	1483	1931	2298	116300	965	1549	2016	2398
100200	839	1352	1763	2100	105600	881	1418	1848	2199	111000	923	1484	1933	2300	116400	966	1550	2017	2399
100300	839	1354	1765	2101	105700	881	1420	1850	2201	111100	924	1485	1935	2302	116500	967	1551	2019	2401
100400	840	1355	1766	2103	105800	882	1421	1851	2203	111200	925	1486	1936	2304	116600	967	1552	2021	2403
100500	841	1356	1768	2105	105900	883	1422	1853	2205	111300	925	1488	1938	2305	116700	968	1553	2022	2405
100600	842	1357	1770	2107	106000	884	1423	1854	2207	111400	926	1489	1939	2307	116800	969	1555	2024	2407
100700	843	1359	1771	2109	106100	885	1424	1856	2209	111500	927	1490	1941	2309	116900	970	1556	2025	2409
100800	843	1360	1773	2111	106200	886	1425	1857	2211	111600	928	1491	1942	2311	117000	970	1557	2027	2411
100900	844	1361	1774	2112	106300	886	1427	1859	2213	111700	928	1492	1944	2313	117100	971	1558	2029	2413
101000	845	1362	1776	2114	106400	887	1428	1860	2215	111800	929	1494	1945	2315	117200	972	1560	2030	2415
101100	846	1363	1778	2116	106500	888	1429	1862	2216	111900	930	1495	1947	2316	117300	972	1561	2032	2417
101200	847	1364	1779	2118	106600	889	1430	1863	2218	112000	931	1496	1948	2318	117400	973	1562	2033	2419
101300	847	1366	1781	2120	106700	890	1431	1865	2220	112100	932	1497	1950	2320	117500	974	1563	2035	2420
101400	848	1367	1782	2121	106800	890	1433	1867	2222	112200	933	1498	1951	2322	117600	975	1565	2037	2422
101500	849	1368	1784	2123	106900	891	1434	1868	2224	112300	933	1500	1953	2324	117700	975	1566	2038	2424
101600	850	1369	1785	2125	107000	892	1435	1870	2226	112400	934	1501	1954	2325	117800	976	1567	2040	2426
101700	851	1370	1787	2127	107100	893	1436	1872	2228	112500	935	1502	1956	2327	117900	977	1568	2042	2428
101800	852	1372	1788	2129	107200	894	1437	1873	2230	112600	936	1503	1957	2329	118000	978	1570	2043	2430
101900	852	1373	1790	2131	107300	894	1439	1875	2232	112700	937	1504	1959	2331	118100	979	1571	2045	2432
102000	853	1374	1791	2133	107400	895	1440	1876	2233	112800	937	1505	1960	2333	118200	980	1572	2046	2434
102100	854	1375	1793	2135	107500	896	1441	1878	2235	112900	938	1507	1962	2335	118300	980	1574	2048	2436
102200	855	1376	1794	2137	107600	897	1442	1880	2237	113000	939	1508	1964	2337	118400	981	1575	2049	2437
102300	855	1378	1796	2138	107700	898	1443	1881	2239	113100	940	1509	1966	2339	118500	982	1576	2051	2439
102400	856	1379	1797	2140	107800	898	1444	1883	2241	113200	941	1511	1967	2341	118600	983	1577	2052	2441
102500	857	1380	1799	2142	107900	899	1446	1884	2243	113300	941	1512	1969	2342	118700	983	1579	2054	2443

Federal Child Support Amounts: Simplified Tables
Montants fédéraux de pensions alimentaires pour enfants: Tables simplifiées

Income/ Revenu ($)	Monthly Award/ Paiement mensuel ($) No. of Children/ Nbre d'enfants				Income/ Revenu ($)	Monthly Award/ Paiement mensuel ($) No. of Children/ Nbre d'enfants				Income/ Revenu ($)	Monthly Award/ Paiement mensuel ($) No. of Children/ Nbre d'enfants				Income/ Revenu ($)	Monthly Award/ Paiement mensuel ($) No. of Children/ Nbre d'enfants			
	1	2	3	4		1	2	3	4		1	2	3	4		1	2	3	4
118800	984	1580	2055	2445	124200	1027	1645	2140	2545	129600	1068	1710	2223	2642	135000	1108	1772	2303	2737
118900	985	1581	2057	2447	124300	1027	1647	2142	2546	129700	1069	1711	2224	2644	135100	1109	1773	2305	2739
119000	986	1582	2058	2448	124400	1028	1648	2143	2548	129800	1070	1712	2226	2646	135200	1110	1774	2306	2741
119100	987	1583	2060	2450	124500	1029	1649	2145	2550	129900	1071	1713	2227	2648	135300	1110	1775	2308	2742
119200	988	1584	2061	2452	124600	1030	1650	2146	2552	130000	1071	1714	2228	2649	135400	1111	1776	2309	2744
119300	988	1586	2063	2454	124700	1030	1652	2148	2554	130100	1072	1715	2229	2651	135500	1112	1778	2311	2746
119400	989	1587	2064	2456	124800	1031	1653	2149	2556	130200	1073	1716	2231	2653	135600	1113	1779	2312	2748
119500	990	1588	2066	2457	124900	1032	1654	2151	2557	130300	1073	1718	2232	2654	135700	1113	1780	2314	2750
119600	991	1589	2067	2459	125000	1033	1655	2152	2559	130400	1074	1719	2234	2656	135800	1114	1781	2315	2751
119700	992	1591	2069	2461	125100	1034	1656	2154	2561	130500	1075	1720	2235	2658	135900	1115	1782	2317	2753
119800	992	1592	2071	2463	125200	1035	1657	2155	2563	130600	1076	1721	2237	2660	136000	1116	1783	2318	2755
119900	993	1593	2072	2465	125300	1035	1659	2157	2565	130700	1076	1722	2238	2661	136100	1117	1784	2319	2757
120000	994	1594	2074	2467	125400	1036	1660	2158	2566	130800	1077	1724	2240	2663	136200	1117	1785	2321	2758
120100	995	1595	2076	2469	125500	1037	1661	2160	2568	130900	1078	1725	2241	2665	136300	1118	1786	2322	2760
120200	996	1596	2077	2471	125600	1038	1662	2161	2570	131000	1079	1726	2243	2667	136400	1119	1788	2324	2762
120300	996	1598	2079	2472	125700	1038	1663	2163	2572	131100	1080	1727	2244	2669	136500	1120	1789	2325	2764
120400	997	1599	2080	2474	125800	1039	1665	2164	2574	131200	1080	1728	2246	2670	136600	1120	1790	2327	2765
120500	998	1600	2082	2476	125900	1040	1666	2166	2576	131300	1081	1729	2247	2672	136700	1121	1791	2328	2767
120600	999	1601	2084	2478	126000	1041	1667	2168	2578	131400	1082	1731	2249	2674	136800	1122	1792	2330	2769
120700	1000	1602	2085	2480	126100	1042	1668	2170	2580	131500	1083	1732	2250	2676	136900	1123	1793	2331	2771
120800	1000	1604	2087	2482	126200	1043	1669	2171	2582	131600	1083	1733	2252	2677	137000	1123	1795	2332	2772
120900	1001	1605	2088	2483	126300	1043	1671	2173	2584	131700	1084	1734	2253	2679	137100	1124	1796	2333	2774
121000	1002	1606	2090	2485	126400	1044	1672	2174	2586	131800	1085	1735	2255	2681	137200	1125	1797	2335	2776
121100	1003	1607	2092	2487	126500	1045	1673	2176	2588	131900	1086	1736	2256	2682	137300	1125	1799	2336	2777
121200	1004	1608	2093	2489	126600	1046	1674	2178	2589	132000	1086	1737	2258	2684	137400	1126	1800	2338	2779
121300	1004	1610	2095	2491	126700	1047	1675	2179	2591	132100	1087	1738	2259	2686	137500	1127	1801	2339	2781
121400	1005	1611	2096	2493	126800	1047	1676	2181	2593	132200	1087	1739	2261	2688	137600	1128	1802	2341	2783
121500	1006	1612	2098	2494	126900	1048	1678	2182	2595	132300	1088	1741	2262	2689	137700	1128	1803	2342	2784
121600	1007	1613	2099	2496	127000	1049	1679	2184	2597	132400	1089	1742	2264	2691	137800	1129	1805	2344	2786
121700	1008	1614	2101	2498	127100	1050	1680	2186	2599	132500	1089	1743	2265	2693	137900	1130	1806	2345	2788
121800	1009	1615	2102	2500	127200	1050	1681	2187	2600	132600	1090	1744	2267	2695	138000	1131	1807	2347	2790
121900	1009	1617	2104	2502	127300	1051	1682	2189	2602	132700	1091	1745	2268	2696	138100	1132	1808	2348	2792
122000	1010	1618	2105	2504	127400	1052	1684	2190	2604	132800	1092	1746	2270	2698	138200	1132	1809	2350	2793
122100	1011	1619	2107	2506	127500	1053	1685	2192	2606	132900	1092	1748	2271	2700	138300	1133	1810	2351	2795
122200	1011	1621	2108	2508	127600	1053	1686	2193	2607	133000	1093	1749	2273	2702	138400	1134	1812	2353	2797
122300	1012	1622	2110	2509	127700	1054	1687	2195	2609	133100	1094	1750	2275	2704	138500	1135	1813	2354	2799
122400	1013	1623	2111	2511	127800	1055	1688	2196	2611	133200	1095	1751	2276	2705	138600	1135	1814	2356	2800
122500	1014	1624	2113	2513	127900	1055	1689	2198	2613	133300	1095	1752	2278	2707	138700	1136	1815	2357	2802
122600	1014	1626	2114	2515	128000	1056	1691	2199	2614	133400	1096	1754	2279	2709	138800	1137	1816	2359	2804
122700	1015	1627	2116	2517	128100	1057	1692	2201	2616	133500	1097	1755	2281	2711	138900	1138	1817	2360	2806
122800	1016	1628	2118	2519	128200	1058	1693	2202	2618	133600	1098	1756	2282	2712	139000	1138	1818	2362	2807
122900	1017	1629	2119	2520	128300	1058	1695	2204	2619	133700	1098	1757	2284	2714	139100	1139	1819	2363	2809
123000	1017	1631	2121	2522	128400	1059	1696	2205	2621	133800	1099	1758	2285	2716	139200	1139	1820	2365	2811
123100	1018	1632	2123	2524	128500	1060	1697	2207	2623	133900	1100	1759	2287	2717	139300	1140	1822	2366	2812
123200	1019	1633	2124	2526	128600	1061	1698	2208	2625	134000	1101	1760	2288	2719	139400	1141	1823	2368	2814
123300	1019	1635	2126	2528	128700	1061	1699	2210	2627	134100	1102	1761	2290	2721	139500	1141	1824	2369	2816
123400	1020	1636	2127	2529	128800	1062	1701	2211	2628	134200	1102	1762	2291	2723	139600	1142	1825	2371	2818
123500	1021	1637	2129	2531	128900	1063	1702	2213	2630	134300	1103	1764	2293	2724	139700	1143	1826	2372	2819
123600	1022	1638	2131	2533	129000	1064	1703	2214	2632	134400	1104	1765	2294	2726	139800	1144	1828	2374	2821
123700	1022	1640	2132	2535	129100	1065	1704	2215	2634	134500	1105	1766	2296	2728	139900	1144	1830	2377	2825
123800	1023	1641	2134	2537	129200	1065	1705	2217	2635	134600	1105	1767	2297	2730	140000	1145	1830	2377	2825
123900	1024	1642	2135	2539	129300	1066	1706	2218	2637	134700	1106	1768	2299	2731	140100	1146	1831	2378	2827
124000	1025	1643	2137	2541	129400	1067	1708	2220	2639	134800	1107	1769	2300	2733	140200	1147	1832	2380	2828
124100	1026	1644	2139	2543	129500	1068	1709	2221	2641	134900	1107	1771	2302	2735	140300	1147	1833	2381	2830

Nova Scotia / Nouvelle-Écosse

Federal Child Support Amounts: Simplified Tables
Montants fédéraux de pensions alimentaires pour enfants: Tables simplifiées

Income/ Revenu ($)	Monthly Award/ Paiement mensuel ($) No. of Children/ N^bre d'enfants				Income/ Revenu ($)	Monthly Award/ Paiement mensuel ($) No. of Children/ N^bre d'enfants				Income/ Revenu ($)	Monthly Award/ Paiement mensuel ($) No. of Children/ N^bre d'enfants			
	1	2	3	4		1	2	3	4		1	2	3	4
140400	1148	1835	2383	2832	143700	1173	1872	2432	2890	147000	1197	1911	2481	2948
140500	1149	1836	2384	2834	143800	1174	1873	2434	2892	147100	1198	1912	2482	2950
140600	1150	1837	2386	2835	143900	1175	1875	2435	2894	147200	1199	1913	2484	2951
140700	1150	1838	2387	2837	144000	1175	1876	2436	2895	147300	1199	1914	2485	2953
140800	1151	1839	2389	2839	144100	1176	1877	2437	2897	147400	1200	1916	2487	2955
140900	1152	1840	2390	2840	144200	1177	1878	2439	2899	147500	1201	1917	2488	2957
141000	1153	1841	2392	2842	144300	1177	1879	2440	2900	147600	1202	1918	2490	2958
141100	1154	1842	2394	2844	144400	1178	1880	2442	2902	147700	1202	1919	2491	2960
141200	1154	1843	2395	2846	144500	1179	1882	2443	2904	147800	1203	1920	2493	2962
141300	1155	1845	2397	2847	144600	1180	1883	2445	2906	147900	1204	1921	2494	2963
141400	1156	1846	2398	2849	144700	1180	1884	2446	2908	148000	1205	1922	2496	2965
141500	1157	1847	2400	2851	144800	1181	1885	2448	2909	148100	1206	1923	2498	2967
141600	1157	1848	2401	2853	144900	1182	1886	2449	2911	148200	1206	1924	2499	2969
141700	1158	1849	2403	2854	145000	1183	1887	2451	2913	148300	1207	1926	2501	2970
141800	1159	1850	2404	2856	145100	1184	1888	2452	2915	148400	1208	1927	2502	2972
141900	1159	1852	2406	2858	145200	1184	1889	2454	2916	148500	1209	1928	2504	2974
142000	1160	1853	2407	2860	145300	1185	1890	2455	2918	148600	1209	1929	2505	2976
142100	1161	1854	2409	2862	145400	1186	1892	2457	2920	148700	1210	1930	2507	2977
142200	1162	1855	2410	2864	145500	1187	1893	2458	2922	148800	1211	1932	2508	2979
142300	1162	1856	2412	2865	145600	1187	1894	2460	2923	148900	1211	1933	2510	2981
142400	1163	1857	2413	2867	145700	1188	1895	2461	2925	149000	1212	1934	2511	2983
142500	1164	1859	2415	2869	145800	1189	1896	2463	2927	149100	1213	1935	2513	2985
142600	1165	1860	2416	2871	145900	1190	1897	2464	2929	149200	1214	1936	2514	2986
142700	1165	1861	2418	2873	146000	1190	1899	2466	2930	149300	1214	1937	2516	2988
142800	1166	1862	2419	2874	146100	1191	1900	2467	2932	149400	1215	1939	2517	2990
142900	1167	1863	2421	2876	146200	1191	1901	2469	2934	149500	1216	1940	2519	2992
143000	1168	1864	2422	2878	146300	1192	1903	2470	2935	149600	1217	1941	2520	2993
143100	1169	1865	2423	2880	146400	1193	1904	2472	2937	149700	1217	1942	2522	2995
143200	1169	1866	2425	2881	146500	1193	1905	2473	2939	149800	1218	1943	2523	2997
143300	1170	1868	2426	2883	146600	1194	1906	2475	2941	149900	1219	1944	2525	2998
143400	1171	1869	2428	2885	146700	1195	1907	2476	2942	150000	1220	1945	2526	3000
143500	1172	1870	2429	2887	146800	1196	1909	2478	2944					
143600	1172	1871	2431	2888	146900	1196	1910	2479	2946					

Monthly Award/Paiement mensuel ($)			
One Child/ Un enfant	Two Children/ Deux enfants	Three Children/ Trois enfants	Four Children/ Quatre enfants
1220 plus 0.76% of income over $150,000	1945 plus 1.14% of income over $150,000	2526 plus 1.52% of income over $150,000	3000 plus 1.70% of income over $150,000
1220 plus 0,76% du revenu dépassant 150 000$	1945 plus 1,14% du revenu dépassant 150 000$	2526 plus 1,52% du revenu dépassant 150 000$	3000 plus 1,70% du revenu dépassant 150 000$

NEW BRUNSWICK

Federal Child Support Amounts: Simplified Tables
Montants fédéraux de pensions alimentaires pour enfants: Tables simplifiées

Income/ Revenu ($)	Monthly Award/ Paiement mensuel ($) No. of Children/ N^bre d'enfants 1	2	3	4	Income/ Revenu ($)	Monthly Award/ Paiement mensuel ($) No. of Children/ N^bre d'enfants 1	2	3	4	Income/ Revenu ($)	Monthly Award/ Paiement mensuel ($) No. of Children/ N^bre d'enfants 1	2	3	4	Income/ Revenu ($)	Monthly Award/ Paiement mensuel ($) No. of Children/ N^bre d'enfants 1	2	3	4
10820	0	0	0	0	16200	139	231	249	266	21600	164	319	443	489	27000	202	379	527	648
10900	3	3	4	4	16300	140	234	252	269	21700	165	320	445	493	27100	203	380	529	650
11000	40	43	46	50	16400	140	237	255	273	21800	166	321	446	497	27200	204	381	530	652
11100	44	47	51	55	16500	140	240	259	276	21900	166	323	448	501	27300	205	382	532	653
11200	48	52	55	60	16600	140	243	262	280	22000	167	324	449	506	27400	206	383	533	655
11300	52	56	60	65	16700	141	246	265	283	22100	168	325	451	510	27500	207	385	535	657
11400	56	60	65	70	16800	141	249	268	287	22200	168	326	452	514	27600	208	386	536	659
11500	60	65	69	75	16900	141	252	272	290	22300	169	327	454	519	27700	209	387	538	661
11600	64	69	74	80	17000	141	255	275	294	22400	169	329	455	523	27800	210	388	539	663
11700	68	73	79	85	17100	141	257	279	298	22500	170	330	457	527	27900	210	389	541	664
11800	72	77	83	90	17200	142	260	283	303	22600	171	331	459	531	28000	211	390	542	666
11900	76	82	88	95	17300	142	262	287	307	22700	171	332	460	536	28100	212	391	544	668
12000	80	86	93	100	17400	142	264	291	311	22800	172	333	462	540	28200	213	393	545	670
12100	83	90	97	104	17500	143	266	295	315	22900	172	334	464	544	28300	214	394	547	672
12200	87	93	101	108	17600	143	269	299	320	23000	173	335	465	548	28400	215	396	548	673
12300	90	97	105	113	17700	143	271	303	324	23100	174	336	467	552	28500	216	397	550	675
12400	93	101	109	117	17800	144	273	306	328	23200	174	337	468	556	28600	216	399	551	677
12500	97	104	112	121	17900	144	276	310	332	23300	175	338	470	561	28700	217	400	553	679
12600	100	108	116	125	18000	144	278	314	337	23400	175	339	471	565	28800	218	402	554	681
12700	103	112	120	130	18100	145	279	318	341	23500	176	341	473	569	28900	219	403	556	683
12800	107	115	124	134	18200	145	280	322	345	23600	176	342	474	573	29000	220	405	557	685
12900	110	119	128	138	18300	146	282	326	350	23700	177	343	476	577	29100	221	406	559	687
13000	113	123	132	142	18400	146	283	330	354	23800	177	344	477	582	29200	222	408	560	689
13100	115	127	136	146	18500	147	284	334	358	23900	178	345	479	586	29300	223	409	562	691
13200	117	130	140	150	18600	147	285	338	362	24000	178	346	480	590	29400	224	411	563	693
13300	119	134	144	154	18700	148	286	342	367	24100	179	347	482	592	29500	225	412	565	694
13400	121	137	147	158	18800	149	287	346	371	24200	179	348	483	594	29600	226	414	566	696
13500	123	141	151	163	18900	149	289	350	375	24300	180	350	485	596	29700	227	415	568	698
13600	125	145	155	167	19000	150	290	354	379	24400	180	351	486	598	29800	228	417	569	700
13700	127	148	159	171	19100	151	291	358	383	24500	181	352	488	600	29900	229	418	571	702
13800	129	152	163	175	19200	151	292	362	387	24600	181	353	489	602	30000	230	420	572	704
13900	131	155	167	179	19300	152	293	366	392	24700	182	354	491	604	30100	231	421	574	706
14000	134	159	171	183	19400	152	295	370	396	24800	182	355	492	606	30200	232	423	576	708
14100	134	163	175	187	19500	153	296	374	400	24900	183	357	494	608	30300	233	424	578	709
14200	134	166	179	191	19600	154	297	378	404	25000	184	358	496	610	30400	234	426	579	711
14300	135	170	182	195	19700	154	298	382	409	25100	185	359	498	612	30500	235	427	581	713
14400	135	173	186	199	19800	155	299	386	413	25200	186	360	499	614	30600	236	429	583	715
14500	135	177	190	203	19900	155	300	389	417	25300	186	361	501	616	30700	236	430	585	717
14600	135	180	194	207	20000	156	301	393	421	25400	187	363	502	618	30800	237	431	587	719
14700	135	184	198	212	20100	157	302	397	425	25500	188	364	504	620	30900	238	433	589	720
14800	135	187	201	216	20200	157	303	401	429	25600	189	365	505	622	31000	239	434	590	722
14900	136	191	205	220	20300	158	304	405	434	25700	190	366	507	623	31100	240	435	592	724
15000	136	194	209	224	20400	158	305	409	438	25800	190	367	509	625	31200	241	437	594	726
15100	136	197	212	227	20500	159	307	413	442	25900	191	368	510	627	31300	242	438	596	728
15200	137	200	216	231	20600	159	308	417	446	26000	192	369	512	629	31400	243	440	597	729
15300	137	203	219	234	20700	160	309	421	450	26100	193	370	514	631	31500	244	441	599	731
15400	137	206	222	238	20800	160	310	425	454	26200	194	371	515	633	31600	245	443	601	733
15500	137	209	225	241	20900	161	311	429	459	26300	195	372	517	635	31700	246	444	603	735
15600	138	212	229	245	21000	161	312	433	463	26400	196	373	518	637	31800	247	446	605	737
15700	138	215	232	248	21100	162	313	435	467	26500	197	374	520	638	31900	248	447	607	739
15800	138	219	235	252	21200	162	314	436	472	26600	198	375	521	640	32000	249	449	609	741
15900	138	222	238	255	21300	163	316	438	476	26700	199	376	523	642	32100	250	450	611	743
16000	139	225	242	259	21400	163	317	440	480	26800	200	377	524	644	32200	251	452	613	745
16100	139	228	245	262	21500	164	318	441	484	26900	201	378	526	646	32300	252	453	614	747

41

New Brunswick / Nouveau-Brunswick

Federal Child Support Amounts: Simplified Tables
Montants fédéraux de pensions alimentaires pour enfants: Tables simplifiées

Income/Revenu ($)	Monthly Award/ Paiement mensuel ($) No. of Children/ N^bre d'enfants				Income/Revenu ($)	Monthly Award/ Paiement mensuel ($) No. of Children/ N^bre d'enfants				Income/Revenu ($)	Monthly Award/ Paiement mensuel ($) No. of Children/ N^bre d'enfants				Income/Revenu ($)	Monthly Award/ Paiement mensuel ($) No. of Children/ N^bre d'enfants			
	1	2	3	4		1	2	3	4		1	2	3	4		1	2	3	4
32400	253	455	616	749	37800	306	535	717	867	43200	359	613	816	982	48600	411	691	914	1098
32500	254	456	618	751	37900	307	536	719	869	43300	360	614	817	984	48700	412	693	916	1100
32600	255	457	620	754	38000	308	538	721	872	43400	361	616	819	986	48800	413	694	918	1102
32700	256	459	621	756	38100	309	539	723	874	43500	362	617	821	988	48900	414	696	920	1104
32800	257	460	623	758	38200	310	541	725	876	43600	363	619	823	990	49000	415	697	922	1107
32900	258	462	625	760	38300	311	542	727	878	43700	364	620	824	993	49100	416	699	924	1109
33000	258	463	627	762	38400	312	544	728	881	43800	365	621	826	995	49200	417	700	926	1111
33100	259	464	629	764	38500	313	545	730	883	43900	366	623	828	997	49300	418	702	928	1114
33200	260	466	631	766	38600	314	547	732	885	44000	366	624	830	999	49400	419	703	930	1116
33300	261	467	633	769	38700	315	548	734	887	44100	367	625	832	1001	49500	420	705	931	1118
33400	262	469	634	771	38800	316	550	736	889	44200	368	627	834	1003	49600	421	706	933	1120
33500	263	470	636	773	38900	317	551	738	891	44300	369	628	835	1005	49700	422	708	935	1123
33600	264	472	638	775	39000	318	552	740	893	44400	370	630	837	1007	49800	423	709	937	1125
33700	265	473	640	778	39100	319	553	742	895	44500	371	631	839	1009	49900	424	711	939	1127
33800	266	475	642	780	39200	320	555	744	897	44600	372	632	841	1011	50000	425	712	941	1129
33900	267	476	644	782	39300	321	556	746	899	44700	373	634	842	1014	50100	426	714	943	1131
34000	268	478	646	784	39400	322	558	747	901	44800	374	635	844	1016	50200	427	715	945	1133
34100	269	479	648	786	39500	323	559	749	904	44900	375	637	846	1018	50300	428	717	947	1136
34200	270	481	650	788	39600	324	560	751	906	45000	376	638	848	1020	50400	429	718	949	1138
34300	271	482	652	791	39700	325	562	753	908	45100	377	639	850	1022	50500	430	720	950	1140
34400	272	484	654	793	39800	326	563	755	910	45200	378	641	852	1024	50600	431	721	952	1142
34500	273	485	656	795	39900	327	565	757	912	45300	379	642	853	1026	50700	432	723	954	1145
34600	274	487	658	797	40000	327	566	758	914	45400	380	644	855	1028	50800	433	724	956	1147
34700	275	488	660	799	40100	328	568	760	916	45500	381	645	857	1030	50900	434	726	958	1149
34800	276	490	662	801	40200	329	569	762	919	45600	382	647	859	1032	51000	435	727	960	1151
34900	277	491	664	804	40300	330	571	764	921	45700	383	648	860	1035	51100	436	728	962	1153
35000	278	493	666	806	40400	331	572	766	923	45800	383	650	862	1037	51200	437	730	964	1155
35100	279	494	668	808	40500	332	574	768	925	45900	384	651	864	1039	51300	438	731	965	1158
35200	280	496	670	811	40600	333	575	770	928	46000	385	653	866	1041	51400	439	733	967	1160
35300	281	497	672	813	40700	334	577	771	930	46100	386	654	868	1043	51500	440	734	969	1162
35400	282	499	674	815	40800	336	578	773	932	46200	387	656	870	1045	51600	441	735	971	1164
35500	283	500	676	817	40900	337	580	775	934	46300	388	657	871	1047	51700	442	737	972	1166
35600	284	502	678	820	41000	338	582	777	937	46400	389	659	873	1049	51800	443	738	974	1169
35700	285	503	680	822	41100	339	583	779	939	46500	390	660	875	1051	51900	444	740	976	1171
35800	286	505	682	824	41200	340	585	781	941	46600	391	662	877	1053	52000	445	741	978	1173
35900	287	506	683	826	41300	341	586	782	943	46700	392	663	878	1056	52100	446	742	980	1175
36000	288	508	685	829	41400	342	588	784	945	46800	393	665	880	1058	52200	447	744	982	1177
36100	289	509	687	831	41500	343	589	786	947	46900	394	666	882	1060	52300	448	745	984	1179
36200	290	511	689	833	41600	344	590	788	950	47000	395	667	884	1062	52400	449	747	985	1182
36300	291	512	691	835	41700	345	592	789	952	47100	396	669	886	1064	52500	450	748	987	1184
36400	292	514	692	837	41800	345	593	791	954	47200	397	670	888	1066	52600	451	749	989	1186
36500	293	515	694	840	41900	346	595	793	956	47300	398	672	890	1069	52700	452	751	991	1188
36600	294	517	696	842	42000	347	596	795	958	47400	399	673	891	1071	52800	453	752	993	1190
36700	295	518	698	844	42100	348	597	797	960	47500	400	675	893	1073	52900	454	753	995	1192
36800	296	520	700	846	42200	349	599	798	962	47600	401	676	895	1075	53000	454	755	997	1194
36900	297	521	702	848	42300	350	600	800	964	47700	402	678	897	1077	53100	455	756	999	1196
37000	298	523	703	850	42400	351	602	802	966	47800	403	679	899	1079	53200	456	758	1001	1198
37100	299	524	705	852	42500	352	603	804	968	47900	404	681	901	1082	53300	457	759	1002	1201
37200	300	526	707	854	42600	353	605	805	970	48000	405	682	903	1084	53400	458	760	1004	1203
37300	301	527	708	856	42700	354	606	807	972	48100	406	684	905	1086	53500	459	762	1006	1205
37400	302	529	710	859	42800	355	607	809	974	48200	407	685	907	1089	53600	460	763	1008	1207
37500	303	530	712	861	42900	356	609	810	976	48300	408	687	909	1091	53700	461	765	1010	1209
37600	304	532	714	863	43000	357	610	812	978	48400	409	688	911	1093	53800	461	766	1012	1211
37700	305	533	715	865	43100	358	611	814	980	48500	410	690	912	1095	53900	462	767	1013	1214

New Brunswick / Nouveau-Brunswick

Federal Child Support Amounts: Simplified Tables
Montants fédéraux de pensions alimentaires pour enfants: Tables simplifiées

Income/Revenu ($)	Monthly Award/Paiement mensuel ($) No. of Children/N^bre d'enfants				Income/Revenu ($)	Monthly Award/Paiement mensuel ($) No. of Children/N^bre d'enfants				Income/Revenu ($)	Monthly Award/Paiement mensuel ($) No. of Children/N^bre d'enfants				Income/Revenu ($)	Monthly Award/Paiement mensuel ($) No. of Children/N^bre d'enfants			
	1	2	3	4		1	2	3	4		1	2	3	4		1	2	3	4
54000	463	769	1015	1216	59400	512	846	1113	1332	64800	561	922	1212	1448	70200	610	999	1310	1564
54100	464	770	1017	1218	59500	512	847	1115	1334	64900	562	924	1213	1450	70300	611	1000	1311	1566
54200	465	772	1019	1220	59600	513	848	1117	1336	65000	563	925	1215	1452	70400	611	1002	1313	1569
54300	466	773	1020	1222	59700	514	850	1119	1338	65100	564	926	1217	1454	70500	612	1003	1315	1571
54400	467	775	1022	1225	59800	515	851	1121	1340	65200	565	928	1219	1456	70600	613	1004	1317	1573
54500	468	776	1024	1227	59900	516	852	1122	1343	65300	566	929	1220	1459	70700	614	1006	1319	1575
54600	469	778	1026	1229	60000	517	854	1124	1345	65400	567	931	1222	1461	70800	615	1007	1320	1577
54700	469	779	1028	1231	60100	518	855	1126	1347	65500	568	932	1224	1463	70900	616	1009	1322	1579
54800	470	781	1030	1233	60200	519	857	1128	1349	65600	569	933	1226	1465	71000	617	1010	1324	1581
54900	471	782	1031	1235	60300	520	858	1129	1351	65700	569	935	1228	1467	71100	618	1011	1326	1583
55000	472	784	1033	1237	60400	520	860	1131	1354	65800	570	936	1229	1469	71200	619	1013	1328	1585
55100	473	785	1035	1239	60500	521	861	1133	1356	65900	571	937	1231	1472	71300	620	1014	1329	1588
55200	474	787	1037	1241	60600	522	863	1135	1358	66000	572	939	1233	1474	71400	620	1016	1331	1590
55300	475	788	1038	1244	60700	523	864	1137	1360	66100	573	940	1235	1476	71500	621	1017	1333	1592
55400	476	790	1040	1246	60800	524	866	1138	1362	66200	574	942	1237	1478	71600	622	1018	1335	1594
55500	477	791	1042	1248	60900	525	867	1140	1364	66300	575	943	1238	1480	71700	623	1020	1336	1596
55600	477	793	1044	1250	61000	526	869	1142	1366	66400	576	944	1240	1483	71800	624	1021	1338	1598
55700	478	794	1046	1252	61100	527	870	1144	1368	66500	577	946	1242	1485	71900	625	1023	1340	1601
55800	479	795	1047	1254	61200	528	872	1146	1370	66600	577	947	1244	1487	72000	626	1024	1342	1603
55900	480	797	1049	1257	61300	529	873	1147	1373	66700	578	949	1245	1489	72100	627	1025	1344	1605
56000	481	798	1051	1259	61400	530	875	1149	1375	66800	579	950	1247	1491	72200	628	1027	1346	1607
56100	482	799	1053	1261	61500	531	876	1151	1377	66900	580	951	1249	1493	72300	629	1028	1348	1609
56200	483	801	1055	1263	61600	532	878	1153	1379	67000	581	953	1251	1495	72400	630	1030	1349	1612
56300	484	802	1056	1265	61700	533	879	1154	1381	67100	582	954	1253	1497	72500	631	1031	1351	1614
56400	485	804	1058	1268	61800	534	881	1156	1383	67200	583	956	1255	1499	72600	632	1032	1353	1616
56500	486	805	1060	1270	61900	535	882	1158	1386	67300	584	957	1257	1502	72700	633	1034	1355	1618
56600	486	807	1062	1272	62000	536	883	1160	1388	67400	585	959	1258	1504	72800	634	1035	1357	1620
56700	487	808	1063	1274	62100	537	884	1162	1390	67500	585	960	1260	1506	72900	635	1036	1359	1622
56800	488	809	1065	1276	62200	538	886	1164	1392	67600	586	962	1262	1508	73000	636	1038	1361	1624
56900	489	811	1067	1278	62300	539	887	1166	1394	67700	587	963	1264	1510	73100	637	1039	1363	1626
57000	490	812	1069	1280	62400	540	889	1167	1397	67800	588	965	1266	1512	73200	638	1041	1364	1628
57100	491	813	1071	1282	62500	541	890	1169	1399	67900	589	966	1268	1515	73300	639	1042	1366	1630
57200	492	815	1073	1284	62600	542	892	1171	1401	68000	590	968	1270	1517	73400	640	1043	1368	1632
57300	493	816	1075	1287	62700	543	893	1173	1403	68100	591	969	1272	1519	73500	641	1045	1370	1634
57400	494	818	1076	1289	62800	544	894	1175	1405	68200	592	971	1274	1521	73600	642	1046	1371	1637
57500	494	819	1078	1291	62900	545	896	1177	1407	68300	593	972	1276	1523	73700	643	1048	1373	1639
57600	495	820	1080	1293	63000	545	897	1179	1409	68400	594	974	1277	1526	73800	644	1049	1375	1641
57700	496	822	1082	1295	63100	546	898	1181	1411	68500	594	975	1279	1528	73900	644	1050	1377	1643
57800	497	823	1084	1297	63200	547	900	1183	1413	68600	595	977	1281	1530	74000	645	1052	1378	1645
57900	498	825	1086	1300	63300	548	901	1185	1416	68700	596	978	1283	1532	74100	646	1053	1380	1647
58000	499	826	1088	1302	63400	549	903	1186	1418	68800	597	980	1285	1534	74200	647	1055	1382	1649
58100	500	827	1090	1304	63500	550	904	1188	1420	68900	598	981	1287	1536	74300	648	1056	1383	1651
58200	501	829	1092	1306	63600	551	905	1190	1422	69000	599	982	1288	1538	74400	649	1057	1385	1654
58300	502	830	1094	1308	63700	552	907	1192	1424	69100	600	983	1290	1540	74500	650	1059	1387	1656
58400	503	832	1095	1311	63800	553	908	1194	1426	69200	601	985	1292	1542	74600	651	1060	1389	1658
58500	503	833	1097	1313	63900	553	910	1196	1429	69300	602	986	1293	1545	74700	652	1062	1390	1660
58600	504	834	1099	1315	64000	554	911	1197	1431	69400	603	988	1295	1547	74800	653	1063	1392	1662
58700	505	836	1101	1317	64100	555	912	1199	1433	69500	603	989	1297	1549	74900	654	1064	1394	1664
58800	506	837	1103	1319	64200	556	914	1201	1435	69600	604	991	1299	1551	75000	654	1066	1396	1667
58900	507	839	1105	1321	64300	557	915	1202	1437	69700	605	992	1301	1553	75100	655	1067	1398	1669
59000	508	840	1106	1323	64400	558	917	1204	1440	69800	606	993	1303	1555	75200	656	1069	1400	1671
59100	509	841	1108	1325	64500	559	918	1206	1442	69900	607	995	1304	1558	75300	657	1070	1401	1673
59200	510	843	1110	1327	64600	560	919	1208	1444	70000	608	996	1306	1560	75400	658	1071	1403	1676
59300	511	844	1111	1330	64700	561	921	1210	1446	70100	609	997	1308	1562	75500	659	1073	1405	1678

NEW BRUNSWICK — CONTINUED

Federal Child Support Amounts: Simplified Tables
Montants fédéraux de pensions alimentaires pour enfants: Tables simplifiées

Income/ Revenu ($)	Monthly Award/ Paiement mensuel ($) No. of Children/ Nbre d'enfants				Income/ Revenu ($)	Monthly Award/ Paiement mensuel ($) No. of Children/ Nbre d'enfants				Income/ Revenu ($)	Monthly Award/ Paiement mensuel ($) No. of Children/ Nbre d'enfants				Income/ Revenu ($)	Monthly Award/ Paiement mensuel ($) No. of Children/ Nbre d'enfants			
	1	2	3	4		1	2	3	4		1	2	3	4		1	2	3	4
75600	660	1074	1407	1680	81000	707	1150	1504	1794	86400	754	1222	1597	1903	91800	799	1292	1688	2011
75700	661	1076	1408	1682	81100	708	1151	1506	1796	86500	754	1224	1599	1905	91900	800	1294	1689	2013
75800	662	1077	1410	1684	81200	709	1153	1508	1798	86600	755	1225	1600	1907	92000	801	1295	1691	2015
75900	663	1078	1412	1686	81300	710	1154	1509	1800	86700	756	1226	1602	1909	92100	802	1296	1693	2017
76000	663	1080	1414	1688	81400	710	1156	1511	1802	86800	757	1228	1604	1911	92200	803	1298	1694	2019
76100	664	1081	1416	1690	81500	711	1157	1513	1804	86900	758	1229	1606	1913	92300	803	1299	1696	2021
76200	665	1083	1418	1692	81600	712	1158	1515	1807	87000	759	1230	1607	1915	92400	804	1300	1698	2023
76300	666	1084	1419	1694	81700	713	1160	1516	1809	87100	760	1231	1609	1917	92500	805	1301	1700	2025
76400	667	1085	1421	1696	81800	714	1161	1518	1811	87200	761	1233	1610	1919	92600	806	1303	1701	2027
76500	668	1087	1423	1699	81900	715	1162	1520	1813	87300	762	1234	1612	1921	92700	807	1304	1703	2029
76600	669	1088	1425	1701	82000	716	1164	1522	1815	87400	762	1235	1614	1923	92800	808	1305	1705	2031
76700	670	1090	1426	1703	82100	717	1165	1524	1817	87500	763	1237	1615	1925	92900	808	1306	1706	2033
76800	671	1091	1428	1705	82200	718	1167	1525	1819	87600	764	1238	1617	1927	93000	809	1308	1708	2034
76900	672	1092	1430	1707	82300	719	1168	1527	1821	87700	765	1239	1619	1929	93100	810	1309	1710	2036
77000	672	1094	1432	1709	82400	719	1169	1529	1823	87800	766	1241	1620	1931	93200	811	1311	1711	2038
77100	673	1095	1434	1711	82500	720	1170	1530	1825	87900	767	1242	1622	1933	93300	812	1312	1713	2040
77200	674	1097	1436	1713	82600	721	1172	1532	1827	88000	767	1243	1623	1935	93400	813	1313	1715	2042
77300	675	1098	1437	1715	82700	722	1173	1534	1829	88100	768	1244	1625	1937	93500	813	1314	1717	2044
77400	675	1100	1439	1717	82800	723	1174	1535	1831	88200	769	1246	1626	1939	93600	814	1316	1718	2046
77500	676	1101	1441	1719	82900	724	1176	1537	1833	88300	769	1247	1628	1941	93700	815	1317	1720	2048
77600	677	1102	1443	1722	83000	725	1177	1539	1835	88400	770	1248	1630	1943	93800	816	1318	1722	2050
77700	678	1104	1444	1724	83100	726	1178	1541	1837	88500	771	1250	1631	1945	93900	817	1319	1724	2052
77800	679	1105	1446	1726	83200	727	1180	1542	1839	88600	772	1251	1633	1947	94000	818	1321	1725	2054
77900	680	1106	1448	1728	83300	727	1181	1544	1841	88700	773	1252	1635	1949	94100	819	1322	1727	2056
78000	680	1108	1450	1730	83400	728	1182	1546	1843	88800	773	1254	1636	1951	94200	820	1324	1728	2058
78100	681	1109	1452	1732	83500	729	1183	1547	1845	88900	774	1255	1638	1953	94300	821	1325	1730	2060
78200	682	1111	1454	1734	83600	730	1185	1549	1847	89000	775	1256	1640	1955	94400	821	1326	1732	2062
78300	683	1112	1455	1736	83700	731	1186	1551	1849	89100	776	1257	1642	1957	94500	822	1328	1733	2064
78400	683	1114	1457	1739	83800	732	1187	1553	1851	89200	777	1259	1643	1959	94600	823	1329	1735	2066
78500	684	1115	1459	1741	83900	732	1189	1554	1853	89300	778	1260	1645	1961	94700	824	1330	1737	2068
78600	685	1116	1461	1743	84000	733	1190	1556	1855	89400	778	1261	1647	1963	94800	825	1332	1738	2070
78700	686	1118	1462	1745	84100	734	1191	1558	1857	89500	779	1263	1648	1965	94900	826	1333	1740	2072
78800	687	1119	1464	1747	84200	735	1193	1559	1859	89600	780	1264	1650	1967	95000	826	1335	1741	2074
78900	688	1120	1466	1749	84300	736	1194	1561	1861	89700	781	1265	1652	1969	95100	827	1336	1743	2076
79000	689	1122	1468	1752	84400	736	1195	1563	1863	89800	782	1266	1653	1971	95200	828	1338	1744	2078
79100	690	1123	1470	1754	84500	737	1196	1565	1865	89900	783	1268	1655	1973	95300	828	1339	1746	2080
79200	691	1125	1472	1756	84600	738	1198	1566	1867	90000	784	1269	1657	1975	95400	829	1340	1748	2082
79300	692	1126	1473	1758	84700	739	1199	1568	1869	90100	785	1270	1659	1977	95500	830	1342	1749	2084
79400	692	1128	1475	1761	84800	740	1200	1570	1871	90200	786	1272	1660	1979	95600	831	1343	1751	2086
79500	693	1129	1477	1763	84900	741	1201	1571	1873	90300	786	1273	1662	1981	95700	832	1344	1753	2088
79600	694	1130	1479	1765	85000	742	1203	1573	1875	90400	787	1274	1664	1983	95800	832	1346	1754	2090
79700	695	1132	1480	1767	85100	743	1204	1575	1877	90500	788	1276	1665	1985	95900	833	1347	1756	2092
79800	696	1133	1482	1769	85200	744	1206	1576	1879	90600	789	1277	1667	1987	96000	834	1348	1758	2094
79900	697	1134	1484	1771	85300	744	1207	1578	1881	90700	790	1278	1669	1989	96100	835	1349	1760	2096
80000	698	1136	1486	1773	85400	745	1208	1580	1883	90800	791	1279	1671	1991	96200	836	1351	1761	2098
80100	699	1137	1488	1775	85500	746	1210	1582	1885	90900	791	1281	1672	1993	96300	837	1352	1763	2100
80200	700	1139	1490	1777	85600	747	1211	1583	1887	91000	792	1282	1674	1995	96400	837	1353	1765	2102
80300	701	1140	1491	1779	85700	748	1213	1585	1889	91100	793	1283	1676	1997	96500	838	1355	1766	2104
80400	701	1142	1493	1781	85800	749	1214	1587	1891	91200	794	1285	1677	1999	96600	839	1356	1768	2106
80500	702	1143	1495	1784	85900	749	1215	1588	1893	91300	795	1286	1679	2001	96700	840	1357	1770	2108
80600	703	1144	1497	1786	86000	750	1217	1590	1895	91400	795	1287	1681	2003	96800	841	1359	1771	2110
80700	704	1146	1498	1788	86100	751	1218	1592	1897	91500	796	1288	1683	2005	96900	842	1360	1773	2112
80800	705	1147	1500	1790	86200	752	1220	1593	1899	91600	797	1290	1684	2007	97000	843	1361	1775	2114
80900	706	1148	1502	1792	86300	753	1221	1595	1901	91700	798	1291	1686	2009	97100	844	1362	1777	2116

44

New Brunswick / Nouveau-Brunswick

Federal Child Support Amounts: Simplified Tables
Montants fédéraux de pensions alimentaires pour enfants: Tables simplifiées

Income/ Revenu ($)	Monthly Award/ Paiement mensuel ($) No. of Children/ Nbre d'enfants				Income/ Revenu ($)	Monthly Award/ Paiement mensuel ($) No. of Children/ Nbre d'enfants				Income/ Revenu ($)	Monthly Award/ Paiement mensuel ($) No. of Children/ Nbre d'enfants				Income/ Revenu ($)	Monthly Award/ Paiement mensuel ($) No. of Children/ Nbre d'enfants			
	1	2	3	4		1	2	3	4		1	2	3	4		1	2	3	4
97200	845	1364	1778	2118	102600	890	1434	1869	2226	108000	936	1505	1961	2333	113400	981	1576	2052	2441
97300	845	1365	1780	2120	102700	891	1435	1871	2228	108100	937	1506	1963	2335	113500	982	1578	2054	2443
97400	846	1366	1782	2122	102800	891	1436	1872	2230	108200	938	1508	1964	2337	113600	983	1579	2055	2445
97500	847	1368	1783	2124	102900	892	1437	1874	2232	108300	939	1509	1966	2339	113700	984	1580	2057	2447
97600	848	1369	1785	2126	103000	893	1439	1876	2234	108400	939	1510	1968	2341	113800	985	1582	2059	2449
97700	849	1370	1787	2128	103100	894	1440	1878	2236	108500	940	1511	1969	2343	113900	985	1583	2060	2451
97800	850	1372	1788	2130	103200	895	1442	1879	2238	108600	941	1513	1971	2345	114000	986	1584	2062	2453
97900	850	1373	1790	2132	103300	896	1443	1881	2240	108700	942	1514	1972	2347	114100	987	1585	2064	2455
98000	851	1374	1792	2134	103400	896	1444	1883	2242	108800	943	1515	1974	2349	114200	988	1587	2065	2457
98100	852	1375	1794	2136	103500	897	1446	1884	2244	108900	944	1517	1976	2351	114300	989	1588	2067	2459
98200	853	1377	1795	2138	103600	898	1447	1886	2246	109000	944	1518	1977	2353	114400	990	1589	2069	2461
98300	854	1378	1797	2140	103700	899	1448	1888	2248	109100	945	1519	1979	2355	114500	990	1591	2071	2463
98400	854	1379	1799	2142	103800	900	1450	1889	2250	109200	946	1521	1980	2357	114600	991	1592	2072	2465
98500	855	1381	1801	2144	103900	901	1451	1891	2252	109300	946	1522	1982	2359	114700	992	1593	2074	2467
98600	856	1382	1802	2146	104000	902	1453	1893	2254	109400	947	1523	1984	2361	114800	993	1595	2076	2469
98700	857	1383	1804	2148	104100	903	1454	1895	2256	109500	948	1524	1985	2363	114900	994	1596	2078	2471
98800	858	1384	1806	2150	104200	904	1456	1896	2258	109600	949	1526	1987	2365	115000	995	1597	2079	2473
98900	859	1386	1807	2152	104300	904	1457	1898	2260	109700	950	1527	1989	2367	115100	996	1598	2081	2475
99000	860	1387	1809	2154	104400	905	1458	1900	2262	109800	950	1528	1990	2369	115200	997	1600	2082	2477
99100	861	1388	1811	2156	104500	906	1460	1901	2264	109900	951	1530	1992	2371	115300	998	1601	2084	2479
99200	862	1390	1812	2158	104600	907	1461	1903	2266	110000	952	1531	1994	2373	115400	998	1602	2086	2481
99300	862	1391	1814	2160	104700	908	1462	1905	2268	110100	953	1532	1996	2375	115500	999	1604	2087	2483
99400	863	1392	1816	2162	104800	908	1464	1906	2270	110200	954	1534	1997	2377	115600	1000	1605	2089	2485
99500	864	1393	1818	2164	104900	909	1465	1908	2272	110300	955	1535	1999	2379	115700	1001	1606	2090	2487
99600	865	1395	1819	2166	105000	910	1466	1910	2274	110400	955	1536	2001	2381	115800	1002	1608	2092	2489
99700	866	1396	1821	2168	105100	911	1467	1912	2276	110500	956	1537	2002	2383	115900	1003	1609	2094	2491
99800	867	1397	1823	2170	105200	912	1469	1913	2278	110600	957	1539	2004	2385	116000	1003	1610	2095	2493
99900	867	1399	1824	2172	105300	913	1470	1915	2280	110700	958	1540	2006	2387	116100	1004	1611	2097	2495
100000	868	1400	1826	2174	105400	913	1471	1917	2282	110800	959	1541	2007	2389	116200	1005	1613	2098	2497
100100	869	1401	1828	2176	105500	914	1473	1918	2284	110900	960	1542	2009	2391	116300	1005	1614	2100	2499
100200	870	1403	1829	2178	105600	915	1474	1920	2286	111000	961	1544	2011	2393	116400	1006	1615	2102	2501
100300	871	1404	1831	2180	105700	916	1475	1922	2288	111100	962	1545	2013	2395	116500	1007	1617	2103	2503
100400	872	1405	1833	2182	105800	917	1477	1924	2290	111200	963	1547	2014	2397	116600	1008	1618	2105	2505
100500	872	1406	1835	2184	105900	918	1478	1925	2292	111300	963	1548	2016	2399	116700	1009	1619	2107	2507
100600	873	1408	1836	2186	106000	919	1479	1927	2293	111400	964	1549	2018	2401	116800	1009	1620	2108	2509
100700	874	1409	1838	2188	106100	920	1480	1929	2295	111500	965	1551	2019	2403	116900	1010	1622	2110	2511
100800	875	1410	1840	2190	106200	921	1482	1930	2297	111600	966	1552	2021	2405	117000	1011	1623	2112	2513
100900	876	1412	1842	2192	106300	921	1483	1932	2299	111700	967	1554	2023	2407	117100	1012	1624	2114	2515
101000	877	1413	1843	2194	106400	922	1484	1934	2301	111800	967	1555	2024	2409	117200	1013	1626	2115	2517
101100	878	1414	1845	2196	106500	923	1486	1936	2303	111900	968	1556	2026	2411	117300	1014	1627	2117	2519
101200	879	1416	1846	2198	106600	924	1487	1937	2305	112000	969	1558	2028	2413	117400	1014	1628	2119	2521
101300	880	1417	1848	2200	106700	925	1488	1939	2307	112100	970	1559	2030	2415	117500	1015	1629	2120	2523
101400	880	1418	1850	2202	106800	926	1490	1941	2309	112200	971	1561	2031	2417	117600	1016	1631	2122	2525
101500	881	1419	1851	2204	106900	926	1491	1942	2311	112300	972	1562	2033	2419	117700	1017	1632	2123	2527
101600	882	1421	1853	2206	107000	927	1492	1944	2313	112400	972	1563	2035	2421	117800	1018	1633	2125	2529
101700	883	1422	1854	2208	107100	928	1493	1946	2315	112500	973	1565	2036	2423	117900	1019	1635	2127	2531
101800	884	1423	1856	2210	107200	929	1495	1947	2317	112600	974	1566	2038	2425	118000	1020	1636	2129	2533
101900	885	1424	1858	2212	107300	930	1496	1949	2319	112700	975	1567	2040	2427	118100	1021	1637	2131	2535
102000	885	1426	1859	2214	107400	931	1497	1951	2321	112800	976	1569	2042	2429	118200	1022	1639	2132	2537
102100	886	1427	1861	2216	107500	931	1499	1953	2323	112900	977	1570	2043	2431	118300	1022	1640	2134	2539
102200	887	1429	1862	2218	107600	932	1500	1954	2325	113000	978	1571	2045	2433	118400	1023	1641	2136	2541
102300	887	1430	1864	2220	107700	933	1501	1956	2327	113100	979	1572	2047	2435	118500	1024	1642	2137	2543
102400	888	1431	1866	2222	107800	934	1502	1958	2329	113200	980	1574	2048	2437	118600	1025	1644	2139	2545
102500	889	1432	1867	2224	107900	935	1504	1960	2331	113300	980	1575	2050	2439	118700	1026	1645	2141	2547

New Brunswick / Nouveau-Brunswick

Federal Child Support Amounts: Simplified Tables
Montants fédéraux de pensions alimentaires pour enfants: Tables simplifiées

Income/ Revenu ($)	Monthly Award/ Paiement mensuel ($) No. of Children/ N^bre d'enfants				Income/ Revenu ($)	Monthly Award/ Paiement mensuel ($) No. of Children/ N^bre d'enfants				Income/ Revenu ($)	Monthly Award/ Paiement mensuel ($) No. of Children/ N^bre d'enfants				Income/ Revenu ($)	Monthly Award/ Paiement mensuel ($) No. of Children/ N^bre d'enfants				Income/ Revenu ($)	Monthly Award/ Paiement mensuel ($) No. of Children/ N^bre d'enfants			
	1	2	3	4		1	2	3	4		1	2	3	4		1	2	3	4		1	2	3	4
118800	1026	1646	2142	2549	124200	1072	1717	2232	2654	129600	1115	1784	2320	2757	135000	1158	1850	2405	2858					
118900	1027	1648	2144	2550	124300	1072	1718	2234	2656	129700	1115	1785	2321	2759	135100	1159	1851	2407	2860					
119000	1028	1649	2146	2552	124400	1073	1719	2235	2658	129800	1116	1787	2323	2761	135200	1159	1853	2408	2862					
119100	1029	1650	2148	2554	124500	1074	1721	2237	2660	129900	1117	1788	2324	2763	135300	1160	1854	2410	2864					
119200	1030	1652	2149	2556	124600	1075	1722	2239	2662	130000	1118	1789	2326	2765	135400	1161	1855	2411	2866					
119300	1031	1653	2151	2558	124700	1076	1723	2240	2664	130100	1119	1790	2328	2767	135500	1162	1856	2413	2867					
119400	1031	1654	2152	2560	124800	1077	1725	2242	2666	130200	1120	1791	2329	2769	135600	1162	1858	2414	2869					
119500	1032	1655	2154	2562	124900	1077	1726	2244	2668	130300	1120	1793	2331	2771	135700	1163	1859	2416	2871					
119600	1033	1657	2156	2564	125000	1078	1727	2245	2670	130400	1121	1794	2332	2773	135800	1164	1860	2417	2873					
119700	1034	1658	2157	2566	125100	1079	1728	2247	2672	130500	1122	1795	2334	2775	135900	1165	1861	2419	2875					
119800	1035	1659	2159	2568	125200	1080	1729	2248	2674	130600	1123	1796	2336	2776	136000	1165	1863	2420	2877					
119900	1036	1661	2160	2570	125300	1080	1731	2250	2676	130700	1123	1797	2337	2778	136100	1166	1864	2422	2879					
120000	1037	1662	2162	2572	125400	1081	1732	2252	2678	130800	1124	1799	2339	2780	136200	1167	1865	2423	2881					
120100	1038	1663	2164	2574	125500	1082	1733	2253	2680	130900	1125	1800	2341	2782	136300	1167	1867	2425	2883					
120200	1039	1665	2165	2576	125600	1083	1734	2255	2682	131000	1126	1801	2342	2784	136400	1168	1868	2426	2884					
120300	1040	1666	2167	2578	125700	1084	1736	2257	2684	131100	1127	1802	2344	2786	136500	1169	1869	2428	2886					
120400	1040	1667	2169	2580	125800	1084	1737	2258	2686	131200	1128	1804	2345	2788	136600	1170	1870	2429	2888					
120500	1041	1668	2170	2582	125900	1085	1738	2260	2688	131300	1128	1805	2347	2790	136700	1170	1872	2431	2890					
120600	1042	1670	2172	2584	126000	1086	1739	2262	2690	131400	1129	1806	2348	2791	136800	1171	1873	2433	2892					
120700	1043	1671	2174	2586	126100	1087	1740	2264	2692	131500	1130	1807	2350	2793	136900	1172	1874	2434	2894					
120800	1044	1672	2175	2588	126200	1088	1742	2265	2694	131600	1131	1809	2351	2795	137000	1173	1875	2436	2895					
120900	1045	1674	2177	2590	126300	1089	1743	2267	2696	131700	1132	1810	2353	2797	137100	1174	1876	2438	2897					
121000	1045	1675	2179	2592	126400	1089	1744	2269	2698	131800	1132	1811	2354	2799	137200	1175	1877	2439	2899					
121100	1046	1676	2181	2594	126500	1090	1745	2271	2700	131900	1133	1812	2356	2801	137300	1175	1879	2441	2901					
121200	1047	1678	2182	2596	126600	1091	1747	2272	2702	132000	1134	1814	2357	2802	137400	1176	1880	2442	2902					
121300	1047	1679	2184	2598	126700	1092	1748	2274	2704	132100	1135	1815	2359	2804	137500	1177	1881	2444	2904					
121400	1048	1680	2186	2600	126800	1093	1749	2276	2706	132200	1136	1816	2360	2806	137600	1178	1882	2446	2906					
121500	1049	1682	2187	2602	126900	1094	1750	2277	2708	132300	1136	1818	2362	2808	137700	1178	1883	2447	2908					
121600	1050	1683	2189	2604	127000	1095	1752	2279	2709	132400	1137	1819	2363	2810	137800	1179	1885	2449	2910					
121700	1051	1684	2191	2606	127100	1096	1753	2281	2711	132500	1138	1820	2365	2811	137900	1180	1886	2450	2912					
121800	1052	1685	2193	2608	127200	1096	1755	2282	2713	132600	1139	1821	2366	2813	138000	1181	1887	2452	2914					
121900	1052	1687	2194	2611	127300	1097	1756	2284	2715	132700	1140	1823	2368	2815	138100	1182	1888	2454	2916					
122000	1053	1688	2196	2613	127400	1098	1757	2285	2717	132800	1140	1824	2370	2817	138200	1183	1889	2455	2918					
122100	1054	1689	2198	2613	127500	1099	1758	2287	2718	132900	1141	1825	2371	2819	138300	1183	1891	2457	2919					
122200	1055	1691	2199	2615	127600	1099	1760	2288	2720	133000	1142	1826	2373	2821	138400	1184	1892	2458	2921					
122300	1055	1692	2201	2617	127700	1100	1761	2290	2722	133100	1143	1827	2375	2823	138500	1185	1893	2460	2923					
122400	1056	1693	2203	2619	127800	1101	1762	2291	2724	133200	1144	1828	2376	2825	138600	1186	1894	2462	2925					
122500	1057	1695	2204	2621	127900	1102	1763	2293	2726	133300	1144	1830	2378	2826	138700	1186	1895	2463	2927					
122600	1058	1696	2206	2623	128000	1102	1765	2294	2728	133400	1145	1831	2379	2828	138800	1187	1897	2465	2928					
122700	1059	1697	2207	2625	128100	1103	1766	2296	2730	133500	1146	1832	2381	2830	138900	1188	1898	2467	2930					
122800	1059	1699	2209	2627	128200	1104	1767	2297	2732	133600	1147	1833	2383	2832	139000	1189	1899	2468	2932					
122900	1060	1700	2211	2629	128300	1104	1769	2299	2733	133700	1148	1834	2384	2834	139100	1190	1900	2470	2934					
123000	1061	1701	2212	2631	128400	1105	1770	2300	2735	133800	1149	1836	2386	2836	139200	1191	1902	2471	2936					
123100	1062	1702	2214	2633	128500	1106	1771	2302	2737	133900	1149	1837	2387	2837	139300	1191	1903	2473	2938					
123200	1063	1704	2215	2635	128600	1107	1772	2303	2739	134000	1150	1838	2389	2839	139400	1192	1904	2474	2939					
123300	1064	1705	2217	2637	128700	1107	1774	2305	2741	134100	1151	1839	2391	2841	139500	1193	1905	2476	2941					
123400	1064	1706	2219	2639	128800	1108	1775	2307	2743	134200	1152	1840	2392	2843	139600	1194	1907	2477	2943					
123500	1065	1708	2220	2641	128900	1109	1776	2308	2744	134300	1152	1842	2394	2845	139700	1195	1908	2479	2945					
123600	1066	1709	2222	2643	129000	1110	1777	2310	2746	134400	1153	1843	2395	2846	139800	1195	1909	2480	2947					
123700	1067	1710	2224	2644	129100	1111	1778	2312	2748	134500	1154	1844	2397	2848	139900	1196	1910	2482	2949					
123800	1068	1712	2225	2646	129200	1112	1779	2313	2750	134600	1155	1845	2399	2850	140000	1197	1912	2483	2951					
123900	1069	1713	2227	2648	129300	1112	1781	2315	2752	134700	1156	1846	2400	2852	140100	1198	1913	2485	2953					
124000	1070	1714	2229	2650	129400	1113	1782	2316	2753	134800	1157	1848	2402	2854	140200	1199	1914	2486	2955					
124100	1071	1715	2231	2652	129500	1114	1783	2318	2755	134900	1157	1849	2404	2856	140300	1199	1916	2488	2957					

NEW BRUNSWICK — CONTINUED

Federal Child Support Amounts: Simplified Tables
Montants fédéraux de pensions alimentaires pour enfants: Tables simplifiées

Income/ Revenu ($)	Monthly Award/ Paiement mensuel ($) No. of Children/ N^bre d'enfants				Income/ Revenu ($)	Monthly Award/ Paiement mensuel ($) No. of Children/ N^bre d'enfants				Income/ Revenu ($)	Monthly Award/ Paiement mensuel ($) No. of Children/ N^bre d'enfants			
	1	2	3	4		1	2	3	4		1	2	3	4
140400	1200	1917	2489	2959	143700	1226	1957	2542	3020	147000	1252	1997	2594	3081
140500	1201	1918	2491	2960	143800	1227	1958	2543	3022	147100	1253	1998	2596	3083
140600	1202	1919	2492	2962	143900	1228	1959	2545	3024	147200	1254	2000	2597	3085
140700	1203	1921	2494	2964	144000	1228	1961	2546	3026	147300	1254	2001	2599	3087
140800	1203	1922	2496	2966	144100	1229	1962	2548	3028	147400	1255	2002	2600	3088
140900	1204	1923	2497	2968	144200	1230	1963	2549	3030	147500	1256	2003	2602	3090
141000	1205	1924	2499	2970	144300	1230	1965	2551	3032	147600	1257	2005	2603	3092
141100	1206	1925	2501	2972	144400	1231	1966	2552	3033	147700	1258	2006	2605	3094
141200	1207	1926	2502	2974	144500	1232	1967	2554	3035	147800	1258	2007	2606	3096
141300	1207	1928	2504	2975	144600	1233	1968	2555	3037	147900	1259	2008	2608	3098
141400	1208	1929	2505	2977	144700	1233	1970	2557	3039	148000	1260	2010	2609	3100
141500	1209	1930	2507	2979	144800	1234	1971	2559	3041	148100	1261	2011	2611	3102
141600	1210	1931	2509	2981	144900	1235	1972	2560	3043	148200	1262	2012	2612	3104
141700	1211	1932	2510	2983	145000	1236	1973	2562	3044	148300	1262	2014	2614	3106
141800	1212	1934	2512	2985	145100	1237	1974	2564	3046	148400	1263	2015	2615	3108
141900	1212	1935	2513	2986	145200	1238	1975	2565	3048	148500	1264	2016	2617	3109
142000	1213	1936	2515	2988	145300	1238	1977	2567	3050	148600	1265	2017	2618	3111
142100	1214	1937	2517	2990	145400	1239	1978	2568	3052	148700	1266	2019	2620	3113
142200	1215	1938	2518	2992	145500	1240	1979	2570	3053	148800	1266	2020	2622	3115
142300	1215	1940	2520	2994	145600	1241	1980	2572	3055	148900	1267	2021	2623	3117
142400	1216	1941	2521	2995	145700	1241	1981	2573	3057	149000	1268	2022	2625	3119
142500	1217	1942	2523	2997	145800	1242	1983	2575	3059	149100	1269	2023	2627	3121
142600	1218	1943	2525	2999	145900	1243	1984	2576	3061	149200	1270	2024	2628	3123
142700	1219	1944	2526	3001	146000	1244	1985	2578	3063	149300	1270	2026	2630	3125
142800	1220	1946	2528	3003	146100	1245	1986	2580	3065	149400	1271	2027	2631	3126
142900	1220	1947	2530	3005	146200	1246	1987	2581	3067	149500	1272	2028	2633	3128
143000	1221	1948	2531	3007	146300	1246	1989	2583	3068	149600	1273	2029	2635	3130
143100	1222	1949	2533	3009	146400	1247	1990	2584	3070	149700	1274	2030	2636	3132
143200	1222	1951	2534	3011	146500	1248	1991	2586	3072	149800	1275	2032	2638	3134
143300	1223	1952	2536	3013	146600	1249	1992	2588	3074	149900	1275	2033	2639	3136
143400	1224	1953	2537	3015	146700	1249	1993	2589	3076	150000	1276	2034	2641	3137
143500	1225	1954	2539	3017	146800	1250	1995	2591	3078					
143600	1225	1956	2540	3018	146900	1251	1996	2593	3079					

Monthly Award/Paiement mensuel ($)			
One Child/ Un enfant	Two Children/ Deux enfants	Three Children/ Trois enfants	Four Children/ Quatre enfants
1276 plus 0.82% of income over $150,000	**2034 plus 1.22%** of income over $150,000	**2641 plus 1.6%** of income over $150,000	**3137 plus 1.84%** of income over $150,000
1276 plus 0,82% du revenu dépassant 150 000$	**2034 plus 1,22%** du revenu dépassant 150 000$	**2641 plus 1,6%** du revenu dépassant 150 000$	**3137 plus 1,84%** du revenu dépassant 150 000$

MANITOBA

Federal Child Support Amounts: Simplified Tables
Montants fédéraux de pensions alimentaires pour enfants: Tables simplifiées

Income/ Revenu ($)	Monthly Award/ Paiement mensuel ($) No. of Children/ N^bre d'enfants				Income/ Revenu ($)	Monthly Award/ Paiement mensuel ($) No. of Children/ N^bre d'enfants				Income/ Revenu ($)	Monthly Award/ Paiement mensuel ($) No. of Children/ N^bre d'enfants				Income/ Revenu ($)	Monthly Award/ Paiement mensuel ($) No. of Children/ N^bre d'enfants			
	1	2	3	4		1	2	3	4		1	2	3	4		1	2	3	4
10820	0	0	0	0	16200	112	200	215	231	21600	138	283	405	453	27000	197	360	497	611
10900	3	3	4	4	16300	112	203	219	235	21700	139	284	406	458	27100	198	361	499	613
11000	37	40	44	47	16400	112	206	222	238	21800	140	286	408	462	27200	199	363	500	614
11100	40	44	48	51	16500	112	209	225	242	21900	141	287	410	466	27300	200	364	502	616
11200	44	47	52	55	16600	112	212	228	245	22000	142	288	411	470	27400	201	365	504	618
11300	47	51	56	60	16700	112	215	231	249	22100	143	289	413	474	27500	202	367	505	620
11400	50	55	60	64	16800	112	218	235	252	22200	144	291	414	479	27600	203	368	507	621
11500	54	58	64	68	16900	112	221	238	256	22300	145	292	416	483	27700	204	369	508	623
11600	57	62	68	72	17000	113	224	241	259	22400	146	294	418	487	27800	205	370	510	625
11700	61	66	72	77	17100	113	226	245	263	22500	147	295	419	491	27900	206	372	512	627
11800	64	69	76	81	17200	113	227	249	267	22600	148	296	421	496	28000	207	373	513	628
11900	67	73	80	85	17300	113	229	253	272	22700	149	298	423	500	28100	208	375	515	630
12000	71	77	83	89	17400	113	231	257	276	22800	150	299	424	504	28200	209	376	516	632
12100	74	80	86	92	17500	113	232	261	280	22900	151	301	426	508	28300	210	378	518	634
12200	77	83	90	96	17600	113	234	265	284	23000	152	302	428	513	28400	211	379	519	636
12300	79	86	93	99	17700	113	236	269	289	23100	153	304	430	517	28500	212	381	521	638
12400	82	89	96	103	17800	113	237	273	293	23200	154	305	431	521	28600	213	382	522	640
12500	85	92	99	106	17900	113	239	277	297	23300	155	307	433	525	28700	214	384	524	642
12600	88	95	103	110	18000	114	241	281	301	23400	156	309	435	529	28800	215	385	525	644
12700	90	98	106	113	18100	114	242	285	305	23500	157	310	437	533	28900	216	387	527	646
12800	93	101	109	117	18200	114	243	289	309	23600	158	312	438	537	29000	217	388	528	648
12900	96	104	112	120	18300	114	244	293	314	23700	159	313	440	541	29100	218	390	530	650
13000	99	107	116	124	18400	114	245	297	318	23800	160	315	442	545	29200	219	391	531	652
13100	100	110	119	127	18500	114	247	301	322	23900	161	317	444	549	29300	220	393	533	654
13200	100	113	122	131	18600	114	248	305	326	24000	163	318	445	553	29400	221	394	535	656
13300	101	116	125	134	18700	114	249	309	331	24100	164	320	447	555	29500	222	396	536	658
13400	101	119	129	138	18800	114	250	313	335	24200	165	321	448	557	29600	223	398	538	660
13500	102	122	132	141	18900	114	251	316	339	24300	166	323	450	559	29700	225	399	540	662
13600	103	125	135	145	19000	115	252	320	343	24400	167	324	452	561	29800	226	401	541	664
13700	103	128	138	148	19100	116	253	324	347	24500	168	326	454	563	29900	227	402	543	666
13800	104	131	141	151	19200	116	254	328	351	24600	170	327	455	566	30000	228	404	545	668
13900	104	134	144	155	19300	117	256	332	356	24700	171	329	457	568	30100	229	406	547	670
14000	105	137	147	158	19400	118	257	336	360	24800	172	330	459	570	30200	230	407	549	672
14100	106	140	150	161	19500	118	258	340	364	24900	173	332	461	572	30300	231	409	551	674
14200	106	143	153	165	19600	119	259	343	368	25000	174	333	462	574	30400	232	410	553	676
14300	107	146	156	168	19700	120	260	347	373	25100	175	335	464	576	30500	233	412	555	678
14400	107	149	159	171	19800	120	261	351	377	25200	176	336	466	578	30600	234	413	557	680
14500	108	152	162	175	19900	121	263	355	381	25300	178	338	468	580	30700	235	415	559	682
14600	108	155	165	178	20000	122	264	359	385	25400	179	339	470	582	30800	236	416	561	684
14700	109	158	169	181	20100	123	265	363	389	25500	180	341	472	584	30900	237	418	563	686
14800	109	160	172	185	20200	124	266	366	394	25600	181	342	474	586	31000	238	419	564	687
14900	110	163	175	188	20300	125	268	370	398	25700	183	344	475	588	31100	239	420	566	689
15000	110	166	178	191	20400	126	269	373	402	25800	184	345	477	590	31200	240	422	568	691
15100	110	169	181	194	20500	127	270	377	406	25900	185	347	479	592	31300	241	423	570	693
15200	110	172	184	198	20600	128	271	380	411	26000	186	349	481	594	31400	242	425	572	695
15300	111	175	187	201	20700	129	272	384	415	26100	187	350	483	596	31500	243	426	574	696
15400	111	177	190	204	20800	130	274	387	419	26200	188	351	484	597	31600	244	428	576	698
15500	111	180	193	207	20900	131	275	391	424	26300	189	352	486	599	31700	245	429	578	700
15600	111	183	196	211	21000	132	276	395	428	26400	190	354	488	601	31800	246	431	580	702
15700	111	186	199	214	21100	133	277	397	432	26500	191	355	489	603	31900	247	432	582	704
15800	112	189	203	217	21200	134	278	398	436	26600	192	356	491	604	32000	248	434	584	706
15900	112	192	206	221	21300	135	280	400	441	26700	193	357	492	606	32100	249	435	586	708
16000	112	194	209	224	21400	136	281	401	445	26800	194	358	494	608	32200	250	437	588	710
16100	112	197	212	228	21500	137	282	403	449	26900	196	359	496	609	32300	251	438	590	712

Manitoba

Federal Child Support Amounts: Simplified Tables
Montants fédéraux de pensions alimentaires pour enfants: Tables simplifiées

Income/ Revenu ($)	Monthly Award/ Paiement mensuel ($) No. of Children/ N^{bre} d'enfants				Income/ Revenu ($)	Monthly Award/ Paiement mensuel ($) No. of Children/ N^{bre} d'enfants				Income/ Revenu ($)	Monthly Award/ Paiement mensuel ($) No. of Children/ N^{bre} d'enfants				Income/ Revenu ($)	Monthly Award/ Paiement mensuel ($) No. of Children/ N^{bre} d'enfants			
	1	2	3	4		1	2	3	4		1	2	3	4		1	2	3	4
32400	252	440	591	714	37800	302	516	687	828	43200	352	592	784	941	48600	400	666	880	1054
32500	253	441	593	716	37900	303	517	689	830	43300	353	593	786	943	48700	400	668	882	1056
32600	254	443	595	718	38000	304	519	691	832	43400	353	594	788	945	48800	401	669	884	1059
32700	255	444	597	721	38100	305	520	693	834	43500	354	596	790	948	48900	402	671	886	1061
32800	256	446	599	723	38200	306	522	695	836	43600	355	597	791	950	49000	403	672	887	1063
32900	257	447	601	725	38300	307	523	696	838	43700	356	599	793	952	49100	404	673	889	1065
33000	258	449	602	727	38400	308	525	698	840	43800	357	600	795	954	49200	405	675	891	1067
33100	259	450	604	729	38500	309	526	700	843	43900	358	601	797	956	49300	406	676	892	1069
33200	260	452	606	731	38600	310	527	702	845	44000	358	603	798	958	49400	407	678	894	1072
33300	261	453	607	733	38700	311	529	703	847	44100	359	604	800	960	49500	408	679	896	1074
33400	262	455	609	735	38800	312	530	705	849	44200	360	606	802	962	49600	409	681	898	1076
33500	263	456	611	737	38900	313	531	707	851	44300	361	607	803	964	49700	409	682	900	1078
33600	264	457	613	739	39000	314	533	709	853	44400	361	608	805	966	49800	410	684	901	1080
33700	265	459	615	742	39100	315	534	711	855	44500	362	610	807	968	49900	411	685	903	1082
33800	266	460	616	744	39200	316	536	713	857	44600	363	611	809	970	50000	412	687	905	1084
33900	267	462	618	746	39300	317	537	714	859	44700	364	612	810	972	50100	413	688	907	1086
34000	267	463	620	748	39400	318	538	716	861	44800	365	614	812	974	50200	414	690	909	1088
34100	268	464	622	750	39500	319	540	718	864	44900	366	615	814	976	50300	415	691	911	1090
34200	269	466	624	752	39600	320	541	720	866	45000	367	616	816	978	50400	416	693	912	1093
34300	270	467	625	754	39700	321	543	722	868	45100	368	617	818	980	50500	417	694	914	1095
34400	271	469	627	756	39800	322	544	723	870	45200	369	619	819	982	50600	417	696	916	1097
34500	272	470	629	758	39900	322	545	725	872	45300	370	620	821	984	50700	418	697	918	1099
34600	272	471	631	761	40000	323	547	727	874	45400	370	621	823	986	50800	419	698	920	1101
34700	273	473	633	763	40100	324	548	729	876	45500	371	623	825	988	50900	420	700	922	1103
34800	274	474	635	765	40200	325	550	731	878	45600	372	624	826	990	51000	421	701	924	1106
34900	275	476	636	767	40300	326	551	733	881	45700	373	625	828	993	51100	422	702	926	1108
35000	276	477	638	769	40400	327	553	735	883	45800	374	627	830	995	51200	423	704	928	1110
35100	277	478	640	771	40500	328	554	736	885	45900	375	628	832	997	51300	424	705	929	1113
35200	278	480	642	773	40600	329	556	738	887	46000	376	630	833	999	51400	425	707	931	1115
35300	279	481	644	775	40700	330	557	740	889	46100	377	631	835	1001	51500	426	708	933	1117
35400	280	483	645	777	40800	331	559	742	892	46200	378	633	836	1003	51600	426	709	935	1119
35500	281	484	647	779	40900	331	560	744	894	46300	379	634	838	1005	51700	427	711	937	1121
35600	282	485	649	782	41000	332	562	746	896	46400	380	636	840	1007	51800	428	712	939	1124
35700	283	487	651	784	41100	333	563	748	898	46500	380	637	841	1010	51900	429	714	940	1126
35800	284	488	653	786	41200	334	565	749	900	46600	381	638	843	1012	52000	430	715	942	1128
35900	285	490	655	788	41300	335	566	751	902	46700	382	640	845	1014	52100	431	716	944	1130
36000	286	491	656	790	41400	336	567	753	904	46800	383	641	847	1016	52200	432	718	946	1132
36100	287	492	658	792	41500	336	569	754	906	46900	384	643	848	1018	52300	433	719	948	1134
36200	288	494	659	794	41600	337	570	756	908	47000	385	644	850	1020	52400	434	721	950	1137
36300	289	495	661	796	41700	338	571	758	910	47100	386	645	852	1022	52500	435	722	951	1139
36400	290	497	663	798	41800	339	573	760	913	47200	387	647	854	1024	52600	435	724	953	1141
36500	291	498	665	800	41900	340	574	761	915	47300	388	648	856	1026	52700	436	725	955	1143
36600	292	499	666	803	42000	341	576	763	917	47400	389	650	857	1029	52800	437	727	957	1145
36700	293	501	668	805	42100	342	577	765	919	47500	390	651	859	1031	52900	438	728	959	1147
36800	294	502	670	807	42200	343	579	767	921	47600	391	653	861	1033	53000	439	730	961	1149
36900	295	504	672	809	42300	344	580	768	923	47700	391	654	863	1035	53100	440	731	963	1151
37000	295	505	673	811	42400	345	581	770	925	47800	392	655	865	1037	53200	441	733	965	1153
37100	296	506	675	813	42500	346	583	772	927	47900	393	657	867	1039	53300	442	734	967	1155
37200	297	508	677	815	42600	346	584	774	929	48000	394	658	869	1041	53400	443	736	968	1158
37300	298	509	678	817	42700	347	585	775	931	48100	395	659	871	1043	53500	443	737	970	1160
37400	299	511	680	819	42800	348	586	777	933	48200	396	661	873	1045	53600	444	738	972	1162
37500	300	512	682	822	42900	349	588	779	935	48300	397	662	875	1048	53700	445	740	974	1164
37600	300	513	684	824	43000	350	589	781	937	48400	398	664	876	1050	53800	446	741	976	1166
37700	301	515	685	826	43100	351	590	783	939	48500	399	665	878	1052	53900	447	743	978	1168

Manitoba

Federal Child Support Amounts: Simplified Tables
Montants fédéraux de pensions alimentaires pour enfants: Tables simplifiées

Income/ Revenu ($)	Monthly Award/ Paiement mensuel ($) No. of Children/ N^bre d'enfants				Income/ Revenu ($)	Monthly Award/ Paiement mensuel ($) No. of Children/ N^bre d'enfants				Income/ Revenu ($)	Monthly Award/ Paiement mensuel ($) No. of Children/ N^bre d'enfants				Income/ Revenu ($)	Monthly Award/ Paiement mensuel ($) No. of Children/ N^bre d'enfants			
	1	2	3	4		1	2	3	4		1	2	3	4		1	2	3	4
54000	448	744	979	1171	59400	496	822	1078	1288	64800	546	900	1177	1405	70200	593	975	1273	1517
54100	449	745	981	1173	59500	497	823	1080	1290	64900	547	901	1179	1407	70300	594	976	1274	1519
54200	450	747	983	1175	59600	498	825	1082	1292	65000	548	903	1181	1409	70400	595	977	1276	1521
54300	451	748	984	1178	59700	499	826	1084	1294	65100	549	904	1183	1411	70500	595	979	1278	1523
54400	452	750	986	1180	59800	500	828	1085	1296	65200	550	906	1185	1413	70600	596	980	1280	1525
54500	452	751	988	1182	59900	501	829	1087	1298	65300	551	907	1187	1415	70700	597	981	1281	1527
54600	453	753	990	1184	60000	502	831	1089	1301	65400	552	909	1188	1418	70800	598	983	1283	1529
54700	454	754	992	1186	60100	503	832	1091	1303	65500	553	910	1190	1420	70900	599	984	1285	1531
54800	455	756	993	1189	60200	504	834	1093	1305	65600	554	912	1192	1422	71000	600	985	1287	1533
54900	456	757	995	1191	60300	505	835	1095	1308	65700	554	913	1194	1424	71100	601	986	1289	1535
55000	457	759	997	1193	60400	506	837	1096	1310	65800	555	914	1196	1426	71200	602	988	1290	1537
55100	458	760	999	1195	60500	507	838	1098	1312	65900	556	916	1198	1428	71300	603	989	1292	1539
55200	459	762	1001	1197	60600	508	840	1100	1314	66000	557	917	1200	1431	71400	603	990	1294	1541
55300	460	763	1003	1199	60700	509	841	1102	1316	66100	558	918	1202	1433	71500	604	992	1296	1543
55400	461	765	1004	1202	60800	510	842	1104	1319	66200	559	920	1204	1435	71600	605	993	1297	1545
55500	461	766	1006	1204	60900	511	844	1106	1321	66300	560	921	1205	1438	71700	606	994	1299	1547
55600	462	768	1008	1206	61000	512	845	1108	1323	66400	561	923	1207	1440	71800	607	995	1301	1549
55700	463	769	1010	1208	61100	513	846	1110	1325	66500	562	924	1209	1442	71900	608	997	1303	1551
55800	464	770	1012	1210	61200	514	848	1112	1327	66600	562	925	1211	1444	72000	608	998	1304	1553
55900	465	772	1014	1212	61300	515	849	1113	1329	66700	563	927	1213	1446	72100	609	999	1306	1555
56000	466	773	1016	1214	61400	516	851	1115	1332	66800	564	928	1215	1449	72200	610	1001	1307	1557
56100	467	774	1018	1216	61500	517	852	1117	1334	66900	565	930	1216	1451	72300	610	1002	1309	1559
56200	468	776	1020	1218	61600	518	853	1119	1336	67000	566	931	1218	1453	72400	611	1003	1311	1561
56300	469	777	1021	1220	61700	519	855	1121	1338	67100	567	932	1220	1455	72500	612	1005	1313	1563
56400	470	779	1023	1223	61800	520	856	1123	1340	67200	568	934	1221	1457	72600	613	1006	1314	1565
56500	470	780	1025	1225	61900	521	858	1124	1342	67300	568	935	1223	1459	72700	614	1008	1316	1567
56600	471	781	1027	1227	62000	521	859	1126	1344	67400	569	936	1225	1461	72800	614	1009	1318	1569
56700	472	783	1029	1229	62100	522	860	1128	1346	67500	570	938	1226	1463	72900	615	1010	1320	1572
56800	473	784	1031	1231	62200	523	862	1130	1348	67600	571	939	1228	1465	73000	616	1012	1321	1574
56900	474	786	1032	1233	62300	524	863	1132	1350	67700	572	941	1230	1467	73100	617	1013	1323	1576
57000	475	787	1034	1236	62400	525	865	1134	1353	67800	572	942	1231	1469	73200	618	1015	1324	1578
57100	476	788	1036	1238	62500	526	866	1135	1355	67900	573	943	1233	1471	73300	619	1016	1326	1580
57200	477	790	1038	1240	62600	527	868	1137	1357	68000	574	945	1235	1473	73400	619	1017	1328	1582
57300	478	791	1040	1243	62700	528	869	1139	1359	68100	575	946	1237	1475	73500	620	1019	1330	1584
57400	478	793	1042	1245	62800	529	871	1141	1361	68200	576	948	1238	1477	73600	621	1020	1331	1586
57500	479	794	1043	1247	62900	529	872	1143	1363	68300	577	949	1240	1479	73700	622	1021	1333	1588
57600	480	796	1045	1249	63000	530	874	1145	1366	68400	577	950	1242	1481	73800	623	1023	1335	1590
57700	481	797	1047	1251	63100	531	875	1147	1368	68500	578	952	1243	1483	73900	624	1024	1337	1592
57800	482	799	1049	1254	63200	532	877	1149	1370	68600	579	953	1245	1485	74000	625	1025	1338	1594
57900	483	800	1051	1256	63300	533	878	1151	1373	68700	580	954	1247	1487	74100	626	1026	1340	1596
58000	484	802	1053	1258	63400	534	880	1152	1375	68800	581	956	1248	1489	74200	627	1028	1341	1598
58100	485	803	1055	1260	63500	535	881	1154	1377	68900	582	957	1250	1491	74300	627	1029	1343	1600
58200	486	805	1057	1262	63600	536	882	1156	1379	69000	583	958	1252	1493	74400	628	1031	1345	1602
58300	487	806	1059	1264	63700	537	884	1158	1381	69100	584	959	1254	1495	74500	629	1032	1347	1604
58400	487	808	1060	1267	63800	537	885	1160	1384	69200	585	961	1255	1497	74600	630	1033	1348	1606
58500	488	809	1062	1269	63900	538	887	1162	1386	69300	585	962	1257	1499	74700	631	1035	1350	1608
58600	489	810	1064	1271	64000	539	888	1163	1388	69400	586	964	1259	1501	74800	632	1036	1352	1610
58700	490	812	1066	1273	64100	540	889	1165	1390	69500	587	965	1260	1503	74900	632	1037	1353	1612
58800	491	813	1068	1275	64200	541	891	1167	1392	69600	588	966	1262	1505	75000	633	1039	1355	1614
58900	492	815	1070	1277	64300	542	892	1168	1394	69700	589	968	1264	1507	75100	634	1040	1357	1616
59000	493	816	1071	1279	64400	543	894	1170	1397	69800	590	969	1265	1509	75200	635	1042	1358	1618
59100	494	817	1073	1281	64500	544	895	1172	1399	69900	590	970	1267	1511	75300	636	1043	1360	1620
59200	495	819	1075	1283	64600	545	897	1174	1401	70000	591	972	1269	1513	75400	637	1044	1362	1622
59300	496	820	1076	1285	64700	545	898	1176	1403	70100	592	973	1271	1515	75500	637	1046	1364	1624

Federal Child Support Amounts: Simplified Tables
Montants fédéraux de pensions alimentaires pour enfants: Tables simplifiées

Income/ Revenu ($)	Monthly Award/ Paiement mensuel ($) No. of Children/ N^{bre} d'enfants 1	2	3	4	Income/ Revenu ($)	Monthly Award/ Paiement mensuel ($) No. of Children/ N^{bre} d'enfants 1	2	3	4	Income/ Revenu ($)	Monthly Award/ Paiement mensuel ($) No. of Children/ N^{bre} d'enfants 1	2	3	4	Income/ Revenu ($)	Monthly Award/ Paiement mensuel ($) No. of Children/ N^{bre} d'enfants 1	2	3	4
75600	638	1047	1365	1626	81000	684	1118	1458	1735	86400	727	1185	1546	1838	91800	769	1251	1632	1939
75700	639	1048	1367	1628	81100	685	1119	1460	1737	86500	728	1186	1547	1839	91900	770	1252	1634	1941
75800	640	1050	1369	1630	81200	686	1121	1461	1739	86600	728	1187	1549	1841	92000	771	1253	1635	1943
75900	641	1051	1370	1632	81300	686	1122	1463	1741	86700	729	1189	1550	1843	92100	772	1254	1637	1945
76000	642	1052	1372	1634	81400	687	1123	1465	1743	86800	730	1190	1552	1845	92200	773	1255	1638	1947
76100	643	1053	1374	1636	81500	688	1125	1467	1745	86900	731	1191	1554	1847	92300	773	1257	1640	1949
76200	644	1055	1375	1638	81600	689	1126	1468	1747	87000	731	1192	1555	1849	92400	774	1258	1642	1951
76300	645	1056	1377	1640	81700	690	1127	1470	1749	87100	732	1193	1557	1851	92500	775	1259	1643	1952
76400	645	1057	1379	1642	81800	691	1129	1472	1751	87200	733	1194	1558	1853	92600	776	1260	1645	1954
76500	646	1059	1380	1644	81900	691	1130	1474	1753	87300	733	1196	1560	1855	92700	777	1261	1647	1956
76600	647	1060	1382	1646	82000	692	1131	1475	1755	87400	734	1197	1562	1857	92800	778	1263	1648	1958
76700	648	1061	1384	1648	82100	693	1132	1477	1757	87500	735	1198	1563	1859	92900	778	1264	1650	1960
76800	649	1062	1386	1650	82200	694	1133	1478	1759	87600	736	1199	1565	1860	93000	779	1265	1651	1962
76900	650	1064	1387	1652	82300	694	1135	1480	1761	87700	736	1201	1566	1862	93100	780	1266	1653	1964
77000	650	1065	1389	1654	82400	695	1136	1482	1763	87800	737	1202	1568	1864	93200	780	1267	1654	1966
77100	651	1066	1391	1656	82500	696	1137	1483	1765	87900	738	1203	1570	1866	93300	781	1269	1656	1968
77200	652	1068	1392	1658	82600	697	1138	1485	1767	88000	739	1204	1571	1868	93400	782	1270	1658	1970
77300	652	1069	1394	1660	82700	698	1140	1486	1768	88100	740	1205	1573	1870	93500	783	1271	1659	1972
77400	653	1070	1396	1662	82800	698	1141	1488	1770	88200	741	1206	1574	1872	93600	783	1272	1661	1973
77500	654	1071	1397	1664	82900	699	1142	1490	1772	88300	741	1208	1576	1874	93700	784	1273	1663	1975
77600	655	1073	1399	1666	83000	700	1143	1491	1774	88400	742	1209	1578	1876	93800	785	1274	1664	1977
77700	656	1074	1401	1668	83100	701	1144	1493	1776	88500	743	1210	1579	1878	93900	786	1276	1666	1979
77800	656	1075	1402	1670	83200	702	1145	1494	1778	88600	744	1211	1581	1880	94000	786	1277	1667	1981
77900	657	1077	1404	1672	83300	702	1147	1496	1780	88700	744	1212	1582	1882	94100	787	1278	1669	1983
78000	658	1078	1406	1674	83400	703	1148	1498	1781	88800	745	1214	1584	1883	94200	788	1280	1670	1985
78100	659	1079	1408	1676	83500	704	1149	1499	1783	88900	746	1215	1586	1885	94300	788	1281	1672	1987
78200	660	1081	1409	1678	83600	705	1150	1501	1785	89000	747	1216	1587	1887	94400	789	1282	1674	1988
78300	661	1082	1411	1680	83700	706	1152	1502	1787	89100	748	1217	1589	1889	94500	790	1283	1675	1990
78400	661	1083	1413	1682	83800	706	1153	1504	1789	89200	749	1218	1590	1891	94600	791	1285	1677	1992
78500	662	1084	1414	1684	83900	707	1154	1506	1791	89300	749	1220	1592	1893	94700	791	1286	1679	1994
78600	663	1086	1416	1686	84000	708	1155	1507	1792	89400	750	1221	1594	1894	94800	792	1287	1680	1996
78700	664	1087	1418	1688	84100	709	1156	1509	1794	89500	751	1222	1595	1896	94900	793	1288	1682	1998
78800	665	1088	1419	1690	84200	710	1157	1510	1796	89600	752	1223	1597	1898	95000	794	1290	1683	1999
78900	666	1089	1421	1692	84300	710	1159	1512	1798	89700	752	1224	1598	1900	95100	795	1291	1685	2001
79000	667	1091	1423	1694	84400	711	1160	1514	1799	89800	753	1225	1600	1902	95200	796	1292	1686	2003
79100	668	1092	1425	1696	84500	712	1161	1515	1801	89900	754	1227	1602	1904	95300	796	1294	1688	2005
79200	669	1094	1426	1698	84600	713	1162	1517	1803	90000	755	1228	1603	1905	95400	797	1295	1690	2006
79300	669	1095	1428	1700	84700	714	1163	1518	1805	90100	756	1229	1605	1907	95500	798	1296	1691	2008
79400	670	1096	1430	1702	84800	715	1165	1520	1807	90200	757	1231	1606	1909	95600	799	1297	1693	2010
79500	671	1097	1431	1704	84900	715	1166	1522	1809	90300	757	1232	1608	1911	95700	799	1299	1695	2012
79600	672	1099	1433	1706	85000	716	1167	1523	1811	90400	758	1233	1610	1912	95800	800	1300	1696	2014
79700	673	1100	1435	1708	85100	717	1168	1525	1813	90500	759	1234	1611	1914	95900	801	1301	1698	2016
79800	673	1101	1436	1710	85200	718	1170	1526	1815	90600	760	1236	1613	1916	96000	802	1302	1699	2018
79900	674	1102	1438	1713	85300	718	1171	1528	1817	90700	761	1237	1614	1918	96100	803	1303	1701	2020
80000	675	1104	1440	1715	85400	719	1172	1530	1819	90800	761	1238	1616	1920	96200	804	1304	1702	2022
80100	676	1105	1442	1717	85500	720	1173	1531	1820	90900	762	1239	1618	1922	96300	804	1306	1704	2024
80200	677	1107	1444	1719	85600	721	1175	1533	1822	91000	763	1241	1619	1924	96400	805	1307	1706	2025
80300	678	1108	1445	1721	85700	722	1176	1534	1824	91100	764	1242	1621	1926	96500	806	1308	1707	2027
80400	678	1109	1447	1723	85800	723	1177	1536	1826	91200	765	1243	1622	1928	96600	807	1309	1709	2029
80500	679	1111	1449	1725	85900	723	1178	1538	1828	91300	765	1245	1624	1930	96700	807	1311	1711	2031
80600	680	1112	1451	1727	86000	724	1180	1539	1830	91400	766	1246	1626	1932	96800	808	1312	1712	2033
80700	681	1113	1452	1729	86100	725	1181	1541	1832	91500	767	1247	1627	1933	96900	809	1313	1714	2035
80800	682	1115	1454	1731	86200	725	1182	1542	1834	91600	768	1248	1629	1935	97000	810	1314	1715	2037
80900	683	1116	1456	1733	86300	726	1184	1544	1836	91700	769	1250	1631	1937	97100	811	1315	1717	2039

Manitoba

Federal Child Support Amounts: Simplified Tables
Montants fédéraux de pensions alimentaires pour enfants: Tables simplifiées

Income/ Revenu ($)	Monthly Award/ Paiement mensuel ($) No. of Children/ N^bre d'enfants				Income/ Revenu ($)	Monthly Award/ Paiement mensuel ($) No. of Children/ N^bre d'enfants				Income/ Revenu ($)	Monthly Award/ Paiement mensuel ($) No. of Children/ N^bre d'enfants				Income/ Revenu ($)	Monthly Award/ Paiement mensuel ($) No. of Children/ N^bre d'enfants			
	1	2	3	4		1	2	3	4		1	2	3	4		1	2	3	4
97200	812	1316	1718	2041	102600	854	1382	1803	2142	108000	897	1449	1890	2244	113400	939	1515	1975	2345
97300	812	1318	1720	2043	102700	854	1383	1805	2144	108100	898	1450	1892	2246	113500	940	1516	1977	2347
97400	813	1319	1722	2045	102800	855	1384	1806	2146	108200	898	1451	1893	2248	113600	941	1517	1979	2349
97500	814	1320	1723	2046	102900	856	1386	1808	2148	108300	899	1453	1895	2250	113700	942	1519	1980	2351
97600	815	1321	1725	2048	103000	857	1387	1810	2150	108400	900	1454	1896	2252	113800	943	1520	1982	2353
97700	816	1322	1727	2050	103100	858	1388	1812	2152	108500	901	1455	1898	2253	113900	943	1521	1984	2355
97800	816	1324	1728	2052	103200	859	1390	1813	2154	108600	901	1456	1899	2255	114000	944	1522	1985	2357
97900	817	1325	1730	2054	103300	859	1391	1815	2156	108700	902	1458	1901	2257	114100	945	1523	1987	2359
98000	818	1326	1731	2056	103400	860	1392	1816	2158	108800	903	1459	1903	2259	114200	946	1524	1988	2361
98100	819	1327	1733	2058	103500	861	1393	1818	2159	108900	904	1460	1904	2261	114300	946	1526	1990	2363
98200	820	1328	1734	2060	103600	862	1395	1819	2161	109000	904	1461	1906	2263	114400	947	1527	1991	2365
98300	820	1330	1736	2062	103700	862	1396	1821	2163	109100	905	1462	1908	2265	114500	948	1528	1993	2366
98400	821	1331	1738	2064	103800	863	1397	1822	2165	109200	906	1463	1909	2267	114600	949	1529	1994	2368
98500	822	1332	1739	2066	103900	864	1398	1824	2167	109300	906	1465	1911	2269	114700	950	1530	1996	2370
98600	823	1333	1741	2067	104000	865	1400	1826	2169	109400	907	1466	1912	2271	114800	951	1532	1997	2372
98700	824	1334	1743	2069	104100	866	1401	1828	2171	109500	908	1467	1914	2272	114900	951	1533	1999	2374
98800	824	1335	1744	2071	104200	867	1402	1829	2173	109600	909	1468	1916	2274	115000	952	1534	2000	2376
98900	825	1337	1746	2073	104300	867	1404	1831	2175	109700	909	1470	1917	2276	115100	953	1535	2002	2378
99000	826	1338	1747	2075	104400	868	1405	1832	2177	109800	910	1471	1919	2278	115200	953	1536	2003	2380
99100	827	1339	1749	2077	104500	869	1406	1834	2179	109900	911	1472	1920	2280	115300	954	1538	2005	2382
99200	828	1341	1750	2079	104600	870	1407	1835	2180	110000	912	1473	1922	2282	115400	955	1539	2006	2384
99300	828	1342	1752	2081	104700	871	1409	1837	2182	110100	913	1474	1924	2284	115500	956	1540	2008	2385
99400	829	1343	1753	2083	104800	871	1410	1838	2184	110200	914	1475	1925	2286	115600	956	1541	2009	2387
99500	830	1344	1755	2085	104900	872	1411	1840	2186	110300	914	1477	1927	2288	115700	957	1542	2011	2389
99600	831	1346	1756	2087	105000	873	1412	1842	2188	110400	915	1478	1928	2290	115800	958	1543	2013	2391
99700	832	1347	1758	2088	105100	874	1413	1844	2190	110500	916	1479	1930	2292	115900	959	1545	2014	2393
99800	833	1348	1759	2090	105200	875	1414	1845	2192	110600	917	1480	1931	2293	116000	959	1546	2016	2395
99900	833	1349	1761	2092	105300	875	1416	1847	2194	110700	917	1481	1933	2295	116100	960	1547	2018	2397
100000	834	1351	1762	2094	105400	876	1417	1848	2196	110800	918	1483	1934	2297	116200	961	1549	2019	2399
100100	835	1352	1764	2096	105500	877	1418	1850	2198	110900	919	1484	1936	2299	116300	961	1550	2021	2401
100200	836	1353	1765	2098	105600	878	1419	1851	2200	111000	920	1485	1937	2301	116400	962	1551	2022	2403
100300	837	1355	1767	2100	105700	879	1420	1853	2201	111100	921	1486	1939	2303	116500	963	1552	2024	2405
100400	837	1356	1768	2101	105800	879	1422	1854	2203	111200	922	1487	1940	2305	116600	964	1554	2026	2406
100500	838	1357	1770	2103	105900	880	1423	1856	2205	111300	922	1489	1942	2307	116700	964	1555	2027	2408
100600	839	1358	1771	2105	106000	881	1424	1858	2207	111400	923	1490	1943	2309	116800	965	1556	2029	2410
100700	840	1360	1773	2107	106100	882	1425	1860	2209	111500	924	1491	1945	2311	116900	966	1557	2030	2412
100800	841	1361	1774	2109	106200	883	1426	1861	2211	111600	925	1492	1946	2313	117000	967	1559	2032	2414
100900	842	1362	1776	2111	106300	883	1428	1863	2213	111700	926	1493	1948	2315	117100	968	1560	2034	2416
101000	842	1363	1778	2112	106400	884	1429	1864	2214	111800	926	1494	1950	2316	117200	969	1561	2035	2418
101100	843	1364	1780	2114	106500	885	1430	1866	2216	111900	927	1496	1951	2318	117300	969	1563	2037	2420
101200	843	1365	1781	2116	106600	886	1431	1867	2218	112000	928	1497	1953	2320	117400	970	1564	2038	2421
101300	844	1367	1783	2118	106700	887	1432	1869	2220	112100	929	1498	1955	2322	117500	971	1565	2040	2423
101400	845	1368	1784	2119	106800	888	1434	1870	2222	112200	930	1500	1956	2324	117600	972	1566	2041	2425
101500	846	1369	1786	2121	106900	888	1435	1872	2224	112300	930	1501	1958	2326	117700	972	1568	2043	2427
101600	846	1370	1787	2123	107000	889	1436	1874	2225	112400	931	1502	1959	2327	117800	973	1569	2044	2429
101700	847	1371	1789	2125	107100	890	1437	1876	2227	112500	932	1503	1961	2329	117900	974	1570	2046	2431
101800	848	1373	1790	2127	107200	891	1439	1877	2229	112600	933	1505	1963	2331	118000	975	1571	2047	2432
101900	849	1374	1792	2129	107300	891	1440	1879	2231	112700	934	1506	1964	2333	118100	976	1572	2049	2434
102000	849	1375	1794	2131	107400	892	1441	1880	2232	112800	934	1507	1966	2335	118200	977	1573	2050	2436
102100	850	1376	1796	2133	107500	893	1442	1882	2234	112900	935	1508	1967	2337	118300	977	1575	2052	2438
102200	851	1377	1797	2135	107600	894	1444	1883	2236	113000	936	1510	1969	2338	118400	978	1576	2053	2439
102300	851	1379	1799	2137	107700	895	1445	1885	2238	113100	937	1511	1971	2340	118500	979	1577	2055	2441
102400	852	1380	1800	2138	107800	896	1446	1886	2240	113200	938	1512	1972	2342	118600	980	1578	2056	2443
102500	853	1381	1802	2140	107900	896	1447	1888	2242	113300	938	1514	1974	2344	118700	981	1580	2058	2445

Federal Child Support Amounts: Simplified Tables
Montants fédéraux de pensions alimentaires pour enfants: Tables simplifiées

Income/ Revenu ($)	Monthly Award/ Paiement mensuel ($) No. of Children/ N^{bre} d'enfants				Income/ Revenu ($)	Monthly Award/ Paiement mensuel ($) No. of Children/ N^{bre} d'enfants				Income/ Revenu ($)	Monthly Award/ Paiement mensuel ($) No. of Children/ N^{bre} d'enfants				Income/ Revenu ($)	Monthly Award/ Paiement mensuel ($) No. of Children/ N^{bre} d'enfants			
	1	2	3	4		1	2	3	4		1	2	3	4		1	2	3	4
118800	981	1581	2059	2447	124200	1024	1646	2145	2549	129600	1065	1711	2228	2648	135000	1105	1774	2308	2745
118900	982	1582	2061	2449	124300	1024	1648	2147	2551	129700	1066	1712	2230	2650	135100	1106	1775	2309	2747
119000	983	1583	2063	2451	124400	1025	1649	2148	2552	129800	1067	1714	2231	2652	135200	1107	1776	2311	2749
119100	984	1584	2065	2453	124500	1026	1650	2150	2554	129900	1067	1715	2233	2654	135300	1107	1777	2312	2750
119200	985	1585	2066	2455	124600	1027	1651	2151	2556	130000	1068	1716	2234	2655	135400	1108	1779	2314	2752
119300	985	1587	2068	2457	124700	1027	1652	2153	2558	130100	1069	1717	2235	2657	135500	1109	1780	2315	2754
119400	986	1588	2069	2458	124800	1028	1653	2154	2560	130200	1070	1718	2237	2659	135600	1110	1781	2317	2756
119500	987	1589	2071	2460	124900	1029	1655	2156	2562	130300	1070	1719	2238	2660	135700	1110	1782	2318	2758
119600	988	1590	2073	2462	125000	1030	1656	2157	2564	130400	1071	1721	2240	2662	135800	1111	1783	2320	2760
119700	989	1591	2074	2464	125100	1031	1657	2159	2566	130500	1072	1722	2241	2664	135900	1112	1784	2321	2761
119800	989	1593	2076	2466	125200	1032	1659	2160	2568	130600	1073	1723	2243	2666	136000	1113	1785	2323	2763
119900	990	1594	2077	2468	125300	1032	1660	2162	2570	130700	1073	1724	2244	2667	136100	1114	1786	2325	2765
120000	991	1595	2079	2470	125400	1033	1661	2163	2571	130800	1074	1725	2246	2669	136200	1114	1787	2326	2766
120100	992	1596	2081	2472	125500	1034	1662	2165	2573	130900	1075	1726	2247	2671	136300	1115	1789	2328	2768
120200	993	1598	2082	2474	125600	1035	1664	2166	2575	131000	1076	1727	2248	2673	136400	1116	1790	2329	2770
120300	993	1599	2084	2476	125700	1035	1665	2168	2577	131100	1077	1728	2249	2675	136500	1117	1791	2331	2772
120400	994	1600	2085	2478	125800	1036	1666	2169	2579	131200	1077	1729	2251	2677	136600	1117	1792	2332	2773
120500	995	1601	2087	2479	125900	1037	1667	2171	2581	131300	1078	1731	2252	2678	136700	1118	1793	2334	2775
120600	996	1603	2089	2481	126000	1038	1669	2173	2583	131400	1079	1732	2254	2680	136800	1119	1794	2335	2777
120700	997	1604	2090	2483	126100	1039	1670	2175	2585	131500	1080	1733	2255	2682	136900	1119	1796	2337	2779
120800	998	1605	2092	2485	126200	1040	1671	2176	2587	131600	1080	1734	2257	2684	137000	1120	1797	2338	2780
120900	998	1606	2094	2487	126300	1040	1673	2178	2589	131700	1081	1735	2258	2685	137100	1121	1798	2340	2782
121000	999	1608	2095	2489	126400	1041	1674	2179	2591	131800	1082	1736	2260	2687	137200	1122	1799	2341	2784
121100	1000	1609	2097	2491	126500	1042	1675	2181	2592	131900	1083	1738	2261	2689	137300	1122	1800	2343	2785
121200	1001	1610	2098	2493	126600	1043	1676	2182	2594	132000	1083	1739	2263	2691	137400	1123	1802	2344	2787
121300	1001	1612	2100	2495	126700	1044	1678	2184	2596	132100	1084	1740	2264	2693	137500	1124	1803	2346	2789
121400	1002	1613	2101	2497	126800	1044	1679	2186	2598	132200	1085	1741	2266	2695	137600	1125	1804	2347	2791
121500	1003	1614	2103	2499	126900	1045	1680	2187	2600	132300	1085	1742	2267	2696	137700	1125	1805	2349	2792
121600	1004	1615	2104	2500	127000	1046	1681	2189	2602	132400	1086	1743	2269	2698	137800	1126	1806	2350	2794
121700	1005	1617	2106	2502	127100	1047	1682	2191	2604	132500	1087	1745	2270	2700	137900	1127	1807	2352	2796
121800	1006	1618	2107	2504	127200	1047	1683	2192	2606	132600	1088	1746	2272	2702	138000	1128	1808	2353	2798
121900	1006	1619	2109	2506	127300	1048	1684	2194	2607	132700	1089	1747	2273	2703	138100	1129	1809	2355	2800
122000	1007	1620	2110	2508	127400	1049	1685	2195	2609	132800	1089	1748	2275	2705	138200	1129	1810	2356	2802
122100	1008	1621	2112	2510	127500	1050	1687	2197	2611	132900	1090	1749	2276	2707	138300	1130	1812	2358	2803
122200	1008	1622	2113	2512	127600	1050	1688	2198	2613	133000	1091	1750	2278	2709	138400	1131	1813	2359	2805
122300	1009	1624	2115	2514	127700	1051	1689	2200	2615	133100	1092	1751	2279	2711	138500	1132	1814	2361	2807
122400	1010	1625	2116	2516	127800	1052	1690	2201	2616	133200	1092	1752	2281	2713	138600	1132	1815	2362	2809
122500	1011	1626	2118	2518	127900	1052	1691	2203	2618	133300	1093	1753	2282	2714	138700	1133	1816	2364	2811
122600	1011	1627	2119	2520	128000	1053	1692	2204	2620	133400	1094	1755	2284	2716	138800	1134	1817	2365	2812
122700	1012	1629	2121	2521	128100	1054	1693	2206	2622	133500	1095	1756	2285	2718	138900	1134	1819	2367	2814
122800	1013	1630	2123	2523	128200	1055	1694	2207	2624	133600	1095	1757	2287	2720	139000	1135	1820	2368	2816
122900	1014	1631	2124	2525	128300	1055	1695	2209	2625	133700	1096	1758	2288	2722	139100	1136	1821	2369	2818
123000	1014	1632	2126	2527	128400	1056	1697	2210	2627	133800	1097	1759	2290	2723	139200	1137	1822	2371	2819
123100	1015	1633	2128	2529	128500	1057	1698	2212	2629	133900	1098	1760	2291	2725	139300	1137	1823	2372	2821
123200	1016	1634	2129	2531	128600	1058	1699	2213	2631	134000	1098	1762	2293	2727	139400	1138	1824	2374	2823
123300	1016	1636	2131	2533	128700	1058	1700	2215	2633	134100	1099	1763	2294	2729	139500	1139	1826	2375	2825
123400	1017	1637	2132	2534	128800	1059	1701	2216	2635	134200	1099	1764	2296	2731	139600	1140	1827	2377	2826
123500	1018	1638	2134	2536	128900	1060	1702	2218	2636	134300	1100	1766	2297	2732	139700	1140	1828	2378	2828
123600	1019	1639	2136	2538	129000	1061	1704	2219	2638	134400	1101	1767	2299	2734	139800	1141	1829	2380	2830
123700	1019	1640	2137	2540	129100	1062	1705	2221	2640	134500	1101	1768	2300	2736	139900	1142	1830	2381	2832
123800	1020	1642	2139	2542	129200	1062	1706	2222	2641	134600	1102	1769	2302	2738	140000	1143	1831	2382	2833
123900	1021	1643	2140	2544	129300	1063	1708	2224	2643	134700	1103	1770	2303	2740	140100	1144	1832	2383	2835
124000	1022	1644	2142	2545	129400	1064	1709	2225	2645	134800	1104	1772	2305	2742	140200	1144	1833	2385	2837
124100	1023	1645	2144	2547	129500	1065	1710	2227	2647	134900	1104	1773	2306	2743	140300	1145	1834	2386	2838

Manitoba

Federal Child Support Amounts: Simplified Tables
Montants fédéraux de pensions alimentaires pour enfants: Tables simplifiées

Income/ Revenu ($)	Monthly Award/ Paiement mensuel ($) No. of Children/ N^bre d'enfants				Income/ Revenu ($)	Monthly Award/ Paiement mensuel ($) No. of Children/ N^bre d'enfants				Income/ Revenu ($)	Monthly Award/ Paiement mensuel ($) No. of Children/ N^bre d'enfants			
	1	2	3	4		1	2	3	4		1	2	3	4
140400	1146	1836	2388	2840	143700	1170	1874	2437	2899	147000	1195	1913	2487	2956
140500	1147	1837	2389	2842	143800	1171	1875	2439	2900	147100	1196	1914	2489	2958
140600	1147	1838	2391	2844	143900	1171	1877	2440	2902	147200	1196	1915	2490	2960
140700	1148	1839	2392	2845	144000	1172	1878	2442	2904	147300	1197	1916	2492	2961
140800	1149	1840	2394	2847	144100	1173	1879	2443	2906	147400	1198	1918	2493	2963
140900	1150	1841	2395	2849	144200	1174	1880	2445	2907	147500	1199	1919	2495	2965
141000	1150	1843	2397	2851	144300	1174	1881	2446	2909	147600	1199	1920	2496	2967
141100	1151	1844	2398	2853	144400	1175	1882	2448	2911	147700	1200	1921	2498	2968
141200	1152	1845	2400	2854	144500	1176	1884	2449	2913	147800	1201	1922	2499	2970
141300	1152	1847	2401	2856	144600	1177	1885	2451	2914	147900	1201	1923	2501	2972
141400	1153	1848	2403	2858	144700	1177	1886	2452	2916	148000	1202	1924	2502	2974
141500	1154	1849	2404	2860	144800	1178	1887	2454	2918	148100	1203	1925	2503	2976
141600	1155	1850	2406	2861	144900	1179	1888	2455	2920	148200	1204	1926	2505	2978
141700	1156	1851	2407	2863	145000	1180	1889	2457	2921	148300	1204	1928	2506	2979
141800	1156	1853	2409	2865	145100	1181	1890	2459	2923	148400	1205	1929	2508	2981
141900	1157	1854	2410	2866	145200	1181	1891	2460	2925	148500	1206	1930	2509	2983
142000	1158	1855	2412	2868	145300	1182	1892	2462	2926	148600	1207	1931	2511	2985
142100	1159	1856	2413	2870	145400	1183	1894	2463	2928	148700	1207	1932	2512	2987
142200	1159	1857	2415	2872	145500	1184	1895	2465	2930	148800	1208	1934	2514	2988
142300	1160	1858	2416	2873	145600	1184	1896	2466	2932	148900	1209	1935	2515	2990
142400	1161	1860	2418	2875	145700	1185	1897	2468	2933	149000	1210	1936	2516	2992
142500	1162	1861	2419	2877	145800	1186	1898	2469	2935	149100	1211	1937	2517	2994
142600	1162	1862	2421	2879	145900	1186	1899	2471	2937	149200	1211	1938	2519	2995
142700	1163	1863	2422	2880	146000	1187	1901	2472	2939	149300	1212	1939	2520	2997
142800	1164	1864	2424	2882	146100	1188	1902	2474	2941	149400	1213	1941	2522	2999
142900	1165	1865	2425	2884	146200	1189	1903	2475	2942	149500	1214	1942	2523	3001
143000	1165	1866	2427	2886	146300	1189	1905	2477	2944	149600	1214	1943	2525	3002
143100	1166	1867	2428	2888	146400	1190	1906	2478	2946	149700	1215	1944	2526	3004
143200	1166	1868	2430	2890	146500	1191	1907	2480	2948	149800	1216	1945	2528	3006
143300	1167	1870	2431	2891	146600	1192	1908	2481	2949	149900	1217	1946	2529	3008
143400	1168	1871	2433	2893	146700	1192	1909	2483	2951	150000	1217	1947	2531	3009
143500	1168	1872	2434	2895	146800	1193	1911	2484	2953					
143600	1169	1873	2436	2897	146900	1194	1912	2486	2954					

Monthly Award/Paiement mensuel ($)			
One Child/ Un enfant	**Two Children/ Deux enfants**	**Three Children/ Trois enfants**	**Four Children/ Quatre enfants**
1217 plus 0.74% of income over $150,000	**1947 plus 1.14%** of income over $150,000	**2531 plus 1.46%** of income over $150,000	**3009 plus 1.74%** of income over $150,000
1217 plus 0,74% du revenu dépassant 150 000$	**1947 plus 1,14%** du revenu dépassant 150 000$	**2531 plus 1,46%** du revenu dépassant 150 000$	**3009 plus 1,74%** du revenu dépassant 150 000$

BRITISH COLUMBIA

British Columbia / Colombie-Britanique

Federal Child Support Amounts: Simplified Tables
Montants fédéraux de pensions alimentaires pour enfants: Tables simplifiées

Income/ Revenu ($)	Monthly Award/ Paiement mensuel ($) No. of Children/ Nbre d'enfants				Income/ Revenu ($)	Monthly Award/ Paiement mensuel ($) No. of Children/ Nbre d'enfants				Income/ Revenu ($)	Monthly Award/ Paiement mensuel ($) No. of Children/ Nbre d'enfants				Income/ Revenu ($)	Monthly Award/ Paiement mensuel ($) No. of Children/ Nbre d'enfants			
	1	2	3	4		1	2	3	4		1	2	3	4		1	2	3	4
10820	5	16	17	19	16200	119	263	283	304	21600	187	345	472	533	27000	239	420	571	694
10900	6	20	22	24	16300	120	266	287	308	21700	188	346	474	537	27100	240	421	573	696
11000	24	71	76	82	16400	122	269	291	312	21800	189	348	476	541	27200	241	422	574	698
11100	26	76	81	88	16500	124	272	294	315	21900	189	349	477	546	27300	242	424	576	700
11200	28	80	86	93	16600	126	275	298	319	22000	190	350	479	550	27400	243	425	577	702
11300	29	85	91	99	16700	128	278	302	323	22100	191	351	481	554	27500	244	426	579	704
11400	31	90	96	104	16800	129	280	305	327	22200	192	353	483	559	27600	245	427	580	706
11500	33	95	101	110	16900	131	283	309	331	22300	193	354	484	563	27700	246	428	582	708
11600	35	99	107	115	17000	133	286	313	335	22400	193	355	486	567	27800	247	430	583	710
11700	37	104	112	121	17100	135	287	317	339	22500	194	357	488	572	27900	248	431	585	712
11800	39	109	117	126	17200	137	288	320	343	22600	195	358	490	576	28000	249	432	586	714
11900	40	114	122	132	17300	139	289	324	347	22700	196	360	492	581	28100	250	434	588	716
12000	42	118	127	137	17400	140	290	327	351	22800	197	361	494	585	28200	251	435	589	718
12100	44	122	131	141	17500	142	290	331	354	22900	198	362	495	589	28300	252	437	591	720
12200	46	125	135	145	17600	144	291	335	358	23000	198	364	497	594	28400	253	438	592	722
12300	47	129	139	149	17700	146	292	338	362	23100	199	365	499	597	28500	254	440	594	724
12400	49	132	142	153	17800	148	293	342	366	23200	200	367	501	601	28600	255	441	595	726
12500	51	136	146	157	17900	150	294	346	370	23300	201	368	502	604	28700	256	443	597	728
12600	53	139	150	161	18000	152	295	349	374	23400	201	369	504	607	28800	257	445	598	730
12700	55	143	154	165	18100	153	296	353	378	23500	202	371	506	611	28900	258	446	600	732
12800	56	147	158	169	18200	155	298	357	383	23600	203	372	508	614	29000	259	448	602	734
12900	58	150	162	173	18300	156	299	362	387	23700	204	373	510	617	29100	260	450	604	736
13000	60	154	166	177	18400	158	300	366	392	23800	205	375	512	621	29200	261	451	605	738
13100	62	158	170	181	18500	159	302	370	396	23900	206	376	513	624	29300	262	453	607	740
13200	64	161	173	185	18600	161	303	374	401	24000	206	377	515	627	29400	263	454	609	742
13300	66	165	177	189	18700	162	305	378	405	24100	207	378	517	629	29500	264	456	610	744
13400	67	168	181	193	18800	163	306	382	410	24200	207	380	519	631	29600	265	457	612	746
13500	69	172	185	197	18900	165	307	387	414	24300	208	381	521	634	29700	266	459	614	748
13600	71	175	188	201	19000	166	309	391	419	24400	209	383	522	636	29800	267	460	615	750
13700	73	179	192	205	19100	167	310	395	424	24500	210	384	524	638	29900	268	462	617	752
13800	75	182	196	210	19200	168	312	399	428	24600	210	385	526	640	30000	269	463	619	754
13900	77	186	200	214	19300	169	313	404	433	24700	211	387	528	642	30100	270	465	621	756
14000	79	189	203	218	19400	169	314	408	437	24800	212	388	530	645	30200	271	466	623	758
14100	81	192	207	222	19500	170	316	412	442	24900	213	389	532	647	30300	272	468	625	760
14200	83	196	210	226	19600	171	317	416	446	25000	213	391	533	649	30400	273	469	627	762
14300	85	199	214	230	19700	172	319	420	451	25100	214	393	535	651	30500	274	471	630	765
14400	86	203	218	234	19800	173	320	425	455	25200	216	394	537	654	30600	275	472	632	767
14500	88	206	221	238	19900	174	321	429	460	25300	217	396	539	656	30700	276	474	634	769
14600	90	210	225	242	20000	174	323	433	464	25400	218	398	541	658	30800	277	475	636	771
14700	92	213	229	246	20100	175	324	436	468	25500	220	399	543	661	30900	278	477	638	773
14800	94	217	233	250	20200	176	326	439	473	25600	221	401	545	663	31000	279	479	640	775
14900	96	220	236	254	20300	176	327	442	477	25700	222	402	547	665	31100	280	481	642	777
15000	97	223	240	257	20400	177	328	444	481	25800	224	404	549	668	31200	281	482	644	779
15100	99	226	244	261	20500	178	330	447	486	25900	225	406	551	670	31300	282	484	646	781
15200	101	230	247	265	20600	179	331	450	490	26000	227	407	553	672	31400	283	485	648	783
15300	102	233	251	269	20700	180	333	453	494	26100	228	408	555	674	31500	284	487	650	785
15400	104	237	254	273	20800	181	334	456	499	26200	229	410	557	676	31600	285	488	652	787
15500	106	240	258	276	20900	181	335	459	503	26300	231	411	558	679	31700	286	490	654	789
15600	108	243	262	280	21000	182	337	461	507	26400	232	412	560	681	31800	287	491	656	791
15700	110	247	265	284	21100	183	338	463	511	26500	233	414	562	683	31900	288	493	658	793
15800	112	250	269	288	21200	184	340	465	516	26600	234	415	564	685	32000	289	495	660	795
15900	113	254	272	292	21300	184	341	466	520	26700	235	416	566	687	32100	290	496	662	797
16000	115	257	276	296	21400	185	342	468	524	26800	237	418	568	689	32200	291	498	664	799
16100	117	260	280	300	21500	186	344	470	529	26900	238	419	569	692	32300	292	499	666	802

BRITISH COLUMBIA — CONTINUED

Federal Child Support Amounts: Simplified Tables
Montants fédéraux de pensions alimentaires pour enfants: Tables simplifiées

Income/ Revenu ($)	Monthly Award/ Paiement mensuel ($) No. of Children/ N^bre d'enfants				Income/ Revenu ($)	Monthly Award/ Paiement mensuel ($) No. of Children/ N^bre d'enfants				Income/ Revenu ($)	Monthly Award/ Paiement mensuel ($) No. of Children/ N^bre d'enfants				Income/ Revenu ($)	Monthly Award/ Paiement mensuel ($) No. of Children/ N^bre d'enfants			
	1	2	3	4		1	2	3	4		1	2	3	4		1	2	3	4
32400	293	501	668	804	37800	345	580	769	924	43200	394	658	870	1042	48600	445	737	971	1162
32500	294	502	670	806	37900	346	581	771	926	43300	395	659	871	1045	48700	446	739	973	1164
32600	295	504	672	808	38000	346	583	773	928	43400	396	661	873	1047	48800	447	740	974	1167
32700	296	505	674	810	38100	347	584	775	930	43500	397	662	875	1049	48900	448	742	976	1169
32800	297	507	675	813	38200	348	586	777	932	43600	398	664	877	1051	49000	449	743	978	1171
32900	298	508	677	815	38300	349	587	779	935	43700	399	665	879	1054	49100	450	745	980	1173
33000	299	510	679	817	38400	350	589	780	937	43800	400	667	881	1056	49200	451	746	982	1176
33100	300	511	681	819	38500	351	590	782	939	43900	401	668	882	1058	49300	452	748	984	1178
33200	301	513	683	821	38600	352	591	784	941	44000	402	670	884	1060	49400	453	749	986	1180
33300	302	514	685	824	38700	352	593	786	944	44100	403	671	886	1062	49500	454	751	988	1183
33400	303	516	687	826	38800	353	594	788	946	44200	404	673	888	1064	49600	455	752	990	1185
33500	303	517	688	828	38900	354	596	790	948	44300	405	674	890	1066	49700	456	754	992	1187
33600	304	519	690	830	39000	355	597	791	950	44400	406	676	892	1069	49800	456	755	994	1190
33700	305	520	692	832	39100	356	598	793	952	44500	407	677	893	1071	49900	457	757	996	1192
33800	306	522	694	834	39200	357	600	795	954	44600	408	679	895	1073	50000	458	758	998	1194
33900	307	523	696	837	39300	358	601	797	957	44700	409	680	897	1075	50100	459	759	1000	1196
34000	308	525	698	839	39400	359	603	799	959	44800	410	681	899	1077	50200	460	761	1002	1199
34100	309	526	700	841	39500	359	604	800	961	44900	410	683	901	1079	50300	461	762	1004	1201
34200	310	528	702	844	39600	360	606	802	963	45000	411	684	903	1081	50400	462	764	1006	1203
34300	311	529	704	846	39700	361	607	804	966	45100	412	685	905	1083	50500	463	765	1008	1206
34400	312	531	706	848	39800	362	609	806	968	45200	413	687	907	1085	50600	464	767	1010	1208
34500	313	532	708	850	39900	363	610	808	970	45300	414	688	909	1088	50700	465	768	1011	1210
34600	314	534	710	853	40000	364	612	810	972	45400	415	690	910	1090	50800	466	770	1013	1213
34700	315	535	711	855	40100	365	614	812	974	45500	416	691	912	1092	50900	467	771	1015	1215
34800	316	536	713	857	40200	366	615	814	977	45600	417	692	914	1094	51000	468	773	1017	1217
34900	317	538	715	859	40300	367	617	816	979	45700	417	694	916	1096	51100	469	774	1019	1219
35000	318	539	717	862	40400	368	618	818	981	45800	418	695	918	1098	51200	470	776	1021	1222
35100	319	540	719	864	40500	369	620	820	984	45900	419	697	920	1101	51300	471	777	1023	1224
35200	320	542	721	866	40600	370	621	822	986	46000	420	698	921	1103	51400	472	779	1025	1226
35300	321	543	723	869	40700	371	623	824	988	46100	421	699	923	1105	51500	473	780	1027	1229
35400	322	545	724	871	40800	372	624	826	991	46200	422	701	925	1107	51600	474	782	1029	1231
35500	323	546	726	873	40900	373	626	828	993	46300	423	702	926	1110	51700	475	783	1031	1233
35600	323	548	728	875	41000	374	627	830	995	46400	424	704	928	1112	51800	476	785	1033	1235
35700	324	549	730	878	41100	375	628	832	997	46500	424	705	930	1114	51900	477	786	1035	1238
35800	326	551	732	880	41200	376	630	834	999	46600	425	707	932	1116	52000	478	788	1037	1240
35900	326	552	734	882	41300	377	631	836	1002	46700	426	708	934	1118	52100	479	790	1039	1242
36000	327	554	735	884	41400	377	632	837	1004	46800	427	710	935	1121	52200	480	791	1041	1245
36100	328	555	737	886	41500	378	634	839	1006	46900	428	711	937	1123	52300	481	793	1043	1247
36200	329	557	739	888	41600	379	635	841	1008	47000	429	713	939	1125	52400	482	794	1045	1249
36300	330	558	741	891	41700	380	637	843	1010	47100	430	715	941	1127	52500	483	796	1047	1252
36400	331	560	742	893	41800	381	638	845	1012	47200	431	716	943	1130	52600	484	797	1049	1254
36500	332	561	744	895	41900	382	639	847	1015	47300	432	718	945	1132	52700	485	799	1050	1256
36600	333	562	746	897	42000	383	641	848	1017	47400	433	719	947	1134	52800	486	800	1052	1258
36700	334	564	748	900	42100	384	642	850	1019	47500	434	721	949	1137	52900	487	802	1054	1261
36800	335	565	750	902	42200	385	644	852	1021	47600	435	722	951	1139	53000	488	804	1056	1263
36900	336	567	752	904	42300	386	645	853	1023	47700	436	724	953	1141	53100	489	806	1058	1265
37000	337	568	754	906	42400	386	646	855	1026	47800	437	725	955	1144	53200	490	807	1060	1268
37100	338	569	756	908	42500	387	648	857	1028	47900	438	727	957	1146	53300	491	809	1062	1270
37200	339	571	758	910	42600	388	649	859	1030	48000	439	728	959	1148	53400	492	810	1064	1272
37300	340	572	760	913	42700	389	651	861	1032	48100	440	730	961	1150	53500	493	812	1066	1274
37400	341	574	762	915	42800	390	652	863	1034	48200	441	731	963	1153	53600	494	813	1068	1277
37500	342	575	764	917	42900	391	653	864	1036	48300	442	733	965	1155	53700	494	815	1070	1279
37600	343	577	765	919	43000	392	655	866	1038	48400	443	734	967	1157	53800	495	816	1072	1281
37700	344	578	767	922	43100	393	656	868	1040	48500	444	736	969	1160	53900	496	818	1074	1284

Federal Child Support Amounts: Simplified Tables
Montants fédéraux de pensions alimentaires pour enfants: Tables simplifiées

Income/ Revenu ($)	Monthly Award/ Paiement mensuel ($) No. of Children/ N^bre d'enfants				Income/ Revenu ($)	Monthly Award/ Paiement mensuel ($) No. of Children/ N^bre d'enfants				Income/ Revenu ($)	Monthly Award/ Paiement mensuel ($) No. of Children/ N^bre d'enfants				Income/ Revenu ($)	Monthly Award/ Paiement mensuel ($) No. of Children/ N^bre d'enfants			
	1	2	3	4		1	2	3	4		1	2	3	4		1	2	3	4
54000	497	819	1076	1286	59400	550	901	1181	1411	64800	603	983	1287	1535	70200	656	1065	1392	1660
54100	498	821	1078	1288	59500	551	903	1183	1414	64900	604	985	1289	1538	70300	657	1067	1394	1662
54200	499	822	1080	1291	59600	552	904	1185	1416	65000	605	986	1291	1540	70400	658	1068	1396	1664
54300	500	824	1082	1293	59700	553	906	1187	1418	65100	606	988	1293	1542	70500	659	1070	1398	1666
54400	501	825	1084	1295	59800	554	907	1189	1421	65200	607	989	1295	1545	70600	660	1071	1400	1669
54500	502	827	1086	1297	59900	555	909	1191	1423	65300	608	991	1297	1547	70700	661	1073	1402	1671
54600	503	828	1087	1300	60000	556	910	1193	1425	65400	609	992	1299	1549	70800	661	1074	1404	1673
54700	504	830	1089	1302	60100	557	912	1195	1427	65500	610	994	1301	1551	70900	662	1076	1406	1675
54800	505	831	1091	1304	60200	558	913	1197	1430	65600	611	995	1303	1554	71000	663	1077	1408	1678
54900	506	833	1093	1307	60300	559	915	1199	1432	65700	612	997	1305	1556	71100	664	1079	1410	1680
55000	507	834	1095	1309	60400	560	916	1201	1434	65800	613	998	1306	1558	71200	665	1080	1412	1683
55100	508	836	1097	1311	60500	561	918	1203	1437	65900	614	1000	1308	1561	71300	666	1082	1414	1685
55200	509	837	1099	1314	60600	562	919	1205	1439	66000	615	1001	1310	1563	71400	667	1083	1416	1687
55300	510	839	1101	1316	60700	563	921	1207	1441	66100	616	1002	1312	1565	71500	668	1085	1418	1689
55400	511	840	1103	1318	60800	564	922	1209	1444	66200	617	1004	1314	1568	71600	669	1086	1420	1692
55500	512	842	1105	1320	60900	565	924	1211	1446	66300	618	1005	1316	1570	71700	670	1088	1421	1694
55600	513	843	1107	1323	61000	566	925	1213	1448	66400	619	1007	1318	1572	71800	671	1089	1423	1696
55700	514	845	1109	1325	61100	567	926	1215	1450	66500	620	1008	1320	1574	71900	672	1091	1425	1698
55800	515	846	1111	1327	61200	568	928	1217	1453	66600	621	1010	1322	1577	72000	673	1092	1427	1701
55900	516	848	1113	1329	61300	569	929	1219	1455	66700	622	1011	1324	1579	72100	674	1093	1429	1703
56000	517	849	1115	1332	61400	570	931	1221	1457	66800	622	1013	1326	1581	72200	675	1095	1431	1705
56100	518	850	1117	1334	61500	571	932	1223	1460	66900	623	1014	1328	1584	72300	676	1096	1433	1708
56200	519	852	1119	1337	61600	572	934	1225	1462	67000	624	1016	1330	1586	72400	677	1098	1435	1710
56300	520	853	1121	1339	61700	573	935	1227	1464	67100	625	1017	1332	1588	72500	678	1099	1436	1712
56400	521	855	1123	1341	61800	574	937	1229	1467	67200	626	1019	1334	1591	72600	679	1101	1438	1714
56500	522	856	1125	1343	61900	575	938	1231	1469	67300	627	1020	1336	1593	72700	680	1102	1440	1716
56600	523	858	1126	1346	62000	576	940	1232	1471	67400	628	1022	1338	1595	72800	681	1104	1442	1718
56700	524	859	1128	1348	62100	577	941	1234	1473	67500	629	1023	1340	1597	72900	682	1105	1444	1721
56800	525	861	1130	1350	62200	578	943	1236	1476	67600	630	1025	1342	1600	73000	683	1107	1446	1723
56900	526	862	1132	1352	62300	579	944	1238	1478	67700	631	1026	1344	1602	73100	684	1108	1448	1725
57000	527	864	1134	1355	62400	580	946	1240	1480	67800	632	1028	1345	1604	73200	685	1110	1450	1728
57100	528	866	1136	1357	62500	581	947	1242	1483	67900	633	1029	1347	1607	73300	686	1111	1452	1730
57200	529	867	1138	1360	62600	582	949	1244	1485	68000	634	1031	1349	1609	73400	687	1113	1454	1732
57300	530	869	1140	1362	62700	583	950	1246	1487	68100	635	1033	1351	1611	73500	688	1114	1456	1734
57400	531	870	1142	1364	62800	584	952	1248	1490	68200	636	1034	1353	1614	73600	689	1116	1457	1737
57500	532	872	1144	1366	62900	584	953	1250	1492	68300	637	1036	1355	1616	73700	690	1117	1459	1739
57600	533	873	1146	1369	63000	585	955	1252	1494	68400	638	1037	1357	1618	73800	691	1119	1461	1741
57700	534	875	1148	1371	63100	586	957	1254	1496	68500	639	1039	1359	1620	73900	692	1120	1463	1743
57800	535	877	1150	1373	63200	587	958	1256	1499	68600	640	1040	1361	1623	74000	692	1121	1465	1746
57900	536	878	1152	1375	63300	588	960	1258	1501	68700	641	1042	1363	1625	74100	693	1122	1467	1748
58000	537	880	1154	1378	63400	589	961	1260	1503	68800	642	1043	1365	1627	74200	694	1124	1469	1750
58100	538	882	1156	1380	63500	590	963	1262	1506	68900	643	1045	1367	1629	74300	695	1125	1471	1753
58200	539	883	1158	1383	63600	591	964	1264	1508	69000	644	1047	1369	1632	74400	696	1127	1472	1755
58300	540	885	1160	1385	63700	592	966	1266	1510	69100	645	1049	1371	1634	74500	697	1128	1474	1757
58400	541	886	1162	1387	63800	593	967	1268	1513	69200	646	1050	1373	1637	74600	697	1130	1476	1759
58500	542	888	1164	1390	63900	594	969	1269	1515	69300	647	1052	1375	1639	74700	698	1131	1478	1762
58600	543	889	1165	1392	64000	595	971	1271	1517	69400	648	1053	1377	1641	74800	699	1133	1480	1764
58700	544	891	1167	1394	64100	596	973	1273	1519	69500	649	1055	1379	1643	74900	700	1134	1482	1766
58800	545	892	1169	1397	64200	597	974	1275	1522	69600	650	1056	1381	1646	75000	701	1136	1483	1768
58900	546	894	1171	1399	64300	598	976	1277	1524	69700	651	1058	1382	1648	75100	702	1137	1485	1770
59000	546	895	1173	1402	64400	599	977	1279	1526	69800	652	1059	1384	1650	75200	703	1139	1487	1772
59100	547	897	1175	1404	64500	600	979	1281	1529	69900	653	1061	1386	1652	75300	704	1140	1489	1775
59200	548	898	1177	1407	64600	601	980	1283	1531	70000	654	1062	1388	1655	75400	705	1142	1490	1777
59300	549	900	1179	1409	64700	602	982	1285	1533	70100	655	1064	1390	1657	75500	706	1143	1492	1779

BRITISH COLUMBIA — CONTINUED

British Columbia / Colombie-Britanique

Federal Child Support Amounts: Simplified Tables
Montants fédéraux de pensions alimentaires pour enfants: Tables simplifiées

Income/ Revenu ($)	Monthly Award/ Paiement mensuel ($) No. of Children/ Nbre d'enfants				Income/ Revenu ($)	Monthly Award/ Paiement mensuel ($) No. of Children/ Nbre d'enfants				Income/ Revenu ($)	Monthly Award/ Paiement mensuel ($) No. of Children/ Nbre d'enfants				Income/ Revenu ($)	Monthly Award/ Paiement mensuel ($) No. of Children/ Nbre d'enfants			
	1	2	3	4		1	2	3	4		1	2	3	4		1	2	3	4
75600	707	1145	1494	1781	81000	758	1223	1596	1901	86400	805	1296	1690	2012	91800	851	1368	1783	2121
75700	708	1146	1496	1784	81100	759	1224	1598	1903	86500	805	1298	1691	2014	91900	852	1370	1784	2124
75800	709	1147	1498	1786	81200	760	1226	1600	1905	86600	806	1299	1693	2016	92000	853	1371	1786	2126
75900	710	1149	1500	1788	81300	761	1227	1602	1908	86700	807	1301	1695	2018	92100	854	1372	1788	2128
76000	711	1150	1502	1790	81400	762	1229	1604	1910	86800	808	1302	1696	2020	92200	855	1374	1789	2130
76100	712	1151	1504	1792	81500	763	1230	1606	1912	86900	809	1303	1698	2022	92300	856	1375	1791	2132
76200	713	1153	1506	1794	81600	764	1232	1607	1914	87000	810	1305	1700	2024	92400	856	1376	1793	2134
76300	714	1154	1508	1797	81700	765	1233	1609	1917	87100	811	1306	1702	2026	92500	857	1378	1794	2136
76400	715	1156	1510	1799	81800	766	1235	1611	1919	87200	812	1308	1704	2028	92600	858	1379	1796	2138
76500	716	1157	1511	1801	81900	767	1236	1613	1921	87300	812	1309	1705	2030	92700	859	1381	1798	2140
76600	717	1159	1513	1803	82000	767	1238	1615	1923	87400	813	1310	1707	2032	92800	860	1382	1799	2142
76700	718	1160	1515	1805	82100	768	1239	1617	1925	87500	814	1312	1709	2034	92900	861	1383	1801	2144
76800	718	1162	1517	1808	82200	769	1241	1618	1927	87600	815	1313	1711	2036	93000	861	1385	1803	2146
76900	719	1163	1519	1810	82300	770	1242	1620	1929	87700	816	1314	1712	2038	93100	862	1386	1805	2148
77000	720	1165	1521	1812	82400	771	1243	1622	1931	87800	817	1316	1714	2041	93200	863	1388	1806	2150
77100	721	1167	1523	1814	82500	772	1245	1624	1933	87900	817	1317	1716	2043	93300	864	1389	1808	2152
77200	722	1168	1525	1816	82600	772	1246	1625	1935	88000	818	1318	1718	2045	93400	865	1390	1810	2154
77300	723	1170	1527	1819	82700	773	1247	1627	1937	88100	819	1319	1720	2047	93500	865	1392	1811	2156
77400	724	1171	1529	1821	82800	774	1249	1629	1939	88200	820	1321	1721	2049	93600	866	1393	1813	2158
77500	724	1173	1531	1823	82900	775	1250	1631	1941	88300	821	1322	1723	2051	93700	867	1394	1815	2160
77600	725	1174	1532	1825	83000	776	1251	1632	1943	88400	821	1323	1725	2053	93800	868	1396	1816	2162
77700	726	1176	1534	1827	83100	777	1252	1634	1945	88500	822	1325	1727	2055	93900	869	1397	1818	2164
77800	727	1177	1536	1830	83200	778	1254	1635	1947	88600	823	1326	1728	2057	94000	870	1398	1820	2166
77900	728	1179	1538	1832	83300	779	1255	1637	1949	88700	824	1327	1730	2059	94100	871	1399	1822	2168
78000	729	1180	1540	1834	83400	779	1256	1639	1951	88800	825	1328	1732	2061	94200	872	1401	1824	2170
78100	730	1181	1542	1836	83500	780	1258	1641	1953	88900	826	1330	1734	2063	94300	872	1402	1825	2172
78200	731	1183	1544	1838	83600	781	1259	1642	1955	89000	827	1331	1735	2065	94400	873	1403	1827	2174
78300	732	1184	1546	1841	83700	782	1261	1644	1957	89100	828	1332	1737	2067	94500	874	1405	1829	2176
78400	733	1186	1547	1843	83800	783	1262	1646	1960	89200	829	1334	1738	2069	94600	875	1406	1831	2178
78500	734	1187	1549	1845	83900	784	1263	1647	1962	89300	830	1335	1740	2071	94700	876	1407	1832	2180
78600	735	1189	1551	1847	84000	784	1265	1649	1964	89400	831	1336	1742	2073	94800	877	1408	1834	2182
78700	736	1190	1553	1849	84100	785	1266	1651	1966	89500	832	1338	1744	2075	94900	877	1410	1836	2184
78800	737	1192	1555	1851	84200	786	1268	1652	1968	89600	832	1339	1745	2077	95000	878	1411	1838	2186
78900	738	1193	1557	1854	84300	787	1269	1654	1970	89700	833	1341	1747	2079	95100	879	1412	1840	2188
79000	739	1194	1558	1856	84400	788	1270	1656	1972	89800	834	1342	1749	2081	95200	880	1414	1841	2190
79100	740	1195	1560	1858	84500	788	1272	1657	1974	89900	835	1343	1751	2083	95300	881	1415	1843	2192
79200	741	1197	1562	1861	84600	789	1273	1659	1976	90000	836	1345	1752	2085	95400	881	1416	1845	2194
79300	742	1198	1564	1863	84700	790	1274	1661	1978	90100	837	1346	1754	2087	95500	882	1418	1847	2196
79400	743	1200	1565	1865	84800	791	1276	1663	1980	90200	838	1348	1755	2089	95600	883	1419	1848	2198
79500	744	1201	1567	1867	84900	792	1277	1664	1982	90300	839	1349	1757	2091	95700	884	1421	1850	2200
79600	745	1203	1569	1870	85000	793	1278	1666	1984	90400	839	1350	1759	2093	95800	885	1422	1852	2202
79700	745	1204	1571	1872	85100	794	1279	1668	1986	90500	840	1352	1761	2095	95900	886	1423	1854	2205
79800	746	1206	1573	1874	85200	795	1281	1669	1988	90600	841	1353	1762	2097	96000	887	1425	1855	2207
79900	747	1207	1575	1876	85300	796	1282	1671	1990	90700	842	1354	1764	2099	96100	888	1426	1857	2209
80000	748	1209	1577	1879	85400	796	1283	1673	1992	90800	843	1356	1766	2101	96200	889	1428	1858	2211
80100	749	1210	1579	1881	85500	797	1285	1674	1994	90900	844	1357	1767	2103	96300	890	1429	1860	2213
80200	750	1212	1581	1883	85600	798	1286	1676	1996	91000	844	1358	1769	2105	96400	891	1430	1862	2215
80300	751	1213	1583	1886	85700	799	1287	1678	1998	91100	845	1359	1771	2107	96500	892	1432	1864	2217
80400	752	1215	1585	1888	85800	800	1288	1679	2000	91200	846	1361	1772	2109	96600	892	1433	1865	2219
80500	753	1216	1586	1890	85900	801	1290	1681	2002	91300	847	1362	1774	2111	96700	893	1434	1867	2221
80600	754	1218	1588	1892	86000	801	1291	1683	2004	91400	848	1363	1776	2113	96800	894	1436	1869	2223
80700	755	1219	1590	1895	86100	802	1292	1685	2006	91500	848	1365	1777	2115	96900	895	1437	1871	2225
80800	756	1220	1592	1897	86200	803	1294	1686	2008	91600	849	1366	1779	2117	97000	896	1438	1872	2227
80900	757	1222	1594	1899	86300	804	1295	1688	2010	91700	850	1367	1781	2119	97100	897	1439	1874	2229

Federal Child Support Amounts: Simplified Tables
Montants fédéraux de pensions alimentaires pour enfants: Tables simplifiées

British Columbia / Colombie-Britanique

Income/ Revenu ($)	Monthly Award/ Paiement mensuel ($) No. of Children/ Nᵇʳᵉ d'enfants 1	2	3	4	Income/ Revenu ($)	Monthly Award/ Paiement mensuel ($) No. of Children/ Nᵇʳᵉ d'enfants 1	2	3	4	Income/ Revenu ($)	Monthly Award/ Paiement mensuel ($) No. of Children/ Nᵇʳᵉ d'enfants 1	2	3	4	Income/ Revenu ($)	Monthly Award/ Paiement mensuel ($) No. of Children/ Nᵇʳᵉ d'enfants 1	2	3	4
97200	898	1441	1875	2231	102600	943	1511	1966	2339	108000	987	1580	2055	2443	113400	1031	1649	2144	2549
97300	899	1442	1877	2233	102700	944	1513	1968	2341	108100	988	1581	2057	2445	113500	1032	1650	2145	2551
97400	899	1443	1879	2235	102800	945	1514	1969	2343	108200	989	1583	2058	2447	113600	1033	1652	2147	2553
97500	900	1445	1881	2237	102900	945	1515	1971	2344	108300	989	1584	2060	2449	113700	1034	1653	2149	2554
97600	901	1446	1882	2239	103000	946	1516	1973	2346	108400	990	1585	2062	2451	113800	1035	1654	2150	2556
97700	902	1447	1884	2241	103100	947	1517	1975	2348	108500	991	1586	2063	2453	113900	1036	1655	2152	2558
97800	903	1448	1886	2243	103200	948	1519	1976	2350	108600	992	1588	2065	2455	114000	1037	1657	2154	2560
97900	904	1450	1887	2245	103300	948	1520	1978	2352	108700	993	1589	2067	2457	114100	1038	1658	2156	2562
98000	904	1451	1889	2247	103400	949	1521	1980	2354	108800	993	1590	2069	2459	114200	1039	1660	2157	2564
98100	905	1452	1891	2249	103500	950	1522	1981	2356	108900	994	1591	2070	2461	114300	1040	1661	2159	2566
98200	906	1454	1892	2251	103600	951	1524	1983	2358	109000	995	1593	2072	2463	114400	1040	1662	2160	2568
98300	907	1455	1894	2253	103700	952	1525	1984	2360	109100	996	1594	2074	2465	114500	1041	1663	2162	2570
98400	908	1456	1896	2255	103800	952	1526	1986	2362	109200	997	1596	2075	2467	114600	1042	1665	2164	2572
98500	908	1458	1897	2257	103900	953	1527	1988	2364	109300	998	1597	2077	2469	114700	1043	1666	2165	2574
98600	909	1459	1899	2259	104000	954	1529	1989	2366	109400	998	1598	2079	2471	114800	1044	1667	2167	2576
98700	910	1461	1901	2261	104100	955	1530	1991	2368	109500	999	1599	2080	2473	114900	1045	1668	2168	2578
98800	911	1462	1903	2263	104200	956	1532	1992	2370	109600	1000	1601	2082	2474	115000	1045	1670	2170	2580
98900	912	1463	1904	2265	104300	956	1533	1994	2372	109700	1001	1602	2084	2476	115100	1046	1671	2172	2582
99000	913	1465	1906	2267	104400	957	1534	1996	2374	109800	1002	1603	2085	2478	115200	1047	1673	2173	2584
99100	914	1466	1908	2269	104500	958	1535	1997	2376	109900	1003	1604	2087	2480	115300	1047	1674	2175	2586
99200	915	1468	1909	2271	104600	959	1537	1999	2378	110000	1004	1606	2088	2482	115400	1048	1675	2177	2588
99300	916	1469	1911	2273	104700	959	1538	2001	2380	110100	1005	1607	2090	2484	115500	1049	1676	2178	2590
99400	916	1470	1913	2275	104800	960	1539	2002	2382	110200	1006	1609	2091	2486	115600	1050	1678	2180	2592
99500	917	1472	1914	2277	104900	961	1541	2004	2384	110300	1007	1610	2093	2488	115700	1051	1679	2182	2594
99600	918	1473	1916	2279	105000	962	1542	2006	2385	110400	1007	1611	2094	2490	115800	1052	1680	2183	2595
99700	919	1474	1918	2281	105100	963	1543	2008	2387	110500	1008	1612	2096	2492	115900	1052	1682	2185	2597
99800	920	1476	1919	2283	105200	964	1545	2009	2389	110600	1009	1614	2098	2494	116000	1053	1683	2187	2599
99900	921	1477	1921	2285	105300	965	1546	2011	2391	110700	1010	1615	2099	2496	116100	1054	1684	2189	2601
100000	921	1478	1923	2288	105400	965	1547	2013	2393	110800	1011	1616	2101	2498	116200	1055	1686	2190	2603
100100	922	1479	1925	2290	105500	966	1549	2014	2394	110900	1012	1618	2102	2500	116300	1055	1687	2192	2605
100200	923	1481	1926	2292	105600	967	1550	2016	2396	111000	1012	1619	2104	2502	116400	1056	1688	2193	2607
100300	923	1482	1928	2294	105700	968	1551	2017	2398	111100	1013	1620	2106	2504	116500	1057	1690	2195	2609
100400	924	1483	1930	2296	105800	969	1552	2019	2400	111200	1014	1622	2107	2506	116600	1058	1691	2197	2611
100500	925	1485	1931	2298	105900	970	1554	2021	2402	111300	1014	1623	2109	2508	116700	1059	1692	2198	2613
100600	926	1486	1933	2300	106000	971	1555	2022	2404	111400	1015	1624	2111	2510	116800	1059	1693	2200	2615
100700	926	1487	1935	2302	106100	972	1556	2024	2406	111500	1016	1626	2112	2512	116900	1060	1695	2202	2617
100800	927	1488	1936	2303	106200	973	1558	2025	2408	111600	1017	1627	2114	2514	117000	1061	1696	2203	2619
100900	928	1490	1938	2305	106300	974	1559	2027	2410	111700	1018	1628	2116	2515	117100	1062	1697	2205	2621
101000	929	1491	1940	2307	106400	974	1560	2029	2412	111800	1019	1630	2117	2517	117200	1063	1699	2206	2623
101100	930	1492	1942	2309	106500	975	1562	2030	2414	111900	1019	1631	2119	2519	117300	1063	1700	2208	2625
101200	931	1494	1943	2311	106600	976	1563	2032	2416	112000	1020	1632	2121	2521	117400	1064	1701	2210	2627
101300	932	1495	1945	2313	106700	977	1564	2034	2418	112100	1021	1633	2123	2523	117500	1065	1703	2211	2629
101400	932	1496	1946	2315	106800	978	1566	2036	2420	112200	1022	1634	2124	2525	117600	1066	1704	2213	2631
101500	933	1498	1948	2317	106900	979	1567	2037	2422	112300	1022	1636	2126	2527	117700	1066	1705	2215	2633
101600	934	1499	1950	2319	107000	979	1568	2039	2424	112400	1023	1637	2127	2529	117800	1067	1707	2216	2635
101700	935	1500	1951	2321	107100	980	1569	2041	2426	112500	1024	1638	2129	2531	117900	1068	1708	2218	2636
101800	936	1502	1953	2323	107200	981	1570	2042	2428	112600	1025	1639	2131	2533	118000	1069	1709	2220	2638
101900	937	1503	1955	2325	107300	981	1572	2044	2430	112700	1026	1641	2132	2535	118100	1070	1710	2222	2640
102000	938	1504	1956	2327	107400	982	1573	2046	2432	112800	1026	1642	2134	2537	118200	1071	1711	2223	2642
102100	939	1505	1958	2329	107500	983	1574	2047	2434	112900	1027	1643	2135	2539	118300	1072	1713	2225	2644
102200	940	1506	1959	2331	107600	984	1575	2049	2435	113000	1028	1644	2137	2541	118400	1072	1714	2226	2646
102300	940	1508	1961	2333	107700	985	1577	2050	2437	113100	1029	1645	2139	2543	118500	1073	1715	2228	2648
102400	941	1509	1963	2335	107800	986	1578	2052	2439	113200	1030	1647	2140	2545	118600	1074	1716	2230	2650
102500	942	1510	1964	2337	107900	986	1579	2054	2441	113300	1031	1648	2142	2547	118700	1075	1718	2231	2652

British Columbia / Colombie-Britanique

Federal Child Support Amounts: Simplified Tables
Montants fédéraux de pensions alimentaires pour enfants: Tables simplifiées

Income/ Revenu ($)	Monthly Award/ Paiement mensuel ($) No. of Children/ Nbre d'enfants				Income/ Revenu ($)	Monthly Award/ Paiement mensuel ($) No. of Children/ Nbre d'enfants				Income/ Revenu ($)	Monthly Award/ Paiement mensuel ($) No. of Children/ Nbre d'enfants				Income/ Revenu ($)	Monthly Award/ Paiement mensuel ($) No. of Children/ Nbre d'enfants			
	1	2	3	4		1	2	3	4		1	2	3	4		1	2	3	4
118800	1076	1719	2233	2654	124200	1121	1788	2322	2759	129600	1164	1855	2408	2861	135000	1206	1921	2493	2961
118900	1077	1720	2235	2656	124300	1121	1789	2324	2761	129700	1164	1856	2410	2863	135100	1207	1922	2495	2963
119000	1078	1721	2236	2658	124400	1122	1790	2326	2763	129800	1165	1857	2412	2865	135200	1208	1923	2496	2965
119100	1079	1722	2238	2660	124500	1123	1791	2327	2765	129900	1166	1859	2413	2867	135300	1208	1925	2498	2967
119200	1080	1724	2239	2662	124600	1124	1793	2329	2766	130000	1167	1860	2415	2869	135400	1209	1926	2499	2969
119300	1080	1725	2241	2664	124700	1125	1794	2330	2768	130100	1168	1861	2417	2871	135500	1210	1927	2501	2970
119400	1081	1726	2243	2666	124800	1125	1795	2332	2770	130200	1169	1863	2418	2873	135600	1211	1928	2503	2972
119500	1082	1727	2244	2668	124900	1126	1796	2334	2772	130300	1169	1864	2420	2874	135700	1211	1929	2504	2974
119600	1083	1729	2246	2670	125000	1127	1798	2335	2774	130400	1170	1865	2421	2876	135800	1212	1930	2506	2976
119700	1084	1730	2248	2672	125100	1128	1799	2337	2776	130500	1171	1866	2423	2878	135900	1213	1932	2507	2978
119800	1085	1731	2249	2674	125200	1129	1801	2338	2778	130600	1172	1868	2425	2880	136000	1214	1933	2509	2980
119900	1085	1732	2251	2675	125300	1129	1802	2340	2780	130700	1173	1869	2426	2882	136100	1215	1934	2511	2982
120000	1086	1734	2253	2677	125400	1130	1803	2342	2782	130800	1173	1870	2428	2884	136200	1216	1935	2512	2984
120100	1087	1735	2255	2679	125500	1131	1804	2343	2784	130900	1174	1871	2429	2885	136300	1216	1937	2514	2986
120200	1088	1737	2256	2681	125600	1132	1806	2345	2786	131000	1175	1873	2431	2887	136400	1217	1938	2515	2987
120300	1088	1738	2258	2683	125700	1133	1807	2347	2788	131100	1176	1874	2433	2889	136500	1218	1939	2517	2989
120400	1089	1739	2260	2685	125800	1133	1808	2349	2790	131200	1177	1875	2434	2891	136600	1219	1940	2518	2991
120500	1090	1740	2261	2686	125900	1134	1810	2350	2792	131300	1177	1877	2436	2893	136700	1220	1941	2520	2993
120600	1091	1742	2263	2688	126000	1135	1811	2352	2794	131400	1178	1878	2437	2895	136800	1220	1942	2521	2995
120700	1092	1743	2264	2690	126100	1136	1812	2354	2796	131500	1179	1879	2439	2896	136900	1221	1944	2523	2997
120800	1092	1744	2266	2692	126200	1137	1814	2355	2798	131600	1180	1880	2440	2898	137000	1222	1945	2524	2998
120900	1093	1746	2268	2694	126300	1138	1815	2357	2800	131700	1181	1882	2442	2900	137100	1223	1946	2526	3000
121000	1094	1747	2269	2696	126400	1138	1816	2359	2802	131800	1182	1883	2443	2902	137200	1224	1948	2527	3002
121100	1095	1748	2271	2698	126500	1139	1817	2360	2804	131900	1182	1884	2445	2904	137300	1224	1949	2529	3004
121200	1096	1750	2272	2700	126600	1140	1819	2362	2806	132000	1183	1885	2446	2906	137400	1225	1950	2530	3006
121300	1096	1751	2274	2702	126700	1141	1820	2364	2807	132100	1184	1886	2448	2908	137500	1226	1951	2532	3007
121400	1097	1752	2276	2704	126800	1142	1821	2365	2809	132200	1185	1887	2449	2910	137600	1227	1953	2533	3009
121500	1098	1754	2277	2706	126900	1143	1823	2367	2811	132300	1185	1889	2451	2911	137700	1228	1954	2535	3011
121600	1099	1755	2279	2708	127000	1144	1824	2368	2813	132400	1186	1890	2452	2913	137800	1229	1955	2536	3013
121700	1099	1756	2281	2710	127100	1145	1825	2370	2815	132500	1187	1891	2454	2915	137900	1229	1956	2538	3015
121800	1100	1757	2282	2712	127200	1145	1826	2371	2817	132600	1188	1892	2455	2917	138000	1230	1958	2540	3017
121900	1101	1759	2284	2714	127300	1146	1828	2373	2819	132700	1189	1894	2457	2919	138100	1231	1959	2542	3019
122000	1102	1760	2286	2716	127400	1147	1829	2374	2820	132800	1190	1895	2459	2921	138200	1231	1960	2543	3021
122100	1103	1761	2288	2718	127500	1148	1830	2376	2822	132900	1190	1896	2460	2922	138300	1232	1962	2545	3023
122200	1104	1763	2289	2720	127600	1148	1831	2378	2824	133000	1191	1897	2462	2924	138400	1233	1963	2546	3024
122300	1105	1764	2291	2722	127700	1149	1833	2379	2826	133100	1192	1898	2464	2926	138500	1234	1964	2548	3026
122400	1105	1765	2293	2724	127800	1150	1834	2381	2828	133200	1192	1899	2465	2928	138600	1234	1965	2550	3028
122500	1106	1767	2294	2726	127900	1151	1835	2382	2830	133300	1193	1901	2467	2930	138700	1235	1967	2551	3030
122600	1107	1768	2296	2727	128000	1151	1836	2384	2832	133400	1194	1902	2468	2932	138800	1236	1968	2553	3032
122700	1108	1769	2297	2729	128100	1152	1837	2386	2834	133500	1195	1903	2470	2933	138900	1237	1969	2554	3034
122800	1109	1771	2299	2731	128200	1153	1838	2387	2836	133600	1195	1904	2472	2935	139000	1237	1970	2556	3035
122900	1110	1772	2301	2733	128300	1153	1840	2389	2837	133700	1196	1906	2473	2937	139100	1238	1971	2558	3037
123000	1111	1773	2302	2735	128400	1154	1841	2390	2839	133800	1197	1907	2475	2939	139200	1239	1972	2559	3039
123100	1112	1774	2304	2737	128500	1155	1842	2392	2841	133900	1198	1908	2477	2941	139300	1239	1974	2561	3041
123200	1113	1775	2305	2739	128600	1156	1843	2393	2843	134000	1198	1909	2478	2943	139400	1240	1975	2562	3043
123300	1114	1777	2307	2741	128700	1156	1844	2395	2845	134100	1199	1910	2480	2945	139500	1241	1976	2564	3044
123400	1114	1778	2309	2743	128800	1157	1846	2396	2847	134200	1200	1911	2481	2947	139600	1242	1977	2565	3046
123500	1115	1779	2310	2745	128900	1158	1847	2398	2848	134300	1200	1913	2483	2948	139700	1242	1979	2567	3048
123600	1116	1780	2312	2747	129000	1159	1848	2399	2850	134400	1201	1914	2484	2950	139800	1243	1980	2568	3050
123700	1117	1782	2314	2749	129100	1160	1849	2401	2852	134500	1202	1915	2486	2952	139900	1244	1981	2570	3052
123800	1118	1783	2315	2751	129200	1161	1850	2402	2854	134600	1203	1916	2487	2954	140000	1245	1982	2571	3054
123900	1119	1784	2317	2753	129300	1161	1852	2404	2856	134700	1203	1917	2489	2956	140100	1246	1983	2573	3056
124000	1119	1785	2319	2755	129400	1162	1853	2405	2857	134800	1204	1919	2490	2958	140200	1247	1984	2574	3058
124100	1120	1786	2321	2757	129500	1163	1854	2407	2859	134900	1205	1920	2492	2959	140300	1247	1986	2576	3060

British Columbia / Colombie-Britanique

Federal Child Support Amounts: Simplified Tables
Montants fédéraux de pensions alimentaires pour enfants: Tables simplifiées

Income/ Revenu ($)	Monthly Award/ Paiement mensuel ($) No. of Children/ N^{bre} d'enfants				Income/ Revenu ($)	Monthly Award/ Paiement mensuel ($) No. of Children/ N^{bre} d'enfants				Income/ Revenu ($)	Monthly Award/ Paiement mensuel ($) No. of Children/ N^{bre} d'enfants			
	1	2	3	4		1	2	3	4		1	2	3	4
140400	1248	1987	2577	3061	143700	1275	2027	2629	3122	147000	1300	2067	2681	3183
140500	1249	1988	2579	3063	143800	1276	2028	2631	3124	147100	1301	2068	2683	3185
140600	1250	1989	2580	3065	143900	1276	2029	2632	3126	147200	1302	2069	2684	3187
140700	1250	1990	2582	3067	144000	1277	2031	2634	3128	147300	1302	2071	2686	3188
140800	1251	1992	2584	3069	144100	1278	2032	2636	3130	147400	1303	2072	2687	3190
140900	1252	1993	2585	3071	144200	1278	2033	2637	3132	147500	1304	2073	2689	3192
141000	1253	1994	2587	3072	144300	1279	2035	2639	3134	147600	1305	2074	2690	3194
141100	1254	1995	2589	3074	144400	1280	2036	2640	3135	147700	1306	2075	2692	3196
141200	1255	1996	2590	3076	144500	1281	2037	2642	3137	147800	1306	2077	2693	3197
141300	1255	1998	2592	3078	144600	1281	2038	2644	3139	147900	1307	2078	2695	3199
141400	1256	1999	2593	3080	144700	1282	2040	2645	3141	148000	1308	2079	2696	3201
141500	1257	2000	2595	3081	144800	1283	2041	2647	3143	148100	1309	2080	2698	3203
141600	1258	2001	2597	3083	144900	1284	2042	2648	3145	148200	1310	2081	2699	3205
141700	1259	2002	2598	3085	145000	1284	2043	2650	3146	148300	1310	2083	2701	3207
141800	1259	2003	2600	3087	145100	1285	2044	2652	3148	148400	1311	2084	2702	3208
141900	1260	2005	2601	3089	145200	1286	2045	2653	3150	148500	1312	2085	2704	3210
142000	1261	2006	2603	3091	145300	1286	2047	2655	3151	148600	1313	2086	2705	3212
142100	1262	2007	2605	3093	145400	1287	2048	2656	3153	148700	1314	2087	2707	3214
142200	1263	2008	2606	3095	145500	1288	2049	2658	3155	148800	1315	2088	2708	3216
142300	1263	2010	2608	3097	145600	1289	2050	2659	3157	148900	1315	2090	2710	3218
142400	1264	2011	2609	3098	145700	1289	2052	2661	3159	149000	1316	2091	2712	3220
142500	1265	2012	2611	3100	145800	1290	2053	2662	3160	149100	1317	2092	2714	3222
142600	1266	2013	2612	3102	145900	1291	2054	2664	3162	149200	1317	2094	2715	3224
142700	1267	2014	2614	3104	146000	1292	2055	2665	3164	149300	1318	2095	2717	3225
142800	1267	2015	2615	3106	146100	1293	2056	2667	3166	149400	1319	2096	2718	3227
142900	1268	2017	2617	3108	146200	1294	2057	2668	3168	149500	1320	2097	2720	3229
143000	1269	2018	2618	3109	146300	1294	2059	2670	3170	149600	1320	2099	2722	3231
143100	1270	2019	2620	3111	146400	1295	2060	2671	3171	149700	1321	2100	2723	3233
143200	1271	2021	2621	3113	146500	1296	2061	2673	3173	149800	1322	2101	2725	3234
143300	1271	2022	2623	3115	146600	1297	2062	2674	3175	149900	1323	2102	2726	3236
143400	1272	2023	2624	3117	146700	1297	2063	2676	3177	150000	1323	2104	2728	3238
143500	1273	2024	2626	3118	146800	1298	2065	2678	3179					
143600	1274	2026	2627	3120	146900	1299	2066	2679	3181					

Monthly Award/Paiement mensuel ($)			
One Child/ Un enfant	Two Children/ Deux enfants	Three Children/ Trois enfants	Four Children/ Quatre enfants
1323 plus 0.74% of income over $150,000	2104 plus 1.26% of income over $150,000	2728 plus 1.58% of income over $150,000	3238 plus 1.80% of income over $150,000
1323 plus 0,74% du revenu dépassant 150 000$	2104 plus 1,26% du revenu dépassant 150 000$	2728 plus 1,58% du revenu dépassant 150 000$	3238 plus 1,80% du revenu dépassant 150 000$

PRINCE EDWARD ISLAND

Federal Child Support Amounts: Simplified Tables
Montants fédéraux de pensions alimentaires pour enfants: Tables simplifiées

Income/ Revenu ($)	Monthly Award/ Paiement mensuel ($) No. of Children/ N^{bre} d'enfants				Income/ Revenu ($)	Monthly Award/ Paiement mensuel ($) No. of Children/ N^{bre} d'enfants				Income/ Revenu ($)	Monthly Award/ Paiement mensuel ($) No. of Children/ N^{bre} d'enfants				Income/ Revenu ($)	Monthly Award/ Paiement mensuel ($) No. of Children/ N^{bre} d'enfants			
	1	2	3	4		1	2	3	4		1	2	3	4		1	2	3	4
10820	0	0	0	0	16200	118	207	222	239	21600	156	300	416	457	27000	218	387	526	639
10900	3	3	4	4	16300	118	210	225	242	21700	157	302	418	462	27100	219	388	528	641
11000	39	42	45	48	16400	118	213	228	245	21800	159	303	420	466	27200	220	390	529	643
11100	43	46	49	52	16500	119	216	231	249	21900	160	305	422	470	27300	221	391	531	645
11200	46	50	53	57	16600	119	219	234	252	22000	161	307	425	475	27400	222	393	533	647
11300	50	54	58	61	16700	119	221	238	255	22100	162	309	427	479	27500	223	394	535	650
11400	53	58	62	66	16800	120	224	241	259	22200	163	310	429	484	27600	224	395	536	652
11500	57	61	66	70	16900	120	227	244	262	22300	165	312	431	488	27700	225	397	538	654
11600	60	65	70	75	17000	120	230	247	265	22400	166	314	434	493	27800	226	398	540	656
11700	64	69	74	79	17100	120	232	251	269	22500	167	315	436	497	27900	227	400	542	658
11800	67	73	78	84	17200	120	235	255	273	22600	168	317	438	501	28000	228	401	543	660
11900	71	77	83	88	17300	121	237	258	277	22700	170	319	440	506	28100	229	403	545	662
12000	74	81	87	93	17400	121	239	262	281	22800	171	320	442	510	28200	230	404	546	664
12100	77	84	90	97	17500	121	242	266	285	22900	172	322	444	515	28300	231	406	548	666
12200	80	87	94	100	17600	121	244	270	290	23000	173	324	446	519	28400	232	408	550	668
12300	83	90	97	104	17700	122	246	273	294	23100	174	326	448	523	28500	233	410	552	670
12400	85	94	101	107	17800	122	249	277	298	23200	175	327	450	528	28600	234	411	553	672
12500	88	97	104	111	17900	122	251	281	302	23300	176	329	452	532	28700	235	413	555	674
12600	91	100	108	115	18000	122	253	285	306	23400	178	331	455	537	28800	236	415	557	676
12700	94	103	111	118	18100	122	254	289	310	23500	179	332	457	541	28900	237	416	559	678
12800	97	106	114	122	18200	123	255	293	314	23600	180	334	459	545	29000	238	418	560	680
12900	100	109	118	125	18300	123	256	297	318	23700	181	336	461	550	29100	239	420	562	682
13000	103	112	121	129	18400	123	257	300	322	23800	182	337	463	554	29200	240	421	563	684
13100	104	115	124	133	18500	123	258	304	327	23900	183	339	465	559	29300	241	423	565	686
13200	105	118	128	136	18600	124	259	308	331	24000	184	341	467	563	29400	242	424	567	688
13300	105	121	131	140	18700	124	260	312	335	24100	185	343	469	566	29500	243	426	569	690
13400	106	124	134	143	18800	124	261	316	339	24200	186	344	471	569	29600	244	427	570	692
13500	107	127	138	147	18900	124	262	320	343	24300	187	346	473	572	29700	245	429	572	694
13600	108	131	141	150	19000	125	263	324	347	24400	189	348	475	575	29800	246	430	574	696
13700	108	134	144	154	19100	126	264	328	351	24500	190	349	478	579	29900	246	432	576	699
13800	109	137	148	158	19200	127	265	332	355	24600	191	351	480	582	30000	247	433	577	701
13900	110	140	151	161	19300	129	266	336	359	24700	192	353	482	585	30100	248	435	579	703
14000	111	143	154	165	19400	130	267	339	363	24800	193	354	484	588	30200	249	436	581	705
14100	111	146	157	168	19500	131	268	343	367	24900	194	356	486	591	30300	250	438	583	707
14200	112	149	161	172	19600	132	269	347	371	25000	196	358	488	594	30400	251	439	585	709
14300	112	152	164	175	19700	133	270	351	375	25100	197	360	490	596	30500	252	441	588	711
14400	112	155	167	179	19800	135	271	355	379	25200	198	361	492	599	30600	253	442	590	714
14500	112	158	170	182	19900	136	272	359	383	25300	200	363	494	601	30700	254	444	592	716
14600	113	162	174	186	20000	137	273	362	387	25400	201	365	496	604	30800	255	445	594	718
14700	113	165	177	189	20100	138	275	366	391	25500	202	366	498	606	30900	256	447	596	720
14800	113	168	180	193	20200	139	276	370	396	25600	203	368	501	608	31000	257	448	598	722
14900	113	171	184	196	20300	141	278	374	400	25700	204	370	503	611	31100	258	450	600	724
15000	114	174	187	200	20400	142	280	378	404	25800	205	371	505	613	31200	259	451	602	726
15100	114	177	190	203	20500	143	281	382	409	25900	207	373	507	616	31300	260	453	604	728
15200	115	179	193	206	20600	144	283	386	413	26000	208	375	509	618	31400	261	454	607	730
15300	115	182	196	210	20700	145	285	390	418	26100	209	376	511	620	31500	262	456	609	733
15400	115	185	199	213	20800	146	286	394	422	26200	210	377	512	622	31600	263	457	611	735
15500	115	188	202	216	20900	148	288	398	426	26300	211	379	514	624	31700	264	459	613	737
15600	116	190	204	219	21000	149	290	402	431	26400	212	380	516	626	31800	265	460	615	739
15700	116	193	207	222	21100	150	292	404	435	26500	213	381	518	628	31900	266	462	617	741
15800	116	196	210	225	21200	151	293	407	440	26600	214	382	519	631	32000	267	463	619	743
15900	117	199	213	229	21300	153	295	409	444	26700	215	384	521	633	32100	268	464	621	745
16000	117	201	216	232	21400	154	297	411	449	26800	216	385	523	635	32200	269	466	623	747
16100	117	204	219	235	21500	155	298	413	453	26900	217	386	525	637	32300	270	467	625	749

Prince Edward Island / Île-du-Prince-Édouard

Federal Child Support Amounts: Simplified Tables
Montants fédéraux de pensions alimentaires pour enfants: Tables simplifiées

Income/ Revenu ($)	Monthly Award/ Paiement mensuel ($) No. of Children/ N^bre d'enfants				Income/ Revenu ($)	Monthly Award/ Paiement mensuel ($) No. of Children/ N^bre d'enfants				Income/ Revenu ($)	Monthly Award/ Paiement mensuel ($) No. of Children/ N^bre d'enfants				Income/ Revenu ($)	Monthly Award/ Paiement mensuel ($) No. of Children/ N^bre d'enfants			
	1	2	3	4		1	2	3	4		1	2	3	4		1	2	3	4
32400	271	469	626	752	37800	317	541	718	865	43200	363	612	811	974	48600	408	683	903	1082
32500	272	470	628	754	37900	318	542	720	867	43300	363	613	813	976	48700	409	685	904	1084
32600	272	471	630	756	38000	318	543	722	869	43400	364	614	815	978	48800	410	686	906	1087
32700	273	473	632	758	38100	319	544	724	871	43500	365	616	816	980	48900	411	688	908	1089
32800	274	474	634	760	38200	320	546	725	873	43600	366	617	818	982	49000	412	689	910	1091
32900	275	476	636	762	38300	321	547	727	875	43700	367	618	819	984	49100	413	690	912	1093
33000	276	477	637	764	38400	322	548	729	877	43800	368	619	821	986	49200	414	692	914	1095
33100	277	478	639	766	38500	322	550	730	879	43900	368	621	823	988	49300	415	693	915	1097
33200	278	480	640	768	38600	323	551	732	881	44000	369	622	824	990	49400	416	695	917	1099
33300	279	481	642	770	38700	324	552	734	883	44100	370	623	826	992	49500	417	696	919	1101
33400	279	482	644	772	38800	325	554	735	885	44200	371	625	827	994	49600	417	698	921	1103
33500	280	484	645	774	38900	326	555	737	887	44300	371	626	829	996	49700	418	699	922	1105
33600	281	485	647	777	39000	327	556	739	890	44400	372	627	831	998	49800	419	700	924	1108
33700	282	486	649	779	39100	328	557	741	892	44500	373	629	832	1000	49900	420	702	926	1110
33800	283	488	650	781	39200	329	559	743	894	44600	374	630	834	1002	50000	421	703	928	1112
33900	284	489	652	783	39300	330	560	744	896	44700	375	631	836	1004	50100	422	704	930	1114
34000	284	490	654	785	39400	330	561	746	898	44800	375	632	837	1006	50200	423	706	932	1116
34100	285	491	656	787	39500	331	563	748	900	44900	376	634	839	1008	50300	424	707	933	1118
34200	286	493	657	789	39600	332	564	750	902	45000	377	635	841	1010	50400	425	709	935	1121
34300	287	494	659	791	39700	333	565	751	904	45100	378	636	843	1012	50500	426	710	937	1123
34400	288	495	661	794	39800	334	566	753	906	45200	379	638	844	1014	50600	426	712	939	1125
34500	288	497	662	796	39900	335	568	755	908	45300	380	639	846	1016	50700	427	713	941	1127
34600	289	498	664	798	40000	335	569	757	910	45400	380	640	848	1018	50800	428	714	942	1129
34700	290	499	666	800	40100	336	570	759	912	45500	381	641	849	1020	50900	429	716	944	1131
34800	291	501	667	802	40200	337	572	761	914	45600	382	643	851	1022	51000	430	717	946	1134
34900	292	502	669	804	40300	338	573	763	916	45700	383	644	853	1024	51100	431	718	948	1136
35000	293	503	671	807	40400	339	575	764	919	45800	384	645	854	1026	51200	432	720	950	1138
35100	294	504	673	809	40500	339	576	766	921	45900	385	647	856	1028	51300	433	721	951	1140
35200	295	506	674	811	40600	340	577	768	923	46000	386	648	858	1030	51400	434	722	953	1143
35300	296	507	676	813	40700	341	579	770	925	46100	387	649	860	1032	51500	435	724	955	1145
35400	296	508	678	816	40800	342	580	772	927	46200	388	651	861	1034	51600	436	725	957	1147
35500	297	509	679	818	40900	343	581	774	929	46300	388	652	863	1036	51700	436	726	959	1149
35600	298	511	681	820	41000	344	583	775	931	46400	389	653	865	1038	51800	437	728	961	1151
35700	299	512	683	822	41100	345	584	777	933	46500	390	654	867	1040	51900	438	729	962	1153
35800	300	513	684	824	41200	346	586	778	935	46600	391	656	868	1042	52000	439	730	964	1155
35900	301	515	686	826	41300	346	587	780	937	46700	392	657	870	1044	52100	440	731	966	1157
36000	301	516	688	828	41400	347	588	782	939	46800	393	658	872	1046	52200	441	733	968	1159
36100	302	517	690	830	41500	348	589	783	941	46900	393	660	873	1047	52300	442	734	969	1161
36200	303	519	691	832	41600	349	591	785	943	47000	394	661	875	1049	52400	443	735	971	1164
36300	304	520	693	834	41700	349	592	786	945	47100	395	662	877	1051	52500	444	737	973	1166
36400	305	521	695	836	41800	350	593	788	947	47200	396	664	878	1053	52600	445	738	975	1168
36500	305	523	696	838	41900	351	594	790	949	47300	397	665	880	1055	52700	445	740	977	1170
36600	306	524	698	841	42000	352	596	791	951	47400	397	667	882	1057	52800	446	741	979	1172
36700	307	526	700	843	42100	353	597	793	953	47500	398	668	884	1059	52900	447	742	980	1174
36800	308	527	701	845	42200	354	599	794	955	47600	399	669	885	1061	53000	448	744	982	1176
36900	309	528	703	847	42300	355	600	796	957	47700	400	671	887	1063	53100	449	745	984	1178
37000	310	530	705	849	42400	355	601	798	959	47800	401	672	889	1065	53200	450	747	985	1180
37100	311	531	707	851	42500	356	602	799	961	47900	402	673	891	1067	53300	451	748	987	1182
37200	312	533	708	853	42600	357	604	801	963	48000	403	675	892	1070	53400	452	749	989	1185
37300	313	534	710	855	42700	358	605	803	965	48100	404	676	894	1072	53500	453	751	991	1187
37400	313	535	712	857	42800	359	606	804	966	48200	405	678	896	1074	53600	454	752	992	1189
37500	314	537	713	859	42900	360	608	806	968	48300	406	679	897	1076	53700	455	754	994	1191
37600	315	538	715	861	43000	361	609	808	970	48400	407	681	899	1078	53800	455	755	996	1193
37700	316	539	717	863	43100	362	610	810	972	48500	407	682	901	1080	53900	456	756	998	1195

Prince Edward Island / Île-du-Prince-Édouard

Federal Child Support Amounts: Simplified Tables
Montants fédéraux de pensions alimentaires pour enfants: Tables simplifiées

Income/ Revenu ($)	Monthly Award/ Paiement mensuel ($) No. of Children/ N^bre d'enfants				Income/ Revenu ($)	Monthly Award/ Paiement mensuel ($) No. of Children/ N^bre d'enfants				Income/ Revenu ($)	Monthly Award/ Paiement mensuel ($) No. of Children/ N^bre d'enfants				Income/ Revenu ($)	Monthly Award/ Paiement mensuel ($) No. of Children/ N^bre d'enfants			
	1	2	3	4		1	2	3	4		1	2	3	4		1	2	3	4
54000	457	758	999	1197	59400	505	832	1096	1310	64800	553	908	1192	1423	70200	599	979	1283	1532
54100	458	759	1001	1199	59500	505	834	1098	1312	64900	553	909	1194	1425	70300	599	980	1285	1534
54200	459	761	1003	1201	59600	506	835	1099	1315	65000	554	910	1195	1428	70400	600	981	1287	1536
54300	460	762	1004	1203	59700	507	836	1101	1317	65100	555	911	1197	1430	70500	601	983	1289	1538
54400	460	764	1006	1206	59800	508	838	1103	1319	65200	556	913	1198	1432	70600	602	984	1290	1540
54500	461	765	1008	1208	59900	509	839	1105	1321	65300	557	914	1200	1434	70700	603	986	1292	1542
54600	462	766	1010	1210	60000	510	841	1106	1323	65400	558	915	1202	1436	70800	604	987	1294	1544
54700	463	768	1011	1212	60100	511	842	1108	1325	65500	558	916	1204	1438	70900	604	988	1295	1546
54800	464	769	1013	1214	60200	512	844	1110	1327	65600	559	918	1205	1440	71000	605	990	1297	1548
54900	465	770	1015	1216	60300	513	845	1111	1329	65700	560	919	1207	1442	71100	606	991	1299	1550
55000	465	772	1017	1218	60400	514	846	1113	1331	65800	561	920	1209	1444	71200	607	993	1300	1552
55100	466	773	1019	1220	60500	514	848	1115	1333	65900	562	922	1211	1446	71300	608	994	1302	1554
55200	467	775	1021	1222	60600	515	849	1117	1335	66000	563	923	1212	1448	71400	608	995	1304	1556
55300	468	776	1022	1224	60700	516	851	1118	1338	66100	564	924	1214	1450	71500	609	997	1306	1558
55400	468	778	1024	1226	60800	517	852	1120	1340	66200	565	926	1215	1452	71600	610	998	1307	1560
55500	469	779	1026	1229	60900	518	853	1122	1342	66300	565	927	1217	1454	71700	611	999	1309	1562
55600	470	780	1028	1231	61000	519	855	1124	1344	66400	566	928	1219	1456	71800	612	1001	1311	1564
55700	471	782	1029	1233	61100	520	856	1126	1346	66500	567	930	1221	1458	71900	613	1002	1312	1566
55800	472	783	1031	1235	61200	521	858	1128	1348	66600	568	931	1222	1460	72000	614	1003	1314	1568
55900	473	785	1033	1237	61300	522	859	1129	1350	66700	569	933	1224	1462	72100	615	1004	1316	1570
56000	474	786	1035	1239	61400	523	861	1131	1352	66800	570	934	1226	1464	72200	616	1006	1317	1572
56100	475	787	1037	1241	61500	524	862	1133	1354	66900	570	935	1228	1466	72300	616	1007	1319	1574
56200	476	789	1039	1243	61600	524	863	1135	1356	67000	571	937	1229	1468	72400	617	1008	1321	1576
56300	477	790	1040	1245	61700	525	865	1136	1359	67100	572	938	1231	1470	72500	618	1010	1323	1578
56400	477	792	1042	1247	61800	526	866	1138	1361	67200	573	940	1232	1472	72600	619	1011	1324	1580
56500	478	793	1044	1250	61900	527	867	1140	1363	67300	574	941	1234	1474	72700	620	1012	1326	1582
56600	479	794	1046	1252	62000	528	869	1142	1365	67400	574	942	1236	1476	72800	621	1014	1328	1584
56700	480	796	1048	1254	62100	529	870	1144	1367	67500	575	944	1238	1478	72900	621	1015	1329	1586
56800	481	797	1049	1256	62200	530	872	1146	1369	67600	576	945	1239	1480	73000	622	1016	1331	1589
56900	482	799	1051	1258	62300	531	873	1147	1371	67700	577	946	1241	1482	73100	623	1017	1333	1591
57000	483	800	1053	1260	62400	532	875	1149	1373	67800	578	948	1243	1484	73200	624	1019	1334	1593
57100	484	801	1055	1262	62500	533	876	1151	1375	67900	579	949	1245	1486	73300	625	1020	1336	1595
57200	485	803	1057	1264	62600	533	877	1153	1377	68000	580	950	1246	1488	73400	625	1021	1338	1597
57300	486	804	1058	1266	62700	534	879	1155	1379	68100	581	951	1248	1490	73500	626	1022	1340	1599
57400	486	806	1060	1268	62800	535	880	1156	1382	68200	582	953	1249	1492	73600	627	1024	1341	1601
57500	487	807	1062	1271	62900	536	882	1158	1384	68300	582	954	1251	1494	73700	628	1025	1343	1603
57600	488	809	1064	1273	63000	537	883	1160	1386	68400	583	955	1253	1496	73800	629	1026	1345	1605
57700	489	810	1066	1275	63100	538	884	1162	1388	68500	584	957	1255	1498	73900	630	1028	1346	1607
57800	490	811	1068	1277	63200	539	886	1164	1390	68600	585	958	1256	1500	74000	631	1029	1348	1609
57900	491	813	1069	1279	63300	540	887	1165	1392	68700	586	959	1258	1502	74100	632	1030	1350	1611
58000	492	814	1071	1281	63400	541	889	1167	1394	68800	587	961	1260	1504	74200	633	1032	1351	1613
58100	493	815	1073	1283	63500	542	890	1169	1396	68900	587	962	1261	1506	74300	633	1033	1353	1615
58200	494	817	1075	1285	63600	543	891	1171	1398	69000	588	963	1263	1508	74400	634	1034	1355	1617
58300	495	818	1076	1287	63700	543	893	1173	1400	69100	589	964	1265	1510	74500	635	1035	1357	1619
58400	496	819	1078	1289	63800	544	894	1175	1402	69200	590	966	1266	1512	74600	636	1037	1358	1621
58500	496	821	1080	1291	63900	545	896	1176	1405	69300	591	967	1268	1514	74700	637	1038	1360	1623
58600	497	822	1082	1294	64000	546	897	1178	1407	69400	591	968	1270	1516	74800	638	1039	1362	1625
58700	498	823	1084	1296	64100	547	898	1180	1409	69500	592	969	1272	1518	74900	638	1040	1363	1627
58800	499	825	1086	1298	64200	548	900	1181	1411	69600	593	971	1273	1520	75000	639	1042	1365	1629
58900	500	826	1087	1300	64300	548	901	1183	1413	69700	594	972	1275	1522	75100	640	1043	1367	1631
59000	501	827	1089	1302	64400	549	902	1185	1415	69800	595	973	1277	1524	75200	641	1045	1368	1633
59100	502	828	1091	1304	64500	550	904	1187	1417	69900	596	975	1278	1526	75300	642	1046	1370	1635
59200	503	830	1092	1306	64600	551	905	1188	1419	70000	597	976	1280	1528	75400	642	1047	1372	1637
59300	504	831	1094	1308	64700	552	906	1190	1421	70100	598	977	1282	1530	75500	643	1049	1374	1639

Prince Edward Island / Île-du-Prince-Édouard

Federal Child Support Amounts: Simplified Tables
Montants fédéraux de pensions alimentaires pour enfants: Tables simplifiées

Income/ Revenu ($)	Monthly Award/ Paiement mensuel ($) No. of Children/ N^bre d'enfants				Income/ Revenu ($)	Monthly Award/ Paiement mensuel ($) No. of Children/ N^bre d'enfants				Income/ Revenu ($)	Monthly Award/ Paiement mensuel ($) No. of Children/ N^bre d'enfants				Income/ Revenu ($)	Monthly Award/ Paiement mensuel ($) No. of Children/ N^bre d'enfants			
	1	2	3	4		1	2	3	4		1	2	3	4		1	2	3	4
75600	644	1050	1375	1641	81000	690	1122	1467	1750	86400	734	1190	1554	1853	91800	778	1257	1639	1954
75700	645	1051	1377	1643	81100	691	1123	1469	1752	86500	735	1191	1556	1855	91900	779	1258	1641	1956
75800	646	1053	1379	1645	81200	692	1125	1470	1754	86600	736	1192	1558	1856	92000	779	1259	1643	1958
75900	647	1054	1380	1647	81300	693	1126	1472	1756	86700	737	1194	1559	1858	92100	780	1260	1645	1960
76000	648	1056	1382	1649	81400	693	1127	1474	1758	86800	738	1195	1561	1860	92200	780	1261	1646	1962
76100	649	1057	1384	1651	81500	694	1129	1475	1760	86900	738	1196	1563	1862	92300	781	1263	1648	1964
76200	650	1059	1385	1653	81600	695	1130	1477	1762	87000	739	1197	1564	1864	92400	782	1264	1649	1966
76300	650	1060	1387	1655	81700	696	1131	1479	1764	87100	740	1198	1566	1866	92500	783	1265	1651	1968
76400	651	1061	1389	1657	81800	697	1132	1480	1766	87200	741	1199	1567	1868	92600	783	1266	1652	1970
76500	652	1063	1390	1659	81900	698	1134	1482	1768	87300	741	1201	1569	1870	92700	784	1267	1654	1971
76600	653	1064	1392	1661	82000	699	1135	1484	1770	87400	742	1202	1571	1872	92800	785	1269	1656	1973
76700	654	1065	1394	1663	82100	700	1136	1486	1772	87500	743	1203	1572	1874	92900	786	1270	1657	1975
76800	654	1067	1396	1665	82200	701	1138	1487	1774	87600	744	1204	1574	1876	93000	786	1271	1659	1977
76900	655	1068	1397	1667	82300	701	1139	1489	1776	87700	745	1205	1575	1878	93100	787	1272	1661	1979
77000	656	1069	1399	1669	82400	702	1140	1490	1777	87800	746	1207	1577	1879	93200	788	1274	1662	1981
77100	657	1070	1401	1671	82500	703	1141	1492	1779	87900	746	1208	1579	1881	93300	788	1275	1664	1983
77200	658	1072	1402	1673	82600	704	1143	1494	1781	88000	747	1209	1580	1883	93400	789	1276	1665	1984
77300	659	1073	1404	1675	82700	705	1144	1495	1783	88100	748	1210	1582	1885	93500	790	1277	1667	1986
77400	659	1074	1406	1677	82800	705	1145	1497	1785	88200	749	1212	1583	1887	93600	791	1279	1668	1988
77500	660	1076	1407	1679	82900	706	1147	1498	1787	88300	749	1213	1585	1889	93700	791	1280	1670	1990
77600	661	1077	1409	1681	83000	707	1148	1500	1788	88400	750	1214	1587	1890	93800	792	1281	1672	1992
77700	662	1078	1411	1683	83100	708	1149	1502	1790	88500	751	1215	1588	1892	93900	793	1282	1673	1994
77800	663	1079	1413	1685	83200	709	1150	1503	1792	88600	752	1217	1590	1894	94000	794	1284	1675	1995
77900	664	1081	1414	1687	83300	709	1152	1505	1794	88700	753	1218	1591	1896	94100	795	1285	1677	1997
78000	665	1082	1416	1689	83400	710	1153	1506	1795	88800	754	1219	1593	1898	94200	796	1286	1678	1999
78100	666	1083	1418	1691	83500	711	1154	1508	1797	88900	754	1220	1595	1900	94300	796	1288	1680	2001
78200	667	1085	1419	1693	83600	712	1155	1510	1799	89000	755	1222	1596	1901	94400	797	1289	1681	2002
78300	667	1086	1421	1695	83700	713	1157	1511	1801	89100	756	1223	1598	1903	94500	798	1290	1683	2004
78400	668	1087	1423	1697	83800	713	1158	1513	1803	89200	757	1224	1599	1905	94600	799	1291	1685	2006
78500	669	1088	1424	1699	83900	714	1159	1514	1805	89300	758	1226	1601	1907	94700	799	1293	1686	2008
78600	670	1090	1426	1701	84000	715	1160	1516	1807	89400	758	1227	1602	1908	94800	800	1294	1688	2010
78700	671	1091	1428	1703	84100	716	1161	1518	1809	89500	759	1228	1604	1910	94900	801	1295	1689	2012
78800	671	1092	1430	1705	84200	717	1162	1519	1811	89600	760	1229	1605	1912	95000	802	1296	1691	2014
78900	672	1093	1431	1707	84300	717	1164	1521	1813	89700	761	1231	1607	1914	95100	803	1297	1693	2016
79000	673	1095	1433	1709	84400	718	1165	1522	1814	89800	762	1232	1608	1916	95200	804	1298	1694	2018
79100	674	1096	1435	1711	84500	719	1166	1524	1816	89900	763	1233	1610	1918	95300	804	1300	1696	2020
79200	675	1098	1436	1713	84600	720	1167	1526	1818	90000	763	1234	1611	1920	95400	805	1301	1697	2022
79300	676	1099	1438	1715	84700	721	1168	1527	1820	90100	764	1235	1613	1922	95500	806	1302	1699	2023
79400	676	1100	1440	1717	84800	722	1170	1529	1822	90200	765	1237	1614	1924	95600	807	1303	1701	2025
79500	677	1102	1441	1719	84900	722	1171	1530	1824	90300	766	1238	1616	1926	95700	807	1304	1702	2027
79600	678	1103	1443	1721	85000	723	1172	1532	1826	90400	766	1239	1617	1928	95800	808	1306	1704	2029
79700	679	1104	1445	1723	85100	724	1173	1534	1828	90500	767	1240	1619	1929	95900	809	1307	1705	2031
79800	680	1106	1447	1725	85200	725	1175	1535	1830	90600	768	1242	1620	1931	96000	810	1308	1707	2033
79900	681	1107	1448	1727	85300	725	1176	1537	1832	90700	769	1243	1622	1933	96100	811	1309	1709	2035
80000	682	1109	1450	1729	85400	726	1177	1538	1834	90800	770	1244	1623	1935	96200	812	1311	1710	2037
80100	683	1110	1452	1731	85500	727	1178	1540	1835	90900	771	1246	1625	1937	96300	812	1312	1712	2039
80200	684	1112	1453	1733	85600	728	1180	1542	1837	91000	771	1247	1627	1939	96400	813	1313	1713	2041
80300	684	1113	1455	1735	85700	729	1181	1543	1839	91100	772	1248	1629	1941	96500	814	1314	1715	2043
80400	685	1114	1457	1737	85800	730	1182	1545	1841	91200	773	1249	1630	1943	96600	815	1316	1717	2044
80500	686	1116	1458	1739	85900	730	1183	1547	1843	91300	774	1251	1632	1945	96700	815	1317	1718	2046
80600	687	1117	1460	1741	86000	731	1185	1548	1845	91400	774	1252	1633	1947	96800	816	1318	1720	2048
80700	688	1118	1462	1743	86100	732	1186	1550	1847	91500	775	1253	1635	1949	96900	817	1319	1721	2050
80800	688	1120	1464	1745	86200	733	1187	1551	1849	91600	776	1254	1636	1950	97000	818	1321	1723	2052
80900	689	1121	1465	1747	86300	733	1189	1553	1851	91700	777	1256	1638	1952	97100	819	1322	1725	2054

Prince Edward Island / Île-du-Prince-Édouard

Federal Child Support Amounts: Simplified Tables
Montants fédéraux de pensions alimentaires pour enfants: Tables simplifiées

Income/ Revenu ($)	Monthly Award/ Paiement mensuel ($) No. of Children/ Nbre d'enfants				Income/ Revenu ($)	Monthly Award/ Paiement mensuel ($) No. of Children/ Nbre d'enfants				Income/ Revenu ($)	Monthly Award/ Paiement mensuel ($) No. of Children/ Nbre d'enfants				Income/ Revenu ($)	Monthly Award/ Paiement mensuel ($) No. of Children/ Nbre d'enfants			
	1	2	3	4		1	2	3	4		1	2	3	4		1	2	3	4
97200	820	1323	1726	2056	102600	861	1388	1809	2155	108000	902	1452	1892	2253	113400	943	1517	1976	2351
97300	820	1325	1728	2058	102700	861	1389	1810	2157	108100	903	1453	1894	2255	113500	944	1518	1978	2353
97400	821	1326	1729	2060	102800	862	1390	1812	2159	108200	904	1454	1895	2257	113600	945	1519	1979	2355
97500	822	1327	1731	2062	102900	863	1391	1813	2160	108300	904	1456	1897	2258	113700	945	1520	1981	2357
97600	823	1328	1733	2064	103000	864	1392	1815	2162	108400	905	1457	1898	2260	113800	946	1521	1982	2358
97700	823	1330	1734	2065	103100	865	1393	1817	2164	108500	906	1458	1900	2262	113900	947	1523	1984	2360
97800	824	1331	1736	2067	103200	865	1394	1818	2166	108600	907	1459	1901	2264	114000	948	1524	1985	2362
97900	825	1332	1738	2069	103300	866	1395	1820	2168	108700	908	1460	1903	2266	114100	949	1525	1987	2364
98000	826	1333	1739	2071	103400	867	1397	1821	2169	108800	909	1461	1904	2268	114200	950	1526	1988	2366
98100	827	1334	1741	2073	103500	868	1398	1823	2171	108900	909	1463	1906	2269	114300	950	1528	1990	2368
98200	828	1336	1742	2075	103600	868	1399	1824	2173	109000	910	1464	1908	2271	114400	951	1529	1991	2369
98300	828	1337	1744	2077	103700	869	1400	1826	2175	109100	911	1465	1910	2273	114500	952	1530	1993	2371
98400	829	1338	1745	2078	103800	870	1401	1827	2177	109200	911	1466	1911	2275	114600	953	1531	1994	2373
98500	830	1339	1747	2080	103900	871	1402	1829	2179	109300	912	1468	1913	2276	114700	953	1532	1996	2375
98600	831	1341	1749	2082	104000	871	1404	1831	2180	109400	913	1469	1914	2278	114800	954	1533	1998	2377
98700	831	1342	1750	2084	104100	872	1405	1833	2182	109500	914	1470	1916	2280	114900	955	1535	1999	2379
98800	832	1343	1752	2086	104200	873	1406	1834	2184	109600	914	1471	1917	2282	115000	956	1536	2001	2381
98900	833	1344	1754	2088	104300	873	1408	1836	2186	109700	915	1472	1919	2284	115100	957	1537	2003	2383
99000	834	1346	1755	2089	104400	874	1409	1837	2187	109800	916	1473	1920	2285	115200	958	1538	2004	2385
99100	835	1347	1757	2091	104500	875	1410	1839	2189	109900	917	1475	1922	2287	115300	958	1540	2006	2387
99200	836	1348	1758	2093	104600	876	1411	1840	2191	110000	917	1476	1923	2289	115400	959	1541	2007	2388
99300	836	1350	1760	2095	104700	877	1412	1842	2193	110100	918	1477	1925	2291	115500	960	1542	2009	2390
99400	837	1351	1761	2096	104800	877	1414	1843	2195	110200	919	1478	1926	2293	115600	961	1543	2010	2392
99500	838	1352	1763	2098	104900	878	1415	1845	2197	110300	919	1480	1928	2294	115700	962	1544	2012	2394
99600	839	1353	1764	2100	105000	879	1416	1846	2198	110400	920	1481	1929	2296	115800	962	1545	2013	2396
99700	839	1355	1766	2102	105100	880	1417	1848	2200	110500	921	1482	1931	2298	115900	963	1547	2015	2398
99800	840	1356	1767	2104	105200	880	1418	1849	2202	110600	922	1483	1932	2300	116000	964	1548	2016	2399
99900	841	1357	1769	2106	105300	881	1420	1851	2203	110700	922	1484	1934	2301	116100	965	1549	2018	2401
100000	842	1358	1770	2108	105400	882	1421	1852	2205	110800	923	1485	1936	2303	116200	965	1550	2019	2403
100100	843	1359	1771	2110	105500	883	1422	1854	2207	110900	924	1487	1937	2305	116300	966	1551	2021	2404
100200	843	1360	1773	2112	105600	883	1423	1856	2209	111000	925	1488	1939	2307	116400	967	1553	2022	2406
100300	844	1361	1774	2113	105700	884	1424	1857	2211	111100	926	1489	1941	2309	116500	968	1554	2024	2408
100400	845	1362	1776	2115	105800	885	1425	1859	2212	111200	927	1490	1942	2311	116600	968	1555	2026	2410
100500	845	1364	1777	2117	105900	886	1427	1860	2214	111300	927	1492	1944	2313	116700	969	1556	2027	2412
100600	846	1365	1779	2119	106000	886	1428	1862	2216	111400	928	1493	1945	2314	116800	970	1557	2029	2414
100700	847	1366	1780	2121	106100	887	1429	1864	2218	111500	929	1494	1947	2316	116900	971	1558	2030	2415
100800	848	1367	1782	2122	106200	888	1430	1865	2220	111600	930	1495	1948	2318	117000	971	1560	2032	2417
100900	848	1368	1783	2124	106300	888	1432	1867	2221	111700	931	1496	1950	2320	117100	972	1561	2034	2419
101000	849	1369	1785	2126	106400	889	1433	1868	2223	111800	931	1497	1951	2322	117200	973	1562	2035	2421
101100	850	1370	1786	2128	106500	890	1434	1870	2225	111900	932	1499	1953	2324	117300	973	1563	2037	2422
101200	850	1371	1788	2130	106600	891	1435	1871	2227	112000	933	1500	1954	2326	117400	974	1565	2038	2424
101300	851	1372	1789	2131	106700	891	1436	1873	2228	112100	934	1501	1956	2328	117500	975	1566	2040	2426
101400	852	1374	1791	2133	106800	892	1437	1874	2230	112200	934	1502	1957	2330	117600	976	1567	2041	2428
101500	852	1375	1792	2135	106900	893	1439	1876	2232	112300	935	1504	1959	2331	117700	976	1568	2043	2430
101600	853	1376	1794	2137	107000	894	1440	1877	2234	112400	936	1505	1960	2333	117800	977	1569	2044	2431
101700	854	1377	1795	2139	107100	895	1441	1878	2236	112500	937	1506	1962	2335	117900	978	1570	2046	2433
101800	854	1378	1797	2140	107200	896	1442	1880	2238	112600	937	1507	1963	2337	118000	979	1572	2047	2435
101900	855	1379	1798	2142	107300	896	1444	1881	2240	112700	938	1508	1965	2339	118100	980	1573	2049	2437
102000	856	1381	1800	2144	107400	897	1445	1883	2241	112800	939	1509	1967	2341	118200	981	1574	2050	2439
102100	857	1382	1801	2146	107500	898	1446	1884	2243	112900	940	1511	1968	2342	118300	981	1575	2052	2441
102200	858	1383	1803	2148	107600	899	1447	1886	2245	113000	940	1512	1970	2344	118400	982	1577	2053	2442
102300	858	1384	1804	2149	107700	900	1448	1887	2247	113100	941	1513	1972	2346	118500	983	1578	2055	2444
102400	859	1385	1806	2151	107800	900	1449	1889	2249	113200	942	1514	1973	2348	118600	984	1579	2056	2446
102500	860	1387	1807	2153	107900	901	1451	1890	2251	113300	942	1516	1975	2349	118700	985	1580	2058	2448

Prince Edward Island / Île-du-Prince-Édouard

Federal Child Support Amounts: Simplified Tables
Montants fédéraux de pensions alimentaires pour enfants: Tables simplifiées

Income/ Revenu ($)	Monthly Award/ Paiement mensuel ($) No. of Children/ N^bre d'enfants				Income/ Revenu ($)	Monthly Award/ Paiement mensuel ($) No. of Children/ N^bre d'enfants				Income/ Revenu ($)	Monthly Award/ Paiement mensuel ($) No. of Children/ N^bre d'enfants				Income/ Revenu ($)	Monthly Award/ Paiement mensuel ($) No. of Children/ N^bre d'enfants			
	1	2	3	4		1	2	3	4		1	2	3	4		1	2	3	4
118800	985	1581	2059	2450	124200	1027	1647	2143	2549	129600	1068	1710	2224	2645	135000	1107	1772	2303	2738
118900	986	1582	2061	2452	124300	1027	1648	2145	2550	129700	1068	1711	2225	2646	135100	1108	1773	2304	2740
119000	987	1584	2062	2454	124400	1028	1649	2146	2552	129800	1069	1712	2227	2648	135200	1108	1774	2306	2741
119100	988	1585	2064	2456	124500	1029	1650	2148	2554	129900	1070	1714	2228	2650	135300	1109	1775	2307	2743
119200	989	1586	2065	2458	124600	1030	1652	2149	2556	130000	1071	1715	2230	2652	135400	1110	1777	2309	2745
119300	989	1587	2067	2460	124700	1030	1653	2151	2558	130100	1072	1716	2232	2654	135500	1110	1778	2310	2747
119400	990	1589	2068	2461	124800	1031	1654	2152	2559	130200	1072	1717	2233	2655	135600	1111	1779	2312	2748
119500	991	1590	2070	2463	124900	1032	1655	2154	2561	130300	1073	1718	2235	2657	135700	1112	1780	2313	2750
119600	992	1591	2071	2465	125000	1033	1657	2155	2563	130400	1074	1720	2236	2659	135800	1112	1781	2315	2752
119700	993	1592	2073	2467	125100	1034	1658	2157	2565	130500	1075	1721	2238	2661	135900	1113	1782	2316	2753
119800	994	1593	2074	2469	125200	1035	1659	2158	2567	130600	1075	1722	2239	2662	136000	1114	1783	2318	2755
119900	994	1594	2076	2471	125300	1035	1661	2160	2568	130700	1076	1723	2241	2664	136100	1115	1784	2319	2757
120000	995	1596	2078	2472	125400	1036	1662	2161	2570	130800	1077	1724	2242	2666	136200	1116	1785	2321	2758
120100	996	1597	2080	2474	125500	1037	1663	2163	2572	130900	1078	1725	2244	2668	136300	1116	1786	2322	2760
120200	996	1598	2081	2476	125600	1038	1664	2165	2574	131000	1078	1726	2245	2669	136400	1117	1787	2324	2762
120300	997	1599	2083	2477	125700	1038	1666	2166	2575	131100	1079	1727	2246	2671	136500	1118	1789	2325	2763
120400	998	1601	2084	2479	125800	1039	1667	2168	2577	131200	1079	1728	2248	2672	136600	1119	1790	2327	2765
120500	999	1602	2086	2481	125900	1040	1668	2169	2579	131300	1080	1729	2249	2674	136700	1119	1791	2328	2767
120600	999	1603	2087	2483	126000	1041	1669	2171	2581	131400	1081	1730	2251	2676	136800	1120	1792	2329	2768
120700	1000	1604	2089	2485	126100	1042	1670	2173	2583	131500	1082	1731	2252	2678	136900	1121	1793	2331	2770
120800	1001	1605	2090	2487	126200	1043	1671	2174	2585	131600	1082	1733	2254	2679	137000	1122	1794	2332	2772
120900	1002	1606	2092	2488	126300	1043	1673	2176	2587	131700	1083	1734	2255	2681	137100	1123	1795	2333	2774
121000	1002	1608	2093	2490	126400	1044	1674	2177	2588	131800	1084	1735	2257	2683	137200	1123	1796	2335	2776
121100	1003	1609	2095	2492	126500	1045	1675	2179	2590	131900	1084	1736	2258	2684	137300	1124	1798	2336	2777
121200	1004	1610	2096	2494	126600	1046	1676	2180	2592	132000	1085	1737	2259	2686	137400	1125	1799	2338	2779
121300	1004	1611	2098	2495	126700	1047	1678	2182	2594	132100	1086	1738	2260	2688	137500	1126	1800	2339	2781
121400	1005	1613	2099	2497	126800	1047	1679	2183	2596	132200	1087	1739	2262	2689	137600	1126	1801	2341	2783
121500	1006	1614	2101	2499	126900	1048	1680	2185	2598	132300	1087	1740	2263	2691	137700	1127	1802	2342	2784
121600	1007	1615	2102	2501	127000	1049	1681	2186	2600	132400	1088	1742	2265	2693	137800	1128	1803	2344	2786
121700	1007	1616	2104	2503	127100	1050	1682	2187	2602	132500	1089	1743	2266	2694	137900	1129	1806	2347	2790
121800	1008	1617	2106	2504	127200	1050	1683	2189	2603	132600	1090	1744	2268	2696	138000	1129	1806	2347	2790
121900	1009	1618	2107	2506	127300	1051	1684	2190	2605	132700	1090	1745	2269	2698	138100	1130	1807	2349	2792
122000	1010	1620	2109	2508	127400	1052	1686	2192	2607	132800	1091	1746	2271	2700	138200	1130	1808	2350	2793
122100	1011	1621	2111	2510	127500	1053	1687	2193	2609	132900	1092	1747	2272	2701	138300	1131	1809	2352	2795
122200	1012	1622	2112	2512	127600	1053	1688	2195	2610	133000	1093	1749	2274	2703	138400	1132	1811	2353	2797
122300	1012	1623	2114	2514	127700	1054	1689	2196	2612	133100	1094	1750	2275	2705	138500	1132	1812	2355	2799
122400	1013	1625	2115	2515	127800	1055	1690	2198	2614	133200	1094	1751	2277	2707	138600	1133	1813	2356	2800
122500	1014	1626	2117	2517	127900	1056	1691	2199	2616	133300	1095	1752	2278	2708	138700	1134	1814	2358	2802
122600	1015	1627	2118	2519	128000	1056	1692	2201	2617	133400	1096	1753	2280	2710	138800	1135	1815	2359	2804
122700	1016	1628	2120	2521	128100	1057	1693	2202	2619	133500	1097	1755	2281	2712	138900	1135	1816	2361	2806
122800	1016	1629	2121	2523	128200	1057	1694	2204	2620	133600	1097	1756	2283	2714	139000	1136	1817	2362	2807
122900	1017	1630	2123	2525	128300	1058	1695	2205	2622	133700	1098	1757	2284	2715	139100	1137	1818	2363	2809
123000	1018	1632	2124	2527	128400	1059	1696	2207	2624	133800	1099	1758	2285	2717	139200	1138	1819	2365	2810
123100	1019	1633	2126	2529	128500	1060	1698	2208	2626	133900	1100	1759	2287	2719	139300	1138	1820	2366	2812
123200	1019	1634	2127	2531	128600	1060	1699	2210	2627	134000	1100	1760	2288	2721	139400	1139	1821	2368	2814
123300	1020	1635	2129	2533	128700	1061	1700	2211	2629	134100	1101	1761	2289	2723	139500	1140	1822	2369	2815
123400	1021	1637	2130	2534	128800	1062	1701	2212	2631	134200	1101	1762	2291	2724	139600	1141	1824	2371	2817
123500	1022	1638	2132	2536	128900	1062	1702	2214	2632	134300	1102	1764	2292	2726	139700	1141	1825	2372	2819
123600	1022	1639	2133	2538	129000	1063	1703	2215	2634	134400	1103	1765	2294	2728	139800	1142	1826	2374	2821
123700	1023	1640	2135	2540	129100	1064	1704	2216	2636	134500	1104	1766	2295	2730	139900	1143	1827	2375	2822
123800	1024	1641	2137	2542	129200	1065	1705	2218	2638	134600	1104	1767	2297	2731	140000	1144	1828	2376	2824
123900	1025	1642	2138	2544	129300	1065	1707	2219	2639	134700	1105	1768	2298	2733	140100	1145	1829	2377	2826
124000	1025	1644	2140	2545	129400	1066	1708	2221	2641	134800	1106	1769	2300	2735	140200	1145	1830	2379	2828
124100	1026	1645	2142	2547	129500	1067	1709	2222	2643	134900	1106	1771	2301	2737	140300	1146	1831	2380	2829

PRINCE EDWARD ISLAND — CONTINUED

Federal Child Support Amounts: Simplified Tables
Montants fédéraux de pensions alimentaires pour enfants: Tables simplifiées

Income/ Revenu ($)	Monthly Award/ Paiement mensuel ($) No. of Children/ N^{bre} d'enfants				Income/ Revenu ($)	Monthly Award/ Paiement mensuel ($) No. of Children/ N^{bre} d'enfants				Income/ Revenu ($)	Monthly Award/ Paiement mensuel ($) No. of Children/ N^{bre} d'enfants			
	1	2	3	4		1	2	3	4		1	2	3	4
140400	1147	1833	2382	2831	143700	1171	1870	2431	2888	147000	1195	1908	2478	2945
140500	1148	1834	2383	2833	143800	1172	1871	2432	2889	147100	1196	1909	2479	2947
140600	1148	1835	2385	2835	143900	1173	1872	2434	2891	147200	1196	1910	2481	2949
140700	1149	1836	2386	2836	144000	1173	1874	2435	2893	147300	1197	1911	2482	2950
140800	1150	1837	2388	2838	144100	1174	1875	2436	2895	147400	1198	1912	2484	2952
140900	1151	1838	2389	2840	144200	1174	1876	2438	2897	147500	1199	1914	2485	2954
141000	1151	1840	2391	2842	144300	1175	1877	2439	2898	147600	1199	1915	2487	2956
141100	1152	1841	2392	2844	144400	1176	1878	2441	2900	147700	1200	1916	2488	2957
141200	1152	1842	2394	2845	144500	1177	1880	2442	2902	147800	1201	1917	2490	2959
141300	1153	1843	2395	2847	144600	1177	1881	2444	2904	147900	1201	1918	2491	2961
141400	1154	1845	2397	2849	144700	1178	1882	2445	2905	148000	1202	1919	2493	2963
141500	1155	1846	2398	2851	144800	1179	1883	2447	2907	148100	1203	1920	2494	2965
141600	1155	1847	2400	2852	144900	1179	1884	2448	2909	148200	1203	1921	2496	2966
141700	1156	1848	2401	2854	145000	1180	1885	2449	2911	148300	1204	1922	2497	2968
141800	1157	1849	2402	2856	145100	1181	1886	2450	2913	148400	1205	1924	2499	2970
141900	1157	1850	2404	2858	145200	1182	1887	2452	2914	148500	1205	1925	2500	2972
142000	1158	1851	2405	2859	145300	1182	1889	2453	2916	148600	1206	1926	2502	2973
142100	1159	1852	2406	2861	145400	1183	1890	2455	2918	148700	1207	1927	2503	2975
142200	1160	1853	2408	2862	145500	1184	1891	2456	2919	148800	1207	1928	2505	2977
142300	1160	1854	2409	2864	145600	1185	1892	2458	2921	148900	1208	1929	2506	2979
142400	1161	1855	2411	2866	145700	1185	1893	2459	2923	149000	1209	1931	2508	2980
142500	1162	1856	2412	2868	145800	1186	1894	2461	2925	149100	1210	1932	2509	2982
142600	1163	1858	2414	2869	145900	1187	1896	2462	2927	149200	1211	1933	2511	2983
142700	1163	1859	2415	2871	146000	1188	1897	2464	2928	149300	1211	1934	2512	2985
142800	1164	1860	2417	2873	146100	1189	1898	2465	2930	149400	1212	1936	2514	2987
142900	1165	1861	2418	2874	146200	1189	1899	2467	2931	149500	1213	1937	2515	2989
143000	1166	1862	2420	2876	146300	1190	1900	2468	2933	149600	1214	1938	2517	2990
143100	1167	1863	2422	2878	146400	1191	1902	2470	2935	149700	1214	1939	2518	2992
143200	1167	1864	2423	2879	146500	1192	1903	2471	2937	149800	1215	1940	2519	2994
143300	1168	1865	2425	2881	146600	1192	1904	2472	2938	149900	1216	1941	2521	2995
143400	1169	1867	2426	2883	146700	1193	1905	2474	2940	150000	1217	1942	2522	2997
143500	1170	1868	2428	2884	146800	1194	1906	2475	2942					
143600	1170	1869	2429	2886	146900	1195	1907	2477	2943					

Monthly Award/Paiement mensuel ($)			
One Child/ Un enfant	Two Children/ Deux enfants	Three Children/ Trois enfants	Four Children/ Quatre enfants
1217 plus 0.76% of income over $150,000	1942 plus 1.12% of income over $150,000	2522 plus 1.42% of income over $150,000	2997 plus 1.72% of income over $150,000
1217 plus 0,76% du revenu dépassant 150 000$	1942 plus 1,12% du revenu dépassant 150 000$	2522 plus 1,42% du revenu dépassant 150 000$	2997 plus 1,72% du revenu dépassant 150 000$

SASKATCHEWAN

Federal Child Support Amounts: Simplified Tables
Montants fédéraux de pensions alimentaires pour enfants: Tables simplifiées

Income/ Revenu ($)	Monthly Award/ Paiement mensuel ($) No. of Children/ N^bre d'enfants				Income/ Revenu ($)	Monthly Award/ Paiement mensuel ($) No. of Children/ N^bre d'enfants				Income/ Revenu ($)	Monthly Award/ Paiement mensuel ($) No. of Children/ N^bre d'enfants				Income/ Revenu ($)	Monthly Award/ Paiement mensuel ($) No. of Children/ N^bre d'enfants			
	1	2	3	4		1	2	3	4		1	2	3	4		1	2	3	4
10820	4	7	7	8	16200	122	237	255	273	21600	167	322	447	501	27000	202	382	532	654
10900	6	11	11	12	16300	124	240	258	277	21700	168	323	449	505	27100	203	383	533	656
11000	23	55	59	63	16400	126	244	261	280	21800	168	325	451	510	27200	203	384	534	657
11100	25	59	64	68	16500	128	247	265	284	21900	169	326	452	514	27300	204	385	536	659
11200	27	64	68	73	16600	129	250	268	287	22000	169	327	454	518	27400	204	386	537	661
11300	29	68	73	78	16700	131	253	271	291	22100	170	328	456	522	27500	205	386	538	662
11400	31	73	78	83	16800	133	256	275	295	22200	170	329	457	527	27600	205	387	539	664
11500	33	77	82	88	16900	135	259	278	298	22300	171	331	459	531	27700	206	388	541	666
11600	34	81	87	93	17000	137	262	282	302	22400	171	332	461	535	27800	206	389	542	667
11700	36	86	92	98	17100	138	264	286	306	22500	172	333	462	540	27900	207	390	543	669
11800	38	90	96	103	17200	138	265	290	311	22600	173	334	464	544	28000	208	391	544	671
11900	40	95	101	108	17300	139	267	294	315	22700	173	335	466	548	28100	209	392	545	673
12000	42	99	106	114	17400	139	269	298	319	22800	174	337	467	552	28200	210	393	547	674
12100	44	103	110	118	17500	140	271	302	323	22900	174	338	469	557	28300	210	395	548	676
12200	46	106	114	122	17600	141	272	306	328	23000	175	339	470	561	28400	211	396	549	677
12300	48	110	118	127	17700	141	274	310	332	23100	176	340	472	565	28500	212	397	550	679
12400	50	114	122	131	17800	142	276	314	336	23200	176	341	473	568	28600	213	398	552	681
12500	52	117	125	135	17900	142	277	318	341	23300	177	343	475	572	28700	213	400	553	682
12600	53	121	129	139	18000	143	279	322	345	23400	178	344	477	576	28800	214	401	554	684
12700	55	125	133	144	18100	144	280	326	349	23500	178	345	478	579	28900	215	402	555	685
12800	57	128	137	148	18200	144	281	330	354	23600	179	346	480	583	29000	216	403	557	687
12900	59	132	141	152	18300	145	283	334	358	23700	180	347	482	587	29100	217	404	558	689
13000	61	135	145	156	18400	146	284	338	362	23800	180	349	483	590	29200	218	405	559	690
13100	63	139	149	160	18500	146	285	342	366	23900	181	350	485	594	29300	219	406	561	692
13200	65	142	153	164	18600	147	286	346	371	24000	182	351	487	598	29400	220	408	562	693
13300	67	146	157	168	18700	148	288	350	375	24100	183	352	489	600	29500	221	409	563	695
13400	69	149	160	173	18800	148	289	355	379	24200	183	353	490	602	29600	222	410	564	696
13500	71	153	164	177	18900	149	290	359	383	24300	184	355	492	604	29700	223	411	566	698
13600	72	157	168	181	19000	150	291	363	388	24400	185	356	493	606	29800	224	412	567	699
13700	74	160	172	185	19100	151	292	367	392	24500	185	357	495	608	29900	225	413	568	701
13800	76	164	176	189	19200	151	293	371	397	24600	186	358	497	610	30000	226	414	569	703
13900	78	167	180	193	19300	152	295	375	401	24700	186	359	498	612	30100	227	415	571	705
14000	80	171	184	197	19400	152	296	379	405	24800	187	360	500	614	30200	228	416	572	706
14100	82	174	187	200	19500	153	297	383	410	24900	188	362	502	616	30300	229	417	574	708
14200	84	177	191	204	19600	154	298	387	414	25000	188	363	503	618	30400	230	418	575	709
14300	86	180	194	207	19700	154	300	391	418	25100	189	364	505	620	30500	231	420	577	711
14400	88	183	197	211	19800	155	301	395	423	25200	190	365	506	622	30600	231	421	579	712
14500	90	186	200	214	19900	156	302	399	427	25300	190	367	508	624	30700	232	422	580	714
14600	91	189	204	218	20000	156	303	403	432	25400	191	368	509	626	30800	233	423	582	715
14700	93	192	207	221	20100	157	304	406	436	25500	192	369	511	628	30900	234	424	584	717
14800	95	195	210	225	20200	157	305	410	441	25600	193	370	512	630	31000	235	425	585	719
14900	97	198	214	228	20300	158	307	413	445	25700	194	371	514	632	31100	236	426	587	721
15000	99	201	217	232	20400	159	308	417	449	25800	194	372	516	634	31200	237	427	588	722
15100	101	204	220	235	20500	159	309	420	454	25900	195	374	517	636	31300	238	429	590	724
15200	103	207	223	239	20600	160	310	423	458	26000	196	375	519	638	31400	239	430	591	725
15300	105	210	226	242	20700	161	311	427	462	26100	197	376	520	640	31500	239	431	593	727
15400	107	213	229	245	20800	161	313	430	467	26200	197	376	522	641	31600	240	432	594	728
15500	109	216	233	249	20900	162	314	434	471	26300	198	377	523	643	31700	241	433	596	730
15600	110	219	236	252	21000	163	315	437	475	26400	198	378	524	644	31800	242	434	597	732
15700	112	222	239	255	21100	164	316	439	479	26500	199	379	525	646	31900	243	436	599	733
15800	114	225	242	259	21200	164	317	440	484	26600	199	379	527	648	32000	244	437	600	735
15900	116	228	245	262	21300	165	319	442	488	26700	200	380	528	649	32100	245	438	601	737
16000	118	231	248	266	21400	166	320	444	492	26800	201	381	529	651	32200	246	439	603	739
16100	120	234	251	270	21500	166	321	446	497	26900	201	382	530	653	32300	247	440	604	740

Federal Child Support Amounts: Simplified Tables
Montants fédéraux de pensions alimentaires pour enfants: Tables simplifiées

Income/ Revenu ($)	Monthly Award/ Paiement mensuel ($) No. of Children/ Nᵇʳᵉ d'enfants				Income/ Revenu ($)	Monthly Award/ Paiement mensuel ($) No. of Children/ Nᵇʳᵉ d'enfants				Income/ Revenu ($)	Monthly Award/ Paiement mensuel ($) No. of Children/ Nᵇʳᵉ d'enfants				Income/ Revenu ($)	Monthly Award/ Paiement mensuel ($) No. of Children/ Nᵇʳᵉ d'enfants			
	1	2	3	4		1	2	3	4		1	2	3	4		1	2	3	4
32400	247	441	606	742	37800	295	510	684	838	43200	342	582	774	934	48600	389	654	868	1042
32500	248	442	607	744	37900	295	511	686	840	43300	342	583	776	935	48700	390	656	870	1044
32600	249	443	609	746	38000	296	512	687	842	43400	343	584	778	937	48800	390	657	872	1046
32700	250	444	610	747	38100	297	513	688	844	43500	344	585	780	939	48900	391	659	873	1049
32800	251	445	612	749	38200	298	515	690	846	43600	345	587	781	941	49000	392	660	875	1051
32900	252	446	613	751	38300	299	516	691	847	43700	346	588	783	943	49100	393	661	877	1053
33000	253	447	615	753	38400	299	517	693	849	43800	347	589	785	945	49200	394	663	879	1055
33100	254	448	616	755	38500	300	519	694	851	43900	347	590	786	946	49300	395	664	880	1057
33200	255	449	618	757	38600	301	520	696	853	44000	348	592	788	948	49400	396	666	882	1060
33300	256	450	619	758	38700	302	521	697	855	44100	349	593	790	950	49500	397	667	884	1062
33400	256	451	621	760	38800	303	522	699	857	44200	350	595	791	952	49600	398	668	886	1064
33500	257	452	622	762	38900	304	524	700	858	44300	351	596	793	954	49700	399	670	888	1066
33600	258	453	624	764	39000	305	525	702	860	44400	352	597	795	956	49800	399	671	890	1068
33700	259	455	625	766	39100	306	526	704	862	44500	352	599	797	958	49900	400	672	891	1070
33800	260	456	627	767	39200	307	528	705	864	44600	353	600	798	960	50000	401	674	893	1072
33900	261	457	628	769	39300	308	529	707	866	44700	354	601	800	962	50100	402	675	895	1074
34000	262	458	630	771	39400	309	530	709	867	44800	355	603	802	964	50200	403	677	897	1076
34100	263	459	631	773	39500	309	532	711	869	44900	356	604	803	966	50300	404	678	898	1078
34200	264	461	633	775	39600	310	533	712	871	45000	357	606	805	968	50400	405	680	900	1080
34300	265	462	634	776	39700	311	535	714	873	45100	358	607	807	970	50500	406	681	902	1083
34400	266	463	636	778	39800	312	536	716	875	45200	359	609	808	972	50600	407	682	904	1085
34500	267	465	637	780	39900	313	537	718	877	45300	359	610	810	974	50700	407	684	906	1087
34600	267	466	639	782	40000	314	539	719	878	45400	360	611	812	976	50800	408	685	907	1089
34700	268	468	640	784	40100	315	540	721	880	45500	361	613	814	978	50900	409	686	909	1091
34800	269	469	641	786	40200	316	542	723	882	45600	362	614	815	980	51000	410	688	911	1093
34900	270	470	643	787	40300	317	543	725	884	45700	363	615	817	982	51100	411	689	913	1095
35000	271	472	644	789	40400	318	545	727	886	45800	364	617	819	984	51200	412	691	915	1097
35100	272	473	645	791	40500	319	546	729	888	45900	364	618	820	986	51300	413	692	916	1100
35200	273	475	647	792	40600	320	547	730	890	46000	365	619	822	988	51400	414	694	918	1102
35300	274	476	648	794	40700	320	549	732	892	46100	366	620	824	990	51500	415	695	920	1104
35400	274	477	650	796	40800	321	550	734	894	46200	367	622	825	992	51600	416	696	922	1106
35500	275	479	651	798	40900	322	552	736	896	46300	368	623	827	994	51700	416	698	924	1108
35600	276	480	653	799	41000	323	553	738	897	46400	369	624	829	996	51800	417	699	925	1110
35700	277	481	654	801	41100	324	554	740	899	46500	369	626	831	998	51900	418	700	927	1113
35800	278	483	656	803	41200	325	556	741	900	46600	370	627	832	1000	52000	419	702	929	1115
35900	279	484	657	805	41300	325	557	743	902	46700	371	628	834	1002	52100	420	703	931	1117
36000	279	485	659	806	41400	326	558	745	904	46800	372	629	836	1004	52200	421	705	933	1119
36100	280	486	660	808	41500	327	559	746	905	46900	373	631	837	1006	52300	422	706	934	1121
36200	281	488	662	810	41600	328	561	748	907	47000	374	632	839	1008	52400	423	707	936	1124
36300	282	489	663	811	41700	329	562	750	909	47100	375	633	841	1010	52500	424	709	938	1126
36400	283	491	665	813	41800	329	563	751	910	47200	376	635	843	1012	52600	425	710	940	1128
36500	283	492	666	815	41900	330	564	753	912	47300	377	636	844	1014	52700	425	712	942	1130
36600	284	493	668	817	42000	331	566	754	913	47400	378	638	846	1016	52800	426	713	943	1132
36700	285	495	669	818	42100	332	567	756	915	47500	379	639	848	1018	52900	427	714	945	1134
36800	286	496	671	820	42200	333	569	757	916	47600	380	640	850	1021	53000	428	716	947	1136
36900	287	497	672	822	42300	334	570	759	918	47700	380	642	852	1023	53100	429	717	949	1138
37000	288	499	673	824	42400	334	571	761	920	47800	381	643	853	1025	53200	430	719	951	1140
37100	289	500	674	826	42500	335	572	762	921	47900	382	644	855	1027	53300	431	720	952	1142
37200	290	502	676	828	42600	336	574	764	923	48000	383	646	857	1029	53400	432	721	954	1144
37300	290	503	677	829	42700	337	575	766	925	48100	384	647	859	1031	53500	433	723	956	1147
37400	291	504	679	831	42800	338	576	767	927	48200	385	649	861	1033	53600	434	724	958	1149
37500	292	506	680	833	42900	339	577	769	928	48300	386	650	862	1036	53700	434	726	960	1151
37600	293	507	681	835	43000	340	579	771	930	48400	387	652	864	1038	53800	435	727	961	1153
37700	294	508	683	837	43100	341	580	773	932	48500	388	653	866	1040	53900	436	728	963	1155

Federal Child Support Amounts: Simplified Tables
Montants fédéraux de pensions alimentaires pour enfants: Tables simplifiées

Income/ Revenu ($)	Monthly Award/ Paiement mensuel ($) No. of Children/ N^bre d'enfants				Income/ Revenu ($)	Monthly Award/ Paiement mensuel ($) No. of Children/ N^bre d'enfants				Income/ Revenu ($)	Monthly Award/ Paiement mensuel ($) No. of Children/ N^bre d'enfants				Income/ Revenu ($)	Monthly Award/ Paiement mensuel ($) No. of Children/ N^bre d'enfants			
	1	2	3	4		1	2	3	4		1	2	3	4		1	2	3	4
54000	437	730	965	1157	59400	486	807	1062	1272	64800	534	882	1161	1388	70200	583	958	1258	1503
54100	438	731	967	1159	59500	487	808	1064	1275	64900	535	884	1162	1390	70300	584	959	1259	1505
54200	439	733	969	1161	59600	487	810	1066	1277	65000	536	885	1164	1392	70400	584	961	1261	1508
54300	440	734	970	1164	59700	488	811	1067	1279	65100	537	886	1166	1394	70500	585	962	1263	1510
54400	441	735	972	1166	59800	489	813	1069	1281	65200	538	888	1168	1396	70600	586	963	1265	1512
54500	442	737	974	1168	59900	490	814	1071	1283	65300	539	889	1169	1398	70700	587	965	1267	1514
54600	442	738	976	1170	60000	491	815	1073	1285	65400	540	891	1171	1400	70800	588	966	1268	1516
54700	443	740	977	1172	60100	492	816	1075	1287	65500	540	892	1173	1403	70900	589	968	1270	1518
54800	444	741	979	1174	60200	493	818	1077	1289	65600	541	894	1175	1405	71000	590	969	1272	1520
54900	445	742	981	1177	60300	494	819	1079	1292	65700	542	895	1177	1407	71100	591	970	1274	1522
55000	446	744	983	1179	60400	495	821	1080	1294	65800	543	896	1179	1409	71200	592	972	1276	1524
55100	447	745	985	1181	60500	495	822	1082	1296	65900	544	898	1180	1411	71300	593	973	1277	1526
55200	448	747	987	1183	60600	496	824	1084	1298	66000	545	899	1182	1413	71400	593	975	1279	1528
55300	449	748	988	1185	60700	497	825	1086	1300	66100	546	900	1184	1415	71500	594	976	1281	1530
55400	450	749	990	1188	60800	498	827	1088	1302	66200	547	902	1186	1417	71600	595	977	1283	1533
55500	451	751	992	1190	60900	499	828	1090	1305	66300	548	903	1187	1420	71700	596	979	1285	1535
55600	451	752	994	1192	61000	500	829	1092	1307	66400	549	905	1189	1422	71800	597	980	1286	1537
55700	452	754	995	1194	61100	501	830	1094	1309	66500	549	906	1191	1424	71900	598	982	1288	1539
55800	453	755	997	1196	61200	502	832	1096	1311	66600	550	907	1193	1426	72000	599	983	1290	1541
55900	454	756	999	1198	61300	503	833	1098	1313	66700	551	909	1195	1428	72100	600	984	1292	1543
56000	455	758	1001	1200	61400	504	835	1099	1316	66800	552	910	1197	1430	72200	601	986	1294	1545
56100	456	759	1003	1202	61500	504	836	1101	1318	66900	553	912	1198	1433	72300	602	987	1295	1547
56200	457	761	1005	1204	61600	505	838	1103	1320	67000	554	913	1200	1435	72400	602	989	1297	1550
56300	458	762	1006	1206	61700	506	839	1105	1322	67100	555	914	1202	1437	72500	603	990	1299	1552
56400	459	763	1008	1208	61800	507	840	1107	1324	67200	556	916	1204	1439	72600	604	991	1301	1554
56500	460	765	1010	1211	61900	508	842	1109	1326	67300	557	917	1205	1441	72700	605	993	1302	1556
56600	460	766	1012	1213	62000	509	843	1110	1328	67400	558	919	1207	1444	72800	606	994	1304	1558
56700	461	768	1013	1215	62100	510	844	1112	1330	67500	558	920	1209	1446	72900	607	995	1306	1560
56800	462	769	1015	1217	62200	511	846	1114	1332	67600	559	921	1211	1448	73000	608	997	1308	1563
56900	463	770	1017	1219	62300	512	847	1116	1334	67700	560	923	1213	1450	73100	609	998	1310	1565
57000	464	772	1019	1221	62400	513	849	1117	1336	67800	561	924	1215	1452	73200	610	1000	1312	1567
57100	465	773	1021	1223	62500	513	850	1119	1339	67900	562	926	1216	1454	73300	611	1001	1313	1569
57200	466	775	1023	1225	62600	514	852	1121	1341	68000	563	927	1218	1456	73400	611	1003	1315	1572
57300	467	776	1024	1228	62700	515	853	1123	1343	68100	564	928	1220	1458	73500	612	1004	1317	1574
57400	468	778	1026	1230	62800	516	854	1125	1345	68200	565	930	1222	1460	73600	613	1005	1319	1576
57500	469	779	1028	1232	62900	517	856	1127	1347	68300	566	931	1223	1462	73700	614	1007	1320	1578
57600	469	781	1030	1234	63000	518	857	1128	1349	68400	567	933	1225	1464	73800	615	1008	1322	1580
57700	470	782	1031	1236	63100	519	858	1130	1351	68500	567	934	1227	1467	73900	616	1009	1324	1582
57800	471	784	1033	1238	63200	520	860	1132	1353	68600	568	935	1229	1469	74000	617	1011	1326	1584
57900	472	785	1035	1241	63300	521	861	1134	1356	68700	569	937	1231	1471	74100	618	1012	1328	1586
58000	473	787	1037	1243	63400	522	863	1135	1358	68800	570	938	1232	1473	74200	619	1014	1330	1588
58100	474	788	1039	1245	63500	522	864	1137	1360	68900	571	940	1234	1475	74300	620	1015	1331	1590
58200	475	790	1041	1247	63600	523	866	1139	1362	69000	572	941	1236	1477	74400	620	1017	1333	1592
58300	476	791	1042	1249	63700	524	867	1141	1364	69100	573	942	1238	1479	74500	621	1018	1335	1594
58400	477	793	1044	1252	63800	525	868	1143	1366	69200	574	944	1240	1481	74600	622	1019	1337	1597
58500	478	794	1046	1254	63900	526	870	1145	1369	69300	575	945	1241	1484	74700	623	1021	1338	1599
58600	478	796	1048	1256	64000	527	871	1146	1371	69400	575	947	1243	1486	74800	624	1022	1340	1601
58700	479	797	1049	1258	64100	528	872	1148	1373	69500	576	948	1245	1488	74900	625	1023	1342	1603
58800	480	799	1051	1260	64200	529	874	1150	1375	69600	577	949	1247	1490	75000	626	1025	1344	1605
58900	481	800	1053	1262	64300	530	875	1151	1377	69700	578	951	1249	1492	75100	627	1026	1346	1607
59000	482	801	1055	1264	64400	531	877	1153	1380	69800	579	952	1250	1494	75200	628	1028	1348	1609
59100	483	802	1057	1266	64500	531	878	1155	1382	69900	580	954	1252	1497	75300	629	1029	1349	1611
59200	484	804	1059	1268	64600	532	880	1157	1384	70000	581	955	1254	1499	75400	629	1031	1351	1614
59300	485	805	1060	1270	64700	533	881	1159	1386	70100	582	956	1256	1501	75500	630	1032	1353	1616

Federal Child Support Amounts: Simplified Tables
Montants fédéraux de pensions alimentaires pour enfants: Tables simplifiées

Income/ Revenu ($)	Monthly Award/ Paiement mensuel ($) No. of Children/ N^{bre} d'enfants				Income/ Revenu ($)	Monthly Award/ Paiement mensuel ($) No. of Children/ N^{bre} d'enfants				Income/ Revenu ($)	Monthly Award/ Paiement mensuel ($) No. of Children/ N^{bre} d'enfants				Income/ Revenu ($)	Monthly Award/ Paiement mensuel ($) No. of Children/ N^{bre} d'enfants			
	1	2	3	4		1	2	3	4		1	2	3	4		1	2	3	4
75600	631	1033	1355	1618	81000	681	1110	1453	1733	86400	726	1181	1545	1843	91800	773	1252	1636	1951
75700	632	1035	1356	1620	81100	682	1111	1455	1735	86500	727	1182	1546	1845	91900	773	1254	1638	1953
75800	633	1036	1358	1622	81200	683	1113	1457	1737	86600	728	1184	1548	1847	92000	774	1255	1640	1955
75900	634	1037	1360	1624	81300	684	1114	1459	1739	86700	729	1185	1550	1849	92100	775	1256	1642	1957
76000	635	1039	1362	1627	81400	685	1116	1460	1742	86800	730	1186	1551	1851	92200	776	1258	1643	1959
76100	636	1040	1364	1629	81500	686	1117	1462	1744	86900	731	1187	1553	1853	92300	777	1259	1645	1961
76200	637	1042	1366	1631	81600	687	1119	1464	1746	87000	732	1189	1555	1855	92400	777	1260	1647	1963
76300	638	1043	1367	1633	81700	688	1120	1466	1748	87100	733	1190	1557	1857	92500	778	1261	1648	1965
76400	638	1044	1369	1636	81800	689	1122	1468	1750	87200	734	1192	1558	1859	92600	779	1263	1650	1967
76500	639	1046	1371	1638	81900	689	1123	1470	1752	87300	734	1193	1560	1861	92700	780	1264	1652	1969
76600	640	1047	1373	1640	82000	690	1124	1471	1755	87400	735	1194	1562	1863	92800	781	1265	1654	1971
76700	641	1049	1374	1642	82100	691	1125	1473	1757	87500	736	1196	1563	1865	92900	782	1266	1655	1973
76800	642	1050	1376	1644	82200	692	1127	1474	1759	87600	737	1197	1565	1867	93000	783	1268	1657	1975
76900	643	1051	1378	1646	82300	693	1128	1476	1761	87700	738	1199	1567	1869	93100	784	1269	1659	1977
77000	644	1053	1380	1648	82400	693	1129	1478	1763	87800	738	1200	1568	1871	93200	785	1271	1660	1979
77100	645	1054	1382	1650	82500	694	1131	1480	1765	87900	739	1201	1570	1873	93300	785	1272	1662	1981
77200	646	1056	1384	1652	82600	695	1132	1481	1767	88000	740	1203	1572	1875	93400	786	1273	1664	1983
77300	647	1057	1385	1654	82700	696	1133	1483	1769	88100	741	1204	1574	1877	93500	787	1275	1665	1985
77400	648	1058	1387	1656	82800	697	1135	1485	1771	88200	742	1206	1575	1879	93600	788	1276	1667	1987
77500	649	1060	1389	1658	82900	698	1136	1487	1773	88300	743	1207	1577	1881	93700	789	1277	1669	1989
77600	650	1061	1391	1661	83000	698	1137	1488	1775	88400	743	1208	1579	1883	93800	790	1279	1671	1991
77700	651	1063	1392	1663	83100	699	1138	1490	1777	88500	744	1210	1580	1885	93900	790	1280	1672	1993
77800	652	1064	1394	1665	83200	700	1140	1491	1779	88600	745	1211	1582	1887	94000	791	1282	1674	1995
77900	653	1065	1396	1667	83300	701	1141	1493	1781	88700	746	1212	1584	1889	94100	792	1283	1676	1997
78000	654	1067	1398	1669	83400	702	1142	1495	1783	88800	747	1214	1585	1891	94200	793	1285	1677	1999
78100	655	1068	1400	1671	83500	702	1144	1497	1785	88900	748	1215	1587	1893	94300	794	1286	1679	2001
78200	656	1070	1402	1673	83600	703	1145	1498	1787	89000	749	1216	1589	1895	94400	794	1287	1681	2003
78300	657	1071	1404	1675	83700	704	1146	1500	1789	89100	750	1217	1591	1897	94500	795	1289	1683	2005
78400	658	1072	1405	1678	83800	705	1148	1502	1791	89200	751	1219	1592	1899	94600	796	1290	1684	2007
78500	659	1074	1407	1680	83900	706	1149	1504	1793	89300	751	1220	1594	1901	94700	797	1291	1686	2009
78600	660	1075	1409	1682	84000	707	1150	1505	1795	89400	752	1221	1596	1903	94800	798	1293	1688	2011
78700	661	1077	1411	1684	84100	708	1151	1507	1797	89500	753	1223	1597	1905	94900	799	1294	1689	2013
78800	662	1078	1413	1686	84200	709	1153	1508	1799	89600	754	1224	1599	1907	95000	800	1295	1691	2015
78900	663	1079	1415	1688	84300	710	1154	1510	1801	89700	755	1225	1601	1909	95100	801	1296	1693	2017
79000	663	1081	1417	1691	84400	710	1155	1512	1803	89800	755	1227	1602	1911	95200	802	1298	1694	2019
79100	664	1082	1419	1693	84500	711	1157	1513	1805	89900	756	1228	1604	1913	95300	802	1299	1696	2021
79200	665	1084	1421	1695	84600	712	1158	1515	1807	90000	757	1229	1606	1915	95400	803	1300	1698	2023
79300	666	1085	1423	1697	84700	713	1159	1517	1809	90100	758	1230	1608	1917	95500	804	1302	1700	2025
79400	667	1086	1424	1700	84800	714	1161	1518	1811	90200	759	1232	1609	1919	95600	805	1303	1701	2027
79500	668	1088	1426	1702	84900	715	1162	1520	1813	90300	760	1233	1611	1921	95700	806	1304	1703	2029
79600	669	1089	1428	1704	85000	715	1163	1521	1815	90400	760	1234	1613	1923	95800	807	1306	1705	2031
79700	670	1091	1430	1706	85100	716	1164	1523	1817	90500	761	1236	1614	1925	95900	807	1307	1706	2033
79800	671	1092	1432	1708	85200	717	1166	1524	1819	90600	762	1237	1616	1927	96000	808	1308	1708	2035
79900	672	1093	1434	1710	85300	717	1167	1526	1821	90700	763	1238	1618	1929	96100	809	1309	1710	2037
80000	672	1095	1435	1712	85400	718	1168	1528	1823	90800	764	1239	1619	1931	96200	810	1311	1711	2039
80100	673	1096	1437	1714	85500	719	1169	1529	1825	90900	765	1241	1621	1933	96300	811	1312	1713	2041
80200	674	1098	1439	1716	85600	720	1171	1531	1827	91000	766	1242	1623	1935	96400	812	1313	1715	2043
80300	675	1099	1441	1718	85700	721	1172	1533	1829	91100	767	1243	1625	1937	96500	812	1314	1717	2045
80400	676	1101	1442	1720	85800	721	1173	1534	1831	91200	768	1245	1626	1939	96600	813	1316	1718	2047
80500	677	1102	1444	1722	85900	722	1175	1536	1833	91300	768	1246	1628	1941	96700	814	1317	1720	2049
80600	678	1104	1446	1725	86000	723	1176	1538	1835	91400	769	1247	1630	1943	96800	815	1318	1722	2051
80700	679	1105	1448	1727	86100	724	1177	1540	1837	91500	770	1248	1631	1945	96900	816	1320	1723	2053
80800	680	1107	1450	1729	86200	725	1179	1541	1839	91600	771	1250	1633	1947	97000	817	1321	1725	2055
80900	680	1108	1452	1731	86300	726	1180	1543	1841	91700	772	1251	1635	1949	97100	818	1322	1727	2057

Federal Child Support Amounts: Simplified Tables
Montants fédéraux de pensions alimentaires pour enfants: Tables simplifiées

Income/ Revenu ($)	Monthly Award/ Paiement mensuel ($) No. of Children/ Nbre d'enfants				Income/ Revenu ($)	Monthly Award/ Paiement mensuel ($) No. of Children/ Nbre d'enfants				Income/ Revenu ($)	Monthly Award/ Paiement mensuel ($) No. of Children/ Nbre d'enfants				Income/ Revenu ($)	Monthly Award/ Paiement mensuel ($) No. of Children/ Nbre d'enfants			
	1	2	3	4		1	2	3	4		1	2	3	4		1	2	3	4
97200	819	1324	1728	2059	102600	864	1395	1820	2167	108000	910	1466	1911	2275	113400	956	1537	2003	2383
97300	819	1325	1730	2061	102700	865	1396	1822	2169	108100	911	1467	1913	2277	113500	956	1538	2005	2385
97400	820	1326	1732	2063	102800	866	1397	1823	2171	108200	912	1469	1914	2279	113600	957	1540	2006	2387
97500	821	1327	1734	2065	102900	867	1399	1825	2173	108300	912	1470	1916	2281	113700	958	1541	2008	2389
97600	822	1329	1735	2067	103000	868	1400	1826	2175	108400	913	1471	1918	2283	113800	959	1542	2010	2391
97700	823	1330	1737	2069	103100	869	1401	1828	2177	108500	914	1472	1919	2285	113900	960	1544	2011	2393
97800	824	1331	1739	2071	103200	870	1403	1829	2179	108600	915	1474	1921	2287	114000	961	1545	2013	2395
97900	824	1333	1740	2073	103300	871	1404	1831	2181	108700	916	1475	1923	2289	114100	962	1546	2015	2397
98000	825	1334	1742	2075	103400	871	1405	1833	2183	108800	917	1476	1924	2291	114200	963	1548	2016	2399
98100	826	1335	1744	2077	103500	872	1406	1834	2185	108900	917	1478	1926	2293	114300	963	1549	2018	2401
98200	827	1337	1745	2079	103600	873	1408	1836	2187	109000	918	1479	1928	2295	114400	964	1550	2020	2403
98300	828	1338	1747	2081	103700	874	1409	1838	2189	109100	919	1480	1930	2297	114500	965	1551	2022	2405
98400	829	1339	1749	2083	103800	875	1410	1839	2191	109200	920	1482	1931	2299	114600	966	1553	2023	2407
98500	829	1341	1751	2085	103900	876	1411	1841	2193	109300	921	1483	1933	2301	114700	967	1554	2025	2409
98600	830	1342	1752	2087	104000	876	1413	1843	2195	109400	921	1484	1935	2303	114800	968	1555	2027	2411
98700	831	1344	1754	2089	104100	877	1414	1845	2197	109500	922	1486	1936	2305	114900	968	1556	2028	2413
98800	832	1345	1756	2091	104200	878	1416	1846	2199	109600	923	1487	1938	2307	115000	969	1558	2030	2416
98900	833	1346	1758	2093	104300	878	1417	1848	2201	109700	924	1489	1940	2309	115100	970	1559	2032	2418
99000	834	1348	1759	2095	104400	879	1418	1850	2203	109800	925	1490	1941	2311	115200	971	1561	2033	2420
99100	835	1349	1761	2097	104500	880	1420	1851	2205	109900	926	1491	1943	2313	115300	971	1562	2035	2422
99200	836	1351	1762	2099	104600	881	1421	1853	2207	110000	927	1493	1945	2315	115400	972	1563	2036	2424
99300	837	1352	1764	2101	104700	882	1422	1855	2209	110100	928	1494	1947	2317	115500	973	1564	2038	2426
99400	837	1353	1766	2103	104800	882	1424	1856	2211	110200	929	1496	1948	2319	115600	974	1566	2040	2428
99500	838	1355	1768	2105	104900	883	1425	1858	2213	110300	929	1497	1950	2321	115700	974	1567	2041	2430
99600	839	1356	1769	2107	105000	884	1427	1860	2215	110400	930	1498	1952	2323	115800	975	1568	2043	2432
99700	840	1357	1771	2109	105100	885	1428	1862	2217	110500	931	1500	1953	2325	115900	976	1569	2045	2434
99800	841	1359	1773	2111	105200	886	1430	1863	2219	110600	932	1501	1955	2327	116000	977	1571	2046	2435
99900	842	1360	1775	2113	105300	887	1431	1865	2221	110700	933	1502	1957	2329	116100	978	1572	2048	2437
100000	842	1361	1776	2115	105400	887	1432	1867	2223	110800	934	1504	1959	2331	116200	979	1574	2049	2439
100100	843	1362	1778	2117	105500	888	1434	1868	2225	110900	934	1505	1960	2333	116300	980	1575	2051	2441
100200	844	1364	1779	2119	105600	889	1435	1870	2227	111000	935	1506	1962	2335	116400	980	1576	2053	2443
100300	845	1365	1781	2121	105700	890	1436	1872	2229	111100	936	1507	1964	2337	116500	981	1577	2054	2444
100400	846	1366	1783	2123	105800	891	1438	1873	2231	111200	937	1509	1965	2339	116600	982	1579	2056	2446
100500	846	1368	1785	2125	105900	892	1439	1875	2233	111300	938	1510	1967	2341	116700	983	1580	2058	2448
100600	847	1369	1786	2127	106000	893	1440	1877	2235	111400	938	1511	1969	2343	116800	984	1581	2059	2450
100700	848	1370	1788	2129	106100	894	1441	1879	2237	111500	939	1513	1970	2345	116900	985	1582	2061	2452
100800	849	1372	1790	2131	106200	895	1443	1880	2239	111600	940	1514	1972	2347	117000	986	1584	2063	2454
100900	850	1373	1792	2133	106300	895	1444	1882	2241	111700	941	1515	1974	2349	117100	987	1585	2065	2456
101000	851	1374	1793	2135	106400	896	1445	1884	2243	111800	942	1517	1976	2351	117200	988	1587	2066	2458
101100	852	1375	1795	2137	106500	897	1447	1885	2245	111900	943	1518	1977	2353	117300	989	1588	2068	2460
101200	853	1377	1796	2139	106600	898	1448	1887	2247	112000	944	1519	1979	2355	117400	989	1589	2070	2462
101300	854	1378	1798	2141	106700	899	1449	1889	2249	112100	945	1520	1981	2357	117500	990	1590	2071	2464
101400	854	1379	1800	2143	106800	899	1451	1890	2251	112200	946	1522	1982	2359	117600	991	1592	2073	2466
101500	855	1381	1802	2145	106900	900	1452	1892	2253	112300	946	1523	1984	2361	117700	992	1593	2074	2468
101600	856	1382	1803	2147	107000	901	1453	1894	2255	112400	947	1524	1986	2363	117800	993	1594	2076	2470
101700	857	1383	1805	2149	107100	902	1454	1896	2257	112500	948	1526	1988	2365	117900	994	1596	2078	2472
101800	858	1384	1807	2151	107200	903	1456	1897	2259	112600	949	1527	1989	2367	118000	994	1597	2079	2474
101900	859	1386	1809	2153	107300	904	1457	1899	2261	112700	950	1528	1991	2369	118100	995	1598	2081	2476
102000	859	1387	1810	2155	107400	904	1458	1901	2263	112800	951	1529	1993	2371	118200	996	1600	2082	2478
102100	860	1388	1812	2157	107500	905	1460	1902	2265	112900	951	1531	1994	2373	118300	996	1601	2084	2480
102200	861	1390	1813	2159	107600	906	1461	1904	2267	113000	952	1532	1996	2375	118400	997	1602	2086	2482
102300	862	1391	1815	2161	107700	907	1462	1906	2269	113100	953	1533	1998	2377	118500	998	1604	2087	2484
102400	863	1392	1817	2163	107800	908	1463	1907	2271	113200	954	1535	1999	2379	118600	999	1605	2089	2486
102500	863	1393	1818	2165	107900	909	1465	1909	2273	113300	955	1536	2001	2381	118700	1000	1606	2091	2487

SASKATCHEWAN — CONTINUED

Federal Child Support Amounts: Simplified Tables
Montants fédéraux de pensions alimentaires pour enfants: Tables simplifiées

Income/ Revenu ($)	Monthly Award/ Paiement mensuel ($) No. of Children/ N^bre d'enfants				Income/ Revenu ($)	Monthly Award/ Paiement mensuel ($) No. of Children/ N^bre d'enfants				Income/ Revenu ($)	Monthly Award/ Paiement mensuel ($) No. of Children/ N^bre d'enfants				Income/ Revenu ($)	Monthly Award/ Paiement mensuel ($) No. of Children/ N^bre d'enfants				Income/ Revenu ($)	Monthly Award/ Paiement mensuel ($) No. of Children/ N^bre d'enfants			
	1	2	3	4		1	2	3	4		1	2	3	4		1	2	3	4		1	2	3	4
118800	1001	1608	2092	2489	124200	1045	1676	2180	2594	129600	1088	1743	2267	2696	135000	1130	1808	2351	2795
118900	1001	1609	2094	2491	124300	1045	1677	2182	2596	129700	1089	1745	2269	2698	135100	1131	1809	2353	2797
119000	1002	1610	2096	2493	124400	1046	1678	2184	2598	129800	1089	1746	2270	2699	135200	1132	1810	2354	2799
119100	1003	1611	2098	2495	124500	1047	1679	2185	2599	129900	1090	1747	2272	2701	135300	1132	1812	2356	2801
119200	1004	1612	2099	2497	124600	1048	1681	2187	2601	130000	1091	1748	2273	2703	135400	1133	1813	2357	2803
119300	1004	1614	2101	2499	124700	1049	1682	2189	2603	130100	1092	1749	2275	2705	135500	1134	1814	2359	2804
119400	1005	1615	2103	2501	124800	1049	1683	2190	2605	130200	1093	1750	2276	2707	135600	1135	1815	2361	2806
119500	1006	1616	2104	2503	124900	1050	1684	2192	2607	130300	1093	1752	2278	2709	135700	1136	1816	2362	2808
119600	1007	1617	2106	2505	125000	1051	1686	2194	2609	130400	1094	1753	2279	2710	135800	1137	1817	2364	2810
119700	1008	1619	2108	2507	125100	1052	1687	2196	2611	130500	1095	1754	2281	2712	135900	1137	1819	2365	2812
119800	1008	1620	2109	2509	125200	1053	1689	2197	2613	130600	1096	1755	2282	2714	136000	1138	1820	2367	2814
119900	1009	1621	2111	2511	125300	1053	1690	2199	2615	130700	1097	1757	2284	2716	136100	1139	1821	2369	2816
120000	1010	1622	2112	2513	125400	1054	1691	2200	2617	130800	1097	1758	2286	2718	136200	1139	1822	2370	2818
120100	1011	1623	2114	2515	125500	1055	1692	2202	2619	130900	1098	1759	2287	2720	136300	1140	1823	2372	2820
120200	1012	1625	2115	2517	125600	1056	1694	2204	2621	131000	1099	1760	2289	2722	136400	1141	1825	2373	2821
120300	1012	1626	2117	2519	125700	1056	1695	2205	2623	131100	1100	1761	2291	2724	136500	1142	1826	2375	2823
120400	1013	1627	2118	2521	125800	1057	1696	2207	2625	131200	1100	1762	2292	2726	136600	1142	1827	2376	2825
120500	1014	1628	2120	2523	125900	1058	1698	2209	2627	131300	1101	1764	2294	2728	136700	1143	1828	2378	2827
120600	1015	1630	2122	2525	126000	1059	1699	2210	2629	131400	1102	1765	2295	2729	136800	1144	1829	2379	2829
120700	1015	1631	2123	2527	126100	1060	1700	2212	2631	131500	1103	1766	2297	2731	136900	1145	1830	2381	2831
120800	1016	1632	2125	2529	126200	1061	1702	2213	2633	131600	1103	1767	2298	2733	137000	1145	1832	2382	2832
120900	1017	1633	2126	2531	126300	1062	1703	2215	2635	131700	1104	1768	2300	2735	137100	1146	1833	2384	2834
121000	1018	1635	2128	2532	126400	1062	1704	2217	2637	131800	1105	1770	2301	2737	137200	1147	1835	2385	2836
121100	1019	1636	2130	2534	126500	1063	1706	2218	2639	131900	1106	1771	2303	2739	137300	1147	1836	2387	2837
121200	1020	1638	2131	2536	126600	1064	1707	2220	2641	132000	1106	1772	2304	2740	137400	1148	1837	2388	2839
121300	1021	1639	2133	2538	126700	1065	1708	2222	2642	132100	1107	1773	2306	2742	137500	1149	1838	2390	2841
121400	1021	1640	2135	2540	126800	1066	1710	2223	2644	132200	1108	1774	2307	2744	137600	1150	1840	2391	2843
121500	1022	1641	2136	2542	126900	1067	1711	2225	2646	132300	1108	1776	2309	2745	137700	1150	1841	2393	2845
121600	1023	1643	2138	2543	127000	1068	1712	2227	2648	132400	1109	1777	2310	2747	137800	1151	1842	2395	2846
121700	1024	1644	2140	2545	127100	1069	1713	2229	2650	132500	1110	1778	2312	2749	137900	1152	1843	2396	2848
121800	1025	1645	2141	2547	127200	1069	1714	2230	2652	132600	1111	1779	2313	2751	138000	1153	1845	2398	2850
121900	1026	1647	2143	2549	127300	1070	1716	2232	2654	132700	1111	1780	2315	2753	138100	1154	1846	2400	2852
122000	1027	1648	2145	2551	127400	1071	1717	2233	2656	132800	1112	1782	2316	2754	138200	1155	1847	2401	2854
122100	1028	1649	2147	2553	127500	1072	1718	2235	2657	132900	1113	1783	2318	2756	138300	1155	1849	2403	2856
122200	1029	1651	2148	2555	127600	1072	1719	2236	2659	133000	1114	1784	2320	2758	138400	1156	1850	2404	2857
122300	1030	1652	2150	2557	127700	1073	1721	2238	2661	133100	1115	1785	2322	2760	138500	1157	1851	2406	2859
122400	1030	1653	2152	2559	127800	1074	1722	2239	2663	133200	1116	1786	2323	2762	138600	1158	1852	2407	2861
122500	1031	1655	2153	2561	127900	1075	1723	2241	2665	133300	1116	1788	2325	2764	138700	1159	1854	2409	2863
122600	1032	1656	2155	2563	128000	1075	1724	2242	2667	133400	1117	1789	2326	2765	138800	1159	1855	2410	2865
122700	1033	1657	2156	2565	128100	1076	1725	2244	2669	133500	1118	1790	2328	2767	138900	1160	1856	2412	2867
122800	1034	1659	2158	2567	128200	1077	1726	2245	2671	133600	1119	1791	2330	2769	139000	1161	1857	2413	2869
122900	1035	1660	2160	2569	128300	1077	1728	2247	2673	133700	1119	1792	2331	2771	139100	1162	1858	2415	2871
123000	1035	1661	2161	2571	128400	1078	1729	2248	2674	133800	1120	1794	2333	2773	139200	1163	1859	2416	2873
123100	1036	1662	2163	2573	128500	1079	1730	2250	2676	133900	1121	1795	2334	2775	139300	1163	1861	2418	2874
123200	1037	1663	2164	2575	128600	1080	1731	2251	2678	134000	1122	1796	2336	2777	139400	1164	1862	2419	2876
123300	1037	1665	2166	2577	128700	1080	1733	2253	2680	134100	1123	1797	2338	2779	139500	1165	1863	2421	2878
123400	1038	1666	2167	2579	128800	1081	1734	2255	2682	134200	1124	1798	2339	2781	139600	1166	1864	2422	2880
123500	1039	1667	2169	2581	128900	1082	1735	2256	2684	134300	1124	1800	2341	2782	139700	1167	1866	2424	2882
123600	1040	1668	2171	2583	129000	1083	1736	2258	2685	134400	1125	1801	2342	2784	139800	1167	1867	2426	2884
123700	1041	1670	2172	2585	129100	1084	1737	2260	2687	134500	1126	1802	2344	2786	139900	1168	1868	2427	2885
123800	1042	1671	2174	2586	129200	1085	1738	2261	2689	134600	1127	1803	2345	2788	140000	1169	1869	2429	2887
123900	1042	1672	2175	2588	129300	1085	1740	2263	2690	134700	1128	1804	2347	2790	140100	1170	1870	2431	2889
124000	1043	1673	2177	2590	129400	1086	1741	2264	2692	134800	1128	1805	2348	2792	140200	1170	1871	2432	2891
124100	1044	1674	2179	2592	129500	1087	1742	2266	2694	134900	1129	1807	2350	2793	140300	1171	1873	2434	2893

SASKATCHEWAN — CONTINUED

Saskatchewan

Federal Child Support Amounts: Simplified Tables
Montants fédéraux de pensions alimentaires pour enfants: Tables simplifiées

Income/ Revenu ($)	Monthly Award/ Paiement mensuel ($) No. of Children/ Nᵇʳᵉ d'enfants				Income/ Revenu ($)	Monthly Award/ Paiement mensuel ($) No. of Children/ Nᵇʳᵉ d'enfants				Income/ Revenu ($)	Monthly Award/ Paiement mensuel ($) No. of Children/ Nᵇʳᵉ d'enfants			
	1	2	3	4		1	2	3	4		1	2	3	4
140400	1172	1874	2435	2895	143700	1198	1913	2487	2955	147000	1223	1953	2538	3016
140500	1173	1875	2437	2896	143800	1198	1915	2488	2957	147100	1224	1954	2540	3018
140600	1173	1876	2438	2898	143900	1199	1916	2490	2959	147200	1225	1956	2541	3020
140700	1174	1878	2440	2900	144000	1200	1917	2491	2961	147300	1225	1957	2543	3021
140800	1175	1879	2441	2902	144100	1201	1918	2493	2963	147400	1226	1958	2544	3023
140900	1176	1880	2443	2904	144200	1202	1919	2494	2965	147500	1227	1959	2546	3025
141000	1176	1881	2444	2906	144300	1202	1921	2496	2967	147600	1228	1961	2547	3027
141100	1177	1882	2446	2908	144400	1203	1922	2497	2968	147700	1229	1962	2549	3029
141200	1178	1883	2447	2910	144500	1204	1923	2499	2970	147800	1229	1963	2550	3031
141300	1178	1885	2449	2912	144600	1205	1924	2501	2972	147900	1230	1964	2552	3032
141400	1179	1886	2450	2913	144700	1206	1925	2502	2974	148000	1231	1966	2553	3034
141500	1180	1887	2452	2915	144800	1207	1926	2504	2976	148100	1232	1967	2555	3036
141600	1181	1888	2453	2917	144900	1207	1928	2505	2978	148200	1233	1968	2556	3038
141700	1181	1889	2455	2919	145000	1208	1929	2507	2979	148300	1233	1970	2558	3040
141800	1182	1891	2456	2921	145100	1209	1930	2509	2981	148400	1234	1971	2559	3042
141900	1183	1892	2458	2923	145200	1209	1931	2510	2983	148500	1235	1972	2561	3043
142000	1184	1893	2460	2924	145300	1210	1933	2512	2984	148600	1236	1973	2562	3045
142100	1185	1894	2462	2926	145400	1211	1934	2513	2986	148700	1237	1975	2564	3047
142200	1186	1895	2463	2928	145500	1212	1935	2515	2988	148800	1237	1976	2566	3049
142300	1186	1897	2465	2929	145600	1212	1936	2516	2990	148900	1238	1977	2567	3051
142400	1187	1898	2466	2931	145700	1213	1937	2518	2992	149000	1239	1978	2569	3053
142500	1188	1899	2468	2933	145800	1214	1938	2519	2993	149100	1240	1979	2571	3055
142600	1189	1900	2470	2935	145900	1215	1940	2521	2995	149200	1240	1980	2572	3057
142700	1189	1901	2471	2937	146000	1215	1941	2522	2997	149300	1241	1982	2574	3059
142800	1190	1903	2473	2938	146100	1216	1942	2524	2999	149400	1242	1983	2575	3060
142900	1191	1904	2474	2940	146200	1217	1943	2525	3001	149500	1243	1984	2577	3062
143000	1192	1905	2476	2942	146300	1217	1944	2527	3003	149600	1243	1985	2578	3064
143100	1193	1906	2478	2944	146400	1218	1946	2528	3004	149700	1244	1987	2580	3066
143200	1194	1907	2479	2946	146500	1219	1947	2530	3006	149800	1245	1988	2581	3068
143300	1194	1909	2481	2948	146600	1220	1948	2531	3008	149900	1246	1989	2583	3070
143400	1195	1910	2482	2949	146700	1220	1949	2533	3010	150000	1246	1990	2584	3071
143500	1196	1911	2484	2951	146800	1221	1950	2535	3012					
143600	1197	1912	2485	2953	146900	1222	1951	2536	3014					

Monthly Award/Paiement mensuel ($)			
One Child/ Un enfant	**Two Children/ Deux enfants**	**Three Children/ Trois enfants**	**Four Children/ Quatre enfants**
1246 plus 0.74% of income over $150,000	**1990 plus 1.24%** of income over $150,000	**2584 plus 1.52%** of income over $150,000	**3071 plus 1.84%** of income over $150,000
1246 plus 0,74% du revenu dépassant 150 000$	**1990 plus 1,24%** du revenu dépassant 150 000$	**2584 plus 1,52%** du revenu dépassant 150 000$	**3071 plus 1,84%** du revenu dépassant 150 000$

ALBERTA

Federal Child Support Amounts: Simplified Tables
Montants fédéraux de pensions alimentaires pour enfants: Tables simplifiées

Income/ Revenu ($)	Monthly Award/ Paiement mensuel ($) No. of Children/ N^bre d'enfants				Income/ Revenu ($)	Monthly Award/ Paiement mensuel ($) No. of Children/ N^bre d'enfants				Income/ Revenu ($)	Monthly Award/ Paiement mensuel ($) No. of Children/ N^bre d'enfants				Income/ Revenu ($)	Monthly Award/ Paiement mensuel ($) No. of Children/ N^bre d'enfants			
	1	2	3	4		1	2	3	4		1	2	3	4		1	2	3	4
10820	0	0	0	0	16200	148	245	264	282	21600	187	342	465	513	27000	222	402	552	674
10900	4	4	4	5	16300	149	249	267	286	21700	187	344	467	517	27100	223	403	553	676
11000	47	51	55	59	16400	150	252	271	290	21800	188	345	469	522	27200	223	404	555	677
11100	51	55	60	64	16500	152	256	275	294	21900	189	346	471	526	27300	224	405	556	679
11200	55	60	65	69	16600	153	259	279	298	22000	189	347	473	530	27400	225	406	557	681
11300	59	64	69	74	16700	154	263	282	302	22100	190	348	475	534	27500	225	407	559	682
11400	63	69	74	79	16800	155	266	286	306	22200	190	350	476	539	27600	226	408	560	684
11500	67	73	79	84	16900	157	270	290	310	22300	191	351	478	543	27700	227	408	561	686
11600	71	77	84	90	17000	158	273	294	315	22400	192	352	480	547	27800	228	409	563	687
11700	76	82	89	95	17100	158	275	298	319	22500	192	353	481	552	27900	228	410	564	689
11800	80	86	93	100	17200	159	278	302	323	22600	193	355	483	556	28000	229	411	565	691
11900	84	90	98	105	17300	159	280	305	327	22700	194	356	485	561	28100	230	412	566	693
12000	88	95	103	110	17400	160	283	309	331	22800	194	357	486	565	28200	230	413	568	694
12100	91	99	107	114	17500	160	285	313	335	22900	195	359	488	569	28300	231	415	569	696
12200	95	102	111	118	17600	161	288	317	339	23000	196	360	490	574	28400	232	416	570	698
12300	98	106	115	123	17700	161	290	321	343	23100	197	361	492	578	28500	232	417	572	699
12400	101	110	119	127	17800	162	292	325	347	23200	197	362	494	583	28600	233	418	573	701
12500	105	113	123	131	17900	162	295	328	351	23300	198	364	495	587	28700	234	419	574	703
12600	108	117	127	135	18000	162	297	332	355	23400	199	365	497	592	28800	234	421	576	704
12700	111	121	131	140	18100	163	298	336	359	23500	199	366	499	596	28900	235	422	577	706
12800	115	124	135	144	18200	163	299	340	364	23600	200	367	501	600	29000	235	423	578	708
12900	118	128	139	148	18300	164	301	344	368	23700	201	369	502	605	29100	236	424	579	710
13000	121	132	142	152	18400	165	302	348	372	23800	201	370	504	609	29200	236	426	581	712
13100	123	136	146	156	18500	165	303	353	377	23900	202	371	506	613	29300	237	427	582	713
13200	124	139	150	160	18600	166	304	357	381	24000	203	372	508	618	29400	237	428	583	715
13300	126	143	153	164	18700	167	305	361	385	24100	204	373	510	620	29500	238	429	585	717
13400	127	147	157	168	18800	167	307	365	390	24200	204	375	511	622	29600	239	431	586	719
13500	129	150	161	173	18900	168	308	369	394	24300	205	376	513	624	29700	239	432	587	720
13600	130	154	165	177	19000	169	309	373	399	24400	206	377	515	626	29800	240	433	589	722
13700	132	157	169	181	19100	170	310	377	403	24500	206	378	517	629	29900	240	434	590	724
13800	133	161	173	185	19200	170	312	381	408	24600	207	380	518	631	30000	241	436	591	726
13900	135	165	176	189	19300	171	313	385	412	24700	208	381	520	633	30100	242	437	593	728
14000	137	168	180	193	19400	172	314	389	417	24800	209	382	522	635	30200	242	438	594	729
14100	137	172	184	197	19500	173	315	393	421	24900	209	383	524	637	30300	243	440	596	731
14200	138	175	188	201	19600	173	317	397	425	25000	210	385	525	639	30400	244	441	598	733
14300	138	179	192	205	19700	174	318	401	430	25100	211	386	526	641	30500	244	442	600	735
14400	139	182	195	209	19800	175	319	405	434	25200	211	387	528	643	30600	245	443	601	736
14500	139	186	199	213	19900	175	320	409	438	25300	212	388	529	644	30700	246	445	603	738
14600	139	189	203	217	20000	176	322	413	443	25400	212	389	531	646	30800	246	446	605	740
14700	140	193	207	221	20100	177	323	417	447	25500	213	390	532	648	30900	247	447	607	742
14800	140	196	211	226	20200	177	325	421	452	25600	214	391	534	650	31000	248	448	608	743
14900	141	200	215	230	20300	178	326	425	456	25700	214	391	535	652	31100	249	449	610	745
15000	141	203	219	234	20400	179	327	429	461	25800	215	392	536	653	31200	249	450	611	746
15100	141	206	223	238	20500	180	328	433	465	25900	215	393	538	655	31300	250	452	613	748
15200	142	210	226	242	20600	180	330	437	469	26000	216	394	539	657	31400	250	453	615	750
15300	142	213	230	246	20700	181	331	441	474	26100	217	395	540	659	31500	251	454	616	752
15400	143	217	234	250	20800	182	332	445	478	26200	217	396	542	660	31600	252	455	618	753
15500	143	220	238	254	20900	182	334	450	483	26300	218	396	543	662	31700	252	457	619	755
15600	143	224	241	258	21000	183	335	454	487	26400	219	397	544	664	31800	253	458	621	757
15700	144	227	245	262	21100	184	336	456	491	26500	219	398	546	665	31900	253	459	623	759
15800	144	231	249	266	21200	184	337	458	496	26600	220	399	547	667	32000	254	460	624	760
15900	145	234	253	270	21300	185	339	460	500	26700	221	400	548	669	32100	255	461	626	762
16000	145	238	256	274	21400	186	340	462	504	26800	221	401	550	670	32200	255	462	627	764
16100	146	242	260	278	21500	186	341	463	509	26900	222	401	551	672	32300	256	464	629	766

ALBERTA — CONTINUED

Federal Child Support Amounts: Simplified Tables
Montants fédéraux de pensions alimentaires pour enfants: Tables simplifiées

Income/Revenu ($)	Monthly Award/Paiement mensuel ($) No. of Children/N^bre d'enfants				Income/Revenu ($)	Monthly Award/Paiement mensuel ($) No. of Children/N^bre d'enfants				Income/Revenu ($)	Monthly Award/Paiement mensuel ($) No. of Children/N^bre d'enfants				Income/Revenu ($)	Monthly Award/Paiement mensuel ($) No. of Children/N^bre d'enfants			
	1	2	3	4		1	2	3	4		1	2	3	4		1	2	3	4
32400	257	465	630	768	37800	294	531	719	874	43200	344	607	818	989	48600	393	683	916	1105
32500	257	466	632	770	37900	295	532	721	877	43300	345	608	819	991	48700	394	685	917	1107
32600	258	467	633	772	38000	296	534	723	879	43400	345	610	821	993	48800	395	686	919	1110
32700	259	468	635	774	38100	297	535	725	881	43500	346	611	823	995	48900	395	688	921	1112
32800	259	470	636	775	38200	298	537	727	883	43600	347	612	825	997	49000	396	689	923	1114
32900	260	471	638	777	38300	299	538	728	885	43700	348	614	827	999	49100	397	690	925	1116
33000	261	472	640	779	38400	299	540	730	888	43800	349	615	829	1001	49200	398	692	927	1119
33100	262	473	642	781	38500	300	541	732	890	43900	350	617	830	1003	49300	399	693	929	1121
33200	262	474	643	783	38600	301	543	734	892	44000	350	618	832	1006	49400	400	695	931	1123
33300	263	475	645	785	38700	302	544	735	894	44100	351	619	834	1008	49500	400	696	933	1125
33400	263	477	646	787	38800	303	546	737	896	44200	352	621	835	1010	49600	401	698	935	1128
33500	264	478	648	789	38900	304	547	739	898	44300	353	622	837	1012	49700	402	699	937	1130
33600	264	479	649	791	39000	305	548	741	900	44400	353	624	839	1015	49800	403	701	938	1132
33700	265	480	651	793	39100	306	549	743	902	44500	354	625	841	1017	49900	404	702	940	1135
33800	265	481	652	794	39200	307	551	745	904	44600	355	627	842	1019	50000	405	703	942	1137
33900	266	482	654	796	39300	308	552	746	906	44700	356	628	844	1021	50100	406	704	944	1139
34000	266	483	656	798	39400	308	554	748	908	44800	357	629	846	1023	50200	407	706	946	1141
34100	267	484	658	800	39500	309	555	750	911	44900	358	631	848	1025	50300	408	707	948	1144
34200	267	485	659	802	39600	310	557	752	913	45000	359	632	849	1028	50400	409	709	949	1146
34300	268	486	661	804	39700	311	558	753	915	45100	360	633	851	1030	50500	410	710	951	1148
34400	268	487	662	806	39800	312	560	755	917	45200	361	635	853	1032	50600	411	712	953	1150
34500	269	489	664	808	39900	313	561	757	919	45300	362	636	854	1034	50700	412	713	955	1153
34600	269	490	665	810	40000	314	562	759	921	45400	362	638	856	1037	50800	413	715	957	1155
34700	270	491	667	812	40100	315	564	761	923	45500	363	639	858	1039	50900	414	716	959	1157
34800	271	492	668	814	40200	316	565	763	926	45600	364	641	860	1041	51000	415	718	960	1159
34900	271	493	670	815	40300	317	567	765	928	45700	365	642	861	1043	51100	416	719	962	1161
35000	272	494	671	817	40400	318	568	767	930	45800	366	644	863	1045	51200	417	721	964	1163
35100	273	495	673	819	40500	319	570	769	932	45900	367	645	865	1047	51300	418	722	966	1166
35200	273	496	674	821	40600	320	571	771	935	46000	368	646	867	1049	51400	419	724	967	1168
35300	274	497	676	823	40700	321	573	773	937	46100	369	647	869	1051	51500	420	725	969	1170
35400	274	498	677	825	40800	322	574	775	939	46200	370	649	871	1053	51600	420	727	971	1172
35500	275	500	679	827	40900	323	576	777	941	46300	371	650	872	1055	51700	421	728	973	1175
35600	276	501	680	829	41000	324	577	779	944	46400	371	651	874	1058	51800	422	730	975	1177
35700	276	502	682	831	41100	325	578	781	946	46500	372	653	876	1060	51900	423	731	977	1179
35800	277	503	683	833	41200	326	580	782	948	46600	373	654	878	1062	52000	424	733	979	1181
35900	277	504	685	834	41300	327	581	784	950	46700	374	655	879	1064	52100	425	734	981	1183
36000	278	505	687	836	41400	328	582	786	952	46800	375	657	881	1066	52200	426	736	983	1185
36100	279	506	689	838	41500	328	584	788	954	46900	376	658	883	1068	52300	427	737	985	1188
36200	280	508	691	840	41600	329	585	789	957	47000	377	659	885	1070	52400	428	739	986	1190
36300	281	509	692	842	41700	330	586	791	959	47100	378	660	887	1072	52500	429	740	988	1192
36400	281	510	694	844	41800	331	588	793	961	47200	379	662	889	1074	52600	430	742	990	1194
36500	282	512	696	847	41900	332	589	795	963	47300	380	663	891	1077	52700	431	743	992	1196
36600	283	513	698	849	42000	333	590	796	965	47400	381	665	893	1079	52800	432	744	994	1198
36700	284	514	699	851	42100	334	591	798	967	47500	382	666	894	1081	52900	433	746	996	1201
36800	285	516	701	853	42200	335	593	800	969	47600	383	668	896	1083	53000	434	747	998	1203
36900	286	517	703	855	42300	336	594	801	971	47700	384	669	898	1086	53100	435	748	1000	1205
37000	287	519	705	857	42400	337	595	803	973	47800	385	671	900	1088	53200	436	750	1002	1208
37100	288	520	707	859	42500	338	597	805	975	47900	386	672	902	1090	53300	437	751	1004	1210
37200	289	522	709	861	42600	339	598	807	977	48000	387	674	904	1092	53400	438	753	1006	1212
37300	290	523	710	864	42700	339	600	808	979	48100	388	676	906	1094	53500	439	754	1007	1214
37400	290	525	712	866	42800	340	601	810	981	48200	389	677	908	1096	53600	440	756	1009	1217
37500	291	526	714	868	42900	341	602	812	983	48300	390	679	910	1099	53700	440	757	1011	1219
37600	292	528	716	870	43000	342	604	814	985	48400	391	680	912	1101	53800	441	759	1013	1221
37700	293	529	717	872	43100	343	605	816	987	48500	392	682	914	1103	53900	442	760	1015	1223

Federal Child Support Amounts: Simplified Tables
Montants fédéraux de pensions alimentaires pour enfants: Tables simplifiées

Income/ Revenu ($)	Monthly Award/ Paiement mensuel ($) No. of Children/ Nbre d'enfants				Income/ Revenu ($)	Monthly Award/ Paiement mensuel ($) No. of Children/ Nbre d'enfants				Income/ Revenu ($)	Monthly Award/ Paiement mensuel ($) No. of Children/ Nbre d'enfants				Income/ Revenu ($)	Monthly Award/ Paiement mensuel ($) No. of Children/ Nbre d'enfants			
	1	2	3	4		1	2	3	4		1	2	3	4		1	2	3	4
54000	443	762	1017	1226	59400	494	842	1119	1346	64800	545	921	1221	1467	70200	596	1000	1323	1587
54100	444	763	1019	1228	59500	495	843	1121	1348	64900	546	923	1223	1469	70300	597	1001	1325	1590
54200	445	765	1021	1230	59600	496	845	1123	1351	65000	547	924	1225	1471	70400	598	1003	1326	1592
54300	446	766	1023	1233	59700	497	846	1125	1353	65100	548	925	1227	1473	70500	599	1004	1328	1594
54400	447	768	1025	1235	59800	498	848	1127	1355	65200	549	927	1229	1476	70600	600	1006	1330	1596
54500	448	769	1026	1237	59900	499	849	1129	1357	65300	550	928	1231	1478	70700	601	1007	1332	1598
54600	449	771	1028	1239	60000	500	850	1130	1360	65400	551	930	1233	1480	70800	602	1009	1334	1601
54700	450	772	1030	1242	60100	501	851	1132	1362	65500	552	931	1235	1482	70900	603	1010	1336	1603
54800	451	774	1032	1244	60200	502	853	1134	1364	65600	553	933	1236	1485	71000	604	1012	1338	1605
54900	452	775	1034	1246	60300	503	854	1136	1367	65700	554	934	1238	1487	71100	605	1014	1340	1607
55000	453	777	1036	1248	60400	504	856	1137	1369	65800	555	935	1240	1489	71200	606	1015	1342	1610
55100	454	778	1038	1250	60500	505	857	1139	1371	65900	556	937	1242	1491	71300	607	1017	1344	1612
55200	455	780	1040	1252	60600	505	859	1141	1373	66000	557	938	1244	1494	71400	608	1018	1346	1614
55300	456	781	1042	1255	60700	506	860	1143	1376	66100	558	939	1246	1496	71500	609	1020	1347	1616
55400	457	783	1044	1257	60800	507	862	1145	1378	66200	559	941	1248	1498	71600	610	1021	1349	1619
55500	458	784	1045	1259	60900	508	863	1147	1380	66300	560	942	1250	1501	71700	610	1023	1351	1621
55600	459	786	1047	1261	61000	509	865	1149	1382	66400	561	944	1252	1503	71800	611	1024	1353	1623
55700	460	787	1049	1263	61100	510	867	1151	1384	66500	562	945	1254	1505	71900	612	1026	1355	1625
55800	460	788	1051	1265	61200	511	868	1153	1386	66600	563	947	1256	1507	72000	613	1027	1357	1628
55900	461	790	1053	1268	61300	512	870	1155	1389	66700	564	948	1257	1510	72100	614	1028	1359	1630
56000	462	791	1055	1270	61400	513	871	1156	1391	66800	565	950	1259	1512	72200	615	1030	1361	1632
56100	463	792	1057	1272	61500	514	873	1158	1393	66900	565	951	1261	1514	72300	616	1031	1363	1635
56200	464	794	1059	1275	61600	515	874	1160	1395	67000	566	953	1263	1516	72400	617	1033	1365	1637
56300	465	795	1061	1277	61700	516	876	1162	1397	67100	567	954	1265	1518	72500	618	1034	1366	1639
56400	466	797	1063	1279	61800	517	877	1164	1400	67200	568	956	1267	1520	72600	619	1036	1368	1641
56500	467	798	1065	1281	61900	518	879	1166	1402	67300	569	957	1269	1523	72700	620	1037	1370	1644
56600	468	800	1066	1284	62000	519	880	1168	1404	67400	570	959	1271	1525	72800	621	1039	1372	1646
56700	469	801	1068	1286	62100	520	881	1170	1406	67500	570	960	1273	1527	72900	622	1040	1374	1648
56800	470	803	1070	1288	62200	521	883	1172	1409	67600	571	962	1275	1529	73000	623	1041	1376	1650
56900	471	804	1072	1290	62300	522	884	1174	1411	67700	572	963	1277	1531	73100	624	1042	1378	1652
57000	472	806	1074	1293	62400	523	886	1176	1413	67800	573	965	1278	1534	73200	625	1044	1380	1654
57100	473	807	1076	1295	62500	524	887	1177	1415	67900	574	966	1280	1536	73300	626	1045	1382	1657
57200	474	809	1078	1297	62600	525	889	1179	1418	68000	575	968	1282	1538	73400	627	1047	1384	1659
57300	475	810	1080	1300	62700	525	890	1181	1420	68100	576	969	1284	1540	73500	628	1048	1385	1661
57400	476	812	1082	1302	62800	526	892	1183	1422	68200	577	971	1286	1543	73600	629	1050	1387	1663
57500	477	813	1084	1304	62900	527	893	1185	1424	68300	578	972	1288	1545	73700	630	1051	1389	1665
57600	478	815	1086	1306	63000	528	894	1187	1427	68400	579	974	1289	1547	73800	630	1053	1391	1668
57700	479	816	1087	1309	63100	529	895	1189	1429	68500	580	975	1291	1549	73900	631	1054	1393	1670
57800	480	818	1089	1311	63200	530	897	1191	1431	68600	581	977	1293	1552	74000	632	1056	1395	1672
57900	480	819	1091	1313	63300	531	898	1193	1434	68700	582	978	1295	1554	74100	633	1058	1397	1674
58000	481	821	1093	1315	63400	532	900	1195	1436	68800	583	979	1297	1556	74200	634	1059	1399	1677
58100	482	823	1095	1317	63500	533	901	1196	1438	68900	584	981	1299	1558	74300	635	1061	1401	1679
58200	483	824	1097	1319	63600	534	903	1198	1440	69000	585	982	1300	1561	74400	636	1062	1403	1681
58300	484	826	1099	1322	63700	535	904	1200	1443	69100	586	983	1302	1563	74500	637	1064	1405	1683
58400	485	827	1101	1324	63800	536	906	1202	1445	69200	587	985	1304	1565	74600	638	1065	1406	1686
58500	485	829	1103	1326	63900	537	907	1204	1447	69300	588	986	1306	1568	74700	639	1067	1408	1688
58600	486	830	1105	1328	64000	538	909	1206	1449	69400	589	988	1307	1570	74800	640	1068	1410	1690
58700	487	832	1107	1330	64100	539	911	1208	1451	69500	590	989	1309	1572	74900	641	1070	1412	1692
58800	488	833	1108	1333	64200	540	912	1210	1453	69600	590	991	1311	1574	75000	642	1071	1414	1695
58900	489	835	1110	1335	64300	541	914	1212	1456	69700	591	992	1313	1577	75100	643	1072	1416	1697
59000	490	836	1112	1337	64400	542	915	1214	1458	69800	592	994	1315	1579	75200	644	1074	1418	1699
59100	491	837	1114	1339	64500	543	917	1215	1460	69900	593	995	1317	1581	75300	645	1075	1420	1702
59200	492	839	1116	1342	64600	544	918	1217	1462	70000	594	997	1319	1583	75400	646	1077	1422	1704
59300	493	840	1118	1344	64700	545	920	1219	1464	70100	595	998	1321	1585	75500	647	1078	1424	1706

ALBERTA — CONTINUED

Federal Child Support Amounts: Simplified Tables
Montants fédéraux de pensions alimentaires pour enfants: Tables simplifiées

Income/ Revenu ($)	Monthly Award/ Paiement mensuel ($) No. of Children/ N^bre d'enfants 1	2	3	4	Income/ Revenu ($)	Monthly Award/ Paiement mensuel ($) No. of Children/ N^bre d'enfants 1	2	3	4	Income/ Revenu ($)	Monthly Award/ Paiement mensuel ($) No. of Children/ N^bre d'enfants 1	2	3	4	Income/ Revenu ($)	Monthly Award/ Paiement mensuel ($) No. of Children/ N^bre d'enfants 1	2	3	4
75600	648	1080	1426	1708	81000	698	1159	1527	1829	86400	747	1235	1624	1943	91800	795	1309	1720	2057
75700	649	1081	1427	1711	81100	699	1160	1529	1831	86500	747	1236	1626	1946	91900	796	1311	1722	2059
75800	650	1083	1429	1713	81200	700	1162	1531	1833	86600	748	1238	1628	1948	92000	797	1312	1724	2061
75900	650	1084	1431	1715	81300	701	1163	1533	1836	86700	749	1239	1630	1950	92100	798	1313	1726	2063
76000	651	1085	1433	1717	81400	702	1165	1535	1838	86800	750	1240	1631	1952	92200	799	1315	1728	2065
76100	652	1086	1435	1719	81500	703	1166	1536	1840	86900	751	1242	1633	1954	92300	800	1316	1729	2067
76200	653	1088	1437	1721	81600	704	1168	1538	1842	87000	752	1243	1635	1956	92400	800	1317	1731	2069
76300	654	1089	1439	1724	81700	705	1169	1540	1845	87100	753	1244	1637	1958	92500	801	1319	1733	2072
76400	655	1091	1441	1726	81800	706	1170	1542	1847	87200	754	1246	1639	1960	92600	802	1320	1735	2074
76500	655	1092	1443	1728	81900	707	1172	1544	1849	87300	755	1247	1640	1962	92700	803	1321	1737	2076
76600	656	1094	1445	1730	82000	708	1173	1546	1851	87400	756	1248	1642	1964	92800	804	1323	1739	2078
76700	657	1095	1447	1732	82100	709	1174	1548	1853	87500	756	1250	1644	1967	92900	805	1324	1740	2080
76800	658	1097	1448	1735	82200	710	1176	1550	1855	87600	757	1251	1646	1969	93000	805	1325	1742	2082
76900	659	1098	1450	1737	82300	711	1177	1551	1857	87700	758	1252	1648	1971	93100	806	1326	1744	2084
77000	660	1100	1452	1739	82400	712	1178	1553	1859	87800	759	1254	1650	1973	93200	807	1328	1745	2086
77100	661	1102	1454	1741	82500	713	1180	1555	1862	87900	760	1255	1651	1975	93300	808	1329	1747	2088
77200	662	1103	1456	1744	82600	714	1181	1557	1864	88000	761	1256	1653	1977	93400	808	1330	1749	2090
77300	663	1105	1458	1746	82700	715	1183	1559	1866	88100	762	1257	1655	1979	93500	809	1332	1751	2093
77400	664	1106	1459	1748	82800	715	1184	1560	1868	88200	763	1259	1656	1981	93600	810	1333	1752	2095
77500	665	1108	1461	1750	82900	716	1185	1562	1870	88300	764	1260	1658	1983	93700	811	1334	1754	2097
77600	666	1109	1463	1753	83000	717	1187	1564	1872	88400	765	1261	1660	1985	93800	812	1336	1756	2099
77700	667	1111	1465	1755	83100	718	1188	1566	1874	88500	765	1263	1662	1988	93900	813	1337	1758	2101
77800	668	1112	1467	1757	83200	719	1190	1568	1876	88600	766	1264	1663	1990	94000	814	1339	1759	2103
77900	669	1114	1469	1759	83300	720	1191	1569	1878	88700	767	1266	1665	1992	94100	815	1340	1761	2105
78000	670	1115	1470	1762	83400	720	1193	1571	1880	88800	768	1267	1667	1994	94200	816	1342	1763	2107
78100	671	1116	1472	1764	83500	721	1194	1573	1883	88900	769	1268	1669	1996	94300	817	1343	1764	2109
78200	672	1118	1474	1766	83600	722	1195	1575	1885	89000	770	1270	1670	1998	94400	817	1344	1766	2111
78300	673	1119	1476	1769	83700	723	1197	1577	1887	89100	771	1271	1672	2000	94500	818	1346	1768	2114
78400	674	1121	1477	1771	83800	724	1198	1579	1889	89200	772	1273	1674	2002	94600	819	1347	1770	2116
78500	675	1122	1479	1773	83900	725	1199	1580	1891	89300	773	1274	1675	2004	94700	820	1349	1771	2118
78600	675	1124	1481	1775	84000	725	1201	1582	1893	89400	774	1276	1677	2006	94800	821	1350	1773	2120
78700	676	1125	1483	1778	84100	726	1202	1584	1895	89500	775	1277	1679	2009	94900	822	1351	1775	2122
78800	677	1126	1485	1780	84200	727	1204	1585	1897	89600	775	1278	1681	2011	95000	823	1353	1777	2124
78900	678	1128	1487	1782	84300	728	1205	1587	1899	89700	776	1280	1682	2013	95100	824	1354	1779	2126
79000	679	1129	1489	1784	84400	728	1207	1589	1901	89800	777	1281	1684	2015	95200	825	1356	1781	2128
79100	680	1130	1491	1786	84500	729	1208	1591	1904	89900	778	1282	1686	2017	95300	826	1357	1782	2130
79200	681	1132	1493	1788	84600	730	1209	1592	1906	90000	779	1284	1688	2019	95400	827	1359	1784	2132
79300	682	1133	1495	1791	84700	731	1211	1594	1908	90100	780	1285	1690	2021	95500	827	1360	1786	2135
79400	683	1135	1496	1793	84800	732	1212	1596	1910	90200	781	1287	1692	2023	95600	828	1361	1788	2137
79500	684	1136	1498	1795	84900	733	1214	1598	1912	90300	782	1288	1693	2025	95700	829	1363	1790	2139
79600	685	1138	1500	1797	85000	734	1215	1599	1914	90400	783	1290	1695	2027	95800	830	1364	1791	2141
79700	686	1139	1502	1799	85100	735	1216	1601	1916	90500	784	1291	1697	2030	95900	831	1365	1793	2143
79800	687	1141	1504	1802	85200	736	1218	1603	1918	90600	785	1292	1699	2032	96000	832	1367	1795	2145
79900	688	1142	1506	1804	85300	737	1219	1604	1920	90700	785	1294	1700	2034	96100	833	1368	1797	2147
80000	689	1144	1508	1806	85400	737	1221	1606	1922	90800	786	1295	1702	2036	96200	834	1370	1799	2149
80100	690	1145	1510	1808	85500	738	1222	1608	1925	90900	787	1297	1704	2038	96300	835	1371	1800	2151
80200	691	1147	1512	1811	85600	739	1223	1610	1927	91000	788	1298	1706	2040	96400	836	1373	1802	2153
80300	692	1148	1514	1813	85700	740	1225	1611	1929	91100	789	1299	1708	2042	96500	836	1374	1804	2156
80400	693	1150	1516	1815	85800	741	1226	1613	1931	91200	790	1301	1710	2044	96600	837	1375	1806	2158
80500	694	1151	1517	1817	85900	742	1228	1615	1933	91300	791	1302	1711	2046	96700	838	1377	1808	2160
80600	695	1153	1519	1820	86000	743	1229	1617	1935	91400	792	1304	1713	2048	96800	839	1378	1810	2162
80700	695	1154	1521	1822	86100	744	1230	1619	1937	91500	793	1305	1715	2051	96900	840	1380	1811	2164
80800	696	1156	1523	1824	86200	745	1232	1621	1939	91600	794	1306	1717	2053	97000	841	1381	1813	2166
80900	697	1157	1525	1827	86300	746	1233	1622	1941	91700	795	1308	1719	2055	97100	842	1382	1815	2168

Alberta

Federal Child Support Amounts: Simplified Tables
Montants fédéraux de pensions alimentaires pour enfants: Tables simplifiées

Income/ Revenu ($)	Monthly Award/ Paiement mensuel ($) No. of Children/ Nᵇʳᵉ d'enfants 1	2	3	4	Income/ Revenu ($)	Monthly Award/ Paiement mensuel ($) No. of Children/ 1	2	3	4	Income/ Revenu ($)	Monthly Award/ Paiement mensuel ($) No. of Children/ 1	2	3	4	Income/ Revenu ($)	Monthly Award/ Paiement mensuel ($) No. of Children/ 1	2	3	4
97200	843	1384	1816	2170	102600	890	1458	1912	2284	108000	939	1533	2008	2397	113400	987	1608	2104	2510
97300	844	1385	1818	2172	102700	891	1460	1914	2286	108100	940	1534	2010	2399	113500	987	1609	2106	2512
97400	845	1387	1820	2174	102800	892	1461	1916	2288	108200	941	1536	2012	2401	113600	988	1610	2108	2515
97500	845	1388	1822	2177	102900	893	1463	1918	2290	108300	942	1537	2013	2403	113700	989	1612	2110	2517
97600	846	1390	1823	2179	103000	894	1464	1919	2292	108400	943	1539	2015	2405	113800	990	1613	2111	2519
97700	847	1391	1825	2181	103100	895	1465	1921	2294	108500	944	1540	2017	2407	113900	991	1615	2113	2521
97800	848	1392	1827	2183	103200	896	1467	1923	2296	108600	945	1541	2019	2410	114000	992	1616	2115	2523
97900	849	1394	1829	2185	103300	897	1468	1924	2298	108700	945	1543	2020	2412	114100	993	1617	2117	2525
98000	850	1395	1830	2187	103400	897	1470	1926	2300	108800	946	1544	2022	2414	114200	994	1619	2119	2527
98100	851	1396	1832	2189	103500	898	1471	1928	2302	108900	947	1546	2024	2416	114300	995	1620	2120	2529
98200	852	1398	1834	2191	103600	899	1473	1930	2305	109000	948	1547	2026	2418	114400	996	1622	2122	2531
98300	853	1399	1835	2193	103700	900	1474	1931	2307	109100	949	1548	2028	2420	114500	996	1623	2124	2533
98400	854	1400	1837	2195	103800	901	1475	1933	2309	109200	950	1550	2030	2422	114600	997	1624	2126	2536
98500	855	1402	1839	2198	103900	902	1477	1935	2311	109300	951	1551	2031	2424	114700	998	1626	2128	2538
98600	855	1403	1841	2200	104000	903	1478	1937	2313	109400	952	1553	2033	2426	114800	999	1627	2130	2540
98700	856	1404	1842	2202	104100	904	1479	1939	2315	109500	953	1554	2035	2428	114900	1000	1629	2131	2542
98800	857	1406	1844	2204	104200	905	1481	1941	2317	109600	954	1556	2037	2431	115000	1001	1630	2133	2544
98900	858	1407	1846	2206	104300	906	1482	1942	2319	109700	955	1557	2039	2433	115100	1002	1631	2135	2546
99000	859	1408	1848	2208	104400	907	1483	1944	2321	109800	955	1558	2040	2435	115200	1003	1633	2136	2548
99100	860	1409	1850	2210	104500	907	1485	1946	2323	109900	956	1560	2042	2437	115300	1004	1634	2138	2550
99200	861	1411	1852	2212	104600	908	1486	1948	2326	110000	957	1561	2044	2439	115400	1005	1636	2140	2552
99300	862	1412	1853	2214	104700	909	1487	1950	2328	110100	958	1562	2046	2441	115500	1005	1637	2142	2554
99400	863	1413	1855	2216	104800	910	1489	1951	2330	110200	959	1564	2048	2443	115600	1006	1639	2143	2557
99500	864	1415	1857	2219	104900	911	1490	1953	2332	110300	960	1565	2049	2445	115700	1007	1640	2145	2559
99600	865	1416	1859	2221	105000	912	1491	1955	2334	110400	960	1566	2051	2447	115800	1008	1641	2147	2561
99700	865	1417	1860	2223	105100	913	1492	1957	2336	110500	961	1568	2053	2449	115900	1009	1643	2149	2563
99800	866	1419	1862	2225	105200	914	1494	1959	2338	110600	962	1569	2055	2452	116000	1010	1644	2150	2565
99900	867	1420	1864	2227	105300	915	1495	1960	2340	110700	963	1570	2057	2454	116100	1011	1645	2152	2567
100000	868	1422	1866	2229	105400	916	1496	1962	2342	110800	964	1572	2059	2456	116200	1012	1647	2154	2569
100100	869	1423	1868	2231	105500	916	1498	1964	2344	110900	965	1573	2060	2458	116300	1013	1648	2155	2571
100200	870	1425	1870	2233	105600	917	1499	1966	2347	111000	965	1574	2062	2460	116400	1014	1649	2157	2573
100300	871	1426	1871	2235	105700	918	1501	1968	2349	111100	966	1575	2064	2462	116500	1015	1651	2159	2575
100400	872	1427	1873	2237	105800	919	1502	1970	2351	111200	967	1577	2065	2464	116600	1015	1652	2161	2578
100500	873	1429	1875	2240	105900	920	1503	1971	2353	111300	968	1578	2067	2466	116700	1016	1653	2162	2580
100600	874	1430	1877	2242	106000	921	1505	1973	2355	111400	968	1579	2069	2468	116800	1017	1655	2164	2582
100700	875	1432	1879	2244	106100	922	1506	1975	2357	111500	969	1581	2071	2470	116900	1018	1656	2166	2584
100800	875	1433	1880	2246	106200	923	1508	1976	2359	111600	970	1582	2072	2473	117000	1019	1657	2168	2586
100900	876	1434	1882	2248	106300	924	1509	1978	2361	111700	971	1584	2074	2475	117100	1020	1658	2170	2588
101000	877	1436	1884	2250	106400	925	1511	1980	2363	111800	972	1585	2076	2477	117200	1021	1660	2172	2590
101100	878	1437	1886	2252	106500	925	1512	1982	2365	111900	973	1586	2078	2479	117300	1022	1661	2173	2592
101200	879	1439	1888	2254	106600	926	1513	1983	2368	112000	974	1588	2079	2481	117400	1023	1662	2175	2594
101300	880	1440	1889	2256	106700	927	1515	1985	2370	112100	975	1589	2081	2483	117500	1024	1664	2177	2596
101400	880	1442	1891	2258	106800	928	1516	1987	2372	112200	976	1591	2083	2485	117600	1025	1665	2179	2599
101500	881	1443	1893	2261	106900	929	1517	1989	2374	112300	977	1592	2084	2487	117700	1025	1667	2180	2601
101600	882	1444	1895	2263	107000	930	1519	1990	2376	112400	977	1594	2086	2489	117800	1026	1668	2182	2603
101700	883	1446	1897	2265	107100	931	1520	1992	2378	112500	978	1595	2088	2491	117900	1027	1669	2184	2605
101800	884	1447	1899	2267	107200	932	1522	1994	2380	112600	979	1596	2090	2494	118000	1028	1671	2186	2607
101900	885	1448	1900	2269	107300	933	1523	1995	2382	112700	980	1598	2091	2496	118100	1029	1672	2188	2609
102000	885	1450	1902	2271	107400	934	1525	1997	2384	112800	981	1599	2093	2498	118200	1030	1674	2190	2611
102100	886	1451	1904	2273	107500	935	1526	1999	2386	112900	982	1600	2095	2500	118300	1031	1675	2191	2613
102200	887	1453	1905	2275	107600	935	1527	2001	2389	113000	983	1602	2097	2502	118400	1032	1677	2193	2615
102300	888	1454	1907	2277	107700	936	1529	2002	2391	113100	984	1603	2099	2504	118500	1033	1678	2195	2617
102400	888	1456	1909	2279	107800	937	1530	2004	2393	113200	985	1605	2101	2506	118600	1034	1679	2197	2619
102500	889	1457	1911	2281	107900	938	1532	2006	2395	113300	986	1606	2102	2508	118700	1035	1681	2199	2622

Federal Child Support Amounts: Simplified Tables
Montants fédéraux de pensions alimentaires pour enfants: Tables simplifiées

Alberta

Income/ Revenu ($)	Monthly Award/ Paiement mensuel ($) No. of Children/ Nbre d'enfants				Income/ Revenu ($)	Monthly Award/ Paiement mensuel ($) No. of Children/ Nbre d'enfants				Income/ Revenu ($)	Monthly Award/ Paiement mensuel ($) No. of Children/ Nbre d'enfants				Income/ Revenu ($)	Monthly Award/ Paiement mensuel ($) No. of Children/ Nbre d'enfants			
	1	2	3	4		1	2	3	4		1	2	3	4		1	2	3	4
118800	1035	1682	2200	2624	124200	1083	1757	2296	2737	129600	1130	1830	2390	2848	135000	1175	1901	2482	2956
118900	1036	1683	2202	2626	124300	1084	1758	2298	2739	129700	1131	1831	2392	2850	135100	1176	1902	2484	2958
119000	1037	1685	2204	2628	124400	1085	1760	2300	2741	129800	1132	1832	2394	2852	135200	1177	1904	2485	2960
119100	1038	1686	2206	2630	124500	1085	1761	2302	2743	129900	1133	1834	2395	2854	135300	1178	1905	2487	2962
119200	1039	1688	2208	2632	124600	1086	1762	2303	2745	130000	1133	1835	2397	2856	135400	1178	1906	2489	2964
119300	1040	1689	2209	2634	124700	1087	1764	2305	2748	130100	1134	1836	2399	2858	135500	1179	1907	2490	2966
119400	1040	1691	2211	2636	124800	1088	1765	2307	2750	130200	1135	1838	2400	2860	135600	1180	1909	2492	2968
119500	1041	1692	2213	2638	124900	1089	1766	2309	2752	130300	1136	1839	2402	2862	135700	1181	1910	2494	2970
119600	1042	1693	2215	2640	125000	1090	1768	2310	2754	130400	1137	1840	2404	2864	135800	1182	1911	2495	2972
119700	1043	1695	2217	2643	125100	1091	1769	2312	2756	130500	1137	1841	2406	2866	135900	1183	1913	2497	2974
119800	1044	1696	2219	2645	125200	1092	1771	2314	2758	130600	1138	1843	2407	2868	136000	1184	1914	2498	2977
119900	1045	1698	2220	2647	125300	1093	1772	2315	2760	130700	1139	1844	2409	2870	136100	1185	1915	2500	2979
120000	1045	1699	2222	2649	125400	1094	1774	2317	2762	130800	1140	1845	2411	2872	136200	1186	1917	2501	2981
120100	1046	1700	2224	2651	125500	1095	1775	2319	2764	130900	1141	1847	2412	2874	136300	1186	1918	2503	2983
120200	1047	1702	2225	2653	125600	1095	1776	2321	2766	131000	1142	1848	2414	2876	136400	1187	1919	2505	2985
120300	1048	1703	2227	2655	125700	1096	1778	2322	2769	131100	1143	1849	2416	2878	136500	1188	1920	2506	2987
120400	1048	1705	2229	2657	125800	1097	1779	2324	2771	131200	1144	1851	2417	2880	136600	1189	1922	2508	2989
120500	1049	1706	2231	2659	125900	1098	1781	2326	2773	131300	1145	1852	2419	2882	136700	1190	1923	2510	2991
120600	1050	1708	2232	2661	126000	1099	1782	2328	2775	131400	1145	1853	2421	2884	136800	1190	1924	2511	2993
120700	1051	1709	2234	2664	126100	1100	1783	2330	2777	131500	1146	1855	2423	2886	136900	1191	1925	2513	2995
120800	1052	1710	2236	2666	126200	1101	1785	2332	2779	131600	1147	1856	2424	2888	137000	1192	1927	2515	2997
120900	1053	1712	2238	2668	126300	1102	1786	2333	2781	131700	1148	1858	2426	2890	137100	1193	1928	2517	2999
121000	1054	1713	2239	2670	126400	1103	1788	2335	2783	131800	1149	1859	2428	2892	137200	1194	1930	2518	3001
121100	1055	1714	2241	2672	126500	1104	1789	2337	2785	131900	1150	1860	2430	2894	137300	1195	1931	2520	3003
121200	1056	1716	2243	2674	126600	1105	1791	2339	2787	132000	1150	1862	2431	2896	137400	1195	1932	2522	3005
121300	1057	1717	2244	2676	126700	1105	1792	2340	2790	132100	1151	1863	2433	2898	137500	1196	1934	2523	3007
121400	1057	1718	2246	2678	126800	1106	1793	2342	2792	132200	1152	1865	2434	2900	137600	1197	1935	2525	3009
121500	1058	1720	2248	2680	126900	1107	1795	2344	2794	132300	1153	1866	2436	2902	137700	1198	1937	2527	3011
121600	1059	1721	2250	2682	127000	1108	1796	2346	2796	132400	1154	1867	2438	2904	137800	1199	1938	2528	3013
121700	1060	1722	2251	2685	127100	1109	1797	2348	2798	132500	1154	1869	2440	2906	137900	1200	1939	2530	3015
121800	1061	1724	2253	2687	127200	1110	1799	2349	2800	132600	1155	1870	2441	2908	138000	1201	1941	2532	3017
121900	1062	1725	2255	2689	127300	1110	1800	2351	2802	132700	1156	1871	2443	2910	138100	1202	1942	2534	3019
122000	1063	1726	2257	2691	127400	1111	1801	2353	2804	132800	1157	1873	2445	2912	138200	1203	1944	2535	3021
122100	1064	1727	2259	2693	127500	1112	1803	2355	2806	132900	1158	1874	2447	2914	138300	1203	1945	2537	3023
122200	1065	1729	2261	2695	127600	1113	1804	2356	2808	133000	1159	1875	2448	2916	138400	1204	1946	2539	3025
122300	1066	1730	2262	2697	127700	1114	1805	2358	2810	133100	1160	1876	2450	2918	138500	1205	1948	2540	3027
122400	1067	1731	2264	2699	127800	1115	1807	2360	2812	133200	1161	1878	2451	2920	138600	1206	1949	2542	3029
122500	1067	1733	2266	2701	127900	1115	1808	2361	2814	133300	1162	1879	2453	2922	138700	1207	1950	2544	3031
122600	1068	1734	2268	2703	128000	1116	1809	2363	2816	133400	1162	1880	2455	2924	138800	1207	1952	2545	3033
122700	1069	1735	2270	2706	128100	1117	1810	2365	2818	133500	1163	1882	2457	2926	138900	1208	1953	2547	3035
122800	1070	1737	2271	2708	128200	1118	1812	2366	2820	133600	1164	1883	2458	2928	139000	1209	1954	2549	3037
122900	1071	1738	2273	2710	128300	1119	1813	2368	2822	133700	1165	1884	2460	2930	139100	1210	1955	2551	3039
123000	1072	1740	2275	2712	128400	1120	1814	2370	2824	133800	1166	1886	2462	2932	139200	1211	1957	2552	3041
123100	1073	1741	2277	2714	128500	1120	1816	2372	2826	133900	1167	1887	2464	2934	139300	1212	1958	2554	3043
123200	1074	1743	2279	2716	128600	1121	1817	2373	2828	134000	1167	1888	2465	2936	139400	1212	1959	2556	3045
123300	1075	1744	2280	2718	128700	1122	1818	2375	2830	134100	1168	1889	2467	2938	139500	1213	1961	2557	3047
123400	1076	1745	2282	2720	128800	1123	1820	2377	2832	134200	1169	1891	2468	2940	139600	1214	1962	2559	3049
123500	1076	1747	2284	2722	128900	1124	1821	2378	2834	134300	1169	1892	2470	2942	139700	1215	1963	2561	3051
123600	1077	1748	2286	2724	129000	1125	1822	2380	2836	134400	1170	1893	2472	2944	139800	1216	1965	2562	3053
123700	1078	1750	2288	2727	129100	1126	1823	2382	2838	134500	1171	1895	2474	2946	139900	1217	1966	2564	3055
123800	1079	1751	2290	2729	129200	1127	1825	2383	2840	134600	1172	1896	2475	2948	140000	1218	1967	2566	3057
123900	1080	1752	2291	2731	129300	1128	1826	2385	2842	134700	1173	1897	2477	2950	140100	1219	1968	2568	3059
124000	1081	1754	2293	2733	129400	1128	1827	2387	2844	134800	1173	1898	2479	2952	140200	1220	1970	2569	3061
124100	1082	1755	2295	2735	129500	1129	1829	2389	2846	134900	1174	1900	2481	2954	140300	1220	1971	2571	3063

81

Alberta

Federal Child Support Amounts: Simplified Tables
Montants fédéraux de pensions alimentaires pour enfants: Tables simplifiées

Income/ Revenu ($)	Monthly Award/ Paiement mensuel ($) No. of Children/ N^{bre} d'enfants				Income/ Revenu ($)	Monthly Award/ Paiement mensuel ($) No. of Children/ N^{bre} d'enfants				Income/ Revenu ($)	Monthly Award/ Paiement mensuel ($) No. of Children/ N^{bre} d'enfants			
	1	2	3	4		1	2	3	4		1	2	3	4
140400	1221	1972	2573	3065	143700	1249	2015	2629	3131	147000	1277	2059	2685	3197
140500	1222	1974	2574	3067	143800	1250	2017	2631	3133	147100	1278	2060	2687	3199
140600	1223	1975	2576	3069	143900	1251	2018	2632	3135	147200	1279	2062	2688	3201
140700	1224	1976	2578	3071	144000	1252	2020	2634	3137	147300	1280	2063	2690	3203
140800	1225	1977	2579	3073	144100	1253	2021	2636	3139	147400	1281	2064	2692	3205
140900	1225	1979	2581	3075	144200	1254	2023	2637	3141	147500	1281	2065	2694	3207
141000	1226	1980	2583	3077	144300	1254	2024	2639	3143	147600	1282	2067	2695	3209
141100	1227	1981	2585	3079	144400	1255	2025	2641	3145	147700	1283	2068	2697	3211
141200	1228	1983	2586	3081	144500	1256	2027	2642	3147	147800	1284	2069	2699	3213
141300	1229	1984	2588	3083	144600	1257	2028	2644	3149	147900	1285	2071	2700	3215
141400	1229	1985	2590	3085	144700	1258	2029	2646	3151	148000	1286	2072	2702	3217
141500	1230	1986	2591	3087	144800	1259	2031	2648	3153	148100	1287	2073	2704	3219
141600	1231	1988	2593	3089	144900	1259	2032	2649	3155	148200	1288	2075	2705	3221
141700	1232	1989	2595	3091	145000	1260	2033	2651	3157	148300	1289	2076	2707	3223
141800	1233	1990	2596	3093	145100	1261	2034	2653	3159	148400	1289	2077	2709	3225
141900	1234	1992	2598	3095	145200	1262	2036	2654	3161	148500	1290	2079	2711	3227
142000	1235	1993	2600	3097	145300	1263	2037	2656	3163	148600	1291	2080	2712	3229
142100	1236	1994	2602	3099	145400	1264	2038	2658	3165	148700	1292	2082	2714	3231
142200	1237	1996	2603	3101	145500	1264	2040	2660	3167	148800	1293	2083	2716	3233
142300	1237	1997	2605	3103	145600	1265	2041	2661	3169	148900	1294	2084	2717	3235
142400	1238	1998	2607	3105	145700	1266	2042	2663	3171	149000	1294	2086	2719	3237
142500	1239	1999	2608	3107	145800	1267	2044	2665	3173	149100	1295	2087	2721	3239
142600	1240	2001	2610	3109	145900	1268	2045	2666	3175	149200	1296	2089	2722	3241
142700	1241	2002	2612	3111	146000	1269	2046	2668	3177	149300	1297	2090	2724	3243
142800	1242	2003	2613	3113	146100	1270	2047	2670	3179	149400	1298	2091	2726	3245
142900	1242	2004	2615	3115	146200	1271	2049	2671	3181	149500	1298	2093	2728	3247
143000	1243	2006	2617	3117	146300	1272	2050	2673	3183	149600	1299	2094	2729	3249
143100	1244	2007	2619	3119	146400	1272	2051	2675	3185	149700	1300	2095	2731	3251
143200	1245	2009	2620	3121	146500	1273	2052	2677	3187	149800	1301	2097	2733	3253
143300	1246	2010	2622	3123	146600	1274	2054	2678	3189	149900	1302	2098	2735	3255
143400	1247	2011	2624	3125	146700	1275	2055	2680	3191	150000	1303	2099	2736	3257
143500	1247	2013	2625	3127	146800	1276	2056	2682	3193					
143600	1248	2014	2627	3129	146900	1277	2058	2683	3195					

Monthly Award/Paiement mensuel ($)			
One Child/ Un enfant	Two Children/ Deux enfants	Three Children/ Trois enfants	Four Children/ Quatre enfants
1303 plus 0.90% of income over $150,000	2099 plus 1.34% of income over $150,000	2736 plus 1.72% of income over $150,000	3257 plus 2.02% of income over $150,000
1303 plus 0,90% du revenu dépassant 150 000$	2099 plus 1,34% du revenu dépassant 150 000$	2736 plus 1,72% du revenu dépassant 150 000$	3257 plus 2,02% du revenu dépassant 150 000$

NEWFOUNDLAND & LABRADOR

Federal Child Support Amounts: Simplified Tables
Montants fédéraux de pensions alimentaires pour enfants: Tables simplifiées

Income/ Revenu ($)	Monthly Award/ Paiement mensuel ($) No. of Children/ N^bre d'enfants				Income/ Revenu ($)	Monthly Award/ Paiement mensuel ($) No. of Children/ N^bre d'enfants				Income/ Revenu ($)	Monthly Award/ Paiement mensuel ($) No. of Children/ N^bre d'enfants				Income/ Revenu ($)	Monthly Award/ Paiement mensuel ($) No. of Children/ N^bre d'enfants			
	1	2	3	4		1	2	3	4		1	2	3	4		1	2	3	4
10820	0	0	0	0	16200	135	234	252	270	21600	154	307	430	475	27000	199	377	525	647
10900	3	4	4	4	16300	136	236	255	273	21700	155	309	431	480	27100	201	379	527	649
11000	42	45	49	52	16400	136	239	257	275	21800	155	310	433	484	27200	202	381	529	652
11100	46	49	54	57	16500	136	241	260	278	21900	156	312	435	489	27300	204	382	531	654
11200	50	54	58	62	16600	136	244	263	281	22000	157	313	437	493	27400	205	384	533	657
11300	54	58	63	67	16700	136	246	265	284	22100	158	314	439	498	27500	207	386	535	659
11400	58	63	68	72	16800	136	249	268	287	22200	159	316	441	502	27600	208	388	537	662
11500	62	67	72	77	16900	137	251	271	290	22300	159	317	443	507	27700	210	390	539	664
11600	66	71	77	82	17000	137	254	273	293	22400	160	318	444	511	27800	211	391	542	667
11700	70	76	81	87	17100	137	256	276	297	22500	161	320	446	516	27900	213	393	544	669
11800	74	80	86	92	17200	137	257	280	300	22600	162	321	448	520	28000	215	395	546	671
11900	78	84	91	97	17300	137	259	283	304	22700	163	322	450	525	28100	217	397	548	673
12000	82	89	95	102	17400	138	261	286	307	22800	163	324	452	529	28200	218	399	550	676
12100	85	93	99	106	17500	138	263	289	311	22900	164	325	454	534	28300	220	401	552	678
12200	89	96	103	110	17600	138	264	293	314	23000	165	326	456	538	28400	221	403	554	681
12300	92	100	107	115	17700	138	266	296	318	23100	166	327	458	543	28500	223	405	557	683
12400	95	104	111	119	17800	138	268	299	321	23200	167	329	460	547	28600	225	407	559	686
12500	99	107	115	123	17900	138	270	303	325	23300	167	330	462	552	28700	226	409	561	688
12600	102	111	119	127	18000	138	271	306	328	23400	168	331	463	556	28800	228	411	563	690
12700	105	114	123	131	18100	138	272	309	332	23500	169	333	465	561	28900	229	413	565	693
12800	109	118	127	135	18200	138	272	313	335	23600	170	334	467	565	29000	231	415	567	695
12900	112	122	131	140	18300	138	273	316	339	23700	171	336	469	570	29100	233	417	569	697
13000	115	125	135	144	18400	138	273	319	342	23800	172	337	471	574	29200	234	419	571	700
13100	117	129	139	148	18500	139	274	323	346	23900	172	338	473	579	29300	236	421	573	702
13200	119	132	143	152	18600	139	274	326	349	24000	173	340	474	583	29400	237	423	575	705
13300	120	136	146	157	18700	139	275	329	353	24100	174	341	476	585	29500	239	425	577	707
13400	122	139	150	161	18800	139	275	332	356	24200	175	343	478	588	29600	240	427	579	709
13500	124	143	154	165	18900	139	276	336	360	24300	175	344	479	590	29700	242	430	581	712
13600	126	147	158	169	19000	139	276	339	363	24400	176	346	481	592	29800	243	432	583	714
13700	127	150	162	173	19100	139	277	343	367	24500	177	347	483	595	29900	245	434	585	717
13800	129	154	166	177	19200	139	278	346	371	24600	178	348	485	597	30000	246	436	587	719
13900	131	157	169	182	19300	140	279	350	375	24700	179	350	487	599	30100	248	438	589	721
14000	133	161	173	186	19400	140	280	354	379	24800	180	351	488	601	30200	249	440	592	724
14100	133	164	177	190	19500	140	280	358	383	24900	180	353	490	604	30300	251	442	594	726
14200	133	168	181	194	19600	140	281	361	387	25000	181	354	492	606	30400	252	444	597	729
14300	133	171	185	198	19700	140	282	365	391	25100	182	355	494	608	30500	254	446	599	731
14400	134	175	188	202	19800	140	283	369	395	25200	183	357	496	610	30600	255	448	602	733
14500	134	178	192	207	19900	141	284	373	399	25300	184	358	497	612	30700	257	450	604	736
14600	134	182	196	211	20000	141	285	376	403	25400	185	359	499	615	30800	259	452	607	738
14700	134	185	200	215	20100	142	286	380	408	25500	186	361	501	617	30900	260	454	609	740
14800	134	189	204	219	20200	143	288	384	412	25600	187	362	503	619	31000	262	456	612	743
14900	134	192	208	223	20300	143	289	389	417	25700	188	363	504	621	31100	264	458	614	745
15000	134	196	212	227	20400	144	290	393	421	25800	189	365	506	623	31200	265	460	617	748
15100	134	199	216	231	20500	145	292	397	426	25900	189	366	508	625	31300	267	462	619	750
15200	134	203	219	234	20600	146	293	401	430	26000	190	367	510	627	31400	268	464	621	752
15300	134	206	223	238	20700	146	295	406	435	26100	191	368	512	629	31500	270	466	624	754
15400	134	209	226	242	20800	147	296	410	439	26200	192	369	513	631	31600	271	468	626	757
15500	135	212	230	246	20900	148	297	414	444	26300	193	370	515	633	31700	273	470	628	759
15600	135	216	233	249	21000	149	299	418	448	26400	193	371	516	635	31800	274	472	631	761
15700	135	219	237	253	21100	150	300	420	453	26500	194	372	518	637	31900	276	474	633	763
15800	135	222	240	257	21200	151	302	422	457	26600	195	373	519	639	32000	277	476	635	766
15900	135	225	244	261	21300	151	303	424	462	26700	196	374	521	641	32100	278	477	637	768
16000	135	229	247	264	21400	152	305	426	466	26800	197	375	522	643	32200	279	479	639	770
16100	135	231	250	267	21500	153	306	428	471	26900	198	376	524	645	32300	280	480	641	772

83

NEWFOUNDLAND & LABRADOR — CONTINUED

Federal Child Support Amounts: Simplified Tables
Montants fédéraux de pensions alimentaires pour enfants: Tables simplifiées

Income/ Revenu ($)	Monthly Award/ Paiement mensuel ($) No. of Children/ Nbre d'enfants				Income/ Revenu ($)	Monthly Award/ Paiement mensuel ($) No. of Children/ Nbre d'enfants				Income/ Revenu ($)	Monthly Award/ Paiement mensuel ($) No. of Children/ Nbre d'enfants				Income/ Revenu ($)	Monthly Award/ Paiement mensuel ($) No. of Children/ Nbre d'enfants				Income/ Revenu ($)	Monthly Award/ Paiement mensuel ($) No. of Children/ Nbre d'enfants			
	1	2	3	4		1	2	3	4		1	2	3	4		1	2	3	4		1	2	3	4
32400	281	482	642	774	37800	328	554	737	885	43200	375	628	829	995	48600	422	700	924	1106					
32500	282	483	644	776	37900	328	556	739	887	43300	375	629	831	997	48700	422	702	926	1108					
32600	282	484	646	778	38000	329	557	740	889	43400	376	630	833	999	48800	423	703	928	1110					
32700	283	486	648	780	38100	330	558	742	891	43500	377	632	834	1001	48900	424	705	929	1112					
32800	284	487	650	783	38200	331	560	743	893	43600	378	633	836	1003	49000	425	706	931	1115					
32900	285	489	652	785	38300	332	561	745	895	43700	379	634	838	1005	49100	426	707	933	1117					
33000	286	490	654	787	38400	332	562	747	897	43800	380	636	839	1007	49200	427	709	935	1119					
33100	287	491	656	789	38500	333	564	749	899	43900	380	637	841	1009	49300	428	710	936	1121					
33200	288	493	657	791	38600	334	565	750	902	44000	381	638	843	1012	49400	429	712	938	1123					
33300	289	494	659	793	38700	335	566	752	904	44100	382	639	845	1014	49500	430	713	940	1126					
33400	290	495	661	795	38800	336	568	754	906	44200	383	641	847	1016	49600	430	714	942	1128					
33500	290	497	663	797	38900	337	569	755	908	44300	384	642	848	1018	49700	431	716	944	1130					
33600	291	498	664	799	39000	338	571	757	910	44400	385	643	850	1020	49800	432	717	946	1132					
33700	292	500	666	801	39100	339	572	759	912	44500	385	644	852	1022	49900	433	719	947	1134					
33800	293	501	668	803	39200	340	574	761	914	44600	386	646	854	1024	50000	434	720	949	1136					
33900	294	502	670	805	39300	341	575	762	916	44700	387	647	855	1026	50100	435	721	951	1138					
34000	295	504	671	807	39400	342	576	764	918	44800	388	648	857	1028	50200	436	723	953	1140					
34100	296	505	673	809	39500	342	578	766	920	44900	389	650	859	1030	50300	437	724	954	1143					
34200	297	507	674	811	39600	343	579	768	922	45000	390	651	861	1032	50400	438	726	956	1145					
34300	298	508	676	813	39700	344	580	769	924	45100	391	652	863	1034	50500	439	727	958	1147					
34400	299	509	678	815	39800	345	581	771	926	45200	392	654	864	1036	50600	439	728	960	1149					
34500	300	511	680	817	39900	346	583	773	928	45300	392	655	866	1038	50700	440	730	962	1151					
34600	300	512	681	819	40000	347	584	775	930	45400	393	656	868	1040	50800	441	731	963	1153					
34700	301	513	683	821	40100	348	585	777	932	45500	394	658	870	1042	50900	442	733	965	1156					
34800	302	515	685	823	40200	349	587	779	934	45600	395	659	871	1044	51000	443	734	967	1158					
34900	303	516	686	825	40300	350	588	781	937	45700	396	661	873	1046	51100	444	735	969	1160					
35000	304	517	688	828	40400	351	590	782	939	45800	397	662	875	1048	51200	445	737	971	1162					
35100	305	518	690	830	40500	352	591	784	941	45900	397	663	877	1050	51300	446	738	972	1164					
35200	306	520	691	832	40600	353	593	786	943	46000	398	665	878	1052	51400	447	740	974	1167					
35300	307	521	693	834	40700	353	594	788	945	46100	399	666	880	1054	51500	447	741	976	1169					
35400	307	523	695	836	40800	354	596	790	948	46200	400	668	881	1056	51600	448	742	978	1171					
35500	308	524	696	838	40900	355	597	792	950	46300	401	669	883	1058	51700	449	744	979	1173					
35600	309	525	698	840	41000	356	599	793	952	46400	401	670	885	1060	51800	450	745	981	1175					
35700	310	527	700	842	41100	357	600	795	954	46500	402	672	887	1062	51900	451	746	983	1177					
35800	311	528	702	844	41200	358	602	796	956	46600	403	673	888	1064	52000	452	748	985	1179					
35900	312	529	703	846	41300	358	603	798	958	46700	404	674	890	1066	52100	453	749	987	1181					
36000	312	531	705	848	41400	359	604	800	960	46800	405	676	892	1068	52200	454	751	989	1183					
36100	313	532	707	850	41500	360	606	801	962	46900	406	677	894	1070	52300	455	752	990	1186					
36200	314	534	709	852	41600	361	607	803	964	47000	407	678	895	1072	52400	456	753	992	1188					
36300	315	535	710	854	41700	362	608	805	966	47100	408	679	897	1074	52500	456	755	994	1190					
36400	316	536	712	856	41800	362	610	807	968	47200	409	681	899	1076	52600	457	756	996	1192					
36500	316	538	714	858	41900	363	611	808	970	47300	410	682	900	1078	52700	458	758	997	1194					
36600	317	539	716	860	42000	364	612	810	972	47400	411	684	902	1080	52800	459	759	999	1196					
36700	318	540	717	862	42100	365	613	812	974	47500	412	685	904	1082	52900	460	760	1001	1199					
36800	319	542	719	865	42200	366	615	813	976	47600	412	686	906	1085	53000	461	762	1003	1201					
36900	320	543	721	867	42300	367	616	815	978	47700	413	688	908	1087	53100	462	763	1005	1203					
37000	321	544	723	869	42400	367	617	817	980	47800	414	689	910	1089	53200	463	765	1007	1205					
37100	322	545	725	871	42500	368	619	818	982	47900	415	691	911	1091	53300	464	766	1009	1207					
37200	323	547	726	873	42600	369	620	820	984	48000	416	692	913	1093	53400	465	768	1010	1210					
37300	323	548	728	875	42700	370	621	821	986	48100	417	693	915	1095	53500	465	769	1012	1212					
37400	324	549	730	877	42800	371	623	823	987	48200	418	695	917	1097	53600	466	771	1014	1214					
37500	325	550	732	879	42900	372	624	825	989	48300	419	696	918	1099	53700	467	772	1016	1216					
37600	326	552	733	881	43000	373	625	826	991	48400	420	698	920	1102	53800	468	774	1018	1218					
37700	327	553	735	883	43100	374	626	828	993	48500	421	699	922	1104	53900	469	775	1020	1220					

NEWFOUNDLAND & LABRADOR — CONTINUED

Federal Child Support Amounts: Simplified Tables
Montants fédéraux de pensions alimentaires pour enfants: Tables simplifiées

Newfoundland & Labrador / Terre-Neuve-et-Labrador

Income/ Revenu ($)	Monthly Award/ Paiement mensuel ($) No. of Children/ Nbre d'enfants				Income/ Revenu ($)	Monthly Award/ Paiement mensuel ($) No. of Children/ Nbre d'enfants				Income/ Revenu ($)	Monthly Award/ Paiement mensuel ($) No. of Children/ Nbre d'enfants				Income/ Revenu ($)	Monthly Award/ Paiement mensuel ($) No. of Children/ Nbre d'enfants			
	1	2	3	4		1	2	3	4		1	2	3	4		1	2	3	4
54000	470	777	1022	1222	59400	520	853	1119	1338	64800	568	928	1216	1453	70200	616	1003	1312	1565
54100	471	778	1024	1224	59500	521	854	1121	1340	64900	569	929	1218	1455	70300	617	1004	1313	1567
54200	472	780	1026	1226	59600	522	855	1123	1342	65000	570	931	1220	1457	70400	618	1005	1315	1569
54300	473	781	1028	1229	59700	523	857	1125	1344	65100	571	932	1222	1459	70500	619	1007	1317	1571
54400	473	783	1029	1231	59800	523	858	1127	1346	65200	572	934	1224	1461	70600	620	1008	1319	1574
54500	474	784	1031	1233	59900	524	859	1129	1348	65300	573	935	1225	1463	70700	621	1009	1320	1576
54600	475	786	1033	1235	60000	525	861	1131	1351	65400	573	937	1227	1466	70800	621	1011	1322	1578
54700	476	787	1035	1237	60100	526	862	1133	1353	65500	574	938	1229	1468	70900	622	1012	1324	1580
54800	477	789	1037	1240	60200	527	864	1135	1355	65600	575	939	1231	1470	71000	623	1013	1326	1582
54900	478	790	1039	1242	60300	528	865	1137	1357	65700	576	941	1233	1472	71100	624	1014	1328	1584
55000	479	791	1040	1244	60400	529	866	1138	1359	65800	577	942	1234	1474	71200	625	1016	1330	1586
55100	480	792	1042	1246	60500	530	868	1140	1362	65900	578	944	1236	1476	71300	626	1017	1331	1588
55200	481	794	1044	1248	60600	531	869	1142	1364	66000	578	945	1238	1478	71400	626	1018	1333	1590
55300	482	795	1045	1250	60700	531	871	1144	1366	66100	579	946	1240	1480	71500	627	1020	1335	1593
55400	482	797	1047	1253	60800	532	872	1146	1368	66200	580	948	1241	1482	71600	628	1021	1337	1595
55500	483	798	1049	1255	60900	533	873	1148	1370	66300	581	949	1243	1484	71700	629	1023	1339	1597
55600	484	800	1051	1257	61000	534	875	1149	1372	66400	581	950	1245	1486	71800	630	1024	1340	1599
55700	485	801	1053	1259	61100	535	876	1151	1374	66500	582	952	1247	1488	71900	631	1025	1342	1601
55800	486	802	1055	1261	61200	536	878	1153	1376	66600	583	953	1248	1490	72000	631	1027	1344	1603
55900	487	804	1056	1263	61300	537	879	1154	1379	66700	584	954	1250	1492	72100	632	1028	1346	1605
56000	488	805	1058	1265	61400	538	881	1156	1381	66800	585	956	1252	1494	72200	633	1030	1347	1607
56100	489	806	1060	1267	61500	539	882	1158	1383	66900	586	957	1254	1496	72300	634	1031	1349	1609
56200	490	808	1062	1269	61600	540	884	1160	1385	67000	587	958	1255	1498	72400	634	1033	1351	1611
56300	491	809	1063	1271	61700	540	885	1162	1387	67100	588	959	1257	1500	72500	635	1034	1353	1614
56400	492	811	1065	1273	61800	541	887	1164	1389	67200	589	961	1259	1502	72600	636	1035	1354	1616
56500	493	812	1067	1276	61900	542	888	1165	1392	67300	590	962	1260	1504	72700	637	1037	1356	1618
56600	494	814	1069	1278	62000	543	890	1167	1394	67400	591	963	1262	1506	72800	638	1038	1358	1620
56700	495	815	1071	1280	62100	544	891	1169	1396	67500	591	965	1264	1508	72900	639	1039	1360	1622
56800	496	816	1072	1282	62200	545	893	1171	1398	67600	592	966	1266	1510	73000	640	1041	1361	1624
56900	497	818	1074	1284	62300	546	894	1172	1400	67700	593	967	1267	1512	73100	641	1042	1363	1626
57000	498	819	1076	1286	62400	547	895	1174	1403	67800	594	969	1269	1514	73200	642	1044	1365	1628
57100	499	820	1078	1288	62500	548	897	1176	1405	67900	595	970	1271	1517	73300	643	1045	1366	1630
57200	500	822	1080	1290	62600	548	898	1178	1407	68000	596	972	1273	1519	73400	644	1047	1368	1633
57300	501	823	1081	1292	62700	549	899	1180	1409	68100	597	973	1275	1521	73500	644	1048	1370	1635
57400	502	825	1083	1295	62800	550	901	1182	1411	68200	598	975	1277	1523	73600	645	1049	1372	1637
57500	503	826	1085	1297	62900	551	902	1183	1413	68300	599	976	1278	1525	73700	646	1051	1373	1639
57600	504	827	1087	1299	63000	552	903	1185	1415	68400	600	978	1280	1527	73800	647	1052	1375	1641
57700	505	829	1089	1301	63100	553	904	1187	1417	68500	600	979	1282	1529	73900	648	1054	1377	1643
57800	506	830	1090	1303	63200	554	906	1188	1419	68600	601	980	1284	1531	74000	649	1055	1379	1645
57900	507	832	1092	1305	63300	555	907	1190	1421	68700	602	982	1286	1533	74100	650	1056	1381	1647
58000	507	833	1094	1308	63400	556	908	1192	1423	68800	603	983	1287	1536	74200	651	1058	1383	1649
58100	508	834	1096	1310	63500	557	910	1194	1426	68900	604	984	1289	1538	74300	652	1059	1384	1651
58200	509	836	1098	1312	63600	557	911	1195	1428	69000	605	986	1291	1540	74400	653	1060	1386	1653
58300	510	837	1099	1314	63700	558	912	1197	1430	69100	606	987	1293	1542	74500	653	1062	1388	1655
58400	511	839	1101	1316	63800	559	914	1199	1432	69200	607	989	1294	1544	74600	654	1063	1390	1657
58500	512	840	1103	1319	63900	560	915	1201	1434	69300	608	990	1296	1546	74700	655	1064	1392	1659
58600	513	841	1105	1321	64000	561	917	1202	1436	69400	609	992	1298	1548	74800	656	1066	1393	1661
58700	514	843	1106	1323	64100	562	918	1204	1438	69500	610	993	1300	1550	74900	657	1067	1395	1663
58800	515	844	1108	1325	64200	563	920	1206	1440	69600	610	994	1301	1552	75000	658	1068	1397	1665
58900	515	846	1110	1327	64300	564	921	1207	1442	69700	611	996	1303	1555	75100	659	1069	1399	1667
59000	516	847	1112	1329	64400	565	923	1209	1444	69800	612	997	1305	1557	75200	660	1071	1400	1669
59100	517	848	1114	1331	64500	566	924	1211	1447	69900	613	999	1307	1559	75300	661	1072	1402	1671
59200	518	850	1116	1333	64600	567	925	1213	1449	70000	614	1000	1308	1561	75400	662	1073	1404	1673
59300	519	851	1118	1335	64700	568	927	1214	1451	70100	615	1001	1310	1563	75500	663	1075	1406	1675

Newfoundland & Labrador / Terre-Neuve-et-Labrador

Federal Child Support Amounts: Simplified Tables
Montants fédéraux de pensions alimentaires pour enfants: Tables simplifiées

Income/ Revenu ($)	Monthly Award/ Paiement mensuel ($) No. of Children/ N^{bre} d'enfants				Income/ Revenu ($)	Monthly Award/ Paiement mensuel ($) No. of Children/ N^{bre} d'enfants				Income/ Revenu ($)	Monthly Award/ Paiement mensuel ($) No. of Children/ N^{bre} d'enfants				Income/ Revenu ($)	Monthly Award/ Paiement mensuel ($) No. of Children/ N^{bre} d'enfants			
	1	2	3	4		1	2	3	4		1	2	3	4		1	2	3	4
75600	663	1076	1407	1677	81000	711	1151	1503	1791	86400	756	1221	1594	1898	91800	800	1290	1682	2003
75700	664	1078	1409	1679	81100	712	1152	1505	1793	86500	757	1222	1595	1900	91900	801	1291	1684	2005
75800	665	1079	1411	1681	81200	713	1154	1506	1795	86600	758	1224	1597	1902	92000	802	1293	1686	2007
75900	666	1080	1413	1683	81300	714	1155	1508	1797	86700	759	1225	1598	1903	92100	803	1294	1688	2009
76000	667	1082	1414	1686	81400	715	1157	1510	1800	86800	760	1226	1600	1905	92200	804	1296	1689	2011
76100	668	1083	1416	1688	81500	716	1158	1512	1802	86900	760	1228	1602	1907	92300	805	1297	1691	2013
76200	669	1085	1418	1690	81600	716	1160	1513	1804	87000	761	1229	1603	1909	92400	805	1298	1692	2015
76300	670	1086	1419	1692	81700	717	1161	1515	1806	87100	762	1230	1605	1911	92500	806	1299	1694	2017
76400	671	1088	1421	1694	81800	718	1162	1517	1808	87200	763	1232	1606	1913	92600	807	1301	1696	2019
76500	672	1089	1423	1696	81900	719	1164	1519	1810	87300	763	1233	1608	1915	92700	808	1302	1697	2021
76600	673	1090	1425	1698	82000	720	1165	1520	1812	87400	764	1234	1610	1917	92800	809	1303	1699	2023
76700	674	1092	1426	1700	82100	721	1166	1522	1814	87500	765	1236	1611	1919	92900	810	1304	1700	2025
76800	674	1093	1428	1703	82200	722	1167	1523	1816	87600	766	1237	1613	1921	93000	811	1306	1702	2027
76900	675	1095	1430	1705	82300	723	1169	1525	1818	87700	767	1238	1615	1923	93100	812	1307	1704	2029
77000	676	1096	1432	1707	82400	723	1170	1527	1820	87800	767	1239	1616	1925	93200	813	1309	1705	2031
77100	677	1097	1434	1709	82500	724	1171	1528	1822	87900	768	1241	1618	1927	93300	813	1310	1707	2033
77200	678	1099	1436	1711	82600	725	1172	1530	1824	88000	769	1242	1620	1929	93400	814	1311	1709	2035
77300	679	1100	1437	1713	82700	726	1174	1532	1826	88100	770	1243	1622	1931	93500	815	1312	1710	2037
77400	679	1102	1439	1715	82800	727	1175	1533	1828	88200	771	1245	1623	1933	93600	816	1314	1712	2039
77500	680	1103	1441	1717	82900	728	1176	1535	1830	88300	772	1246	1625	1935	93700	817	1315	1714	2040
77600	681	1104	1443	1719	83000	728	1177	1537	1831	88400	772	1247	1627	1937	93800	818	1316	1715	2042
77700	682	1106	1445	1722	83100	729	1178	1539	1833	88500	773	1249	1628	1939	93900	818	1318	1717	2044
77800	683	1107	1446	1724	83200	730	1180	1540	1835	88600	774	1250	1630	1940	94000	819	1319	1719	2046
77900	684	1109	1448	1726	83300	730	1181	1542	1837	88700	775	1251	1631	1942	94100	820	1320	1721	2048
78000	684	1110	1450	1728	83400	731	1182	1543	1839	88800	776	1253	1633	1944	94200	821	1322	1722	2050
78100	685	1111	1452	1730	83500	732	1183	1545	1841	88900	777	1254	1635	1946	94300	821	1323	1724	2052
78200	686	1113	1453	1732	83600	733	1185	1547	1843	89000	778	1255	1636	1948	94400	822	1324	1726	2054
78300	687	1114	1455	1734	83700	734	1186	1548	1845	89100	779	1256	1638	1950	94500	823	1325	1727	2056
78400	687	1115	1457	1736	83800	734	1187	1550	1847	89200	780	1258	1639	1952	94600	824	1327	1729	2058
78500	688	1117	1459	1738	83900	735	1188	1551	1849	89300	781	1259	1641	1954	94700	825	1328	1731	2060
78600	689	1118	1460	1741	84000	736	1190	1553	1851	89400	781	1260	1643	1956	94800	825	1329	1733	2062
78700	690	1119	1462	1743	84100	737	1191	1555	1853	89500	782	1262	1644	1958	94900	826	1331	1734	2064
78800	691	1121	1464	1745	84200	738	1193	1556	1855	89600	783	1263	1646	1960	95000	827	1332	1736	2066
78900	692	1122	1466	1747	84300	738	1194	1558	1857	89700	784	1264	1648	1962	95100	828	1333	1738	2068
79000	693	1123	1467	1749	84400	739	1195	1560	1859	89800	785	1266	1649	1964	95200	829	1335	1739	2070
79100	694	1124	1469	1751	84500	740	1196	1561	1861	89900	786	1267	1651	1966	95300	830	1336	1741	2072
79200	695	1126	1471	1753	84600	741	1198	1563	1863	90000	786	1268	1653	1968	95400	830	1337	1743	2074
79300	696	1127	1472	1755	84700	741	1199	1565	1865	90100	787	1269	1655	1970	95500	831	1339	1744	2076
79400	697	1128	1474	1757	84800	742	1200	1566	1866	90200	788	1270	1656	1972	95600	832	1340	1746	2077
79500	697	1130	1476	1760	84900	743	1201	1568	1868	90300	788	1272	1658	1974	95700	833	1341	1747	2079
79600	698	1131	1478	1762	85000	744	1203	1570	1870	90400	789	1273	1659	1976	95800	834	1342	1749	2081
79700	699	1133	1479	1764	85100	745	1204	1572	1872	90500	790	1274	1661	1978	95900	835	1344	1751	2083
79800	700	1134	1481	1766	85200	746	1206	1573	1874	90600	791	1275	1663	1980	96000	836	1345	1752	2085
79900	701	1135	1483	1768	85300	747	1207	1575	1876	90700	792	1277	1664	1982	96100	837	1346	1754	2087
80000	702	1137	1485	1770	85400	747	1208	1577	1878	90800	792	1278	1666	1984	96200	838	1348	1755	2089
80100	703	1138	1487	1772	85500	748	1209	1578	1880	90900	793	1279	1668	1986	96300	839	1349	1757	2091
80200	704	1140	1489	1774	85600	749	1211	1580	1882	91000	794	1280	1669	1988	96400	839	1350	1759	2093
80300	705	1141	1490	1776	85700	750	1212	1582	1884	91100	795	1281	1671	1990	96500	840	1352	1760	2095
80400	706	1143	1492	1778	85800	751	1213	1584	1886	91200	796	1283	1672	1992	96600	841	1353	1762	2097
80500	706	1144	1494	1781	85900	752	1215	1585	1888	91300	796	1284	1674	1994	96700	842	1354	1764	2099
80600	707	1145	1496	1783	86000	753	1216	1587	1890	91400	797	1285	1676	1996	96800	843	1356	1765	2101
80700	708	1147	1498	1785	86100	754	1217	1589	1892	91500	798	1286	1677	1998	96900	844	1357	1767	2103
80800	709	1148	1499	1787	86200	755	1219	1590	1894	91600	799	1288	1679	2000	97000	844	1358	1769	2105
80900	710	1150	1501	1789	86300	755	1220	1592	1896	91700	799	1289	1681	2002	97100	845	1359	1771	2107

Newfoundland & Labrador / Terre-Neuve-et-Labrador

Federal Child Support Amounts: Simplified Tables
Montants fédéraux de pensions alimentaires pour enfants: Tables simplifiées

Income/ Revenu ($)	Monthly Award/ Paiement mensuel ($) No. of Children/ N^bre d'enfants				Income/ Revenu ($)	Monthly Award/ Paiement mensuel ($) No. of Children/ N^bre d'enfants				Income/ Revenu ($)	Monthly Award/ Paiement mensuel ($) No. of Children/ N^bre d'enfants				Income/ Revenu ($)	Monthly Award/ Paiement mensuel ($) No. of Children/ N^bre d'enfants				Income/ Revenu ($)	Monthly Award/ Paiement mensuel ($) No. of Children/ N^bre d'enfants			
	1	2	3	4		1	2	3	4		1	2	3	4		1	2	3	4		1	2	3	4
97200	846	1361	1772	2109	102600	890	1430	1861	2214	108000	935	1499	1951	2320	113400	979	1569	2041	2426					
97300	846	1362	1774	2111	102700	890	1431	1863	2216	108100	936	1500	1953	2322	113500	980	1571	2042	2428					
97400	847	1363	1776	2113	102800	891	1432	1864	2218	108200	937	1502	1954	2324	113600	981	1572	2044	2430					
97500	848	1365	1777	2115	102900	892	1434	1866	2220	108300	937	1503	1956	2326	113700	982	1573	2045	2432					
97600	849	1366	1779	2117	103000	893	1435	1868	2222	108400	938	1504	1957	2328	113800	983	1575	2047	2434					
97700	850	1367	1780	2119	103100	894	1436	1870	2224	108500	939	1505	1959	2330	113900	984	1576	2049	2436					
97800	851	1369	1782	2121	103200	895	1438	1871	2226	108600	940	1507	1961	2332	114000	985	1577	2050	2438					
97900	851	1370	1784	2123	103300	896	1439	1873	2228	108700	941	1508	1962	2334	114100	986	1578	2052	2440					
98000	852	1371	1785	2125	103400	896	1440	1875	2230	108800	941	1509	1964	2336	114200	987	1579	2053	2442					
98100	853	1372	1787	2127	103500	897	1442	1876	2232	108900	942	1510	1966	2338	114300	988	1581	2055	2444					
98200	854	1373	1788	2129	103600	898	1443	1878	2234	109000	943	1512	1967	2340	114400	988	1582	2057	2446					
98300	854	1375	1790	2131	103700	899	1444	1880	2236	109100	944	1513	1969	2342	114500	989	1583	2058	2448					
98400	855	1376	1792	2133	103800	900	1445	1882	2238	109200	945	1515	1970	2344	114600	990	1584	2060	2450					
98500	856	1377	1793	2135	103900	901	1447	1883	2240	109300	945	1516	1972	2346	114700	991	1586	2062	2452					
98600	857	1378	1795	2137	104000	902	1448	1885	2242	109400	946	1517	1974	2348	114800	992	1587	2063	2453					
98700	858	1380	1797	2139	104100	903	1449	1887	2244	109500	947	1518	1975	2350	114900	993	1588	2065	2455					
98800	858	1381	1798	2141	104200	904	1451	1888	2246	109600	948	1520	1977	2352	115000	993	1589	2067	2457					
98900	859	1382	1800	2142	104300	904	1452	1890	2248	109700	948	1521	1979	2353	115100	994	1590	2069	2459					
99000	860	1383	1802	2144	104400	905	1453	1892	2250	109800	949	1522	1980	2355	115200	995	1592	2070	2461					
99100	861	1384	1804	2146	104500	906	1455	1893	2252	109900	950	1524	1982	2357	115300	995	1593	2072	2463					
99200	862	1386	1805	2148	104600	907	1456	1895	2254	110000	951	1525	1984	2359	115400	996	1594	2074	2465					
99300	863	1387	1807	2150	104700	908	1457	1896	2256	110100	952	1526	1986	2361	115500	997	1595	2075	2467					
99400	863	1388	1808	2152	104800	909	1459	1898	2258	110200	953	1528	1987	2363	115600	998	1597	2077	2469					
99500	864	1389	1810	2154	104900	909	1460	1900	2260	110300	954	1529	1989	2365	115700	999	1598	2078	2471					
99600	865	1391	1812	2156	105000	910	1461	1901	2262	110400	954	1530	1990	2367	115800	1000	1599	2080	2473					
99700	866	1392	1813	2158	105100	911	1462	1903	2264	110500	955	1531	1992	2369	115900	1000	1600	2082	2475					
99800	867	1393	1815	2160	105200	912	1464	1904	2266	110600	956	1533	1994	2371	116000	1001	1602	2083	2477					
99900	868	1394	1817	2162	105300	912	1465	1906	2268	110700	957	1534	1995	2373	116100	1002	1603	2085	2479					
100000	869	1396	1818	2164	105400	913	1466	1908	2270	110800	958	1535	1997	2375	116200	1003	1605	2086	2481					
100100	870	1397	1820	2166	105500	914	1468	1909	2272	110900	959	1537	1998	2377	116300	1003	1606	2088	2483					
100200	871	1399	1821	2168	105600	915	1469	1911	2274	111000	960	1538	2000	2379	116400	1004	1607	2090	2485					
100300	872	1400	1823	2170	105700	916	1470	1913	2276	111100	961	1539	2002	2381	116500	1005	1608	2091	2487					
100400	872	1401	1825	2172	105800	916	1472	1914	2278	111200	962	1541	2003	2383	116600	1006	1610	2093	2489					
100500	873	1402	1826	2174	105900	917	1473	1916	2280	111300	962	1542	2005	2385	116700	1007	1611	2095	2492					
100600	874	1404	1828	2176	106000	918	1474	1918	2281	111400	963	1543	2007	2387	116800	1007	1612	2096	2492					
100700	875	1405	1830	2177	106100	919	1475	1920	2283	111500	964	1545	2008	2389	116900	1008	1613	2098	2494					
100800	876	1406	1831	2179	106200	920	1476	1921	2285	111600	965	1546	2010	2391	117000	1009	1615	2100	2496					
100900	877	1407	1833	2181	106300	921	1478	1923	2287	111700	966	1547	2012	2393	117100	1010	1616	2102	2498					
101000	877	1409	1835	2183	106400	921	1479	1925	2289	111800	967	1548	2013	2395	117200	1011	1618	2103	2500					
101100	878	1410	1837	2185	106500	922	1480	1926	2291	111900	967	1550	2015	2397	117300	1012	1619	2105	2502					
101200	879	1412	1838	2187	106600	923	1481	1928	2293	112000	968	1551	2017	2399	117400	1012	1620	2106	2504					
101300	879	1413	1840	2189	106700	924	1483	1929	2295	112100	969	1552	2019	2401	117500	1013	1621	2108	2506					
101400	880	1414	1841	2191	106800	925	1484	1931	2297	112200	970	1554	2020	2403	117600	1014	1623	2110	2508					
101500	881	1415	1843	2193	106900	926	1485	1933	2299	112300	970	1555	2022	2405	117700	1015	1624	2111	2510					
101600	882	1417	1845	2195	107000	927	1486	1934	2301	112400	971	1556	2024	2407	117800	1016	1625	2113	2512					
101700	883	1418	1846	2197	107100	928	1487	1936	2303	112500	972	1558	2025	2409	117900	1017	1627	2115	2514					
101800	883	1419	1848	2199	107200	929	1489	1937	2305	112600	973	1559	2027	2411	118000	1018	1628	2116	2516					
101900	884	1421	1849	2201	107300	930	1490	1939	2307	112700	974	1560	2029	2413	118100	1019	1629	2118	2518					
102000	885	1422	1851	2203	107400	930	1491	1941	2309	112800	974	1562	2031	2415	118200	1020	1631	2119	2520					
102100	886	1423	1853	2205	107500	931	1492	1942	2311	112900	975	1563	2032	2417	118300	1021	1632	2121	2522					
102200	887	1425	1854	2207	107600	932	1494	1944	2313	113000	976	1564	2034	2418	118400	1021	1633	2123	2524					
102300	887	1426	1856	2209	107700	933	1495	1946	2315	113100	977	1565	2036	2420	118500	1022	1634	2124	2526					
102400	888	1427	1858	2211	107800	934	1496	1947	2316	113200	978	1567	2037	2422	118600	1023	1636	2126	2527					
102500	889	1428	1859	2213	107900	935	1497	1949	2318	113300	979	1568	2039	2424	118700	1024	1637	2128	2529					

Federal Child Support Amounts: Simplified Tables
Montants fédéraux de pensions alimentaires pour enfants: Tables simplifiées

Income/ Revenu ($)	Monthly Award/ Paiement mensuel ($) No. of Children/ Nᵇʳᵉ d'enfants				Income/ Revenu ($)	Monthly Award/ Paiement mensuel ($) No. of Children/ Nᵇʳᵉ d'enfants				Income/ Revenu ($)	Monthly Award/ Paiement mensuel ($) No. of Children/ Nᵇʳᵉ d'enfants				Income/ Revenu ($)	Monthly Award/ Paiement mensuel ($) No. of Children/ Nᵇʳᵉ d'enfants				Income/ Revenu ($)	Monthly Award/ Paiement mensuel ($) No. of Children/ Nᵇʳᵉ d'enfants			
	1	2	3	4		1	2	3	4		1	2	3	4		1	2	3	4		1	2	3	4
118800	1025	1638	2129	2531	124200	1069	1708	2219	2637	129600	1113	1776	2307	2740	135000	1155	1842	2391	2841					
118900	1026	1640	2131	2533	124300	1070	1709	2221	2639	129700	1114	1777	2308	2742	135100	1156	1843	2393	2843					
119000	1026	1641	2133	2535	124400	1070	1710	2223	2641	129800	1114	1778	2310	2744	135200	1157	1844	2394	2845					
119100	1027	1642	2135	2537	124500	1071	1711	2224	2643	129900	1115	1779	2312	2746	135300	1157	1846	2396	2847					
119200	1028	1644	2136	2539	124600	1072	1713	2226	2645	130000	1116	1781	2313	2748	135400	1158	1847	2397	2848					
119300	1028	1645	2138	2541	124700	1073	1714	2227	2647	130100	1117	1782	2315	2750	135500	1159	1848	2399	2850					
119400	1029	1646	2139	2543	124800	1074	1715	2229	2649	130200	1118	1783	2316	2752	135600	1160	1849	2401	2852					
119500	1030	1648	2141	2545	124900	1075	1716	2231	2651	130300	1118	1785	2318	2753	135700	1161	1851	2402	2854					
119600	1031	1649	2143	2547	125000	1076	1718	2232	2653	130400	1119	1786	2319	2755	135800	1161	1852	2404	2856					
119700	1032	1650	2144	2549	125100	1077	1719	2234	2655	130500	1120	1787	2321	2757	135900	1162	1853	2405	2858					
119800	1032	1651	2146	2551	125200	1078	1721	2235	2657	130600	1121	1788	2322	2759	136000	1163	1854	2407	2859					
119900	1033	1653	2147	2553	125300	1079	1722	2237	2659	130700	1122	1790	2324	2761	136100	1164	1855	2409	2861					
120000	1034	1654	2149	2555	125400	1079	1723	2239	2661	130800	1123	1791	2325	2763	136200	1165	1856	2410	2863					
120100	1035	1655	2151	2557	125500	1080	1724	2240	2663	130900	1123	1792	2327	2764	136300	1165	1858	2412	2865					
120200	1036	1657	2152	2559	125600	1081	1726	2242	2664	131000	1124	1793	2328	2766	136400	1166	1859	2413	2867					
120300	1036	1658	2154	2561	125700	1082	1727	2244	2666	131100	1125	1794	2330	2768	136500	1167	1860	2415	2868					
120400	1037	1659	2156	2563	125800	1083	1728	2245	2668	131200	1125	1795	2331	2770	136600	1168	1861	2417	2870					
120500	1038	1661	2157	2565	125900	1084	1730	2247	2670	131300	1126	1797	2333	2772	136700	1169	1862	2418	2872					
120600	1039	1662	2159	2567	126000	1084	1731	2249	2672	131400	1127	1798	2334	2773	136800	1169	1864	2420	2874					
120700	1039	1663	2161	2569	126100	1085	1732	2251	2674	131500	1128	1799	2336	2775	136900	1170	1865	2422	2876					
120800	1040	1665	2162	2571	126200	1086	1734	2252	2676	131600	1128	1800	2337	2777	137000	1171	1866	2423	2878					
120900	1041	1666	2164	2573	126300	1086	1735	2254	2678	131700	1129	1801	2339	2779	137100	1172	1867	2425	2880					
121000	1042	1667	2166	2575	126400	1087	1736	2255	2680	131800	1130	1803	2341	2781	137200	1173	1868	2426	2882					
121100	1043	1668	2168	2577	126500	1088	1737	2257	2682	131900	1131	1804	2342	2783	137300	1173	1870	2428	2883					
121200	1044	1670	2169	2579	126600	1089	1739	2259	2684	132000	1131	1805	2344	2785	137400	1174	1871	2429	2885					
121300	1045	1671	2171	2581	126700	1090	1740	2260	2686	132100	1132	1806	2346	2787	137500	1175	1872	2431	2887					
121400	1045	1672	2173	2583	126800	1090	1741	2262	2688	132200	1133	1807	2347	2789	137600	1176	1873	2432	2889					
121500	1046	1674	2174	2585	126900	1091	1743	2264	2690	132300	1133	1809	2349	2790	137700	1177	1874	2434	2891					
121600	1047	1675	2176	2587	127000	1092	1744	2265	2692	132400	1134	1810	2350	2792	137800	1178	1875	2435	2893					
121700	1048	1676	2178	2589	127100	1093	1745	2267	2694	132500	1135	1811	2352	2794	137900	1178	1877	2437	2894					
121800	1049	1678	2180	2591	127200	1094	1746	2268	2696	132600	1136	1812	2354	2796	138000	1179	1878	2438	2896					
121900	1050	1679	2181	2592	127300	1094	1748	2270	2698	132700	1136	1813	2355	2798	138100	1180	1879	2440	2898					
122000	1051	1680	2183	2594	127400	1095	1749	2271	2700	132800	1137	1815	2357	2799	138200	1181	1881	2441	2900					
122100	1052	1681	2185	2596	127500	1096	1750	2273	2702	132900	1138	1816	2358	2801	138300	1182	1882	2443	2902					
122200	1053	1682	2186	2598	127600	1097	1751	2274	2703	133000	1139	1817	2360	2803	138400	1182	1883	2444	2903					
122300	1053	1684	2188	2600	127700	1097	1752	2276	2705	133100	1140	1818	2362	2805	138500	1183	1884	2446	2905					
122400	1054	1685	2190	2602	127800	1098	1754	2278	2707	133200	1141	1820	2363	2807	138600	1184	1886	2447	2907					
122500	1055	1686	2191	2604	127900	1099	1755	2279	2709	133300	1141	1821	2365	2809	138700	1185	1887	2449	2909					
122600	1056	1687	2193	2606	128000	1100	1756	2281	2711	133400	1142	1822	2366	2810	138800	1186	1888	2451	2911					
122700	1057	1689	2194	2608	128100	1101	1757	2283	2713	133500	1143	1823	2368	2812	138900	1187	1889	2452	2913					
122800	1058	1690	2196	2610	128200	1102	1758	2284	2715	133600	1144	1825	2369	2814	139000	1187	1891	2454	2915					
122900	1058	1691	2198	2612	128300	1102	1760	2286	2717	133700	1144	1826	2371	2816	139100	1188	1892	2456	2917					
123000	1059	1692	2199	2614	128400	1103	1761	2287	2718	133800	1145	1827	2372	2818	139200	1188	1893	2457	2919					
123100	1060	1693	2201	2616	128500	1104	1762	2289	2720	133900	1146	1828	2374	2820	139300	1189	1895	2459	2921					
123200	1061	1695	2202	2618	128600	1105	1763	2291	2722	134000	1147	1830	2375	2822	139400	1190	1896	2460	2923					
123300	1061	1696	2204	2620	128700	1106	1764	2292	2724	134100	1148	1831	2377	2824	139500	1191	1897	2462	2925					
123400	1062	1697	2206	2622	128800	1106	1765	2294	2726	134200	1149	1832	2378	2826	139600	1191	1898	2464	2926					
123500	1063	1698	2207	2624	128900	1107	1767	2295	2728	134300	1149	1834	2380	2828	139700	1192	1900	2465	2928					
123600	1064	1700	2209	2626	129000	1108	1768	2297	2729	134400	1150	1835	2381	2830	139800	1193	1901	2467	2930					
123700	1065	1701	2211	2627	129100	1109	1769	2299	2731	134500	1151	1836	2383	2831	139900	1194	1902	2468	2932					
123800	1065	1702	2212	2629	129200	1110	1771	2300	2733	134600	1152	1837	2384	2833	140000	1194	1903	2470	2934					
123900	1066	1703	2214	2631	129300	1110	1772	2302	2735	134700	1152	1839	2386	2835	140100	1195	1904	2472	2936					
124000	1067	1705	2216	2633	129400	1111	1773	2303	2737	134800	1153	1840	2387	2837	140200	1196	1905	2473	2938					
124100	1068	1706	2218	2635	129500	1112	1774	2305	2738	134900	1154	1841	2389	2839	140300	1196	1907	2475	2940					

Newfoundland & Labrador / Terre-Neuve-et-Labrador

Federal Child Support Amounts: Simplified Tables
Montants fédéraux de pensions alimentaires pour enfants: Tables simplifiées

Income/ Revenu ($)	Monthly Award/ Paiement mensuel ($) No. of Children/ Nbre d'enfants				Income/ Revenu ($)	Monthly Award/ Paiement mensuel ($) No. of Children/ Nbre d'enfants				Income/ Revenu ($)	Monthly Award/ Paiement mensuel ($) No. of Children/ Nbre d'enfants			
	1	2	3	4		1	2	3	4		1	2	3	4
140400	1197	1908	2476	2941	143700	1224	1949	2528	3002	147000	1249	1989	2580	3064
140500	1198	1909	2478	2943	143800	1224	1950	2530	3004	147100	1250	1990	2582	3066
140600	1199	1910	2479	2945	143900	1225	1951	2531	3006	147200	1251	1991	2583	3068
140700	1199	1911	2481	2947	144000	1226	1952	2533	3008	147300	1251	1993	2585	3070
140800	1200	1913	2482	2949	144100	1227	1953	2535	3010	147400	1252	1994	2586	3071
140900	1201	1914	2484	2951	144200	1228	1954	2536	3012	147500	1253	1995	2588	3073
141000	1202	1915	2485	2952	144300	1228	1956	2538	3013	147600	1254	1996	2590	3075
141100	1203	1916	2487	2954	144400	1229	1957	2539	3015	147700	1254	1998	2591	3077
141200	1204	1917	2488	2956	144500	1230	1958	2541	3017	147800	1255	1999	2593	3079
141300	1204	1919	2490	2958	144600	1231	1959	2542	3019	147900	1256	2000	2595	3081
141400	1205	1920	2491	2960	144700	1232	1961	2544	3021	148000	1257	2001	2596	3082
141500	1206	1921	2493	2961	144800	1233	1962	2545	3022	148100	1258	2002	2598	3084
141600	1207	1922	2494	2963	144900	1233	1963	2547	3024	148200	1259	2003	2599	3086
141700	1207	1923	2496	2965	145000	1234	1964	2548	3026	148300	1259	2005	2601	3088
141800	1208	1924	2497	2967	145100	1235	1965	2550	3028	148400	1260	2006	2602	3090
141900	1209	1926	2499	2969	145200	1236	1966	2551	3030	148500	1261	2007	2604	3091
142000	1210	1927	2501	2971	145300	1236	1968	2553	3032	148600	1262	2008	2605	3093
142100	1211	1928	2503	2973	145400	1237	1969	2554	3033	148700	1262	2010	2607	3095
142200	1212	1930	2504	2975	145500	1238	1970	2556	3035	148800	1263	2011	2608	3097
142300	1212	1931	2506	2976	145600	1239	1971	2557	3037	148900	1264	2012	2610	3099
142400	1213	1932	2507	2978	145700	1240	1972	2559	3039	149000	1265	2013	2611	3101
142500	1214	1933	2509	2980	145800	1241	1974	2560	3041	149100	1266	2014	2613	3103
142600	1215	1935	2510	2982	145900	1241	1975	2562	3043	149200	1267	2015	2614	3105
142700	1216	1936	2512	2984	146000	1242	1976	2564	3045	149300	1267	2017	2616	3106
142800	1216	1937	2514	2986	146100	1243	1977	2566	3047	149400	1268	2018	2617	3108
142900	1217	1938	2515	2987	146200	1243	1979	2567	3049	149500	1269	2019	2619	3110
143000	1218	1940	2517	2989	146300	1244	1980	2569	3051	149600	1270	2020	2620	3112
143100	1219	1941	2519	2991	146400	1245	1981	2570	3053	149700	1271	2021	2622	3114
143200	1220	1942	2520	2993	146500	1246	1982	2572	3054	149800	1271	2023	2624	3116
143300	1220	1944	2522	2995	146600	1246	1984	2574	3056	149900	1272	2024	2625	3117
143400	1221	1945	2523	2996	146700	1247	1985	2575	3058	150000	1273	2025	2627	3119
143500	1222	1946	2525	2998	146800	1248	1986	2577	3060					
143600	1223	1947	2527	3000	146900	1249	1987	2578	3062					

Monthly Award/Paiement mensuel ($)			
One Child/ Un enfant	Two Children/ Deux enfants	Three Children/ Trois enfants	Four Children/ Quatre enfants
1273 plus 0.78% of income over $150,000	2025 plus 1.20% of income over $150,000	2627 plus 1.58% of income over $150,000	3119 plus 1.82% of income over $150,000
1273 plus 0,78% du revenu dépassant 150 000$	2025 plus 1,20% du revenu dépassant 150 000$	2627 plus 1,58% du revenu dépassant 150 000$	3119 plus 1.82% du revenu dépassant 150 000$

YUKON

Federal Child Support Amounts: Simplified Tables
Montants fédéraux de pensions alimentaires pour enfants: Tables simplifiées

Income/ Revenu ($)	Monthly Award/ Paiement mensuel ($) No. of Children/ Nᵇʳᵉ d'enfants 1	2	3	4	Income/ Revenu ($)	Monthly Award/ Paiement mensuel ($) No. of Children/ Nᵇʳᵉ d'enfants 1	2	3	4	Income/ Revenu ($)	Monthly Award/ Paiement mensuel ($) No. of Children/ Nᵇʳᵉ d'enfants 1	2	3	4	Income/ Revenu ($)	Monthly Award/ Paiement mensuel ($) No. of Children/ Nᵇʳᵉ d'enfants 1	2	3	4	Income/ Revenu ($)	Monthly Award/ Paiement mensuel ($) No. of Children/ Nᵇʳᵉ d'enfants 1	2	3	4
10820	0	0	0	0	16200	141	233	251	269	21600	175	330	454	502	27000	219	395	545	667
10900	3	3	4	4	16300	141	236	255	273	21700	176	332	456	506	27100	220	396	546	669
11000	40	43	46	50	16400	142	240	259	277	21800	177	333	458	510	27200	221	397	548	671
11100	44	47	51	55	16500	142	243	263	281	21900	177	334	459	515	27300	222	398	549	673
11200	48	52	55	60	16600	142	247	266	285	22000	178	335	461	519	27400	223	399	551	675
11300	52	56	60	65	16700	143	250	270	290	22100	179	336	463	523	27500	224	400	552	677
11400	56	60	65	70	16800	143	254	274	294	22200	179	338	464	528	27600	225	402	554	678
11500	60	65	69	75	16900	144	257	277	298	22300	180	339	466	532	27700	226	403	555	680
11600	64	69	74	80	17000	144	261	281	302	22400	181	340	468	536	27800	227	404	557	682
11700	68	73	79	85	17100	145	263	285	306	22500	182	341	469	541	27900	229	405	558	684
11800	72	77	83	90	17200	145	266	289	311	22600	182	343	471	545	28000	230	406	559	686
11900	76	82	88	95	17300	146	268	293	315	22700	183	344	473	549	28100	231	408	560	688
12000	80	86	93	100	17400	147	270	297	319	22800	184	345	475	554	28200	232	409	562	690
12100	83	90	97	104	17500	147	273	301	324	22900	184	347	476	558	28300	233	411	563	692
12200	87	93	101	108	17600	148	275	305	328	23000	185	348	478	563	28400	234	412	565	693
12300	90	97	105	112	17700	149	278	309	332	23100	186	349	480	567	28500	235	414	566	695
12400	93	100	109	116	17800	149	280	313	337	23200	186	350	481	572	28600	236	415	568	697
12500	97	104	112	121	17900	150	282	318	341	23300	187	352	483	576	28700	237	417	569	699
12600	100	107	116	125	18000	151	285	322	345	23400	188	353	485	580	28800	238	418	571	701
12700	103	111	120	129	18100	152	286	326	349	23500	188	354	486	584	28900	239	420	572	703
12800	107	114	124	133	18200	152	288	330	354	23600	189	355	488	589	29000	240	422	574	704
12900	110	118	128	137	18300	153	289	334	358	23700	190	357	490	593	29100	241	424	575	706
13000	113	122	132	141	18400	154	290	338	363	23800	190	358	492	597	29200	242	425	577	708
13100	115	125	136	145	18500	155	291	342	367	23900	191	359	493	602	29300	243	427	578	710
13200	118	129	140	149	18600	155	293	347	371	24000	191	360	495	606	29400	244	428	580	711
13300	120	132	144	153	18700	156	294	351	376	24100	192	361	497	608	29500	245	430	581	713
13400	122	136	147	157	18800	157	295	355	380	24200	192	362	498	610	29600	246	431	583	715
13500	125	139	151	161	18900	157	296	359	384	24300	193	364	500	612	29700	247	433	584	717
13600	127	143	155	166	19000	158	298	363	389	24400	194	365	502	614	29800	248	435	586	719
13700	129	146	159	170	19100	159	299	367	393	24500	194	366	503	616	29900	249	436	587	721
13800	132	150	163	174	19200	159	300	371	398	24600	195	367	505	618	30000	250	438	588	723
13900	134	153	167	178	19300	160	302	375	402	24700	196	368	507	620	30100	251	440	590	725
14000	136	157	170	182	19400	161	303	379	406	24800	196	370	509	622	30200	252	441	592	727
14100	136	160	174	186	19500	161	304	383	411	24900	197	371	510	624	30300	253	443	594	729
14200	136	164	177	190	19600	162	305	387	415	25000	198	372	512	626	30400	254	444	596	731
14300	136	167	181	194	19700	162	306	391	419	25100	199	373	514	628	30500	255	446	598	733
14400	136	171	185	198	19800	163	308	395	424	25200	200	375	516	630	30600	256	448	600	734
14500	136	174	189	202	19900	164	309	399	428	25300	201	376	517	633	30700	257	449	602	736
14600	137	178	192	206	20000	164	310	403	432	25400	202	377	519	635	30800	258	451	604	738
14700	137	181	196	210	20100	165	311	407	436	25500	204	379	521	637	30900	259	452	607	740
14800	137	185	200	214	20200	165	313	411	441	25600	205	380	523	639	31000	260	454	609	742
14900	137	188	204	218	20300	166	314	415	445	25700	206	381	525	641	31100	261	456	611	744
15000	137	192	207	222	20400	167	315	419	449	25800	207	383	526	643	31200	262	457	613	746
15100	137	195	211	226	20500	167	316	423	454	25900	208	384	528	646	31300	263	459	615	748
15200	138	199	214	230	20600	168	318	427	458	26000	209	386	530	648	31400	264	460	617	749
15300	138	202	218	234	20700	169	319	431	463	26100	210	387	531	650	31500	265	462	619	751
15400	138	206	222	238	20800	169	320	435	467	26200	211	388	533	652	31600	266	463	621	753
15500	138	209	225	242	20900	170	321	439	471	26300	212	389	534	654	31700	267	465	623	755
15600	139	212	229	246	21000	171	323	444	476	26400	213	390	536	656	31800	268	466	625	757
15700	139	216	233	249	21100	172	324	446	480	26500	214	391	537	657	31900	269	468	627	759
15800	139	219	237	253	21200	172	325	447	485	26600	215	392	539	659	32000	270	469	629	760
15900	139	222	240	257	21300	173	327	449	489	26700	216	392	540	661	32100	271	470	631	762
16000	140	226	244	261	21400	174	328	451	493	26800	217	393	542	663	32200	272	472	633	764
16100	140	229	248	265	21500	174	329	452	498	26900	218	394	543	665	32300	273	473	635	766

YUKON — CONTINUED

Federal Child Support Amounts: Simplified Tables
Montants fédéraux de pensions alimentaires pour enfants: Tables simplifiées

Income/ Revenu ($)	Monthly Award/ Paiement mensuel ($) No. of Children/ Nᵇʳᵉ d'enfants				Income/ Revenu ($)	Monthly Award/ Paiement mensuel ($) No. of Children/ Nᵇʳᵉ d'enfants				Income/ Revenu ($)	Monthly Award/ Paiement mensuel ($) No. of Children/ Nᵇʳᵉ d'enfants				Income/ Revenu ($)	Monthly Award/ Paiement mensuel ($) No. of Children/ Nᵇʳᵉ d'enfants			
	1	2	3	4		1	2	3	4		1	2	3	4		1	2	3	4
32400	274	475	637	769	37800	325	555	738	888	43200	375	633	839	1007	48600	424	709	936	1123
32500	275	476	639	771	37900	326	557	740	891	43300	376	634	840	1009	48700	425	710	938	1125
32600	276	478	641	773	38000	327	558	742	893	43400	377	636	842	1011	48800	426	712	940	1128
32700	277	479	642	775	38100	328	559	744	895	43500	377	637	844	1013	48900	427	713	942	1130
32800	278	481	644	777	38200	329	561	746	898	43600	378	639	846	1016	49000	428	715	944	1132
32900	279	482	646	779	38300	330	562	748	900	43700	379	640	848	1018	49100	429	717	946	1134
33000	280	484	648	782	38400	331	564	749	902	43800	380	641	849	1020	49200	430	718	948	1137
33100	281	485	650	784	38500	332	565	751	904	43900	381	643	851	1022	49300	431	720	950	1139
33200	282	487	652	786	38600	333	567	753	907	44000	382	644	853	1024	49400	432	721	951	1141
33300	283	488	654	789	38700	334	568	755	909	44100	383	645	855	1026	49500	433	723	953	1143
33400	284	490	656	791	38800	334	570	757	911	44200	384	647	857	1028	49600	434	724	955	1146
33500	285	491	657	793	38900	335	571	759	913	44300	385	648	858	1030	49700	434	726	957	1148
33600	286	493	659	795	39000	336	572	761	916	44400	386	650	860	1032	49800	435	727	959	1150
33700	287	494	661	797	39100	337	573	763	918	44500	386	651	862	1034	49900	436	729	961	1152
33800	287	496	663	799	39200	338	575	765	920	44600	387	653	864	1036	50000	437	730	963	1155
33900	288	497	665	802	39300	339	576	767	923	44700	388	654	866	1039	50100	438	731	965	1157
34000	289	499	667	804	39400	340	578	769	925	44800	389	655	867	1041	50200	439	733	967	1159
34100	290	500	669	806	39500	341	579	770	927	44900	390	657	869	1043	50300	440	734	969	1162
34200	291	502	671	809	39600	342	581	772	929	45000	391	658	871	1045	50400	441	736	970	1164
34300	292	503	673	811	39700	343	582	774	932	45100	392	659	873	1047	50500	442	737	972	1166
34400	293	505	675	813	39800	344	584	776	934	45200	393	661	875	1049	50600	443	739	974	1168
34500	293	506	676	815	39900	345	585	778	936	45300	394	662	876	1051	50700	444	740	976	1171
34600	294	508	678	818	40000	346	587	780	938	45400	395	664	878	1054	50800	445	742	978	1173
34700	295	509	680	820	40100	347	589	782	940	45500	396	665	880	1056	50900	446	743	980	1175
34800	296	511	682	822	40200	348	590	784	943	45600	396	667	882	1058	51000	447	744	982	1177
34900	297	512	684	824	40300	349	592	786	945	45700	397	668	884	1060	51100	448	745	984	1179
35000	298	514	686	827	40400	350	593	788	948	45800	398	670	885	1062	51200	449	747	986	1182
35100	299	515	688	829	40500	351	595	790	950	45900	399	671	887	1064	51300	450	748	988	1184
35200	300	517	690	831	40600	352	597	792	952	46000	400	672	889	1067	51400	451	750	989	1186
35300	301	518	692	834	40700	353	598	794	955	46100	401	673	891	1069	51500	452	751	991	1188
35400	302	520	694	836	40800	354	600	796	957	46200	402	675	893	1071	51600	453	753	993	1191
35500	303	521	696	838	40900	355	601	798	960	46300	403	676	894	1073	51700	453	754	995	1193
35600	304	523	697	840	41000	356	603	800	962	46400	404	677	896	1076	51800	454	756	997	1195
35700	305	524	699	843	41100	357	604	802	964	46500	405	679	898	1078	51900	455	757	999	1198
35800	306	525	701	845	41200	358	606	804	966	46600	405	680	900	1080	52000	456	759	1001	1200
35900	307	527	703	847	41300	359	607	805	968	46700	406	681	902	1082	52100	457	760	1003	1202
36000	308	528	705	849	41400	359	608	807	970	46800	407	683	904	1084	52200	458	762	1005	1204
36100	309	529	707	851	41500	360	610	809	972	46900	408	684	905	1086	52300	459	763	1007	1207
36200	310	531	709	853	41600	361	611	811	974	47000	409	685	907	1088	52400	460	765	1008	1209
36300	311	532	710	856	41700	362	612	813	976	47100	410	686	909	1090	52500	461	766	1010	1211
36400	312	534	712	858	41800	363	614	814	978	47200	411	688	911	1092	52600	462	768	1012	1213
36500	313	535	714	860	41900	364	615	816	980	47300	412	689	912	1095	52700	463	769	1014	1216
36600	313	537	716	862	42000	364	616	818	982	47400	413	691	914	1097	52800	464	771	1016	1218
36700	314	538	718	864	42100	365	617	820	984	47500	414	692	916	1099	52900	465	772	1018	1220
36800	315	540	720	867	42200	366	619	821	986	47600	414	694	918	1101	53000	466	774	1020	1222
36900	316	541	721	869	42300	367	620	823	988	47700	415	695	920	1104	53100	467	776	1022	1224
37000	317	543	723	871	42400	367	622	825	990	47800	416	697	922	1106	53200	468	777	1024	1226
37100	318	545	725	873	42500	368	623	827	992	47900	417	698	923	1108	53300	469	779	1026	1229
37200	319	546	727	875	42600	369	624	828	994	48000	418	700	925	1110	53400	470	780	1027	1231
37300	320	548	729	878	42700	370	626	830	996	48100	419	701	927	1112	53500	471	782	1029	1233
37400	321	549	730	880	42800	371	627	832	998	48200	420	703	929	1114	53600	472	783	1031	1235
37500	322	551	732	882	42900	372	628	834	1001	48300	421	704	931	1117	53700	472	785	1033	1237
37600	323	552	734	884	43000	373	630	835	1003	48400	422	706	932	1119	53800	473	786	1035	1240
37700	324	554	736	886	43100	374	631	837	1005	48500	423	707	934	1121	53900	474	788	1037	1242

Federal Child Support Amounts: Simplified Tables
Montants fédéraux de pensions alimentaires pour enfants: Tables simplifiées

Income/ Revenu ($)	Monthly Award/ Paiement mensuel ($) No. of Children/ Nbre d'enfants				Income/ Revenu ($)	Monthly Award/ Paiement mensuel ($) No. of Children/ Nbre d'enfants				Income/ Revenu ($)	Monthly Award/ Paiement mensuel ($) No. of Children/ Nbre d'enfants				Income/ Revenu ($)	Monthly Award/ Paiement mensuel ($) No. of Children/ Nbre d'enfants			
	1	2	3	4		1	2	3	4		1	2	3	4		1	2	3	4
54000	475	789	1039	1244	59400	527	868	1142	1366	64800	578	948	1244	1487	70200	629	1028	1347	1608
54100	476	790	1041	1246	59500	528	869	1143	1368	64900	579	949	1246	1489	70300	630	1030	1349	1610
54200	477	792	1043	1249	59600	529	871	1145	1370	65000	580	951	1248	1491	70400	631	1031	1351	1612
54300	478	793	1045	1251	59700	530	872	1147	1373	65100	581	953	1250	1493	70500	632	1033	1353	1614
54400	479	795	1046	1253	59800	530	874	1149	1375	65200	582	954	1252	1496	70600	633	1034	1354	1617
54500	480	796	1048	1255	59900	531	875	1151	1377	65300	583	956	1254	1498	70700	634	1036	1356	1619
54600	481	798	1050	1258	60000	532	877	1153	1379	65400	584	957	1256	1500	70800	635	1037	1358	1621
54700	482	799	1052	1260	60100	533	878	1155	1381	65500	585	959	1257	1502	70900	636	1039	1360	1623
54800	483	801	1054	1262	60200	534	880	1157	1383	65600	586	960	1259	1505	71000	637	1040	1362	1626
54900	484	802	1056	1264	60300	535	881	1159	1386	65700	587	962	1261	1507	71100	638	1041	1364	1628
55000	485	803	1058	1267	60400	536	883	1161	1388	65800	588	963	1263	1509	71200	639	1043	1366	1630
55100	486	804	1060	1269	60500	537	884	1162	1390	65900	588	965	1265	1512	71300	640	1044	1368	1633
55200	487	806	1062	1271	60600	538	886	1164	1392	66000	589	966	1267	1514	71400	641	1046	1370	1635
55300	488	807	1064	1274	60700	539	887	1166	1394	66100	590	967	1269	1516	71500	642	1047	1372	1637
55400	489	809	1065	1276	60800	540	889	1168	1397	66200	591	969	1271	1518	71600	643	1049	1373	1639
55500	490	810	1067	1278	60900	541	890	1170	1399	66300	592	970	1273	1521	71700	644	1050	1375	1642
55600	491	812	1069	1280	61000	542	892	1172	1401	66400	593	972	1275	1523	71800	645	1052	1377	1644
55700	492	813	1071	1282	61100	543	894	1174	1403	66500	594	973	1276	1525	71900	646	1053	1379	1646
55800	492	815	1073	1285	61200	544	895	1176	1406	66600	595	975	1278	1527	72000	646	1054	1381	1648
55900	493	816	1075	1287	61300	545	897	1178	1408	66700	596	976	1280	1530	72100	647	1055	1383	1650
56000	494	818	1077	1289	61400	546	898	1180	1410	66800	597	977	1282	1532	72200	648	1057	1385	1653
56100	495	819	1079	1291	61500	547	900	1181	1412	66900	598	979	1284	1534	72300	649	1058	1387	1655
56200	496	821	1081	1294	61600	548	901	1183	1415	67000	599	980	1286	1536	72400	650	1060	1389	1657
56300	497	822	1083	1296	61700	549	903	1185	1417	67100	600	981	1288	1538	72500	650	1061	1391	1659
56400	498	824	1084	1298	61800	549	904	1187	1419	67200	601	983	1290	1540	72600	651	1063	1392	1662
56500	499	825	1086	1300	61900	550	906	1189	1421	67300	602	984	1292	1543	72700	652	1064	1394	1664
56600	500	827	1088	1303	62000	551	907	1191	1424	67400	603	986	1294	1545	72800	653	1066	1396	1666
56700	501	828	1090	1305	62100	552	908	1193	1426	67500	604	987	1295	1547	72900	654	1067	1398	1669
56800	502	830	1092	1307	62200	553	910	1195	1428	67600	605	989	1297	1549	73000	655	1069	1400	1671
56900	503	831	1094	1309	62300	554	911	1197	1431	67700	606	990	1299	1551	73100	656	1070	1402	1673
57000	504	833	1096	1312	62400	555	913	1199	1433	67800	607	992	1301	1554	73200	657	1072	1404	1675
57100	505	835	1098	1314	62500	556	914	1200	1435	67900	607	993	1303	1556	73300	658	1073	1406	1678
57200	506	836	1100	1316	62600	557	916	1202	1437	68000	608	995	1305	1558	73400	659	1075	1408	1680
57300	507	838	1102	1319	62700	558	917	1204	1439	68100	609	996	1307	1560	73500	660	1076	1410	1682
57400	508	839	1103	1321	62800	559	918	1206	1442	68200	610	998	1309	1563	73600	661	1078	1411	1684
57500	509	841	1105	1323	62900	560	920	1208	1444	68300	611	999	1311	1565	73700	662	1079	1413	1687
57600	510	842	1107	1325	63000	561	921	1210	1446	68400	612	1001	1313	1567	73800	663	1081	1415	1689
57700	511	844	1109	1328	63100	562	922	1212	1448	68500	613	1002	1314	1569	73900	664	1082	1417	1691
57800	511	845	1111	1330	63200	563	924	1214	1451	68600	614	1004	1316	1572	74000	665	1084	1419	1693
57900	512	847	1113	1332	63300	564	925	1216	1453	68700	615	1005	1318	1574	74100	666	1086	1421	1695
58000	513	848	1115	1334	63400	565	927	1218	1455	68800	616	1007	1320	1576	74200	667	1087	1423	1697
58100	514	849	1117	1336	63500	566	928	1219	1457	68900	617	1008	1322	1578	74300	668	1089	1425	1700
58200	515	851	1119	1339	63600	567	930	1221	1460	69000	618	1010	1324	1581	74400	669	1090	1427	1702
58300	516	852	1121	1341	63700	568	931	1223	1462	69100	619	1011	1326	1583	74500	670	1092	1429	1704
58400	517	854	1123	1343	63800	569	933	1225	1464	69200	620	1013	1328	1585	74600	670	1093	1430	1706
58500	518	855	1124	1345	63900	569	934	1227	1466	69300	621	1014	1330	1588	74700	671	1095	1432	1708
58600	519	857	1126	1348	64000	570	936	1229	1469	69400	622	1016	1332	1590	74800	672	1096	1434	1711
58700	520	858	1128	1350	64100	571	937	1231	1471	69500	623	1017	1334	1592	74900	673	1098	1436	1713
58800	521	859	1130	1352	64200	572	939	1233	1473	69600	624	1019	1335	1594	75000	674	1099	1438	1715
58900	522	861	1132	1355	64300	573	940	1235	1476	69700	625	1020	1337	1596	75100	675	1100	1440	1717
59000	523	862	1134	1357	64400	574	942	1237	1478	69800	626	1022	1339	1599	75200	676	1102	1442	1720
59100	524	863	1136	1359	64500	575	943	1238	1480	69900	627	1023	1341	1601	75300	677	1103	1444	1722
59200	525	865	1138	1361	64600	576	945	1240	1482	70000	627	1025	1343	1603	75400	678	1105	1446	1724
59300	526	866	1140	1364	64700	577	946	1242	1485	70100	628	1027	1345	1605	75500	679	1106	1448	1726

Yukon

Federal Child Support Amounts: Simplified Tables
Montants fédéraux de pensions alimentaires pour enfants: Tables simplifiées

Income/ Revenu ($)	Monthly Award/ Paiement mensuel ($) No. of Children/ N^bre d'enfants				Income/ Revenu ($)	Monthly Award/ Paiement mensuel ($) No. of Children/ N^bre d'enfants				Income/ Revenu ($)	Monthly Award/ Paiement mensuel ($) No. of Children/ N^bre d'enfants				Income/ Revenu ($)	Monthly Award/ Paiement mensuel ($) No. of Children/ N^bre d'enfants			
	1	2	3	4		1	2	3	4		1	2	3	4		1	2	3	4
75600	680	1108	1449	1729	81000	731	1187	1552	1850	86400	778	1260	1646	1962	91800	824	1331	1739	2071
75700	681	1109	1451	1731	81100	732	1188	1554	1852	86500	779	1261	1647	1964	91900	825	1333	1741	2073
75800	682	1111	1453	1733	81200	733	1190	1556	1854	86600	780	1263	1649	1966	92000	826	1334	1742	2075
75900	683	1112	1455	1735	81300	734	1191	1558	1857	86700	781	1264	1651	1968	92100	827	1335	1744	2077
76000	684	1113	1457	1738	81400	735	1193	1560	1859	86800	782	1265	1652	1970	92200	828	1337	1745	2079
76100	685	1114	1459	1740	81500	736	1194	1562	1861	86900	782	1267	1654	1972	92300	829	1338	1747	2081
76200	686	1116	1461	1742	81600	737	1196	1564	1863	87000	783	1268	1656	1974	92400	829	1339	1749	2083
76300	687	1117	1463	1745	81700	738	1197	1565	1865	87100	784	1269	1658	1976	92500	830	1341	1751	2085
76400	688	1119	1465	1747	81800	739	1199	1567	1868	87200	785	1271	1659	1978	92600	831	1342	1752	2087
76500	689	1120	1467	1749	81900	740	1200	1569	1870	87300	786	1272	1661	1980	92700	832	1344	1754	2089
76600	689	1122	1469	1751	82000	741	1202	1571	1872	87400	786	1273	1663	1982	92800	833	1345	1756	2091
76700	690	1123	1470	1753	82100	742	1203	1573	1874	87500	787	1275	1664	1984	92900	834	1346	1758	2093
76800	691	1125	1472	1756	82200	743	1205	1574	1876	87600	788	1276	1666	1986	93000	834	1348	1759	2095
76900	692	1126	1474	1758	82300	744	1206	1576	1878	87700	789	1278	1668	1988	93100	835	1349	1761	2097
77000	693	1128	1476	1760	82400	745	1207	1578	1880	87800	790	1279	1669	1990	93200	836	1351	1762	2099
77100	694	1129	1478	1762	82500	746	1209	1580	1882	87900	791	1280	1671	1992	93300	837	1352	1764	2101
77200	695	1131	1480	1765	82600	746	1210	1581	1884	88000	792	1282	1673	1994	93400	838	1353	1766	2103
77300	696	1132	1482	1767	82700	747	1211	1583	1886	88100	793	1283	1675	1996	93500	838	1355	1768	2105
77400	697	1134	1484	1769	82800	748	1213	1585	1889	88200	794	1285	1676	1998	93600	839	1356	1769	2107
77500	698	1135	1486	1771	82900	749	1214	1587	1891	88300	794	1286	1678	2000	93700	840	1357	1771	2109
77600	699	1137	1488	1774	83000	750	1215	1588	1893	88400	795	1287	1680	2002	93800	841	1359	1773	2111
77700	700	1138	1489	1776	83100	751	1216	1590	1895	88500	796	1289	1681	2004	93900	842	1360	1775	2113
77800	701	1140	1491	1778	83200	752	1218	1591	1897	88600	797	1290	1683	2006	94000	843	1361	1776	2115
77900	702	1141	1493	1780	83300	753	1219	1593	1899	88700	798	1291	1685	2008	94100	844	1362	1778	2117
78000	703	1143	1495	1783	83400	753	1220	1595	1901	88800	799	1293	1686	2010	94200	845	1364	1779	2119
78100	704	1145	1497	1785	83500	754	1222	1597	1903	88900	799	1294	1688	2012	94300	845	1365	1781	2121
78200	705	1146	1499	1787	83600	755	1223	1598	1905	89000	800	1295	1690	2014	94400	846	1367	1783	2123
78300	706	1148	1501	1790	83700	756	1225	1600	1907	89100	801	1296	1692	2016	94500	847	1368	1785	2125
78400	707	1149	1503	1792	83800	757	1226	1602	1909	89200	802	1298	1694	2018	94600	848	1369	1786	2127
78500	708	1151	1505	1794	83900	758	1227	1603	1911	89300	803	1299	1695	2020	94700	849	1371	1788	2129
78600	708	1152	1507	1796	84000	758	1229	1605	1913	89400	804	1300	1697	2022	94800	850	1372	1790	2131
78700	709	1154	1508	1799	84100	759	1230	1607	1915	89500	804	1302	1699	2024	94900	850	1373	1791	2133
78800	710	1155	1510	1801	84200	760	1232	1608	1917	89600	805	1303	1701	2026	95000	851	1375	1793	2135
78900	711	1157	1512	1803	84300	760	1233	1610	1919	89700	806	1304	1702	2028	95100	852	1376	1795	2137
79000	712	1158	1514	1805	84400	761	1234	1612	1921	89800	807	1306	1704	2030	95200	853	1378	1796	2139
79100	713	1159	1516	1807	84500	762	1236	1613	1923	89900	808	1307	1706	2032	95300	854	1379	1798	2141
79200	714	1161	1518	1810	84600	763	1237	1615	1925	90000	809	1308	1708	2034	95400	854	1380	1800	2143
79300	715	1162	1520	1812	84700	764	1238	1617	1927	90100	810	1309	1710	2036	95500	855	1382	1801	2145
79400	716	1164	1522	1814	84800	764	1240	1618	1929	90200	811	1311	1711	2038	95600	856	1383	1803	2147
79500	717	1165	1524	1816	84900	765	1241	1620	1931	90300	812	1312	1713	2040	95700	857	1384	1805	2149
79600	718	1167	1526	1819	85000	766	1242	1622	1933	90400	812	1313	1715	2042	95800	858	1386	1807	2151
79700	719	1168	1527	1821	85100	767	1243	1624	1935	90500	813	1315	1717	2044	95900	859	1387	1808	2153
79800	720	1170	1529	1823	85200	768	1245	1625	1937	90600	814	1316	1718	2046	96000	860	1388	1810	2156
79900	721	1171	1531	1826	85300	769	1246	1627	1939	90700	815	1317	1720	2048	96100	861	1389	1812	2158
80000	722	1172	1533	1828	85400	769	1247	1629	1941	90800	816	1318	1722	2050	96200	862	1391	1813	2160
80100	723	1173	1535	1830	85500	770	1249	1630	1943	90900	817	1320	1724	2053	96300	863	1392	1815	2162
80200	724	1175	1537	1832	85600	771	1250	1632	1945	91000	817	1321	1725	2055	96400	864	1393	1817	2164
80300	725	1176	1539	1835	85700	772	1251	1634	1947	91100	818	1322	1727	2057	96500	865	1395	1818	2166
80400	726	1178	1541	1837	85800	773	1252	1635	1949	91200	819	1324	1728	2059	96600	865	1396	1820	2168
80500	727	1179	1543	1839	85900	774	1254	1637	1952	91300	820	1325	1730	2061	96700	866	1397	1822	2170
80600	727	1181	1545	1841	86000	775	1255	1639	1954	91400	821	1326	1732	2063	96800	867	1398	1823	2172
80700	728	1182	1546	1844	86100	776	1256	1641	1956	91500	822	1327	1734	2065	96900	868	1400	1825	2174
80800	729	1184	1548	1846	86200	777	1258	1642	1958	91600	822	1329	1735	2067	97000	869	1401	1827	2176
80900	730	1185	1550	1848	86300	777	1259	1644	1960	91700	823	1330	1737	2069	97100	870	1402	1829	2178

Federal Child Support Amounts: Simplified Tables
Montants fédéraux de pensions alimentaires pour enfants: Tables simplifiées

Income/ Revenu ($)	Monthly Award/ Paiement mensuel ($) No. of Children/ N^bre d'enfants				Income/ Revenu ($)	Monthly Award/ Paiement mensuel ($) No. of Children/ N^bre d'enfants				Income/ Revenu ($)	Monthly Award/ Paiement mensuel ($) No. of Children/ N^bre d'enfants				Income/ Revenu ($)	Monthly Award/ Paiement mensuel ($) No. of Children/ N^bre d'enfants			
	1	2	3	4		1	2	3	4		1	2	3	4		1	2	3	4
97200	871	1404	1831	2180	102600	917	1476	1924	2290	108000	963	1549	2017	2400	113400	1009	1621	2110	2510
97300	872	1405	1832	2182	102700	918	1478	1926	2292	108100	964	1550	2019	2402	113500	1010	1623	2112	2512
97400	872	1406	1834	2184	102800	919	1479	1928	2294	108200	965	1552	2020	2404	113600	1011	1624	2113	2514
97500	873	1408	1836	2186	102900	920	1480	1930	2296	108300	966	1553	2022	2406	113700	1012	1625	2115	2516
97600	874	1409	1838	2188	103000	920	1482	1931	2298	108400	966	1554	2024	2408	113800	1013	1627	2117	2518
97700	875	1411	1839	2191	103100	921	1483	1933	2300	108500	967	1556	2026	2410	113900	1014	1628	2118	2520
97800	876	1412	1841	2193	103200	922	1485	1934	2302	108600	968	1557	2027	2412	114000	1015	1629	2120	2522
97900	877	1413	1843	2195	103300	923	1486	1936	2304	108700	969	1558	2029	2414	114100	1016	1630	2122	2524
98000	877	1415	1845	2197	103400	924	1487	1938	2306	108800	970	1560	2031	2416	114200	1017	1632	2123	2526
98100	878	1416	1847	2199	103500	924	1489	1940	2308	108900	971	1561	2032	2418	114300	1018	1633	2125	2528
98200	879	1418	1848	2201	103600	925	1490	1941	2310	109000	972	1562	2034	2420	114400	1019	1634	2127	2530
98300	880	1419	1850	2203	103700	926	1491	1943	2313	109100	973	1563	2036	2422	114500	1020	1636	2128	2532
98400	881	1420	1852	2205	103800	927	1493	1945	2315	109200	974	1565	2037	2424	114600	1020	1637	2130	2534
98500	881	1422	1854	2207	103900	928	1494	1946	2317	109300	975	1566	2039	2426	114700	1021	1638	2132	2536
98600	882	1423	1855	2209	104000	929	1495	1948	2319	109400	976	1567	2041	2428	114800	1022	1639	2133	2538
98700	883	1424	1857	2211	104100	930	1496	1950	2321	109500	977	1568	2042	2430	114900	1023	1641	2135	2540
98800	884	1426	1859	2213	104200	931	1498	1951	2323	109600	977	1570	2044	2432	115000	1024	1642	2137	2542
98900	885	1427	1861	2215	104300	931	1499	1953	2325	109700	978	1571	2046	2434	115100	1025	1643	2139	2544
99000	886	1428	1862	2217	104400	932	1500	1955	2327	109800	979	1572	2048	2437	115200	1026	1645	2141	2546
99100	887	1429	1864	2219	104500	933	1501	1956	2329	109900	980	1574	2049	2439	115300	1027	1646	2142	2548
99200	888	1431	1865	2221	104600	934	1503	1958	2331	110000	981	1575	2051	2441	115400	1027	1647	2144	2550
99300	888	1432	1867	2223	104700	935	1504	1960	2333	110100	982	1576	2053	2443	115500	1028	1649	2146	2552
99400	889	1433	1869	2225	104800	936	1505	1962	2335	110200	983	1578	2055	2445	115600	1029	1650	2148	2554
99500	890	1434	1871	2227	104900	936	1507	1963	2337	110300	984	1579	2056	2447	115700	1030	1652	2149	2556
99600	891	1436	1872	2229	105000	937	1508	1965	2339	110400	984	1580	2058	2449	115800	1031	1653	2151	2558
99700	892	1437	1874	2231	105100	938	1509	1967	2341	110500	985	1582	2060	2451	115900	1032	1654	2153	2560
99800	893	1438	1876	2233	105200	939	1511	1968	2343	110600	986	1583	2062	2453	116000	1032	1656	2155	2563
99900	893	1440	1877	2235	105300	940	1512	1970	2345	110700	987	1585	2063	2455	116100	1033	1657	2157	2565
100000	894	1441	1879	2237	105400	940	1513	1972	2347	110800	988	1586	2065	2457	116200	1034	1659	2158	2567
100100	895	1442	1881	2239	105500	941	1515	1973	2349	110900	989	1587	2067	2459	116300	1035	1660	2160	2569
100200	896	1444	1882	2241	105600	942	1516	1975	2351	111000	989	1589	2069	2461	116400	1036	1661	2162	2571
100300	897	1445	1884	2243	105700	943	1517	1977	2353	111100	990	1590	2071	2463	116500	1036	1663	2164	2573
100400	897	1446	1886	2245	105800	944	1519	1978	2355	111200	991	1592	2072	2465	116600	1037	1664	2165	2575
100500	898	1448	1887	2247	105900	945	1520	1980	2357	111300	992	1593	2074	2467	116700	1038	1665	2167	2577
100600	899	1449	1889	2249	106000	946	1522	1982	2359	111400	993	1594	2076	2469	116800	1039	1667	2169	2579
100700	900	1450	1891	2252	106100	947	1523	1984	2361	111500	993	1596	2078	2471	116900	1040	1668	2171	2581
100800	901	1452	1892	2254	106200	948	1525	1986	2363	111600	994	1597	2079	2473	117000	1041	1669	2172	2583
100900	902	1453	1894	2256	106300	949	1526	1987	2365	111700	995	1598	2081	2475	117100	1042	1670	2174	2585
101000	903	1455	1896	2258	106400	950	1527	1989	2367	111800	996	1600	2083	2477	117200	1043	1672	2175	2587
101100	904	1456	1898	2260	106500	950	1529	1991	2369	111900	997	1601	2085	2479	117300	1043	1673	2177	2589
101200	905	1458	1900	2262	106600	951	1530	1993	2371	112000	998	1602	2086	2481	117400	1044	1675	2179	2591
101300	906	1459	1901	2264	106700	952	1531	1994	2373	112100	999	1603	2088	2483	117500	1045	1676	2181	2593
101400	907	1460	1903	2266	106800	953	1533	1996	2376	112200	1000	1605	2089	2485	117600	1046	1677	2182	2595
101500	907	1462	1905	2268	106900	954	1534	1998	2378	112300	1000	1606	2091	2487	117700	1047	1679	2184	2598
101600	908	1463	1907	2270	107000	955	1535	2000	2380	112400	1001	1608	2093	2489	117800	1048	1680	2186	2600
101700	909	1464	1908	2272	107100	956	1536	2002	2382	112500	1002	1609	2095	2491	117900	1048	1681	2187	2602
101800	910	1466	1910	2274	107200	957	1538	2003	2384	112600	1003	1610	2096	2493	118000	1049	1683	2189	2604
101900	911	1467	1912	2276	107300	957	1539	2005	2386	112700	1004	1612	2098	2495	118100	1050	1684	2191	2606
102000	912	1468	1914	2278	107400	958	1541	2007	2388	112800	1005	1613	2100	2497	118200	1051	1686	2192	2608
102100	913	1469	1916	2280	107500	959	1542	2009	2390	112900	1005	1614	2102	2500	118300	1052	1687	2194	2610
102200	914	1471	1917	2282	107600	960	1543	2010	2392	113000	1006	1616	2103	2502	118400	1052	1688	2196	2612
102300	915	1472	1919	2284	107700	961	1545	2012	2394	113100	1007	1617	2105	2504	118500	1053	1690	2197	2614
102400	915	1473	1921	2286	107800	962	1546	2014	2396	113200	1008	1619	2106	2506	118600	1054	1691	2199	2616
102500	916	1475	1923	2288	107900	962	1547	2016	2398	113300	1009	1620	2108	2508	118700	1055	1692	2201	2618

Federal Child Support Amounts: Simplified Tables
Montants fédéraux de pensions alimentaires pour enfants: Tables simplifiées

Income/ Revenu ($)	Monthly Award/ Paiement mensuel ($) No. of Children/ N^{bre} d'enfants				Income/ Revenu ($)	Monthly Award/ Paiement mensuel ($) No. of Children/ N^{bre} d'enfants				Income/ Revenu ($)	Monthly Award/ Paiement mensuel ($) No. of Children/ N^{bre} d'enfants				Income/ Revenu ($)	Monthly Award/ Paiement mensuel ($) No. of Children/ N^{bre} d'enfants				Income/ Revenu ($)	Monthly Award/ Paiement mensuel ($) No. of Children/ N^{bre} d'enfants			
	1	2	3	4		1	2	3	4		1	2	3	4		1	2	3	4		1	2	3	4
118800	1056	1694	2203	2620	124200	1103	1766	2296	2730	129600	1148	1835	2386	2836	135000	1191	1903	2472	2938					
118900	1057	1695	2204	2622	124300	1104	1767	2297	2732	129700	1149	1836	2387	2838	135100	1192	1904	2474	2940					
119000	1058	1696	2206	2624	124400	1105	1768	2299	2734	129800	1150	1838	2389	2840	135200	1193	1905	2475	2942					
119100	1059	1697	2208	2626	124500	1105	1770	2301	2736	129900	1150	1839	2390	2842	135300	1193	1907	2477	2944					
119200	1060	1699	2210	2628	124600	1106	1771	2303	2738	130000	1151	1840	2392	2843	135400	1194	1908	2478	2946					
119300	1061	1700	2211	2630	124700	1107	1772	2304	2740	130100	1152	1841	2394	2845	135500	1195	1909	2480	2948					
119400	1062	1701	2213	2632	124800	1108	1773	2306	2742	130200	1153	1843	2395	2847	135600	1196	1910	2482	2949					
119500	1063	1703	2215	2634	124900	1109	1775	2308	2744	130300	1153	1844	2397	2849	135700	1197	1912	2483	2951					
119600	1063	1704	2217	2636	125000	1110	1776	2310	2746	130400	1154	1845	2398	2850	135800	1197	1913	2485	2953					
119700	1064	1705	2218	2638	125100	1111	1777	2312	2748	130500	1155	1846	2400	2852	135900	1198	1914	2486	2955					
119800	1065	1706	2220	2640	125200	1112	1779	2313	2750	130600	1156	1848	2402	2854	136000	1199	1915	2488	2957					
119900	1066	1708	2222	2642	125300	1113	1780	2315	2752	130700	1157	1849	2403	2856	136100	1200	1916	2490	2959					
120000	1067	1709	2224	2644	125400	1113	1781	2317	2754	130800	1158	1850	2405	2858	136200	1201	1918	2491	2961					
120100	1068	1710	2226	2646	125500	1114	1783	2319	2756	130900	1158	1851	2406	2860	136300	1201	1919	2493	2963					
120200	1069	1712	2227	2648	125600	1115	1784	2320	2758	131000	1159	1853	2408	2862	136400	1202	1920	2494	2965					
120300	1070	1713	2229	2650	125700	1116	1786	2322	2760	131100	1160	1854	2410	2864	136500	1203	1921	2496	2967					
120400	1070	1714	2231	2652	125800	1117	1787	2324	2762	131200	1161	1855	2411	2866	136600	1204	1923	2498	2968					
120500	1071	1716	2233	2654	125900	1118	1788	2326	2764	131300	1161	1857	2413	2868	136700	1205	1924	2499	2970					
120600	1072	1717	2234	2656	126000	1118	1790	2327	2766	131400	1162	1858	2414	2869	136800	1205	1925	2501	2972					
120700	1073	1719	2236	2659	126100	1119	1791	2329	2768	131500	1163	1859	2416	2871	136900	1206	1927	2502	2974					
120800	1074	1720	2238	2661	126200	1120	1793	2330	2770	131600	1164	1860	2418	2873	137000	1207	1928	2504	2976					
120900	1075	1721	2240	2663	126300	1121	1794	2332	2772	131700	1165	1861	2419	2875	137100	1208	1929	2506	2978					
121000	1075	1723	2241	2665	126400	1121	1795	2334	2774	131800	1166	1863	2421	2877	137200	1209	1930	2507	2980					
121100	1076	1724	2243	2667	126500	1122	1797	2336	2776	131900	1166	1864	2422	2879	137300	1209	1932	2509	2982					
121200	1077	1726	2244	2669	126600	1123	1798	2337	2778	132000	1167	1865	2424	2881	137400	1210	1933	2510	2984					
121300	1078	1727	2246	2671	126700	1124	1799	2339	2780	132100	1168	1866	2426	2883	137500	1211	1934	2512	2986					
121400	1079	1728	2248	2673	126800	1125	1801	2341	2783	132200	1169	1868	2427	2885	137600	1212	1935	2514	2988					
121500	1079	1730	2250	2675	126900	1126	1802	2342	2785	132300	1169	1869	2429	2887	137700	1213	1937	2515	2989					
121600	1080	1731	2251	2677	127000	1127	1803	2344	2787	132400	1170	1870	2430	2889	137800	1213	1938	2517	2991					
121700	1081	1732	2253	2679	127100	1128	1804	2346	2789	132500	1171	1871	2432	2890	137900	1214	1939	2518	2993					
121800	1082	1734	2255	2681	127200	1129	1806	2347	2791	132600	1172	1873	2434	2892	138000	1215	1940	2520	2995					
121900	1083	1735	2257	2683	127300	1129	1807	2349	2793	132700	1173	1874	2435	2894	138100	1216	1941	2522	2997					
122000	1084	1736	2258	2685	127400	1130	1808	2350	2795	132800	1174	1875	2437	2896	138200	1217	1942	2523	2999					
122100	1085	1737	2260	2687	127500	1131	1809	2352	2797	132900	1174	1876	2438	2898	138300	1217	1944	2525	3001					
122200	1086	1739	2261	2689	127600	1132	1811	2354	2799	133000	1175	1878	2440	2900	138400	1218	1945	2526	3003					
122300	1086	1740	2263	2691	127700	1133	1812	2355	2801	133100	1176	1879	2442	2902	138500	1219	1946	2528	3005					
122400	1087	1742	2265	2693	127800	1134	1813	2357	2802	133200	1177	1880	2443	2904	138600	1220	1947	2530	3007					
122500	1088	1743	2267	2695	127900	1134	1815	2358	2804	133300	1177	1882	2445	2906	138700	1221	1948	2531	3009					
122600	1089	1744	2268	2697	128000	1135	1816	2360	2806	133400	1178	1883	2446	2908	138800	1221	1950	2533	3010					
122700	1090	1746	2270	2699	128100	1136	1817	2362	2808	133500	1179	1884	2448	2909	138900	1222	1951	2534	3012					
122800	1091	1747	2272	2701	128200	1137	1818	2363	2810	133600	1180	1885	2450	2911	139000	1223	1952	2536	3014					
122900	1091	1748	2273	2703	128300	1137	1820	2365	2812	133700	1181	1887	2451	2913	139100	1224	1953	2538	3016					
123000	1092	1750	2275	2705	128400	1138	1821	2366	2814	133800	1182	1888	2453	2915	139200	1225	1955	2539	3018					
123100	1093	1751	2277	2707	128500	1139	1822	2368	2816	133900	1182	1889	2454	2917	139300	1225	1956	2541	3020					
123200	1094	1753	2278	2709	128600	1140	1823	2370	2818	134000	1183	1890	2456	2919	139400	1226	1957	2542	3022					
123300	1095	1754	2280	2711	128700	1141	1825	2371	2820	134100	1184	1891	2458	2921	139500	1227	1958	2544	3024					
123400	1095	1755	2282	2713	128800	1142	1826	2373	2822	134200	1185	1893	2459	2923	139600	1228	1960	2546	3026					
123500	1096	1757	2283	2715	128900	1142	1827	2374	2823	134300	1185	1894	2461	2925	139700	1229	1961	2547	3028					
123600	1097	1758	2285	2717	129000	1143	1828	2376	2825	134400	1186	1895	2462	2927	139800	1229	1962	2549	3030					
123700	1098	1759	2287	2720	129100	1144	1829	2378	2827	134500	1187	1896	2464	2928	139900	1230	1963	2550	3031					
123800	1099	1761	2288	2722	129200	1145	1830	2379	2829	134600	1188	1898	2466	2930	140000	1231	1965	2552	3033					
123900	1100	1762	2290	2724	129300	1145	1832	2381	2831	134700	1189	1899	2467	2932	140100	1232	1966	2554	3035					
124000	1101	1763	2292	2726	129400	1146	1833	2382	2832	134800	1190	1900	2469	2934	140200	1233	1967	2555	3037					
124100	1102	1764	2294	2728	129500	1147	1834	2384	2834	134900	1190	1902	2470	2936	140300	1233	1969	2557	3039					

YUKON — CONTINUED

Federal Child Support Amounts: Simplified Tables
Montants fédéraux de pensions alimentaires pour enfants: Tables simplifiées

Income/ Revenu ($)	Monthly Award/ Paiement mensuel ($) No. of Children/ Nbre d'enfants				Income/ Revenu ($)	Monthly Award/ Paiement mensuel ($) No. of Children/ Nbre d'enfants				Income/ Revenu ($)	Monthly Award/ Paiement mensuel ($) No. of Children/ Nbre d'enfants			
	1	2	3	4		1	2	3	4		1	2	3	4
140400	1234	1970	2558	3040	143700	1261	2011	2611	3102	147000	1287	2052	2664	3165
140500	1235	1971	2560	3042	143800	1261	2012	2613	3104	147100	1288	2053	2666	3167
140600	1236	1972	2562	3044	143900	1262	2014	2614	3106	147200	1289	2054	2667	3169
140700	1237	1973	2563	3046	144000	1263	2015	2616	3108	147300	1289	2056	2669	3171
140800	1237	1975	2565	3048	144100	1264	2016	2618	3110	147400	1290	2057	2670	3173
140900	1238	1976	2566	3050	144200	1265	2017	2619	3112	147500	1291	2058	2672	3175
141000	1239	1977	2568	3051	144300	1265	2019	2621	3114	147600	1292	2059	2674	3176
141100	1240	1978	2570	3053	144400	1266	2020	2622	3116	147700	1293	2060	2675	3178
141200	1241	1980	2571	3055	144500	1267	2021	2624	3117	147800	1293	2062	2677	3180
141300	1241	1981	2573	3057	144600	1268	2022	2626	3119	147900	1294	2063	2678	3182
141400	1242	1982	2574	3058	144700	1269	2024	2627	3121	148000	1295	2064	2680	3184
141500	1243	1983	2576	3060	144800	1269	2025	2629	3123	148100	1296	2065	2682	3186
141600	1244	1985	2578	3062	144900	1270	2026	2630	3125	148200	1297	2067	2683	3188
141700	1245	1986	2579	3064	145000	1271	2027	2632	3127	148300	1297	2068	2685	3190
141800	1245	1987	2581	3066	145100	1272	2028	2634	3129	148400	1298	2069	2686	3192
141900	1246	1988	2582	3068	145200	1273	2030	2635	3131	148500	1299	2070	2688	3194
142000	1247	1990	2584	3070	145300	1273	2031	2637	3133	148600	1300	2072	2690	3196
142100	1248	1991	2586	3072	145400	1274	2032	2638	3135	148700	1301	2073	2691	3197
142200	1249	1992	2587	3074	145500	1275	2033	2640	3136	148800	1301	2074	2693	3199
142300	1249	1994	2589	3076	145600	1276	2035	2642	3138	148900	1302	2075	2694	3201
142400	1250	1995	2590	3077	145700	1277	2036	2643	3140	149000	1303	2077	2696	3203
142500	1251	1996	2592	3079	145800	1277	2037	2645	3142	149100	1304	2078	2698	3205
142600	1252	1997	2594	3081	145900	1278	2039	2646	3144	149200	1305	2079	2699	3207
142700	1253	1999	2595	3083	146000	1279	2040	2648	3146	149300	1305	2081	2701	3209
142800	1253	2000	2597	3085	146100	1280	2041	2650	3148	149400	1306	2082	2702	3211
142900	1254	2001	2598	3087	146200	1281	2042	2651	3150	149500	1307	2083	2704	3213
143000	1255	2002	2600	3089	146300	1281	2044	2653	3152	149600	1308	2084	2706	3215
143100	1256	2003	2602	3091	146400	1282	2045	2654	3154	149700	1309	2085	2707	3217
143200	1257	2005	2603	3093	146500	1283	2046	2656	3156	149800	1309	2087	2709	3218
143300	1257	2006	2605	3095	146600	1284	2047	2658	3157	149900	1310	2088	2710	3220
143400	1258	2007	2606	3096	146700	1285	2049	2659	3159	150000	1311	2089	2712	3222
143500	1259	2008	2608	3098	146800	1285	2050	2661	3161					
143600	1260	2010	2610	3100	146900	1286	2051	2662	3163					

Monthly Award/Paiement mensuel ($)			
One Child/ Un enfant	Two Children/ Deux enfants	Three Children/ Trois enfants	Four Children/ Quatre enfants
1311 plus 0.82% of income over $150,000	2089 plus 1.22% of income over $150,000	2712 plus 1.60% of income over $150,000	3222 plus 1.92% of income over $150,000
1311 plus 0,82% du revenu dépassant 150 000$	2089 plus 1,22% du revenu dépassant 150 000$	2712 plus 1,60% du revenu dépassant 150 000$	3222 plus 1,92% du revenu dépassant 150 000$

NORTHWEST TERRITORIES

Federal Child Support Amounts: Simplified Tables
Montants fédéraux de pensions alimentaires pour enfants: Tables simplifiées

Income/ Revenu ($)	Monthly Award/ Paiement mensuel ($) No. of Children/ N^bre d'enfants				Income/ Revenu ($)	Monthly Award/ Paiement mensuel ($) No. of Children/ N^bre d'enfants				Income/ Revenu ($)	Monthly Award/ Paiement mensuel ($) No. of Children/ N^bre d'enfants				Income/ Revenu ($)	Monthly Award/ Paiement mensuel ($) No. of Children/ N^bre d'enfants				Income/ Revenu ($)	Monthly Award/ Paiement mensuel ($) No. of Children/ N^bre d'enfants			
	1	2	3	4		1	2	3	4		1	2	3	4		1	2	3	4		1	2	3	4
10820	6	14	15	16	16200	129	248	267	286	21600	185	344	471	534	27000	234	418	572	697					
10900	8	18	19	20	16300	131	251	271	290	21700	186	345	472	539	27100	235	419	574	699					
11000	26	62	67	71	16400	132	255	275	294	21800	187	346	474	544	27200	236	421	575	701					
11100	28	66	72	76	16500	134	258	279	298	21900	188	348	476	549	27300	237	422	577	703					
11200	30	71	76	81	16600	136	261	282	302	22000	188	349	478	553	27400	238	423	579	705					
11300	32	75	81	86	16700	138	265	286	306	22100	189	350	480	558	27500	239	424	580	707					
11400	34	79	86	91	16800	140	268	290	310	22200	190	352	482	562	27600	240	426	582	710					
11500	36	84	91	96	16900	142	271	294	314	22300	191	353	484	567	27700	241	427	583	712					
11600	38	88	95	101	17000	144	275	297	318	22400	191	355	486	572	27800	242	428	585	714					
11700	40	92	100	106	17100	145	276	301	323	22500	192	356	488	577	27900	243	429	587	716					
11800	42	96	105	111	17200	146	278	306	327	22600	193	358	490	581	28000	244	431	588	718					
11900	44	101	110	116	17300	147	279	310	332	22700	194	359	492	586	28100	245	433	590	720					
12000	46	105	114	122	17400	148	281	315	337	22800	195	361	494	591	28200	246	434	591	722					
12100	48	109	118	126	17500	148	282	319	341	22900	196	362	496	596	28300	247	436	593	724					
12200	50	112	122	130	17600	149	284	324	346	23000	197	364	498	600	28400	248	438	595	726					
12300	52	116	126	135	17700	150	285	328	351	23100	198	365	500	603	28500	249	439	596	729					
12400	54	120	130	139	17800	151	287	332	356	23200	199	367	502	606	28600	250	441	598	731					
12500	56	123	134	143	17900	152	288	337	360	23300	200	368	504	609	28700	251	443	600	733					
12600	58	127	138	147	18000	153	290	341	365	23400	201	370	506	613	28800	252	444	601	735					
12700	60	131	142	152	18100	154	291	345	370	23500	201	371	508	616	28900	253	446	603	737					
12800	62	134	146	156	18200	155	293	350	374	23600	202	373	510	619	29000	255	448	605	739					
12900	64	138	149	160	18300	156	294	354	379	23700	203	374	512	622	29100	256	450	607	741					
13000	66	142	153	164	18400	157	296	358	384	23800	204	376	514	625	29200	257	451	609	743					
13100	68	145	157	168	18500	158	297	363	389	23900	205	377	516	628	29300	258	453	610	745					
13200	70	149	160	172	18600	158	299	367	393	24000	206	379	518	631	29400	259	455	612	747					
13300	72	152	164	176	18700	159	300	371	398	24100	207	380	520	633	29500	260	456	614	749					
13400	74	156	168	180	18800	160	302	376	403	24200	208	382	522	636	29600	261	458	616	752					
13500	76	159	172	184	18900	161	303	380	407	24300	209	383	524	638	29700	262	460	617	754					
13600	78	162	175	188	19000	162	305	384	412	24400	210	385	526	640	29800	263	461	619	756					
13700	80	166	179	192	19100	163	306	388	417	24500	210	386	528	643	29900	264	463	621	758					
13800	82	169	183	195	19200	164	308	393	421	24600	211	388	530	645	30000	265	464	623	760					
13900	84	173	186	199	19300	165	309	397	426	24700	212	389	532	647	30100	266	466	625	762					
14000	86	176	190	203	19400	166	311	401	431	24800	213	391	534	650	30200	267	467	627	764					
14100	88	179	194	207	19500	167	312	406	436	24900	214	392	535	652	30300	268	469	629	766					
14200	90	183	197	211	19600	168	314	410	440	25000	215	394	537	654	30400	269	470	631	768					
14300	92	186	201	214	19700	168	315	415	445	25100	216	395	539	656	30500	270	472	633	770					
14400	94	189	204	218	19800	169	317	419	450	25200	217	397	541	659	30600	271	474	635	773					
14500	96	192	208	222	19900	170	318	423	454	25300	218	398	543	661	30700	272	475	637	775					
14600	98	196	211	226	20000	171	320	428	459	25400	219	400	545	663	30800	274	477	639	777					
14700	100	199	215	229	20100	172	322	431	464	25500	221	401	546	665	30900	275	479	641	779					
14800	102	202	218	233	20200	173	323	434	468	25600	222	402	548	668	31000	276	480	643	781					
14900	104	206	222	237	20300	174	325	437	473	25700	223	404	550	670	31100	277	482	645	783					
15000	105	209	225	241	20400	175	326	440	478	25800	224	405	552	672	31200	278	483	647	785					
15100	107	212	229	245	20500	176	328	443	483	25900	225	407	554	674	31300	279	485	649	787					
15200	109	215	232	248	20600	177	329	446	487	26000	226	408	556	677	31400	280	486	651	789					
15300	111	219	236	252	20700	178	331	450	492	26100	227	409	558	679	31500	281	488	653	791					
15400	113	222	239	256	20800	178	332	453	497	26200	228	410	559	681	31600	282	490	655	793					
15500	115	225	243	260	20900	179	334	456	501	26300	228	411	561	683	31700	283	491	657	796					
15600	117	228	246	263	21000	180	335	459	506	26400	229	412	562	685	31800	284	493	660	798					
15700	119	232	250	267	21100	181	336	461	511	26500	230	413	564	687	31900	285	494	662	800					
15800	121	235	253	271	21200	182	338	463	515	26600	231	414	566	689	32000	286	496	664	802					
15900	123	238	257	274	21300	183	339	465	520	26700	232	415	567	691	32100	287	498	666	804					
16000	125	241	260	278	21400	183	341	467	525	26800	233	416	569	693	32200	288	499	668	807					
16100	127	244	264	282	21500	184	342	469	530	26900	233	417	570	695	32300	289	501	670	809					

Northwest Territories / Territoires du Nord-Ouest

Federal Child Support Amounts: Simplified Tables
Montants fédéraux de pensions alimentaires pour enfants: Tables simplifiées

Income/ Revenu ($)	Monthly Award/ Paiement mensuel ($) No. of Children/ Nᵇʳᵉ d'enfants				Income/ Revenu ($)	Monthly Award/ Paiement mensuel ($) No. of Children/ Nᵇʳᵉ d'enfants				Income/ Revenu ($)	Monthly Award/ Paiement mensuel ($) No. of Children/ Nᵇʳᵉ d'enfants				Income/ Revenu ($)	Monthly Award/ Paiement mensuel ($) No. of Children/ Nᵇʳᵉ d'enfants			
	1	2	3	4		1	2	3	4		1	2	3	4		1	2	3	4
32400	290	502	672	811	37800	343	584	777	935	43200	393	663	879	1054	48600	444	742	980	1175
32500	291	504	674	813	37900	344	585	779	937	43300	394	664	880	1056	48700	445	744	982	1177
32600	292	505	676	816	38000	345	587	781	940	43400	395	666	882	1059	48800	446	745	984	1179
32700	293	507	678	818	38100	346	589	783	942	43500	396	667	884	1061	48900	447	747	986	1182
32800	294	509	680	820	38200	347	590	785	944	43600	397	668	886	1063	49000	448	748	988	1184
32900	295	510	682	822	38300	348	592	787	947	43700	398	670	888	1065	49100	449	750	990	1186
33000	296	512	684	825	38400	349	593	789	949	43800	399	671	890	1067	49200	450	751	992	1189
33100	297	514	686	827	38500	350	595	791	951	43900	400	673	891	1069	49300	451	753	994	1191
33200	298	515	688	830	38600	351	596	792	953	44000	401	674	893	1072	49400	452	754	996	1193
33300	299	517	690	832	38700	352	598	794	956	44100	402	675	895	1074	49500	453	756	998	1196
33400	300	518	692	834	38800	353	599	796	958	44200	403	677	897	1076	49600	454	757	1000	1198
33500	301	520	694	836	38900	354	601	798	960	44300	404	678	899	1079	49700	455	759	1002	1200
33600	302	521	696	839	39000	354	602	800	962	44400	405	680	901	1081	49800	456	760	1003	1202
33700	303	523	698	841	39100	355	603	802	964	44500	406	681	902	1083	49900	457	762	1005	1205
33800	304	524	700	843	39200	356	605	804	966	44600	407	683	904	1085	50000	458	763	1007	1207
33900	305	526	702	845	39300	357	606	806	969	44700	408	684	906	1087	50100	459	764	1009	1209
34000	306	527	704	848	39400	358	608	807	971	44800	408	686	908	1089	50200	460	766	1011	1212
34100	307	529	706	850	39500	359	609	809	973	44900	409	687	910	1092	50300	461	767	1013	1214
34200	308	530	708	853	39600	359	611	811	975	45000	410	689	912	1094	50400	462	769	1015	1216
34300	309	532	710	855	39700	360	612	813	978	45100	411	690	914	1096	50500	463	770	1017	1218
34400	310	533	712	857	39800	361	614	815	980	45200	412	692	916	1098	50600	464	772	1019	1221
34500	311	535	714	859	39900	362	615	817	982	45300	413	693	917	1101	50700	464	773	1021	1223
34600	312	536	716	862	40000	363	616	818	984	45400	414	695	919	1103	50800	465	775	1023	1225
34700	313	538	718	864	40100	364	618	820	986	45500	415	696	921	1105	50900	466	776	1025	1228
34800	314	539	719	866	40200	365	619	822	989	45600	415	698	923	1107	51000	467	778	1027	1230
34900	315	541	721	868	40300	366	621	824	991	45700	416	699	925	1109	51100	468	779	1029	1232
35000	316	542	723	871	40400	367	622	826	993	45800	417	700	927	1111	51200	469	781	1031	1235
35100	317	543	725	873	40500	368	624	828	996	45900	418	702	928	1114	51300	470	782	1033	1237
35200	318	545	727	876	40600	369	626	830	998	46000	419	703	930	1116	51400	471	784	1035	1239
35300	319	546	729	878	40700	370	627	832	1000	46100	420	704	932	1118	51500	472	785	1037	1241
35400	320	548	731	880	40800	371	629	834	1002	46200	421	706	934	1120	51600	473	787	1039	1244
35500	321	549	733	882	40900	372	630	836	1005	46300	422	707	936	1123	51700	474	788	1040	1246
35600	322	551	735	885	41000	373	632	838	1007	46400	423	709	938	1125	51800	475	790	1042	1248
35700	323	552	737	887	41100	374	633	840	1009	46500	423	710	939	1127	51900	476	791	1044	1251
35800	323	554	739	889	41200	375	635	842	1011	46600	424	712	941	1129	52000	477	793	1046	1253
35900	324	555	741	891	41300	376	636	844	1013	46700	425	713	943	1131	52100	478	795	1048	1255
36000	325	557	743	894	41400	376	638	845	1016	46800	426	715	945	1134	52200	479	796	1050	1258
36100	326	558	745	896	41500	377	639	847	1018	46900	427	716	947	1136	52300	480	798	1052	1260
36200	327	560	747	899	41600	378	641	849	1020	47000	428	718	949	1138	52400	481	799	1054	1262
36300	328	561	749	901	41700	379	642	851	1022	47100	429	720	951	1140	52500	482	801	1056	1264
36400	329	563	751	903	41800	380	643	853	1024	47200	430	721	953	1143	52600	483	802	1058	1267
36500	330	564	753	905	41900	381	645	855	1026	47300	431	723	955	1145	52700	484	804	1060	1269
36600	331	566	755	908	42000	382	646	857	1029	47400	432	724	957	1147	52800	485	805	1062	1271
36700	332	567	757	910	42100	383	647	859	1031	47500	433	726	959	1150	52900	486	807	1064	1273
36800	333	569	758	912	42200	384	649	861	1033	47600	434	727	961	1152	53000	487	809	1066	1276
36900	334	570	760	914	42300	385	650	863	1035	47700	435	729	962	1154	53100	488	811	1068	1278
37000	335	572	762	917	42400	385	652	864	1037	47800	436	730	964	1156	53200	489	812	1070	1281
37100	336	573	764	919	42500	386	653	866	1040	47900	437	732	966	1159	53300	490	814	1072	1283
37200	337	575	766	922	42600	387	655	868	1042	48000	438	733	968	1161	53400	491	815	1074	1285
37300	338	576	768	924	42700	388	656	870	1044	48100	439	735	970	1163	53500	492	817	1076	1288
37400	339	578	770	926	42800	389	657	872	1046	48200	440	736	972	1166	53600	493	818	1077	1290
37500	340	579	771	928	42900	390	659	874	1048	48300	441	738	974	1168	53700	494	820	1079	1292
37600	341	581	773	931	43000	391	660	875	1050	48400	442	739	976	1170	53800	495	821	1081	1295
37700	342	582	775	933	43100	392	661	877	1052	48500	443	741	978	1173	53900	496	823	1083	1297

Federal Child Support Amounts: Simplified Tables
Montants fédéraux de pensions alimentaires pour enfants: Tables simplifiées

Income/ Revenu ($)	Monthly Award/ Paiement mensuel ($) No. of Children/ Nᵇʳᵉ d'enfants				Income/ Revenu ($)	Monthly Award/ Paiement mensuel ($) No. of Children/ Nᵇʳᵉ d'enfants				Income/ Revenu ($)	Monthly Award/ Paiement mensuel ($) No. of Children/ Nᵇʳᵉ d'enfants				Income/ Revenu ($)	Monthly Award/ Paiement mensuel ($) No. of Children/ Nᵇʳᵉ d'enfants			
	1	2	3	4		1	2	3	4		1	2	3	4		1	2	3	4
54000	497	824	1085	1300	59400	550	906	1191	1424	64800	603	988	1297	1550	70200	655	1069	1401	1673
54100	498	826	1087	1302	59500	551	908	1193	1426	64900	603	990	1299	1552	70300	656	1070	1403	1675
54200	499	827	1089	1305	59600	552	909	1195	1429	65000	604	991	1301	1554	70400	657	1072	1405	1677
54300	500	829	1091	1307	59700	552	911	1197	1431	65100	605	992	1303	1556	70500	658	1073	1407	1679
54400	501	830	1093	1309	59800	553	912	1199	1433	65200	606	994	1305	1559	70600	659	1075	1409	1682
54500	502	832	1095	1312	59900	554	914	1201	1436	65300	607	995	1307	1561	70700	659	1076	1411	1684
54600	503	833	1097	1314	60000	555	915	1203	1438	65400	608	997	1309	1563	70800	660	1078	1413	1686
54700	504	835	1099	1316	60100	556	916	1205	1440	65500	609	998	1311	1566	70900	661	1079	1415	1689
54800	505	836	1101	1319	60200	557	918	1207	1443	65600	610	1000	1313	1568	71000	662	1081	1417	1691
54900	506	838	1103	1321	60300	558	919	1209	1445	65700	611	1001	1315	1570	71100	663	1082	1419	1693
55000	507	839	1105	1323	60400	559	921	1211	1447	65800	612	1003	1317	1573	71200	664	1084	1421	1696
55100	508	840	1107	1325	60500	560	922	1213	1449	65900	613	1004	1318	1575	71300	665	1085	1423	1698
55200	509	842	1109	1328	60600	561	924	1215	1452	66000	614	1006	1320	1577	71400	666	1087	1425	1700
55300	510	843	1111	1330	60700	562	925	1216	1454	66100	615	1007	1322	1579	71500	667	1088	1427	1703
55400	511	845	1113	1332	60800	563	927	1218	1456	66200	616	1009	1324	1582	71600	668	1090	1429	1705
55500	512	846	1115	1335	60900	564	928	1220	1459	66300	617	1010	1326	1584	71700	669	1091	1431	1707
55600	513	848	1117	1337	61000	565	930	1222	1461	66400	618	1012	1328	1586	71800	670	1093	1433	1710
55700	514	849	1119	1339	61100	566	932	1224	1463	66500	619	1013	1329	1589	71900	671	1094	1435	1712
55800	515	851	1121	1342	61200	567	933	1226	1466	66600	620	1015	1331	1591	72000	672	1096	1436	1714
55900	515	852	1123	1344	61300	568	935	1228	1468	66700	621	1016	1333	1593	72100	673	1097	1438	1716
56000	516	854	1125	1346	61400	569	936	1230	1470	66800	622	1018	1335	1595	72200	674	1099	1440	1718
56100	517	855	1127	1348	61500	570	938	1232	1472	66900	623	1019	1337	1598	72300	675	1100	1442	1721
56200	518	857	1129	1351	61600	571	939	1234	1475	67000	624	1021	1339	1600	72400	676	1102	1444	1723
56300	519	858	1131	1353	61700	572	941	1236	1477	67100	625	1022	1341	1602	72500	677	1103	1446	1725
56400	520	860	1133	1355	61800	573	943	1238	1479	67200	626	1024	1343	1604	72600	678	1105	1448	1727
56500	521	861	1135	1358	61900	574	944	1240	1481	67300	627	1025	1345	1607	72700	679	1106	1449	1730
56600	522	863	1137	1360	62000	575	946	1242	1484	67400	628	1027	1347	1609	72800	680	1108	1451	1732
56700	523	864	1139	1362	62100	576	948	1244	1486	67500	629	1028	1349	1611	72900	681	1109	1453	1734
56800	524	866	1141	1365	62200	577	949	1246	1489	67600	630	1030	1351	1613	73000	682	1111	1455	1736
56900	525	867	1142	1367	62300	578	951	1248	1491	67700	630	1031	1353	1616	73100	683	1112	1457	1738
57000	526	869	1144	1369	62400	579	952	1250	1493	67800	631	1033	1355	1618	73200	684	1114	1459	1741
57100	527	871	1146	1371	62500	580	954	1252	1496	67900	632	1034	1357	1620	73300	685	1115	1461	1743
57200	528	872	1148	1374	62600	581	955	1253	1498	68000	633	1036	1359	1622	73400	686	1117	1463	1745
57300	529	874	1150	1376	62700	582	957	1255	1500	68100	634	1037	1361	1624	73500	687	1118	1464	1747
57400	530	875	1152	1378	62800	583	958	1257	1503	68200	635	1039	1363	1627	73600	688	1120	1466	1750
57500	531	877	1154	1381	62900	584	960	1259	1505	68300	636	1040	1365	1629	73700	689	1121	1468	1752
57600	532	878	1156	1383	63000	585	961	1261	1508	68400	637	1042	1367	1631	73800	689	1123	1470	1754
57700	533	880	1158	1385	63100	586	963	1263	1510	68500	638	1043	1369	1633	73900	690	1124	1472	1756
57800	534	881	1160	1387	63200	587	964	1265	1513	68600	639	1045	1371	1636	74000	691	1126	1474	1759
57900	535	883	1162	1390	63300	588	966	1267	1515	68700	640	1046	1373	1638	74100	692	1127	1476	1761
58000	536	885	1164	1392	63400	589	967	1269	1517	68800	641	1048	1374	1640	74200	693	1129	1478	1763
58100	537	887	1166	1394	63500	590	969	1271	1520	68900	642	1049	1376	1642	74300	694	1130	1480	1766
58200	538	888	1168	1397	63600	591	970	1273	1522	69000	643	1051	1378	1645	74400	695	1132	1481	1768
58300	539	890	1170	1399	63700	592	972	1275	1524	69100	644	1052	1380	1647	74500	696	1133	1483	1770
58400	540	891	1172	1401	63800	593	973	1277	1527	69200	645	1054	1382	1650	74600	697	1135	1485	1772
58500	541	893	1174	1404	63900	594	975	1279	1529	69300	646	1055	1384	1652	74700	698	1136	1487	1774
58600	542	894	1176	1406	64000	595	976	1281	1531	69400	647	1057	1386	1654	74800	699	1138	1489	1776
58700	543	896	1178	1408	64100	596	978	1283	1533	69500	648	1058	1388	1656	74900	700	1139	1491	1779
58800	544	897	1179	1410	64200	597	979	1285	1536	69600	649	1060	1389	1659	75000	701	1141	1493	1781
58900	545	899	1181	1413	64300	598	981	1287	1538	69700	650	1061	1391	1661	75100	702	1142	1495	1783
59000	546	900	1183	1415	64400	599	982	1289	1540	69800	651	1063	1393	1663	75200	703	1144	1497	1785
59100	547	902	1185	1417	64500	600	984	1291	1543	69900	652	1064	1395	1665	75300	704	1145	1498	1788
59200	548	903	1187	1420	64600	601	985	1293	1545	70000	653	1066	1397	1668	75400	705	1147	1500	1790
59300	549	905	1189	1422	64700	602	987	1295	1547	70100	654	1067	1399	1670	75500	706	1148	1502	1792

Northwest Territories / Territoires du Nord-Ouest

Federal Child Support Amounts: Simplified Tables
Montants fédéraux de pensions alimentaires pour enfants: Tables simplifiées

Income/ Revenu ($)	Monthly Award/ Paiement mensuel ($) No. of Children/ Nbre d'enfants				Income/ Revenu ($)	Monthly Award/ Paiement mensuel ($) No. of Children/ Nbre d'enfants				Income/ Revenu ($)	Monthly Award/ Paiement mensuel ($) No. of Children/ Nbre d'enfants				Income/ Revenu ($)	Monthly Award/ Paiement mensuel ($) No. of Children/ Nbre d'enfants			
	1	2	3	4		1	2	3	4		1	2	3	4		1	2	3	4
75600	707	1150	1504	1794	81000	755	1226	1603	1911	86400	802	1299	1696	2021	91800	849	1371	1788	2131
75700	708	1151	1506	1796	81100	756	1227	1605	1913	86500	803	1301	1698	2023	91900	849	1372	1790	2133
75800	709	1152	1508	1799	81200	757	1229	1607	1915	86600	804	1302	1700	2025	92000	850	1374	1792	2135
75900	710	1154	1509	1801	81300	758	1230	1609	1917	86700	805	1303	1701	2028	92100	851	1375	1794	2137
76000	710	1155	1511	1803	81400	758	1232	1610	1920	86800	806	1305	1703	2030	92200	852	1377	1796	2139
76100	711	1156	1513	1805	81500	759	1233	1612	1922	86900	806	1306	1705	2032	92300	853	1378	1797	2141
76200	712	1158	1515	1807	81600	760	1234	1614	1924	87000	807	1307	1707	2034	92400	853	1379	1799	2143
76300	713	1159	1516	1809	81700	761	1236	1616	1926	87100	808	1308	1709	2036	92500	854	1381	1801	2145
76400	714	1161	1518	1812	81800	762	1237	1618	1928	87200	809	1310	1710	2038	92600	855	1382	1803	2147
76500	715	1162	1520	1814	81900	763	1239	1620	1930	87300	810	1311	1712	2040	92700	856	1383	1804	2149
76600	716	1163	1522	1816	82000	764	1240	1621	1932	87400	810	1312	1714	2042	92800	857	1385	1806	2151
76700	717	1165	1524	1818	82100	765	1241	1623	1934	87500	811	1314	1716	2044	92900	858	1386	1808	2153
76800	717	1166	1525	1820	82200	766	1243	1624	1936	87600	812	1315	1717	2046	93000	859	1387	1810	2155
76900	718	1168	1527	1822	82300	767	1244	1626	1938	87700	813	1316	1719	2048	93100	860	1388	1812	2157
77000	719	1169	1529	1824	82400	767	1246	1628	1940	87800	814	1317	1721	2050	93200	861	1390	1813	2159
77100	720	1170	1531	1826	82500	768	1247	1630	1942	87900	815	1319	1723	2052	93300	861	1391	1815	2161
77200	721	1172	1533	1828	82600	769	1248	1631	1944	88000	816	1320	1724	2054	93400	862	1392	1817	2163
77300	722	1173	1535	1831	82700	770	1250	1633	1946	88100	817	1321	1726	2056	93500	863	1393	1819	2165
77400	723	1175	1536	1833	82800	771	1251	1635	1948	88200	818	1323	1727	2058	93600	864	1395	1820	2167
77500	724	1176	1538	1835	82900	772	1252	1637	1950	88300	819	1324	1729	2060	93700	865	1396	1822	2169
77600	725	1177	1540	1837	83000	773	1254	1638	1952	88400	820	1325	1731	2062	93800	866	1397	1824	2172
77700	725	1179	1542	1839	83100	774	1255	1640	1954	88500	821	1327	1733	2064	93900	866	1399	1826	2174
77800	726	1180	1544	1841	83200	775	1257	1641	1956	88600	821	1328	1734	2066	94000	867	1400	1827	2176
77900	727	1181	1546	1844	83300	776	1258	1643	1958	88700	822	1330	1736	2068	94100	868	1401	1829	2178
78000	728	1183	1548	1846	83400	777	1259	1645	1960	88800	823	1331	1738	2070	94200	869	1403	1830	2180
78100	729	1184	1550	1848	83500	777	1261	1647	1962	88900	824	1332	1740	2072	94300	870	1404	1832	2182
78200	730	1186	1552	1850	83600	778	1262	1648	1964	89000	825	1334	1741	2074	94400	870	1405	1834	2184
78300	731	1187	1553	1852	83700	779	1263	1650	1966	89100	826	1335	1743	2076	94500	871	1407	1836	2186
78400	732	1189	1555	1854	83800	780	1265	1652	1968	89200	827	1337	1744	2078	94600	872	1408	1837	2188
78500	733	1190	1557	1857	83900	781	1266	1653	1971	89300	828	1338	1746	2080	94700	873	1410	1839	2190
78600	733	1192	1559	1859	84000	782	1267	1655	1973	89400	828	1339	1748	2082	94800	874	1411	1841	2192
78700	734	1193	1561	1861	84100	783	1268	1657	1975	89500	829	1341	1750	2084	94900	875	1412	1843	2194
78800	735	1195	1563	1863	84200	784	1270	1658	1977	89600	830	1342	1751	2086	95000	876	1414	1844	2196
78900	736	1196	1564	1865	84300	785	1271	1660	1979	89700	831	1343	1753	2088	95100	877	1415	1846	2198
79000	737	1198	1566	1867	84400	785	1272	1662	1981	89800	832	1345	1755	2090	95200	878	1417	1847	2200
79100	738	1199	1568	1869	84500	786	1274	1663	1983	89900	833	1346	1756	2092	95300	879	1418	1849	2202
79200	739	1201	1570	1871	84600	787	1275	1665	1985	90000	833	1347	1758	2094	95400	880	1419	1851	2204
79300	740	1202	1571	1873	84700	788	1276	1667	1987	90100	834	1348	1760	2096	95500	880	1421	1853	2206
79400	741	1204	1573	1876	84800	789	1277	1669	1989	90200	835	1350	1761	2098	95600	881	1422	1854	2208
79500	741	1205	1575	1878	84900	790	1279	1670	1991	90300	836	1351	1763	2100	95700	882	1423	1856	2210
79600	742	1207	1577	1880	85000	790	1280	1672	1993	90400	837	1352	1765	2102	95800	883	1425	1858	2212
79700	743	1208	1579	1882	85100	791	1281	1674	1995	90500	837	1354	1766	2104	95900	884	1426	1859	2214
79800	744	1210	1580	1884	85200	792	1283	1675	1997	90600	838	1355	1768	2106	96000	885	1427	1861	2216
79900	745	1211	1582	1886	85300	793	1284	1677	1999	90700	839	1356	1770	2108	96100	886	1428	1863	2218
80000	746	1212	1584	1889	85400	794	1286	1679	2001	90800	840	1357	1772	2110	96200	887	1430	1864	2220
80100	747	1213	1586	1891	85500	794	1287	1680	2003	90900	841	1359	1773	2113	96300	888	1431	1866	2222
80200	748	1215	1588	1893	85600	795	1288	1682	2005	91000	842	1360	1775	2115	96400	888	1432	1868	2224
80300	749	1216	1590	1896	85700	796	1290	1684	2007	91100	843	1361	1777	2117	96500	889	1433	1869	2226
80400	750	1218	1592	1898	85800	797	1291	1685	2009	91200	844	1363	1778	2119	96600	890	1435	1871	2228
80500	750	1219	1593	1900	85900	798	1292	1687	2011	91300	844	1364	1780	2121	96700	891	1436	1873	2230
80600	751	1221	1595	1902	86000	799	1294	1689	2013	91400	845	1365	1782	2123	96800	892	1437	1875	2232
80700	752	1222	1597	1904	86100	800	1295	1691	2015	91500	846	1367	1783	2125	96900	893	1439	1876	2234
80800	753	1223	1599	1907	86200	801	1297	1693	2017	91600	847	1368	1785	2127	97000	893	1440	1878	2236
80900	754	1225	1601	1909	86300	801	1298	1694	2019	91700	848	1370	1787	2129	97100	894	1441	1880	2238

Federal Child Support Amounts: Simplified Tables
Montants fédéraux de pensions alimentaires pour enfants: Tables simplifiées

Income/ Revenu ($)	Monthly Award/ Paiement mensuel ($) No. of Children/ Nᵇʳᵉ d'enfants				Income/ Revenu ($)	Monthly Award/ Paiement mensuel ($) No. of Children/ Nᵇʳᵉ d'enfants				Income/ Revenu ($)	Monthly Award/ Paiement mensuel ($) No. of Children/ Nᵇʳᵉ d'enfants				Income/ Revenu ($)	Monthly Award/ Paiement mensuel ($) No. of Children/ Nᵇʳᵉ d'enfants			
	1	2	3	4		1	2	3	4		1	2	3	4		1	2	3	4
97200	895	1443	1881	2240	102600	941	1515	1974	2350	108000	988	1587	2067	2460	113400	1034	1659	2160	2569
97300	896	1444	1883	2242	102700	942	1517	1976	2352	108100	989	1588	2069	2462	113500	1035	1660	2162	2571
97400	897	1445	1885	2244	102800	943	1518	1978	2354	108200	990	1590	2070	2464	113600	1036	1662	2163	2573
97500	897	1447	1886	2246	102900	944	1519	1979	2356	108300	991	1591	2072	2466	113700	1037	1663	2165	2575
97600	898	1448	1888	2248	103000	945	1521	1981	2358	108400	991	1592	2074	2468	113800	1038	1664	2167	2577
97700	899	1449	1890	2250	103100	946	1522	1983	2360	108500	992	1594	2075	2470	113900	1039	1666	2168	2579
97800	900	1451	1891	2252	103200	947	1524	1984	2362	108600	993	1595	2077	2472	114000	1039	1667	2170	2581
97900	901	1452	1893	2255	103300	947	1525	1986	2364	108700	994	1597	2079	2474	114100	1040	1668	2172	2583
98000	902	1454	1895	2257	103400	948	1526	1988	2366	108800	995	1598	2081	2476	114200	1041	1670	2173	2585
98100	903	1455	1897	2259	103500	949	1528	1989	2368	108900	996	1599	2082	2478	114300	1042	1671	2175	2587
98200	904	1457	1899	2261	103600	950	1529	1991	2370	109000	996	1601	2084	2480	114400	1043	1672	2177	2589
98300	904	1458	1900	2263	103700	951	1530	1993	2372	109100	997	1602	2086	2482	114500	1043	1674	2178	2591
98400	905	1459	1902	2265	103800	952	1532	1994	2374	109200	998	1604	2087	2484	114600	1044	1675	2180	2593
98500	906	1461	1904	2267	103900	952	1533	1996	2376	109300	999	1605	2089	2486	114700	1045	1676	2182	2595
98600	907	1462	1906	2269	104000	953	1534	1998	2378	109400	1000	1606	2091	2488	114800	1046	1678	2184	2598
98700	908	1463	1907	2271	104100	954	1535	2000	2380	109500	1000	1608	2092	2490	114900	1047	1679	2185	2600
98800	909	1465	1909	2273	104200	955	1537	2002	2382	109600	1001	1609	2094	2492	115000	1048	1681	2187	2602
98900	909	1466	1911	2275	104300	956	1538	2003	2384	109700	1002	1610	2096	2494	115100	1049	1682	2190	2604
99000	910	1467	1913	2277	104400	956	1539	2005	2386	109800	1003	1612	2097	2496	115200	1050	1684	2190	2606
99100	911	1468	1915	2279	104500	957	1541	2007	2388	109900	1004	1613	2099	2498	115300	1050	1685	2192	2608
99200	912	1470	1916	2281	104600	958	1542	2009	2390	110000	1005	1614	2101	2500	115400	1051	1686	2194	2610
99300	913	1471	1918	2283	104700	959	1543	2010	2392	110100	1006	1615	2103	2502	115500	1052	1688	2195	2612
99400	913	1473	1920	2285	104800	960	1544	2012	2394	110200	1007	1617	2105	2504	115600	1053	1689	2197	2614
99500	914	1474	1922	2287	104900	961	1546	2014	2396	110300	1007	1618	2106	2506	115700	1054	1690	2199	2616
99600	915	1475	1923	2289	105000	962	1547	2016	2399	110400	1008	1619	2108	2508	115800	1055	1692	2200	2618
99700	916	1477	1925	2291	105100	963	1548	2018	2401	110500	1009	1620	2110	2510	115900	1055	1693	2202	2620
99800	917	1478	1927	2293	105200	964	1550	2019	2403	110600	1010	1622	2112	2512	116000	1056	1694	2204	2622
99900	918	1479	1929	2295	105300	964	1551	2021	2405	110700	1011	1623	2113	2514	116100	1057	1695	2206	2624
100000	919	1481	1930	2297	105400	965	1552	2023	2407	110800	1012	1624	2115	2516	116200	1058	1697	2208	2626
100100	920	1482	1932	2299	105500	966	1554	2025	2409	110900	1012	1626	2117	2518	116300	1059	1698	2209	2628
100200	921	1484	1933	2301	105600	967	1555	2026	2411	111000	1013	1627	2119	2520	116400	1059	1699	2211	2630
100300	922	1485	1935	2303	105700	968	1557	2028	2413	111100	1014	1628	2121	2522	116500	1060	1700	2213	2632
100400	923	1486	1937	2305	105800	969	1558	2030	2415	111200	1015	1630	2122	2524	116600	1061	1702	2215	2634
100500	924	1488	1939	2307	105900	969	1559	2032	2417	111300	1016	1631	2124	2526	116700	1062	1703	2216	2636
100600	924	1489	1940	2309	106000	970	1561	2033	2419	111400	1016	1632	2126	2528	116800	1063	1704	2218	2638
100700	925	1490	1942	2311	106100	971	1562	2035	2421	111500	1017	1634	2128	2530	116900	1064	1706	2220	2640
100800	926	1492	1944	2314	106200	972	1564	2036	2423	111600	1018	1635	2129	2532	117000	1065	1707	2222	2642
100900	927	1493	1946	2316	106300	973	1565	2038	2425	111700	1019	1637	2131	2534	117100	1066	1708	2224	2644
101000	928	1494	1947	2318	106400	973	1566	2040	2427	111800	1020	1638	2133	2536	117200	1067	1710	2225	2646
101100	929	1495	1949	2320	106500	974	1568	2042	2429	111900	1021	1639	2135	2538	117300	1067	1711	2227	2648
101200	930	1497	1950	2322	106600	975	1569	2043	2431	112000	1022	1641	2136	2541	117400	1068	1712	2229	2650
101300	931	1498	1952	2324	106700	976	1570	2045	2433	112100	1023	1642	2138	2543	117500	1069	1714	2231	2652
101400	931	1499	1954	2326	106800	977	1572	2047	2435	112200	1024	1644	2139	2545	117600	1070	1715	2232	2654
101500	932	1501	1956	2328	106900	978	1573	2049	2437	112300	1025	1645	2141	2547	117700	1071	1716	2234	2656
101600	933	1502	1957	2330	107000	979	1574	2050	2439	112400	1026	1646	2143	2549	117800	1072	1718	2236	2658
101700	934	1503	1959	2332	107100	980	1575	2052	2441	112500	1027	1648	2145	2551	117900	1072	1719	2238	2660
101800	935	1505	1961	2334	107200	981	1577	2053	2443	112600	1027	1649	2146	2553	118000	1073	1721	2239	2662
101900	936	1506	1962	2336	107300	982	1578	2055	2445	112700	1028	1650	2148	2555	118100	1074	1722	2241	2664
102000	936	1507	1964	2338	107400	983	1579	2057	2447	112800	1029	1652	2150	2557	118200	1075	1724	2242	2666
102100	937	1508	1966	2340	107500	983	1581	2059	2449	112900	1030	1653	2152	2559	118300	1076	1725	2244	2668
102200	938	1510	1967	2342	107600	984	1582	2060	2451	113000	1031	1654	2153	2561	118400	1076	1726	2246	2670
102300	939	1511	1969	2344	107700	985	1583	2062	2453	113100	1032	1655	2155	2563	118500	1077	1728	2248	2672
102400	940	1513	1971	2346	107800	986	1584	2064	2456	113200	1033	1657	2156	2565	118600	1078	1729	2249	2674
102500	940	1514	1972	2348	107900	987	1586	2065	2458	113300	1034	1658	2158	2567	118700	1079	1730	2251	2676

Federal Child Support Amounts: Simplified Tables
Montants fédéraux de pensions alimentaires pour enfants: Tables simplifiées

Income/ Revenu ($)	Monthly Award/ Paiement mensuel ($) No. of Children/ Nᵇʳᵉ d'enfants				Income/ Revenu ($)	Monthly Award/ Paiement mensuel ($) No. of Children/ Nᵇʳᵉ d'enfants				Income/ Revenu ($)	Monthly Award/ Paiement mensuel ($) No. of Children/ Nᵇʳᵉ d'enfants				Income/ Revenu ($)	Monthly Award/ Paiement mensuel ($) No. of Children/ Nᵇʳᵉ d'enfants			
	1	2	3	4		1	2	3	4		1	2	3	4		1	2	3	4
118800	1080	1732	2253	2678	124200	1126	1803	2343	2786	129600	1170	1870	2431	2890	135000	1212	1937	2517	2991
118900	1081	1733	2255	2680	124300	1126	1804	2345	2788	129700	1171	1871	2433	2892	135100	1213	1938	2519	2993
119000	1082	1734	2256	2683	124400	1127	1805	2347	2790	129800	1171	1873	2434	2894	135200	1214	1939	2520	2995
119100	1083	1735	2258	2685	124500	1128	1807	2348	2792	129900	1172	1874	2436	2896	135300	1214	1941	2522	2997
119200	1084	1737	2259	2687	124600	1129	1808	2350	2794	130000	1173	1875	2437	2897	135400	1215	1942	2523	2999
119300	1085	1738	2261	2689	124700	1130	1809	2352	2796	130100	1174	1876	2439	2899	135500	1216	1943	2525	3001
119400	1086	1740	2263	2691	124800	1130	1811	2354	2798	130200	1175	1878	2440	2901	135600	1217	1944	2526	3003
119500	1086	1741	2265	2693	124900	1131	1812	2355	2800	130300	1175	1879	2442	2903	135700	1217	1945	2528	3004
119600	1087	1742	2266	2695	125000	1132	1813	2357	2802	130400	1176	1880	2443	2904	135800	1218	1947	2529	3006
119700	1088	1744	2268	2697	125100	1133	1814	2359	2804	130500	1177	1881	2445	2906	135900	1219	1948	2531	3008
119800	1089	1745	2270	2699	125200	1134	1816	2360	2806	130600	1178	1883	2446	2908	136000	1220	1949	2532	3010
119900	1090	1746	2271	2701	125300	1135	1817	2362	2808	130700	1179	1884	2448	2910	136100	1221	1950	2534	3012
120000	1091	1748	2273	2703	125400	1135	1818	2364	2810	130800	1180	1885	2449	2912	136200	1222	1952	2535	3014
120100	1092	1749	2275	2705	125500	1136	1820	2365	2812	130900	1180	1886	2451	2914	136300	1222	1953	2537	3016
120200	1093	1751	2276	2707	125600	1137	1821	2367	2814	131000	1181	1888	2453	2916	136400	1223	1954	2538	3017
120300	1094	1752	2278	2709	125700	1138	1822	2368	2816	131100	1182	1889	2455	2918	136500	1224	1955	2540	3019
120400	1094	1753	2280	2711	125800	1139	1824	2370	2818	131200	1183	1890	2456	2920	136600	1225	1957	2541	3021
120500	1095	1755	2281	2713	125900	1140	1825	2372	2820	131300	1183	1892	2458	2922	136700	1225	1958	2543	3023
120600	1096	1756	2283	2715	126000	1141	1826	2373	2822	131400	1184	1893	2459	2924	136800	1226	1959	2544	3025
120700	1097	1757	2285	2717	126100	1142	1827	2375	2824	131500	1185	1894	2461	2925	136900	1227	1960	2546	3027
120800	1098	1759	2287	2719	126200	1143	1828	2376	2826	131600	1186	1895	2462	2927	137000	1228	1962	2548	3028
120900	1099	1760	2288	2721	126300	1143	1830	2378	2828	131700	1187	1897	2464	2929	137100	1229	1963	2550	3030
121000	1099	1761	2290	2723	126400	1144	1831	2380	2830	131800	1188	1898	2466	2931	137200	1230	1964	2551	3032
121100	1100	1762	2292	2725	126500	1145	1832	2381	2832	131900	1188	1899	2467	2933	137300	1230	1966	2553	3034
121200	1101	1764	2293	2727	126600	1146	1833	2383	2834	132000	1189	1900	2469	2935	137400	1231	1967	2554	3036
121300	1101	1765	2295	2729	126700	1147	1835	2385	2836	132100	1190	1901	2471	2937	137500	1232	1968	2556	3037
121400	1102	1766	2297	2731	126800	1148	1836	2386	2838	132200	1191	1902	2472	2939	137600	1233	1969	2557	3039
121500	1103	1768	2298	2733	126900	1148	1837	2388	2839	132300	1192	1904	2474	2940	137700	1233	1971	2559	3041
121600	1104	1769	2300	2735	127000	1149	1838	2390	2841	132400	1192	1905	2475	2942	137800	1234	1972	2561	3043
121700	1105	1770	2302	2737	127100	1150	1839	2392	2843	132500	1193	1906	2477	2944	137900	1235	1973	2562	3045
121800	1105	1772	2304	2739	127200	1151	1841	2393	2845	132600	1194	1907	2479	2946	138000	1236	1974	2564	3047
121900	1106	1773	2305	2741	127300	1151	1842	2395	2847	132700	1195	1908	2480	2948	138100	1237	1975	2566	3049
122000	1107	1774	2307	2743	127400	1152	1843	2396	2848	132800	1196	1910	2482	2950	138200	1238	1976	2567	3051
122100	1108	1775	2309	2745	127500	1153	1844	2398	2850	132900	1197	1911	2483	2951	138300	1238	1978	2569	3053
122200	1109	1777	2310	2747	127600	1154	1846	2400	2852	133000	1197	1912	2485	2953	138400	1239	1979	2570	3055
122300	1110	1778	2312	2749	127700	1155	1847	2401	2854	133100	1198	1913	2487	2955	138500	1240	1980	2572	3057
122400	1110	1779	2314	2751	127800	1155	1848	2403	2856	133200	1198	1915	2488	2957	138600	1241	1981	2574	3058
122500	1111	1781	2315	2753	127900	1156	1849	2404	2858	133300	1199	1916	2490	2959	138700	1242	1983	2575	3060
122600	1112	1782	2317	2755	128000	1157	1851	2406	2860	133400	1200	1917	2491	2960	138800	1242	1984	2577	3062
122700	1113	1783	2318	2757	128100	1158	1852	2408	2862	133500	1201	1918	2493	2962	138900	1243	1985	2578	3064
122800	1114	1785	2320	2759	128200	1159	1853	2409	2864	133600	1201	1920	2495	2964	139000	1244	1986	2580	3066
122900	1115	1786	2322	2761	128300	1159	1855	2411	2866	133700	1202	1921	2496	2966	139100	1245	1987	2582	3068
123000	1116	1787	2323	2763	128400	1160	1856	2412	2868	133800	1203	1922	2498	2968	139200	1246	1988	2583	3070
123100	1117	1788	2325	2765	128500	1161	1857	2414	2870	133900	1204	1923	2499	2970	139300	1246	1990	2585	3072
123200	1118	1790	2326	2767	128600	1162	1858	2416	2871	134000	1204	1925	2501	2972	139400	1247	1991	2586	3073
123300	1118	1791	2328	2769	128700	1163	1860	2417	2873	134100	1205	1926	2503	2974	139500	1248	1992	2588	3075
123400	1119	1792	2330	2771	128800	1163	1861	2419	2875	134200	1206	1927	2504	2976	139600	1249	1993	2590	3077
123500	1120	1794	2331	2773	128900	1164	1862	2421	2877	134300	1206	1929	2506	2978	139700	1250	1994	2591	3079
123600	1121	1795	2333	2775	129000	1165	1863	2422	2879	134400	1207	1930	2507	2980	139800	1250	1995	2593	3081
123700	1122	1796	2335	2777	129100	1166	1864	2424	2881	134500	1208	1931	2509	2981	139900	1251	1997	2595	3083
123800	1123	1798	2336	2779	129200	1167	1865	2425	2883	134600	1209	1932	2511	2983	140000	1252	1998	2596	3084
123900	1123	1799	2338	2781	129300	1167	1867	2427	2885	134700	1209	1934	2512	2985	140100	1253	1999	2598	3086
124000	1124	1800	2340	2782	129400	1168	1868	2428	2886	134800	1210	1935	2514	2987	140200	1254	2001	2599	3088
124100	1125	1801	2342	2784	129500	1169	1869	2430	2888	134900	1211	1936	2516	2989	140300	1254	2002	2601	3090

Northwest Territories / Territoires du Nord-Ouest

Federal Child Support Amounts: Simplified Tables

Montants fédéraux de pensions alimentaires pour enfants: Tables simplifiées

Income/ Revenu ($)	Monthly Award/ Paiement mensuel ($) No. of Children/ Nbre d'enfants				Income/ Revenu ($)	Monthly Award/ Paiement mensuel ($) No. of Children/ Nbre d'enfants				Income/ Revenu ($)	Monthly Award/ Paiement mensuel ($) No. of Children/ Nbre d'enfants			
	1	2	3	4		1	2	3	4		1	2	3	4
140400	1255	2003	2602	3091	143700	1282	2044	2654	3153	147000	1307	2085	2706	3215
140500	1256	2004	2604	3093	143800	1283	2045	2656	3155	147100	1308	2086	2708	3217
140600	1257	2006	2605	3095	143900	1284	2046	2657	3157	147200	1309	2087	2709	3219
140700	1258	2007	2607	3097	144000	1284	2048	2659	3159	147300	1309	2089	2711	3221
140800	1258	2008	2608	3099	144100	1285	2049	2661	3161	147400	1310	2090	2712	3223
140900	1259	2009	2610	3101	144200	1285	2050	2662	3163	147500	1311	2091	2714	3224
141000	1260	2011	2611	3103	144300	1286	2052	2664	3165	147600	1312	2092	2715	3226
141100	1261	2012	2613	3105	144400	1287	2053	2665	3167	147700	1312	2094	2717	3228
141200	1262	2013	2614	3107	144500	1288	2054	2667	3168	147800	1313	2095	2718	3230
141300	1262	2015	2616	3109	144600	1288	2055	2669	3170	147900	1314	2096	2720	3232
141400	1263	2016	2617	3111	144700	1289	2057	2670	3172	148000	1315	2097	2722	3234
141500	1264	2017	2619	3112	144800	1290	2058	2672	3174	148100	1316	2098	2724	3236
141600	1265	2018	2620	3114	144900	1291	2059	2673	3176	148200	1317	2099	2725	3238
141700	1266	2020	2622	3116	145000	1291	2060	2675	3178	148300	1317	2101	2727	3240
141800	1267	2021	2623	3118	145100	1292	2061	2677	3180	148400	1318	2102	2728	3242
141900	1267	2022	2625	3120	145200	1293	2062	2678	3182	148500	1319	2103	2730	3244
142000	1268	2023	2627	3122	145300	1293	2064	2680	3183	148600	1320	2104	2731	3245
142100	1269	2024	2629	3124	145400	1294	2065	2681	3185	148700	1320	2105	2733	3247
142200	1270	2025	2630	3126	145500	1295	2066	2683	3187	148800	1321	2107	2735	3249
142300	1270	2027	2632	3127	145600	1296	2067	2685	3189	148900	1322	2108	2736	3251
142400	1271	2028	2633	3129	145700	1296	2068	2686	3191	149000	1323	2109	2738	3253
142500	1272	2029	2635	3131	145800	1297	2070	2688	3193	149100	1324	2110	2740	3255
142600	1273	2030	2636	3133	145900	1298	2071	2690	3194	149200	1325	2111	2741	3257
142700	1274	2031	2638	3135	146000	1299	2072	2691	3196	149300	1325	2113	2743	3259
142800	1275	2033	2640	3137	146100	1300	2073	2693	3198	149400	1326	2114	2744	3260
142900	1275	2034	2641	3138	146200	1301	2075	2694	3200	149500	1327	2115	2746	3262
143000	1276	2035	2643	3140	146300	1301	2076	2696	3202	149600	1328	2116	2748	3264
143100	1277	2036	2645	3142	146400	1302	2077	2697	3203	149700	1329	2117	2749	3266
143200	1278	2038	2646	3144	146500	1303	2078	2699	3205	149800	1329	2118	2751	3268
143300	1279	2039	2648	3146	146600	1304	2080	2700	3207	149900	1330	2120	2752	3270
143400	1279	2040	2649	3147	146700	1304	2081	2702	3209	150000	1331	2121	2754	3271
143500	1280	2041	2651	3149	146800	1305	2082	2703	3211					
143600	1281	2043	2653	3151	146900	1306	2083	2705	3213					

Monthly Award/Paiement mensuel ($)			
One Child/ Un enfant	Two Children/ Deux enfants	Three Children/ Trois enfants	Four Children/ Quatre enfants
1331 plus 0.78% of income over $150,000	2121 plus 1.18% of income over $150,000	2754 plus 1.60% of income over $150,000	3271 plus 1.84% of income over $150,000
1331 plus 0,78% du revenu dépassant 150 000$	2121 plus 1,18% du revenu dépassant 150 000$	2754 plus 1,60% du revenu dépassant 150 000$	3271 plus 1,84% du revenu dépassant 150 000$

NUNAVUT

Federal Child Support Amounts: Simplified Tables
Montants fédéraux de pensions alimentaires pour enfants: Tables simplifiées

Income/ Revenu ($)	Monthly Award/ Paiement mensuel ($) No. of Children/ N^bre d'enfants				Income/ Revenu ($)	Monthly Award/ Paiement mensuel ($) No. of Children/ N^bre d'enfants				Income/ Revenu ($)	Monthly Award/ Paiement mensuel ($) No. of Children/ N^bre d'enfants				Income/ Revenu ($)	Monthly Award/ Paiement mensuel ($) No. of Children/ N^bre d'enfants			
	1	2	3	4		1	2	3	4		1	2	3	4		1	2	3	4
10820	0	0	0	0	16200	177	269	290	310	21600	197	361	490	572	27000	225	415	574	703
10900	2	2	2	2	16300	177	274	294	316	21700	197	362	492	577	27100	226	416	576	705
11000	20	22	23	25	16400	177	278	299	321	21800	197	363	493	581	27200	227	418	577	707
11100	25	28	29	31	16500	178	283	304	326	21900	197	363	495	586	27300	228	419	579	710
11200	30	33	35	38	16600	178	287	309	331	22000	198	364	496	591	27400	230	421	581	712
11300	35	39	41	44	16700	178	292	314	336	22100	198	365	497	594	27500	231	422	583	714
11400	40	44	47	51	16800	179	296	318	342	22200	199	366	499	598	27600	232	424	584	716
11500	46	50	53	57	16900	179	301	323	347	22300	199	367	500	601	27700	233	425	586	718
11600	51	55	59	63	17000	179	305	328	352	22400	199	368	502	604	27800	234	427	588	721
11700	56	61	65	70	17100	179	307	333	357	22500	199	369	503	607	27900	235	428	590	723
11800	61	66	71	76	17200	180	309	337	362	22600	200	370	505	611	28000	237	430	591	725
11900	66	72	77	83	17300	180	310	342	367	22700	200	370	506	614	28100	238	432	593	727
12000	71	77	83	89	17400	180	312	347	372	22800	200	371	508	617	28200	239	433	595	729
12100	75	82	88	94	17500	181	314	351	377	22900	201	372	509	620	28300	241	435	596	731
12200	80	86	93	100	17600	181	316	356	382	23000	201	373	511	624	28400	242	437	598	734
12300	84	91	98	105	17700	182	318	361	387	23100	201	374	512	626	28500	243	439	600	736
12400	89	96	103	111	17800	182	320	365	392	23200	201	375	514	628	28600	244	440	602	738
12500	93	101	109	116	17900	182	321	370	397	23300	202	376	515	630	28700	245	442	603	740
12600	97	105	114	122	18000	183	323	375	402	23400	202	377	517	631	28800	247	444	605	742
12700	102	110	119	127	18100	183	324	380	407	23500	202	378	518	633	28900	248	446	607	744
12800	106	115	124	132	18200	184	325	384	412	23600	202	378	520	635	29000	249	447	609	746
12900	111	119	129	138	18300	184	326	389	417	23700	203	379	521	637	29100	250	449	611	748
13000	115	124	134	143	18400	185	328	393	422	23800	203	380	522	639	29200	251	450	613	750
13100	119	129	139	148	18500	185	329	398	426	23900	203	381	524	641	29300	252	452	614	753
13200	123	133	144	154	18600	186	330	402	431	24000	203	382	525	642	29400	254	454	616	755
13300	128	138	149	159	18700	186	331	407	436	24100	203	383	526	644	29500	255	456	618	757
13400	132	142	154	164	18800	187	332	412	441	24200	204	384	528	646	29600	256	457	620	759
13500	136	147	159	169	18900	187	333	416	446	24300	204	385	529	648	29700	257	459	622	761
13600	140	152	164	175	19000	188	334	421	451	24400	204	386	531	649	29800	258	461	623	763
13700	145	156	169	180	19100	188	335	426	456	24500	204	386	532	651	29900	259	463	625	766
13800	149	161	174	185	19200	189	336	430	461	24600	205	387	534	653	30000	260	464	627	768
13900	153	165	178	191	19300	189	337	435	466	24700	205	388	535	655	30100	261	466	629	770
14000	157	170	183	196	19400	190	338	439	470	24800	205	389	537	657	30200	262	467	631	772
14100	159	175	188	201	19500	190	340	444	475	24900	205	390	538	659	30300	264	469	633	775
14200	160	179	193	206	19600	191	341	448	480	25000	206	391	540	661	30400	265	471	635	777
14300	162	184	198	212	19700	191	342	453	485	25100	207	392	542	663	30500	266	473	638	779
14400	163	188	203	217	19800	191	343	457	490	25200	208	393	543	665	30600	267	474	640	781
14500	165	193	208	222	19900	192	344	462	495	25300	208	394	545	667	30700	268	476	642	783
14600	166	197	212	227	20000	192	345	466	499	25400	209	396	547	669	30800	269	478	644	786
14700	168	202	217	232	20100	192	346	468	504	25500	210	397	548	671	30900	271	479	646	788
14800	169	206	222	238	20200	193	347	469	508	25600	211	398	550	673	31000	272	481	648	790
14900	171	211	227	243	20300	193	348	471	513	25700	211	399	551	675	31100	273	483	650	792
15000	172	215	232	248	20400	193	349	472	517	25800	212	400	553	677	31200	274	484	652	794
15100	172	219	237	253	20500	193	350	474	522	25900	213	401	555	679	31300	275	486	654	796
15200	173	224	242	258	20600	194	351	476	527	26000	214	403	556	681	31400	276	488	657	799
15300	173	228	246	263	20700	194	352	477	531	26100	215	404	558	683	31500	278	489	659	801
15400	174	233	251	269	20800	194	353	479	536	26200	216	405	560	685	31600	279	491	661	803
15500	174	237	256	274	20900	194	354	481	540	26300	217	407	561	687	31700	280	493	663	805
15600	174	242	261	279	21000	195	355	482	545	26400	218	408	563	690	31800	281	495	665	807
15700	175	246	266	284	21100	195	356	483	550	26500	220	409	565	692	31900	282	496	667	809
15800	175	251	271	289	21200	196	357	485	554	26600	221	410	567	694	32000	283	498	670	811
15900	175	255	275	294	21300	196	358	486	559	26700	222	412	569	696	32100	284	500	672	813
16000	176	260	280	300	21400	196	359	488	563	26800	223	413	570	698	32200	285	501	674	816
16100	176	265	285	305	21500	196	360	489	568	26900	224	414	572	700	32300	286	503	676	818

Nunavut

Federal Child Support Amounts: Simplified Tables
Montants fédéraux de pensions alimentaires pour enfants: Tables simplifiées

Income/ Revenu ($)	Monthly Award/ Paiement mensuel ($) No. of Children/ Nbre d'enfants				Income/ Revenu ($)	Monthly Award/ Paiement mensuel ($) No. of Children/ Nbre d'enfants				Income/ Revenu ($)	Monthly Award/ Paiement mensuel ($) No. of Children/ Nbre d'enfants				Income/ Revenu ($)	Monthly Award/ Paiement mensuel ($) No. of Children/ Nbre d'enfants			
	1	2	3	4		1	2	3	4		1	2	3	4		1	2	3	4
32400	288	505	678	821	37800	354	599	794	955	43200	413	686	906	1085	48600	465	768	1010	1208
32500	289	506	681	823	37900	355	600	796	957	43300	414	687	908	1087	48700	466	770	1012	1211
32600	290	508	683	825	38000	356	602	799	960	43400	415	689	910	1089	48800	467	771	1014	1213
32700	291	510	685	828	38100	357	604	801	963	43500	416	690	912	1092	48900	468	773	1016	1215
32800	292	511	687	830	38200	359	606	803	965	43600	417	692	914	1094	49000	469	774	1018	1218
32900	293	513	689	832	38300	360	607	806	968	43700	417	693	916	1096	49100	470	776	1020	1220
33000	295	515	691	835	38400	361	609	808	970	43800	418	695	918	1098	49200	471	777	1022	1223
33100	296	517	693	837	38500	363	611	810	973	43900	419	696	920	1101	49300	472	779	1024	1225
33200	297	518	695	840	38600	364	613	812	976	44000	420	698	921	1103	49400	473	780	1026	1228
33300	298	520	697	842	38700	365	615	815	978	44100	421	699	923	1105	49500	474	782	1028	1230
33400	300	522	699	844	38800	367	617	817	981	44200	422	701	925	1107	49600	475	783	1030	1232
33500	301	523	701	847	38900	368	618	819	983	44300	423	702	927	1110	49700	476	785	1032	1235
33600	302	525	703	849	39000	369	620	821	986	44400	424	704	929	1112	49800	477	787	1034	1237
33700	303	526	705	851	39100	370	622	823	989	44500	425	705	931	1114	49900	478	788	1037	1239
33800	304	528	707	854	39200	371	624	825	991	44600	426	707	933	1116	50000	479	790	1039	1242
33900	305	530	709	856	39300	373	625	828	994	44700	427	708	935	1119	50100	480	792	1041	1244
34000	306	531	711	858	39400	374	627	830	996	44800	428	710	937	1121	50200	481	793	1043	1247
34100	307	533	713	860	39500	375	629	832	999	44900	429	711	938	1123	50300	482	795	1045	1249
34200	308	534	715	863	39600	376	631	834	1001	45000	430	713	940	1125	50400	483	796	1047	1252
34300	309	536	717	865	39700	378	633	836	1004	45100	431	714	942	1127	50500	484	798	1049	1254
34400	311	538	719	868	39800	379	634	838	1006	45200	432	716	944	1130	50600	485	800	1051	1256
34500	312	539	722	870	39900	380	636	841	1009	45300	433	717	946	1132	50700	486	801	1053	1259
34600	313	541	724	872	40000	381	638	843	1011	45400	434	719	948	1134	50800	487	803	1055	1261
34700	314	542	726	875	40100	382	640	845	1014	45500	435	720	950	1136	50900	488	804	1057	1263
34800	315	544	728	877	40200	383	641	847	1016	45600	435	722	952	1139	51000	489	806	1059	1266
34900	316	546	730	879	40300	384	643	849	1019	45700	436	723	953	1141	51100	490	808	1061	1268
35000	317	547	732	882	40400	385	645	851	1021	45800	437	725	955	1143	51200	491	809	1063	1271
35100	318	549	734	885	40500	386	646	854	1024	45900	438	726	957	1146	51300	492	811	1065	1273
35200	320	551	736	887	40600	388	648	856	1026	46000	439	728	959	1148	51400	493	812	1067	1276
35300	321	553	739	890	40700	389	649	858	1029	46100	440	729	961	1150	51500	494	814	1069	1278
35400	322	554	741	892	40800	390	651	860	1031	46200	441	731	963	1152	51600	495	816	1071	1280
35500	323	556	743	895	40900	391	653	862	1034	46300	442	732	965	1155	51700	496	817	1073	1283
35600	325	558	745	897	41000	392	654	864	1036	46400	443	734	967	1157	51800	497	819	1075	1285
35700	326	560	748	900	41100	393	655	866	1038	46500	444	735	969	1159	51900	498	821	1077	1288
35800	327	562	750	902	41200	394	657	868	1040	46600	445	737	970	1161	52000	500	822	1079	1290
35900	329	564	752	905	41300	395	658	870	1043	46700	446	738	972	1164	52100	501	824	1081	1292
36000	330	566	754	908	41400	396	660	872	1045	46800	447	740	974	1166	52200	502	825	1083	1295
36100	331	568	756	911	41500	397	661	874	1047	46900	448	741	976	1168	52300	503	827	1085	1297
36200	333	570	758	913	41600	397	663	875	1049	47000	449	743	978	1170	52400	504	828	1087	1300
36300	334	572	761	916	41700	398	664	877	1052	47100	450	745	980	1172	52500	505	830	1089	1302
36400	335	573	763	918	41800	399	666	879	1054	47200	451	746	982	1175	52600	506	831	1091	1304
36500	337	575	765	921	41900	400	667	881	1056	47300	452	748	984	1177	52700	507	833	1094	1307
36600	338	577	767	923	42000	401	669	883	1058	47400	453	749	986	1179	52800	508	834	1096	1309
36700	339	579	769	926	42100	402	670	885	1060	47500	454	751	988	1182	52900	509	836	1098	1312
36800	340	581	772	929	42200	403	672	887	1062	47600	455	753	990	1184	53000	510	837	1100	1314
36900	342	583	774	931	42300	404	673	889	1065	47700	456	754	992	1186	53100	511	839	1102	1316
37000	343	584	776	934	42400	405	675	891	1067	47800	457	756	994	1189	53200	512	840	1104	1319
37100	344	586	778	937	42500	406	676	893	1069	47900	458	757	996	1191	53300	513	842	1106	1321
37200	346	588	781	939	42600	407	678	895	1071	48000	459	759	998	1194	53400	514	843	1108	1324
37300	347	589	783	942	42700	408	679	896	1074	48100	460	761	1000	1196	53500	515	845	1110	1326
37400	348	591	785	944	42800	409	680	898	1076	48200	461	762	1002	1199	53600	516	846	1112	1328
37500	350	593	787	947	42900	410	682	900	1078	48300	462	764	1004	1201	53700	517	848	1114	1331
37600	351	595	790	950	43000	411	683	902	1080	48400	463	765	1006	1204	53800	518	849	1116	1333
37700	352	597	792	952	43100	412	684	904	1082	48500	464	767	1008	1206	53900	519	851	1118	1336

Federal Child Support Amounts: Simplified Tables
Montants fédéraux de pensions alimentaires pour enfants: Tables simplifiées

Income/ Revenu ($)	Monthly Award/ Paiement mensuel ($) No. of Children/ N^{bre} d'enfants				Income/ Revenu ($)	Monthly Award/ Paiement mensuel ($) No. of Children/ N^{bre} d'enfants				Income/ Revenu ($)	Monthly Award/ Paiement mensuel ($) No. of Children/ N^{bre} d'enfants				Income/ Revenu ($)	Monthly Award/ Paiement mensuel ($) No. of Children/ N^{bre} d'enfants			
	1	2	3	4		1	2	3	4		1	2	3	4		1	2	3	4
54000	520	853	1120	1338	59400	575	938	1229	1468	64800	625	1018	1333	1591	70200	674	1098	1437	1715
54100	521	855	1122	1340	59500	576	940	1231	1470	64900	626	1020	1335	1594	70300	675	1099	1439	1717
54200	522	856	1124	1343	59600	577	942	1233	1473	65000	627	1021	1337	1596	70400	676	1101	1441	1719
54300	523	858	1126	1345	59700	578	943	1235	1475	65100	628	1022	1339	1598	70500	677	1102	1442	1722
54400	524	859	1128	1348	59800	579	945	1237	1477	65200	629	1024	1341	1601	70600	678	1104	1444	1724
54500	525	861	1130	1350	59900	580	946	1239	1480	65300	630	1025	1343	1603	70700	679	1105	1446	1726
54600	526	862	1132	1352	60000	581	948	1241	1482	65400	631	1027	1344	1605	70800	680	1107	1448	1729
54700	527	864	1134	1355	60100	582	950	1243	1484	65500	632	1028	1346	1608	70900	681	1108	1450	1731
54800	528	866	1136	1357	60200	583	951	1245	1487	65600	633	1030	1348	1610	71000	682	1110	1452	1733
54900	529	867	1138	1360	60300	584	953	1247	1489	65700	634	1031	1350	1612	71100	683	1111	1454	1735
55000	530	869	1140	1362	60400	585	954	1249	1491	65800	635	1033	1352	1615	71200	684	1113	1456	1737
55100	531	871	1142	1364	60500	586	956	1251	1494	65900	635	1034	1354	1617	71300	685	1114	1458	1740
55200	532	872	1144	1367	60600	587	957	1253	1496	66000	636	1036	1356	1619	71400	686	1116	1459	1742
55300	533	874	1146	1369	60700	587	959	1255	1498	66100	637	1037	1358	1621	71500	687	1117	1461	1744
55400	534	875	1148	1372	60800	588	960	1257	1501	66200	638	1039	1360	1623	71600	688	1119	1463	1746
55500	535	877	1150	1374	60900	589	962	1259	1503	66300	639	1040	1362	1626	71700	689	1120	1465	1749
55600	536	879	1152	1376	61000	590	963	1261	1505	66400	640	1042	1364	1628	71800	690	1121	1467	1751
55700	537	880	1154	1379	61100	591	964	1263	1507	66500	641	1043	1366	1630	71900	690	1123	1469	1753
55800	538	882	1156	1381	61200	592	966	1265	1509	66600	642	1045	1368	1632	72000	691	1124	1471	1755
55900	539	883	1158	1384	61300	593	967	1267	1512	66700	642	1046	1370	1635	72100	692	1125	1473	1757
56000	540	885	1160	1386	61400	594	969	1269	1514	66800	643	1048	1372	1637	72200	693	1127	1475	1760
56100	541	887	1162	1388	61500	595	970	1271	1516	66900	644	1049	1374	1639	72300	694	1128	1477	1762
56200	542	888	1164	1391	61600	595	972	1273	1518	67000	645	1051	1376	1641	72400	695	1130	1479	1764
56300	543	890	1166	1393	61700	596	973	1275	1521	67100	646	1053	1378	1643	72500	696	1131	1481	1766
56400	544	892	1168	1396	61800	597	975	1276	1523	67200	647	1054	1380	1646	72600	697	1133	1483	1769
56500	545	893	1170	1398	61900	598	976	1278	1525	67300	648	1056	1382	1648	72700	697	1134	1485	1771
56600	546	895	1172	1400	62000	599	977	1280	1527	67400	649	1057	1384	1650	72800	698	1136	1487	1773
56700	547	896	1174	1403	62100	600	978	1282	1529	67500	650	1059	1386	1652	72900	699	1137	1489	1775
56800	548	898	1176	1405	62200	601	980	1284	1532	67600	650	1060	1388	1655	73000	700	1139	1491	1778
56900	549	900	1179	1408	62300	602	981	1286	1534	67700	651	1062	1390	1657	73100	701	1141	1493	1780
57000	550	901	1181	1410	62400	603	983	1288	1536	67800	652	1063	1391	1659	73200	702	1142	1495	1783
57100	551	903	1183	1412	62500	603	984	1290	1538	67900	653	1065	1393	1661	73300	703	1144	1497	1785
57200	552	904	1185	1415	62600	604	986	1292	1541	68000	654	1066	1395	1664	73400	704	1145	1499	1787
57300	553	906	1187	1417	62700	605	987	1293	1543	68100	655	1067	1397	1666	73500	705	1147	1501	1790
57400	554	907	1189	1420	62800	606	989	1295	1545	68200	656	1069	1399	1669	73600	706	1148	1503	1792
57500	555	909	1191	1422	62900	607	990	1297	1547	68300	657	1070	1401	1671	73700	707	1150	1505	1795
57600	556	910	1193	1424	63000	608	992	1299	1550	68400	658	1072	1403	1673	73800	708	1152	1507	1797
57700	557	912	1195	1427	63100	609	994	1301	1552	68500	658	1073	1405	1675	73900	709	1153	1509	1799
57800	558	913	1197	1429	63200	610	995	1303	1555	68600	659	1075	1407	1678	74000	710	1155	1511	1802
57900	559	915	1199	1432	63300	611	997	1305	1557	68700	660	1076	1408	1680	74100	711	1157	1513	1804
58000	560	916	1201	1434	63400	612	998	1307	1559	68800	661	1078	1410	1682	74200	712	1158	1515	1807
58100	561	918	1203	1436	63500	612	1000	1309	1561	68900	662	1079	1412	1685	74300	713	1160	1517	1809
58200	562	919	1205	1439	63600	613	1001	1310	1564	69000	663	1080	1414	1687	74400	714	1161	1519	1811
58300	563	921	1207	1441	63700	614	1003	1312	1566	69100	664	1081	1416	1689	74500	715	1163	1521	1814
58400	564	922	1209	1444	63800	615	1004	1314	1568	69200	665	1083	1418	1692	74600	716	1164	1523	1816
58500	565	924	1211	1446	63900	616	1006	1316	1571	69300	666	1084	1420	1694	74700	717	1166	1525	1818
58600	566	925	1213	1448	64000	617	1007	1318	1573	69400	667	1086	1422	1696	74800	718	1167	1527	1821
58700	567	927	1215	1451	64100	618	1008	1320	1575	69500	667	1087	1424	1699	74900	719	1169	1529	1823
58800	568	929	1217	1453	64200	619	1010	1322	1578	69600	668	1089	1425	1701	75000	720	1170	1530	1825
58900	569	930	1219	1456	64300	620	1011	1324	1580	69700	669	1090	1427	1703	75100	721	1171	1532	1827
59000	571	932	1221	1458	64400	621	1013	1326	1582	69800	670	1092	1429	1705	75200	722	1173	1534	1830
59100	572	934	1223	1460	64500	622	1014	1327	1585	69900	671	1093	1431	1708	75300	723	1174	1536	1832
59200	573	935	1225	1463	64600	623	1016	1329	1587	70000	672	1095	1433	1710	75400	724	1176	1538	1834
59300	574	937	1227	1465	64700	624	1017	1331	1589	70100	673	1096	1435	1712	75500	725	1177	1540	1837

Federal Child Support Amounts: Simplified Tables
Montants fédéraux de pensions alimentaires pour enfants: Tables simplifiées

Income/ Revenu ($)	Monthly Award/ Paiement mensuel ($) No. of Children/ Nbre d'enfants				Income/ Revenu ($)	Monthly Award/ Paiement mensuel ($) No. of Children/ Nbre d'enfants				Income/ Revenu ($)	Monthly Award/ Paiement mensuel ($) No. of Children/ Nbre d'enfants				Income/ Revenu ($)	Monthly Award/ Paiement mensuel ($) No. of Children/ Nbre d'enfants			
	1	2	3	4		1	2	3	4		1	2	3	4		1	2	3	4
75600	726	1179	1542	1839	81000	778	1261	1647	1963	86400	828	1338	1745	2079	91800	876	1413	1844	2195
75700	727	1180	1544	1841	81100	779	1263	1649	1965	86500	829	1339	1747	2082	91900	877	1415	1846	2197
75800	728	1182	1546	1843	81200	780	1264	1651	1968	86600	829	1340	1749	2084	92000	878	1416	1847	2199
75900	729	1183	1548	1846	81300	781	1266	1653	1970	86700	830	1342	1750	2086	92100	879	1417	1849	2201
76000	730	1185	1550	1848	81400	782	1267	1655	1972	86800	831	1343	1752	2088	92200	880	1419	1851	2203
76100	731	1187	1552	1850	81500	783	1269	1657	1975	86900	832	1345	1754	2090	92300	881	1420	1853	2205
76200	732	1188	1554	1853	81600	784	1270	1658	1977	87000	833	1346	1756	2092	92400	882	1422	1854	2207
76300	733	1190	1556	1855	81700	785	1272	1660	1979	87100	834	1347	1758	2094	92500	882	1423	1856	2210
76400	734	1191	1558	1857	81800	786	1273	1662	1981	87200	835	1349	1760	2096	92600	883	1424	1858	2212
76500	735	1193	1560	1860	81900	787	1275	1664	1984	87300	836	1350	1761	2099	92700	884	1426	1860	2214
76600	736	1194	1562	1862	82000	788	1276	1666	1986	87400	837	1352	1763	2101	92800	885	1427	1862	2216
76700	737	1196	1564	1865	82100	789	1277	1668	1988	87500	838	1353	1765	2103	92900	886	1428	1864	2218
76800	738	1197	1566	1867	82200	790	1279	1670	1990	87600	838	1354	1767	2105	93000	887	1430	1865	2220
76900	739	1199	1568	1869	82300	791	1280	1671	1992	87700	839	1356	1768	2107	93100	888	1431	1867	2222
77000	740	1201	1570	1872	82400	792	1282	1673	1995	87800	840	1357	1770	2109	93200	889	1433	1869	2224
77100	741	1203	1572	1874	82500	793	1283	1675	1997	87900	841	1359	1772	2112	93300	890	1434	1870	2227
77200	742	1204	1574	1877	82600	794	1285	1677	1999	88000	842	1360	1774	2114	93400	891	1436	1872	2229
77300	743	1206	1576	1879	82700	794	1286	1679	2001	88100	843	1361	1776	2116	93500	891	1437	1874	2231
77400	744	1207	1578	1881	82800	795	1287	1680	2003	88200	844	1363	1778	2118	93600	892	1438	1876	2233
77500	745	1209	1580	1884	82900	796	1289	1682	2005	88300	845	1364	1779	2120	93700	893	1440	1878	2235
77600	746	1210	1582	1886	83000	797	1290	1684	2007	88400	846	1366	1781	2123	93800	894	1441	1880	2237
77700	747	1212	1584	1888	83100	798	1291	1686	2009	88500	847	1367	1783	2125	93900	895	1442	1881	2240
77800	748	1213	1585	1891	83200	799	1293	1688	2011	88600	847	1368	1785	2127	94000	896	1444	1883	2242
77900	749	1215	1587	1893	83300	800	1294	1689	2013	88700	848	1370	1786	2129	94100	897	1445	1885	2244
78000	749	1216	1589	1895	83400	801	1296	1691	2015	88800	849	1371	1788	2131	94200	898	1447	1887	2246
78100	750	1217	1591	1897	83500	802	1297	1693	2018	88900	850	1373	1790	2133	94300	899	1448	1888	2248
78200	751	1219	1593	1900	83600	803	1299	1695	2020	89000	851	1374	1792	2135	94400	900	1450	1890	2251
78300	752	1220	1595	1902	83700	803	1300	1696	2022	89100	852	1375	1794	2137	94500	900	1451	1892	2253
78400	753	1222	1597	1904	83800	804	1301	1698	2024	89200	853	1377	1796	2139	94600	901	1452	1894	2255
78500	754	1223	1599	1907	83900	805	1303	1700	2026	89300	854	1378	1798	2141	94700	902	1454	1896	2257
78600	755	1225	1601	1909	84000	806	1304	1702	2028	89400	855	1380	1799	2143	94800	903	1455	1898	2259
78700	756	1226	1603	1911	84100	807	1305	1704	2030	89500	856	1381	1801	2146	94900	904	1456	1899	2261
78800	757	1228	1605	1914	84200	808	1307	1706	2032	89600	856	1382	1803	2148	95000	905	1458	1901	2263
78900	758	1229	1607	1916	84300	809	1308	1707	2035	89700	857	1384	1805	2150	95100	906	1459	1903	2265
79000	759	1231	1609	1918	84400	810	1310	1709	2037	89800	858	1385	1807	2152	95200	907	1461	1905	2267
79100	760	1232	1611	1920	84500	811	1311	1711	2039	89900	859	1387	1809	2154	95300	908	1462	1906	2269
79200	761	1234	1613	1922	84600	812	1313	1713	2041	90000	860	1388	1811	2156	95400	909	1463	1908	2271
79300	762	1235	1615	1925	84700	812	1314	1714	2043	90100	861	1389	1813	2158	95500	909	1465	1910	2274
79400	763	1237	1617	1927	84800	813	1315	1716	2045	90200	862	1391	1815	2160	95600	910	1466	1912	2276
79500	764	1238	1619	1929	84900	814	1317	1718	2048	90300	863	1392	1817	2163	95700	911	1468	1914	2278
79600	765	1240	1621	1931	85000	815	1318	1720	2050	90400	864	1394	1818	2165	95800	912	1469	1916	2280
79700	766	1241	1623	1934	85100	816	1319	1722	2052	90500	865	1395	1820	2167	95900	913	1470	1917	2282
79800	767	1243	1624	1936	85200	817	1321	1724	2054	90600	865	1396	1822	2169	96000	914	1472	1919	2284
79900	768	1244	1626	1938	85300	818	1322	1725	2056	90700	866	1398	1824	2171	96100	915	1473	1921	2286
80000	769	1246	1628	1940	85400	819	1324	1727	2059	90800	867	1399	1826	2173	96200	916	1475	1923	2288
80100	770	1248	1630	1942	85500	820	1325	1729	2061	90900	868	1401	1828	2176	96300	917	1476	1924	2291
80200	771	1249	1632	1945	85600	821	1326	1731	2063	91000	869	1402	1829	2178	96400	918	1477	1926	2293
80300	772	1251	1634	1947	85700	821	1328	1732	2065	91100	870	1403	1831	2180	96500	918	1479	1928	2295
80400	773	1252	1636	1949	85800	822	1329	1734	2067	91200	871	1405	1833	2182	96600	919	1480	1930	2297
80500	774	1254	1638	1951	85900	823	1331	1736	2069	91300	872	1406	1835	2184	96700	920	1482	1932	2299
80600	775	1255	1640	1954	86000	824	1332	1738	2071	91400	873	1408	1836	2187	96800	921	1483	1933	2301
80700	776	1257	1641	1956	86100	825	1333	1740	2073	91500	874	1409	1838	2189	96900	922	1484	1935	2304
80800	777	1258	1643	1958	86200	826	1335	1742	2075	91600	874	1410	1840	2191	97000	923	1486	1937	2306
80900	777	1260	1645	1960	86300	827	1336	1743	2077	91700	875	1412	1842	2193	97100	924	1487	1939	2308

Nunavut

Federal Child Support Amounts: Simplified Tables
Montants fédéraux de pensions alimentaires pour enfants: Tables simplifiées

Income/ Revenu ($)	Monthly Award/ Paiement mensuel ($) No. of Children/ Nbre d'enfants				Income/ Revenu ($)	Monthly Award/ Paiement mensuel ($) No. of Children/ Nbre d'enfants				Income/ Revenu ($)	Monthly Award/ Paiement mensuel ($) No. of Children/ Nbre d'enfants				Income/ Revenu ($)	Monthly Award/ Paiement mensuel ($) No. of Children/ Nbre d'enfants			
	1	2	3	4		1	2	3	4		1	2	3	4		1	2	3	4
97200	925	1489	1941	2310	102600	973	1566	2038	2425	108000	1022	1641	2136	2540	113400	1072	1717	2233	2655
97300	926	1490	1942	2312	102700	974	1567	2039	2427	108100	1023	1642	2138	2542	113500	1073	1718	2235	2657
97400	927	1491	1944	2315	102800	975	1569	2041	2429	108200	1024	1644	2140	2544	113600	1074	1719	2237	2660
97500	927	1493	1946	2317	102900	976	1570	2043	2432	108300	1025	1645	2142	2547	113700	1075	1721	2239	2662
97600	928	1494	1948	2319	103000	977	1571	2045	2434	108400	1025	1647	2143	2549	113800	1076	1722	2241	2664
97700	929	1496	1950	2321	103100	978	1572	2047	2436	108500	1026	1648	2145	2551	113900	1076	1724	2242	2666
97800	930	1497	1951	2323	103200	979	1574	2049	2438	108600	1027	1649	2147	2553	114000	1077	1725	2244	2668
97900	931	1498	1953	2325	103300	980	1575	2050	2440	108700	1028	1651	2149	2555	114100	1078	1726	2246	2670
98000	932	1500	1955	2327	103400	980	1577	2052	2443	108800	1029	1652	2151	2557	114200	1079	1728	2248	2672
98100	933	1501	1957	2329	103500	981	1578	2054	2445	108900	1030	1654	2153	2560	114300	1080	1729	2249	2674
98200	934	1503	1959	2331	103600	982	1580	2056	2447	109000	1031	1655	2154	2562	114400	1081	1731	2251	2677
98300	935	1504	1960	2333	103700	983	1581	2057	2449	109100	1032	1656	2156	2564	114500	1082	1732	2253	2679
98400	936	1505	1962	2335	103800	984	1583	2059	2451	109200	1033	1658	2158	2566	114600	1083	1733	2255	2681
98500	936	1507	1964	2338	103900	985	1584	2061	2453	109300	1034	1659	2160	2568	114700	1084	1735	2257	2683
98600	937	1508	1966	2340	104000	986	1585	2063	2455	109400	1035	1661	2161	2571	114800	1085	1736	2258	2685
98700	938	1510	1968	2342	104100	987	1586	2065	2457	109500	1036	1662	2163	2573	114900	1085	1738	2260	2687
98800	939	1511	1969	2344	104200	988	1588	2067	2459	109600	1037	1663	2165	2575	115000	1086	1739	2262	2690
98900	940	1512	1971	2346	104300	989	1589	2068	2461	109700	1038	1665	2167	2577	115100	1087	1740	2264	2692
99000	941	1514	1973	2348	104400	989	1591	2070	2463	109800	1039	1666	2169	2579	115200	1088	1742	2266	2694
99100	942	1515	1975	2350	104500	990	1592	2072	2466	109900	1040	1668	2171	2581	115300	1089	1743	2267	2696
99200	943	1517	1977	2352	104600	991	1594	2074	2468	110000	1041	1669	2172	2583	115400	1090	1745	2269	2699
99300	944	1518	1978	2355	104700	992	1595	2075	2470	110100	1042	1670	2174	2585	115500	1091	1746	2271	2701
99400	945	1519	1980	2357	104800	993	1596	2077	2472	110200	1043	1672	2176	2587	115600	1092	1747	2273	2703
99500	945	1521	1982	2359	104900	994	1598	2079	2474	110300	1044	1673	2178	2589	115700	1093	1749	2275	2705
99600	946	1522	1984	2361	105000	995	1599	2081	2476	110400	1045	1675	2179	2591	115800	1093	1750	2276	2707
99700	947	1523	1986	2363	105100	996	1600	2083	2478	110500	1046	1676	2181	2594	115900	1094	1751	2278	2709
99800	948	1525	1987	2365	105200	997	1602	2085	2480	110600	1047	1677	2183	2596	116000	1095	1753	2280	2711
99900	949	1526	1989	2368	105300	998	1603	2086	2483	110700	1048	1679	2185	2598	116100	1096	1754	2282	2713
100000	950	1528	1991	2370	105400	998	1605	2088	2485	110800	1049	1680	2187	2600	116200	1097	1756	2284	2715
100100	951	1529	1993	2372	105500	999	1606	2090	2487	110900	1050	1682	2189	2602	116300	1098	1757	2285	2717
100200	952	1531	1995	2374	105600	1000	1608	2092	2489	111000	1050	1683	2190	2604	116400	1099	1759	2287	2719
100300	953	1532	1996	2376	105700	1001	1609	2093	2491	111100	1051	1684	2192	2606	116500	1100	1760	2289	2721
100400	954	1534	1998	2379	105800	1002	1610	2095	2493	111200	1052	1686	2194	2608	116600	1101	1761	2291	2724
100500	954	1535	2000	2381	105900	1003	1612	2097	2496	111300	1053	1687	2195	2610	116700	1102	1763	2293	2726
100600	955	1537	2002	2383	106000	1004	1613	2099	2498	111400	1054	1689	2197	2613	116800	1102	1764	2294	2728
100700	956	1538	2004	2385	106100	1005	1614	2101	2500	111500	1055	1690	2199	2615	116900	1103	1765	2296	2730
100800	957	1540	2005	2387	106200	1006	1616	2103	2502	111600	1056	1691	2201	2617	117000	1104	1767	2298	2732
100900	958	1541	2007	2389	106300	1007	1617	2104	2504	111700	1057	1693	2203	2619	117100	1105	1768	2300	2734
101000	959	1543	2009	2391	106400	1007	1619	2106	2507	111800	1058	1694	2205	2621	117200	1106	1770	2302	2736
101100	960	1544	2011	2393	106500	1008	1620	2108	2509	111900	1059	1696	2206	2623	117300	1107	1771	2303	2738
101200	961	1546	2013	2395	106600	1009	1622	2110	2511	112000	1059	1697	2208	2626	117400	1108	1773	2305	2741
101300	962	1547	2014	2397	106700	1010	1623	2111	2513	112100	1060	1698	2210	2628	117500	1109	1774	2307	2743
101400	962	1549	2016	2399	106800	1011	1624	2113	2515	112200	1061	1700	2212	2630	117600	1110	1775	2309	2745
101500	963	1550	2018	2402	106900	1012	1626	2115	2517	112300	1062	1701	2213	2632	117700	1111	1777	2311	2747
101600	964	1552	2020	2404	107000	1013	1627	2117	2519	112400	1063	1703	2215	2635	117800	1111	1778	2312	2749
101700	965	1553	2021	2406	107100	1014	1628	2119	2521	112500	1064	1704	2217	2637	117900	1112	1779	2314	2751
101800	966	1555	2023	2408	107200	1015	1630	2121	2523	112600	1065	1705	2219	2639	118000	1113	1781	2316	2754
101900	967	1556	2025	2410	107300	1016	1631	2123	2525	112700	1066	1707	2221	2641	118100	1114	1782	2318	2756
102000	968	1557	2027	2412	107400	1016	1633	2124	2527	112800	1067	1708	2223	2643	118200	1115	1784	2320	2758
102100	969	1558	2029	2414	107500	1017	1634	2126	2530	112900	1067	1710	2224	2645	118300	1116	1785	2321	2760
102200	970	1560	2031	2416	107600	1018	1636	2128	2532	113000	1068	1711	2226	2647	118400	1117	1786	2323	2763
102300	971	1561	2032	2419	107700	1019	1637	2130	2534	113100	1069	1712	2228	2649	118500	1118	1788	2325	2765
102400	971	1563	2034	2421	107800	1020	1638	2132	2536	113200	1070	1714	2230	2651	118600	1119	1789	2327	2767
102500	972	1564	2036	2423	107900	1021	1640	2134	2538	113300	1071	1715	2231	2653	118700	1119	1791	2329	2769

Federal Child Support Amounts: Simplified Tables
Montants fédéraux de pensions alimentaires pour enfants: Tables simplifiées

Income/ Revenu ($)	Monthly Award/ Paiement mensuel ($) No. of Children/ N^bre d'enfants 1	2	3	4	Income/ Revenu ($)	Monthly Award/ Paiement mensuel ($) No. of Children/ N^bre d'enfants 1	2	3	4	Income/ Revenu ($)	Monthly Award/ Paiement mensuel ($) No. of Children/ N^bre d'enfants 1	2	3	4	Income/ Revenu ($)	Monthly Award/ Paiement mensuel ($) No. of Children/ N^bre d'enfants 1	2	3	4
118800	1120	1792	2330	2771	124200	1169	1869	2428	2886	129600	1216	1941	2522	2996	135000	1260	2011	2611	3102
118900	1121	1793	2332	2773	124300	1170	1870	2429	2888	129700	1217	1942	2523	2998	135100	1261	2012	2613	3104
119000	1122	1795	2334	2775	124400	1171	1872	2431	2891	129800	1218	1943	2525	3000	135200	1262	2013	2614	3106
119100	1123	1796	2336	2777	124500	1172	1873	2433	2893	129900	1219	1944	2527	3002	135300	1262	2015	2616	3108
119200	1124	1798	2338	2779	124600	1172	1875	2435	2895	130000	1219	1946	2528	3004	135400	1263	2016	2617	3110
119300	1125	1799	2339	2781	124700	1173	1876	2436	2897	130100	1220	1947	2530	3006	135500	1264	2017	2619	3112
119400	1126	1800	2341	2783	124800	1174	1878	2438	2899	130200	1221	1949	2531	3008	135600	1265	2018	2621	3114
119500	1127	1802	2343	2785	124900	1175	1879	2440	2901	130300	1221	1950	2533	3010	135700	1266	2020	2622	3116
119600	1128	1803	2345	2788	125000	1176	1880	2442	2903	130400	1222	1951	2535	3012	135800	1266	2021	2624	3118
119700	1128	1805	2346	2790	125100	1177	1881	2444	2905	130500	1223	1952	2536	3014	135900	1267	2022	2626	3120
119800	1129	1806	2348	2792	125200	1178	1883	2446	2907	130600	1224	1954	2538	3016	136000	1268	2023	2627	3122
119900	1130	1807	2350	2794	125300	1179	1884	2448	2909	130700	1225	1955	2540	3018	136100	1269	2024	2629	3124
120000	1131	1809	2352	2796	125400	1180	1886	2449	2911	130800	1226	1956	2541	3020	136200	1270	2026	2630	3126
120100	1132	1810	2354	2798	125500	1181	1887	2451	2913	130900	1226	1957	2543	3022	136300	1271	2027	2632	3128
120200	1133	1812	2356	2800	125600	1181	1889	2453	2916	131000	1227	1959	2545	3024	136400	1271	2028	2634	3130
120300	1134	1813	2357	2802	125700	1182	1890	2455	2918	131100	1228	1960	2547	3026	136500	1272	2029	2635	3132
120400	1135	1814	2359	2805	125800	1183	1892	2457	2920	131200	1229	1962	2548	3028	136600	1273	2031	2637	3134
120500	1136	1816	2361	2807	125900	1184	1893	2459	2922	131300	1229	1963	2550	3030	136700	1274	2032	2639	3136
120600	1137	1817	2363	2809	126000	1185	1894	2461	2924	131400	1230	1964	2551	3032	136800	1275	2033	2640	3138
120700	1137	1819	2364	2811	126100	1186	1895	2463	2926	131500	1231	1965	2553	3034	136900	1276	2034	2642	3139
120800	1138	1820	2366	2813	126200	1187	1897	2465	2928	131600	1232	1967	2555	3035	137000	1277	2036	2644	3141
120900	1139	1821	2368	2815	126300	1188	1898	2467	2930	131700	1233	1968	2556	3037	137100	1278	2037	2646	3143
121000	1140	1823	2370	2818	126400	1189	1900	2468	2933	131800	1233	1969	2558	3039	137200	1279	2039	2647	3145
121100	1141	1824	2372	2820	126500	1190	1901	2470	2935	131900	1234	1971	2560	3041	137300	1280	2040	2649	3147
121200	1142	1826	2374	2822	126600	1190	1903	2472	2937	132000	1235	1972	2561	3043	137400	1280	2041	2650	3149
121300	1143	1827	2375	2824	126700	1191	1904	2474	2939	132100	1236	1973	2563	3045	137500	1281	2042	2652	3151
121400	1144	1828	2377	2827	126800	1192	1906	2476	2941	132200	1237	1975	2564	3047	137600	1282	2044	2654	3153
121500	1145	1830	2379	2829	126900	1193	1907	2478	2943	132300	1238	1976	2566	3049	137700	1283	2045	2655	3155
121600	1146	1831	2381	2831	127000	1194	1908	2479	2946	132400	1238	1977	2568	3051	137800	1284	2046	2657	3157
121700	1146	1833	2382	2833	127100	1195	1909	2481	2948	132500	1239	1979	2569	3053	137900	1285	2047	2658	3159
121800	1147	1834	2384	2835	127200	1196	1911	2482	2950	132600	1240	1980	2571	3055	138000	1285	2049	2660	3161
121900	1148	1835	2386	2837	127300	1196	1912	2484	2952	132700	1241	1981	2573	3057	138100	1286	2050	2662	3163
122000	1149	1837	2388	2839	127400	1197	1913	2486	2954	132800	1242	1982	2574	3059	138200	1287	2052	2663	3165
122100	1150	1838	2390	2841	127500	1198	1915	2487	2956	132900	1243	1984	2576	3061	138300	1287	2053	2665	3167
122200	1151	1840	2392	2843	127600	1199	1916	2489	2958	133000	1244	1985	2578	3063	138400	1288	2054	2667	3169
122300	1152	1841	2393	2845	127700	1200	1917	2490	2959	133100	1245	1986	2580	3065	138500	1289	2055	2668	3171
122400	1153	1842	2395	2847	127800	1200	1919	2492	2961	133200	1246	1988	2581	3067	138600	1290	2057	2670	3173
122500	1154	1844	2397	2849	127900	1201	1920	2494	2963	133300	1247	1989	2583	3069	138700	1291	2058	2672	3175
122600	1154	1845	2399	2852	128000	1202	1921	2495	2965	133400	1247	1990	2584	3071	138800	1291	2059	2673	3176
122700	1155	1846	2400	2854	128100	1203	1922	2497	2967	133500	1248	1992	2586	3073	138900	1292	2061	2675	3178
122800	1156	1848	2402	2856	128200	1204	1923	2498	2969	133600	1249	1993	2588	3075	139000	1293	2062	2677	3180
122900	1157	1849	2404	2858	128300	1205	1925	2500	2971	133700	1250	1994	2589	3077	139100	1294	2063	2679	3182
123000	1158	1851	2406	2860	128400	1205	1926	2502	2973	133800	1251	1996	2591	3079	139200	1295	2065	2680	3184
123100	1159	1852	2408	2862	128500	1206	1927	2503	2975	133900	1252	1997	2593	3081	139300	1295	2066	2682	3186
123200	1160	1854	2410	2864	128600	1207	1928	2505	2977	134000	1252	1998	2594	3083	139400	1296	2067	2684	3188
123300	1161	1855	2411	2866	128700	1208	1930	2507	2979	134100	1253	1999	2596	3085	139500	1297	2069	2686	3190
123400	1162	1857	2413	2869	128800	1209	1931	2508	2981	134200	1254	2001	2597	3087	139600	1298	2070	2687	3192
123500	1163	1858	2415	2871	128900	1210	1932	2510	2983	134300	1254	2002	2599	3089	139700	1298	2071	2689	3194
123600	1163	1860	2417	2873	129000	1211	1933	2512	2985	134400	1255	2003	2601	3091	139800	1299	2072	2691	3196
123700	1164	1861	2418	2875	129100	1212	1934	2514	2987	134500	1256	2005	2602	3093	139900	1300	2074	2692	3198
123800	1165	1863	2420	2877	129200	1213	1936	2515	2989	134600	1257	2006	2604	3095	140000	1301	2075	2694	3200
123900	1166	1864	2422	2879	129300	1214	1937	2517	2991	134700	1258	2007	2606	3097	140100	1302	2076	2696	3202
124000	1167	1866	2424	2882	129400	1214	1938	2519	2993	134800	1259	2009	2607	3099	140200	1303	2078	2697	3204
124100	1168	1867	2426	2884	129500	1215	1939	2520	2995	134900	1259	2010	2609	3101	140300	1304	2079	2699	3206

Nunavut

Federal Child Support Amounts: Simplified Tables
Montants fédéraux de pensions alimentaires pour enfants: Tables simplifiées

Income/ Revenu ($)	Monthly Award/ Paiement mensuel ($) No. of Children/ N^bre d'enfants				Income/ Revenu ($)	Monthly Award/ Paiement mensuel ($) No. of Children/ N^bre d'enfants				Income/ Revenu ($)	Monthly Award/ Paiement mensuel ($) No. of Children/ N^bre d'enfants			
	1	2	3	4		1	2	3	4		1	2	3	4
140400	1304	2080	2701	3208	143700	1331	2122	2755	3272	147000	1359	2165	2809	3336
140500	1305	2082	2702	3210	143800	1332	2123	2757	3274	147100	1360	2166	2811	3338
140600	1306	2083	2704	3212	143900	1333	2124	2758	3276	147200	1361	2168	2812	3340
140700	1307	2084	2706	3214	144000	1334	2126	2760	3278	147300	1362	2169	2814	3342
140800	1308	2086	2707	3215	144100	1335	2127	2762	3280	147400	1362	2170	2816	3344
140900	1309	2087	2709	3217	144200	1336	2129	2763	3282	147500	1363	2172	2817	3346
141000	1310	2088	2710	3219	144300	1337	2130	2765	3284	147600	1364	2173	2819	3348
141100	1311	2089	2712	3221	144400	1337	2131	2767	3286	147700	1365	2174	2821	3350
141200	1312	2091	2713	3223	144500	1338	2132	2768	3288	147800	1366	2176	2822	3352
141300	1312	2092	2715	3225	144600	1339	2134	2770	3289	147900	1367	2177	2824	3354
141400	1313	2093	2717	3227	144700	1340	2135	2771	3291	148000	1368	2178	2826	3356
141500	1314	2095	2718	3229	144800	1341	2136	2773	3293	148100	1369	2179	2828	3358
141600	1315	2096	2720	3231	144900	1342	2138	2775	3295	148200	1370	2180	2829	3360
141700	1316	2097	2722	3233	145000	1343	2139	2776	3297	148300	1371	2182	2831	3362
141800	1317	2099	2724	3235	145100	1344	2140	2778	3299	148400	1371	2183	2833	3364
141900	1317	2100	2725	3237	145200	1345	2142	2779	3301	148500	1372	2184	2834	3366
142000	1318	2101	2727	3239	145300	1345	2143	2781	3303	148600	1373	2185	2836	3368
142100	1319	2102	2729	3241	145400	1346	2144	2783	3305	148700	1374	2187	2837	3370
142200	1320	2103	2730	3243	145500	1347	2145	2784	3307	148800	1375	2188	2839	3372
142300	1320	2105	2732	3245	145600	1348	2147	2786	3309	148900	1376	2189	2841	3374
142400	1321	2106	2734	3247	145700	1349	2148	2788	3311	149000	1376	2190	2842	3376
142500	1322	2107	2735	3249	145800	1350	2149	2789	3313	149100	1377	2191	2844	3378
142600	1323	2108	2737	3251	145900	1350	2151	2791	3315	149200	1378	2193	2845	3380
142700	1324	2110	2739	3252	146000	1351	2152	2793	3317	149300	1378	2194	2847	3382
142800	1324	2111	2740	3254	146100	1352	2153	2795	3319	149400	1379	2195	2849	3384
142900	1325	2112	2742	3256	146200	1353	2155	2796	3321	149500	1380	2196	2850	3386
143000	1326	2113	2743	3258	146300	1353	2156	2798	3323	149600	1381	2198	2852	3388
143100	1327	2114	2745	3260	146400	1354	2157	2800	3325	149700	1382	2199	2854	3390
143200	1328	2116	2746	3262	146500	1355	2159	2801	3327	149800	1383	2200	2855	3392
143300	1328	2117	2748	3264	146600	1356	2160	2803	3328	149900	1383	2201	2857	3394
143400	1329	2118	2750	3266	146700	1357	2161	2804	3330	150000	1384	2203	2859	3395
143500	1330	2119	2751	3268	146800	1357	2162	2806	3332					
143600	1331	2121	2753	3270	146900	1358	2164	2808	3334					

Monthly Award/Paiement mensuel ($)			
One Child/ Un enfant	Two Children/ Deux enfants	Three Children/ Trois enfants	Four Children/ Quatre enfants
1384 plus 0.82% of income over $150,000	2203 plus 1.26% of income over $150,000	2859 plus 1.68% of income over $150,000	3395 plus 1.94% of income over $150,000
1384 plus 0,82% du revenu dépassant 150 000$	2203 plus 1,26% du revenu dépassant 150 000$	2859 plus 1,68% du revenu dépassant 150 000$	3395 plus 1,94% du revenu dépassant 150 000$

110

SEPARATION AGREEMENT

THIS AGREEMENT made the_____ day of_____, 20_____

BETWEEN:

_____,

of the City of _____, in the

Province/Territory of _____

(referred to in this Agreement as "the Husband")

AND:

_____,

of the City of _____, in the

Province/Territory of _____

(referred to in this Agreement as "the Wife")

RECITALS

WHEREAS:

A.   The parties were married to each other at_____, in the Province/Territory of _____, on the _____ day of _____, _____.

B.   The parties have_____ children as follows:

Name of Child	Age	Date of Birth
_____	_____	_____
_____	_____	_____
_____	_____	_____
_____	_____	_____

C.   The Husband and the Wife agree to live separate and apart and have lived apart since the _____ day of_____, _____, and intend to continue to live separate and apart according to the terms and conditions described in this agreement.

D.   The assets and liabilities of the Husband and the Wife are completely and accurately described at Schedule A attached to the back of this agreement.

E.   The Husband and the Wife intend this agreement to be —

(i)   a final settlement of their respective rights to and in property owned jointly and/or separately by them; and

(ii)   a final settlement of the issues of custody, access, guardianship, and support.

NOW THEREFORE THE HUSBAND AND THE WIFE AGREE AS FOLLOWS:

GENERAL

1.   The Husband and the Wife will continue to live separate and apart, and neither will annoy, disturb, or interfere with the other person.

2. This agreement and everything contained in it shall continue to govern the relationship between the Husband and the Wife, notwithstanding subsequent divorce, dissolution, or annulment of the marriage, by any order or instrument.

3. This agreement and everything contained in it shall be governed by the Federal *Divorce Act*, and the laws of the Province/Territory of_____.

4. Any part or provision of this agreement that is found to be void, voidable, or otherwise unenforceable shall be severable from the agreement, and the remainder of the agreement following that finding shall continue in full force and effect.

5. This agreement may only be amended or varied by a court order, or by written agreement between the Husband and the Wife, which amendment or agreement shall be duly executed by the Husband and the Wife by unrelated or independent persons.

CUSTODY, ACCESS, AND GUARDIANSHIP

6. (a) The Husband and/or Wife shall have sole/joint custody and the Husband/Wife shall have primary residency of the following child/ren:

Name of Child	Age	Date of Birth
_____	_____	_____
_____	_____	_____
_____	_____	_____
_____	_____	_____

(b) The Husband and/or the Wife shall have reasonable and liberal access to the child/ren on the following terms:

(i) _____
_____ ;

(ii) _____
_____ ;

(iii) _____
_____ ;

(iv) _____
_____ .

7. The Husband and the Wife have joint guardianship of the child/ren above described and further agree as follows:

(a) _____
_____ ;

(b) _____
_____ ;

(c) _____
_____ .

SUPPORT

8. The Husband/Wife shall pay to the Wife/Husband, for his/her own support, the sum of $_____ per month, commencing on the _____ day of _____, 20_____, and continuing on each and every month thereafter until the _____ day of _____, 20_____, (or) until such time as the Wife/Husband dies, remarries, or commences cohabitation with another person, in what is generally referred to as a common-law relationship, whichever shall occur first.

9. The Husband/Wife shall pay to the Wife/Husband for the maintenance of the infant child/ren of the marriage, namely —

Name of Child	Age	Date of Birth
_____	_____	_____
_____	_____	_____
_____	_____	_____
_____	_____	_____

    the sum of $_____ per month (net of tax), based on the payor's Guideline income of $_____, such payments to be made on the _____ day of _____, 20_____, and continuing on the_____ day of each and every month thereafter, for so long as each child of the marriage remains a child of the marriage.

10. In addition to the amount above described, the Husband/Wife shall pay to the Wife/Husband, for special expenses, the sum of $_____, to be paid at the same time as the payment described in paragraph 9.

ASSETS AND LIABILITIES

11.   (a)   The Husband shall hereafter own and possess the following assets:

Description	Approximate Value
Household items:	
Vehicles:	
Savings/RRSPs:	
Other:	

11.　(b)　The Wife shall hereafter own and possess the following assets:

Description	Approximate Value
Household items:	
Vehicles:	
Savings/RRSPs:	
Other:	

12.　(a)　The Husband shall and does hereafter accept sole and exclusive liability for the following debts:

Institution	Balance	Payments
(i)		
(ii)		
(iii)		

and does now indemnify and save harmless the Wife of and from any and all liability thereunder.

　(b)　The Wife shall and does hereafter accept sole and exclusive liability for the following debts:

Institution	Balance	Payments
(i)		
(ii)		
(iii)		

and does now indemnify and save harmless the Husband of and from any and all liability thereunder.

13.　Neither the Husband nor the Wife shall hereafter pledge the credit of the other or bind the other for debt.

MATRIMONIAL HOME AT: _____

14.   (a)   The Husband/Wife shall have a licence to exclusive occupation and possession of the matrimonial home situate and being at _____ without the obligation to pay rent, until such time as the Husband and the Wife mutually agree to sell the home. If the parties cannot later agree when the home is to be sold, either of them may apply to Court for further determination of same. When the home is sold, the equity or loss resulting therefrom, following the payment of all accounts of real estate commission, mortgage, taxes, and other just discounts, shall be divided equally between the Husband and the Wife.

OR

    (b)   Forthwith upon execution of this agreement, the Husband/Wife shall purchase from the Wife/Husband, all interest, right, and title to and in the matrimonial home upon the following terms and conditions:

        (i)   the payment to the Wife/Husband of the sum of $_____

        (ii)   (other terms and conditions): _____

_____

OR

    (c)   On the_____ day of_____, 20_____, the matrimonial home shall be listed for sale and sold as soon thereafter as is reasonable. Until sale, the Husband/Wife shall have a licence to exclusive occupation and possession of the matrimonial home, absent rent. For so long as the Husband/Wife is in occupation and possession of the matrimonial home, the Wife/Husband shall maintain all accounts of mortgage, maintain all taxes, insurance, heat, water, and other charges, and keep the matrimonial home fully insured. Upon sale, the proceeds of sale obtained in accordance with this paragraph shall be distributed as follows:

        (i)   first, to real estate commission

        (ii)   second, to all accounts of mortgage

	(iii)	third, to all taxes, utilities, and other adjustments and discounts
	(iv)	fourth, the balance, if any, to be divided equally between the Husband and the Wife

OR

(d)   On or about the _____ day of _____, 20____, the matrimonial home was sold and proceeds were divided to the satisfaction of the Husband and the Wife, and as a consequence, the Husband and the Wife agree that their respective rights to share in such proceeds have been satisfied, and each agrees not to claim or bring any claim in respect thereto, with respect to property laws in their Province/Territory.

15.   This agreement adequately and completely provides for the present and future needs of the Husband and the Wife, and each covenants and agrees that the arrangement herein described constitutes a full, complete, and final settlement of all rights, causes, claims, and demands with respect to support and property.

ACCEPTANCE

16.   The Husband and the Wife further acknowledge and agree that —

    (a)   each and every recital of fact contained herein is true and accurate;

    (b)   they each have general knowledge of the other's affairs, assets, and liabilities;

    (c)   they have each read and understood this agreement;

    (d)   they each sign this agreement as free agents;

    (e)   this agreement has been executed without any pressure, influence, or intimidation by anyone; and

(f)   they have each received full and independent legal advice with respect to this agreement and the alternatives available to the execution of it.

OR

being aware of their entitlement to full and independent legal advice, they have, nonetheless, chosen to waive same and elect to proceed with the execution of this agreement absent such advice.

IN WITNESS WHEREOF the Husband and the Wife set their hands this _____ day of _____, 20_____, at the City of _____, in the Province/Territory of _____.

SIGNED BY THE HUSBAND   )
in the presence of:)
)
_____   )
(Signature of Witness)   )
)   _____
)   Signature of Husband
_____   )
(Print Name)   )
)
_____   )
(Address)   )
)
_____   )
(Occupation)   )

SIGNED BY THE WIFE   )
in the presence of:)
)
_____   )
(Signature of Witness)   )
)   _____
)   Signature of Wife
_____   )
(Print Name)   )
)
_____   )
(Address)   )
)
_____   )
(Occupation)   )

SCHEDULE A

ASSETS AND LIABILITIES OF THE SPOUSES

LIST OF ASSETS		LIST OF LIABILITIES	
Description	Approximate Value	Description	Approximate Balance Owing
1.		1.	
2.		2.	
3.		3.	
4.		4.	
5.		5.	
6.		6.	
7.		7.	
8.		8.	
9.		9.	
10.		10.	

DOWNLOAD KIT

Please enter the URL you see in the box below into your computer web browser to access and download the kit.

> ## www.self-counsel.com/updates/separate/15kit.htm

The download kit includes:

- Sample separation agreement
- Sample separation agreement for same-sex couples
- Blank separation agreements for your use

* * *

IMPORTANT

Laws may change frequently or without notice. The forms and information in this book may be updated from time to time to ensure compliance with laws and regulations. Please install the download kit included with this book and click the "Check for Updates" link to ensure you are working with the most up-to-date forms and information.